CHINA
AT WAR

CHINA AT WAR

HANS VAN DE VEN

TRIUMPH AND TRAGEDY IN THE
EMERGENCE OF THE NEW CHINA
1937–1952

P

PROFILE BOOKS

First published in Great Britain in 2017 by
Profile Books Ltd
3 Holford Yard
Bevin Way
London WC1X 9HD
www.profilebooks.com

1 3 5 7 9 10 8 6 4 2

Typeset in Minion by MacGuru Ltd

Printed and bound in Great Britain by Clays, St Ives plc

A CIP catalogue record for this book is available from the British Library.

ISBN 978 1 78125 194 2
eISBN 978 1 78283 016 0

FSC
www.fsc.org
MIX
Paper from
responsible sources
FSC® C018072

CONTENTS

MAPS

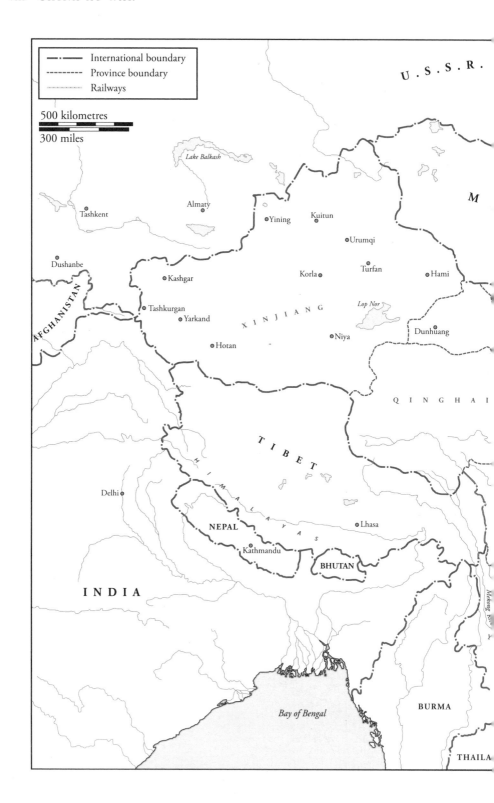

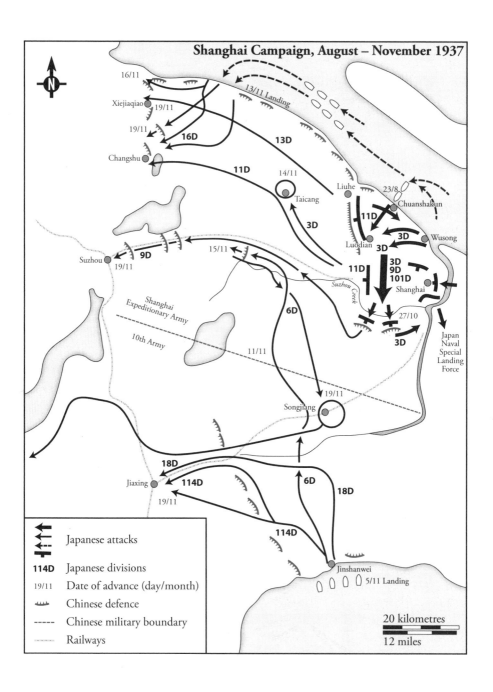

Shanghai Campaign, August – November 1937

N

16/11

Xiejiaqiao 19/11

19/11

16D   **13D**

13/11 Landing

Changshu

11D   14/11

Taicang   Liuhe   23/8   Chuanshakun

11D

3D   **11D**   **3D**

Luodian   **3D**

Suzhou   **9D**   15/11   **11D**   **3D**
                                   9D
19/11   Suzhou Creek   **101D**   Shanghai

Shanghai
Expeditionary
Army   **6D**   27/10

10th Army   **3D**

11/11   Japan
             Naval
             Special
             Landing
             Force

19/11

Songjiang

18D

Jiaxing   **114D**   **6D**   **18D**

19/11

114D

Jinshanwei
0 0 0 0 0 5/11 Landing

Japanese attacks

114D Japanese divisions

19/11   Date of advance (day/month)

Chinese defence

-----   Chinese military boundary

Railways

20 kilometres

12 miles

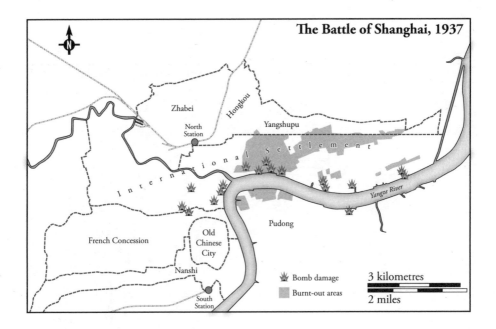

The Battle of Shanghai, 1937

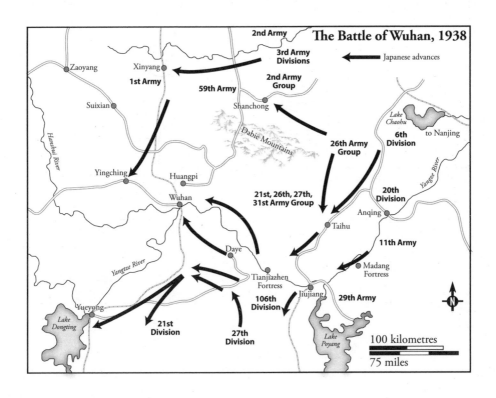

The Battle of Wuhan, 1938

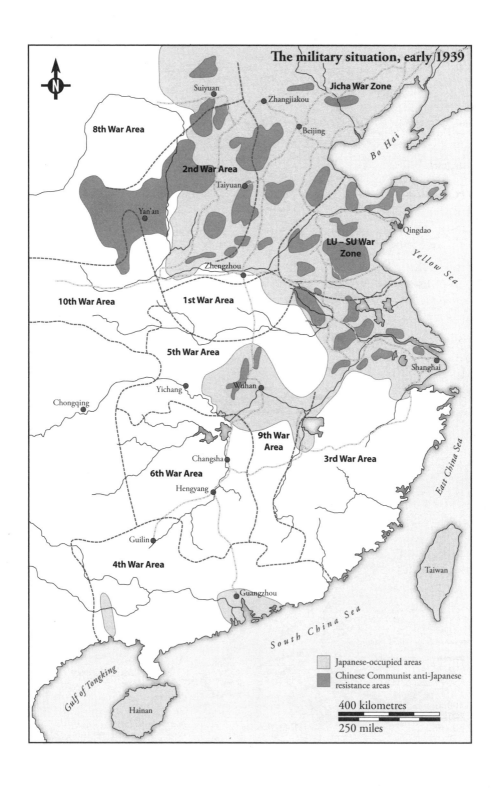

The military situation, early 1939

8th War Area

Suiyuan

Zhangjiakou

Jicha War Zone

Beijing

Bo Hai

2nd War Area

Taiyuan

Yan'an

Qingdao

LU – SU War Zone

Zhengzhou

Yellow Sea

10th War Area

1st War Area

5th War Area

Shanghai

Yichang

Wuhan

Chongqing

9th War Area

Changsha

3rd War Area

6th War Area

Hengyang

East China Sea

Guilin

Taiwan

4th War Area

Guangzhou

South China Sea

Gulf of Tongking

Hainan

Japanese-occupied areas

Chinese Communist anti-Japanese resistance areas

400 kilometres

250 miles

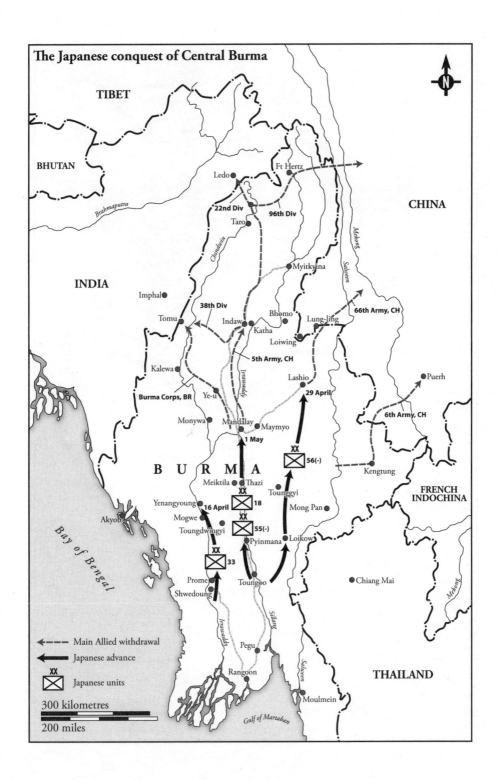

The Japanese conquest of Central Burma

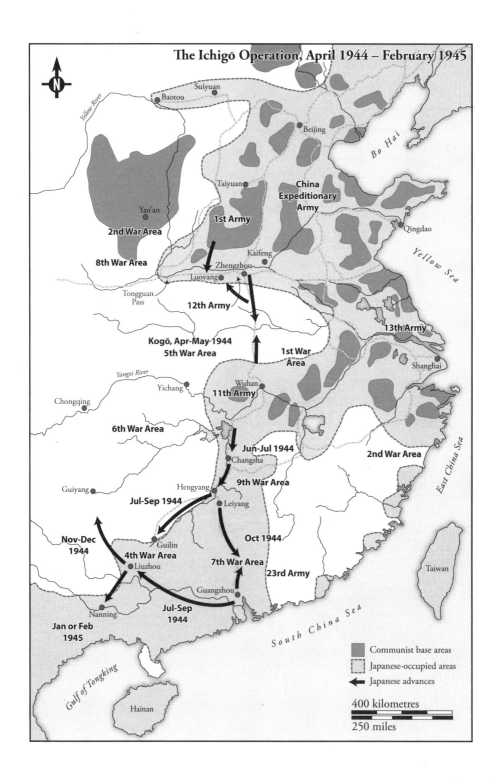

The Ichigō Operation, April 1944 – February 1945

Yellow River

Baotou

Suiyuan

Beijing

Bo Hai

Taiyuan

China
Expeditionary
Army

Qingdao

Yan'an

1st Army

Kaifeng

Yellow Sea

2nd War Area

Zhengzhou

8th War Area

Luoyang

Tongguan
Pass

12th Army

13th Army

Kogō, Apr-May 1944
5th War Area

1st War
Area

Shanghai

Yangzi River

Yichang

Wuhan

Chongqing

11th Army

6th War Area

Jun-Jul 1944

2nd War Area

Changsha

Guiyang

9th War Area

East China Sea

Hengyang

Jul-Sep 1944

Leiyang

Nov-Dec
1944

Oct 1944

Guilin

4th War Area

Liuzhou

7th War Area

23rd Army

Taiwan

Guangzhou

Nanning

Jul-Sep
1944

Jan or Feb
1945

South China Sea

Gulf of Tongking

Hainan

Communist base areas

Japanese-occupied areas

Japanese advances

400 kilometres

250 miles

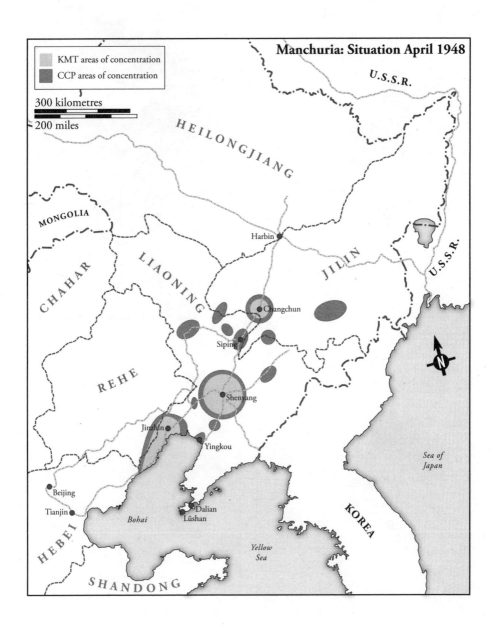

Manchuria: Situation April 1948

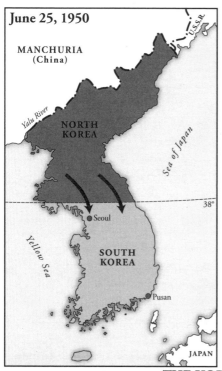

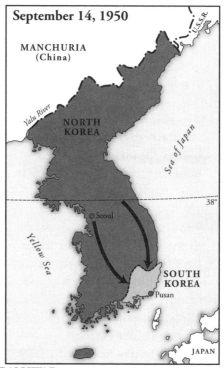

THE KOREAN WAR

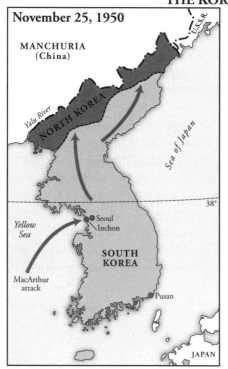

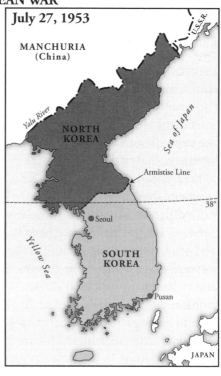

INTRODUCTION

> … I the Lord thy God am a jealous God,
> visiting the iniquity of the fathers upon the children
> unto the third and fourth generation of them that hate me.
>
> Deuteronomy 5:9

> The world war which is approaching with irresistible force will review the
> Chinese problem together with all other problems of colonial domination.
> For it is in this that the real task of the second world war will consist: to
> divide the planet anew in accord with the new relationship of imperialist
> forces. The principal arena of struggle will, of course, not be that
> Lilliputian bath-tub, the Mediterranean, nor even the Atlantic Ocean, but
> the basin of the Pacific.
>
> Leon Trotsky, foreword, in Harold Isaacs, *The Tragedy of the Chinese Revolution*
> (1938)[1]

Coming to grips with China's wartime history poses extraordinary challenges, not least because so much fighting took place in such a vast country
over such a long period of time, from 1937 to 1945. In resisting Japanese aggression, China fought a war whose moral contours were simple and during which
the country made enormous sacrifices to ensure its survival. This was the
warfare of Herodotus's *The Histories*, of a civilisation defending itself against
the depredations of a barbaric aggressor. However, there was also more or less
simultaneously a civil war, of the kind that Thucydides portrayed in his *History
of the Peloponnesian War*, with instances of gross brutality, lawlessness, social
mayhem, cynical betrayals and Machiavellian struggles for power. Civil wars
raise different issues from wars between countries. In national wars, such as
between Prussia and France in 1870, Spain and the Netherlands between 1568
and 1648, or even the First and Second World Wars, the goals are straightforward and nations come together. In civil wars, charismatic leadership, an
ability to inspire, political shrewdness, managerial skill and a strong dose of
ruthlessness are usually needed, first to force an outcome and make it stick, and
then to bring calm to a society that has just torn itself apart.

Today, China recounts its wartime history in the Herodotean mode. This is a
recent departure. In the early decades of the People's Republic of China (PRC),

China's recent past was constructed as a revolution in which the Chinese Communists had triumphed against great odds, freeing the country from the brutal tyranny of the Nationalists led by Chiang Kaishek, Japanese aggression and Western imperialism. Public attention was focused on events such as: the founding of the Chinese Communist Party (CCP) in 1921; the 1927 purge that left thousands of Communists dead; the emergence during the Second World War of Yan'an, the Communist capital, as a beacon of hope in a sea of Nationalist corruption and oppression; and the final defeat of the Nationalists in three great battles: the Liaoshen Campaign for control of Manchuria from May to November 1948, the battles for Beijing and Tianjin that lasted from 29 November 1948 until 31 January 1949, and the Huaihai Campaign in north China from 6 November 1948 to 10 January 1949. The history of the Communist revolution stood centre stage.

Now it is China's victory over Japan that takes the limelight. The Second World War (or the War of Resistance, as it is still usually called in China) is portrayed as the time when the New China was born, when the country managed to come together to prevail over enormous odds and safeguard a civilisation threatened with extinction. That today's leaders of the People's Republic choose to portray the country's war history as its finest hour is entirely understandable. Globally the Second World War has come to be regarded as something of an axial moment out of which the modern world emerged, providing not only its geopolitical contours but also its moral bearings. Many countries, including the United State of America, Russia and the United Kingdom, have put victory to use to enhance the national feel-good factor; why should China not do so, too?

The change, as so often in post-Mao China, was the result of initiatives at the local level, in this instance beginning in the universities. In the early 1980s, after Deng Xiaoping's rise to power, academic historians in the People's Republic, especially at Nanjing University, initiated a reassessment of the Nationalists' role during the War of Resistance. Using archival sources preserved in that city, they argued that, especially during the first phase of the war, it was the Nationalists rather than the Communists who bore the brunt of the fighting. In so doing, they overturned decades of silence about the enormous sacrifices the Nationalists and their armies had made in the service of the country.

Soon after, museums opened in places of significance in the war: at Nanjing, where the Nanjing Massacre Museum welcomed its first visitors in 1985 and where in the foothills of Purple Mountain the names of slain Chinese, as well as Russian and American airmen, are inscribed on memorial walls; in Shenyang, where the September 18 Memorial Museum, named after the date in 1931 on which the Japanese occupation of Manchuria began, was inaugurated in 1991; at Marco Polo Bridge, where, on 7 July 1937, the first shots of the War of

Resistance were fired; and in Chongqing, the city in western China to which the Nationalists retreated in 1938, and where Nationalist government buildings as well as the residences of Nationalist leaders have been restored and opened to the public.

Many cities now house memorial parks for the war dead, including Guang-zhou, Shanghai, Hengyang, Guilin, Changde, Harbin, Shanggao and others. The war now features in movies, TV documentaries, memoirs and video games. In schools, students learn about the Second World War in China in Patriotic Education programmes. This trend culminated in the decision, taken by China's highest law-making body, the National People's Congress, to enshrine the new narrative in law. In February 2014 it decided that from then on China would mark its 'victory in the Chinese people's War of Resistance against Japan' every 3 September. Showcasing the inclusivity of the new narra-tive, both Communist and Nationalist veterans flanked President Xi Jinping as he presided over the commemorations held in September 2015. A year later, the seventieth anniversary of China's victory was celebrated with a huge military parade in Beijing.

There are real positives to this development. As Oxford historian Rana Mitter has noted, it has facilitated the healing of wounds resulting from decades of class struggle during which millions of Chinese people died.[2] It has given a new dignity to all those who were connected in one way or another with the Nationalists, distrusted during the Cultural Revolution and before as 'bour-geois running dogs', 'counter-revolutionaries', 'big tigers' or 'bad elements'. They, and their descendants, can now hold their heads up high in public.

This new understanding of the Second World War does more than further national reconciliation. The appeals of Maoism have long faded and even eco-nomic success, no matter how stellar, no longer suffices as a source of national pride for the country or of political legitimacy for its leaders. Commemorating the war fits the PRC government's efforts to move beyond ideology and eco-nomic success to promote a common national identity and proclaim its new international stature. To achieve these aims, the leadership has taken a series of steps, ranging from staging spectacles such as the 2008 Beijing Olympics and the 2010 Shanghai World Expo and reforming the national football league with the aim of making Chinese football internationally competitive, to instituting a uniform nationwide examination for university admissions and enforcing a standard pronunciation of Chinese through its schools. To construct an inspiring account of how the New China emerged from the Second World War furthers this project in modern statecraft.

China's leaders today are of course well aware that presiding over commem-orative events associated with this version of China's history burnishes their image by association.[3] One of their aims in emphasising China's role in the war against Japan is also to suggest equivalence with the Western Allies, the message being that if China could be trusted by the international community then, the same should be true now. Hence their pressure to talk about a 'world-wide anti-fascist war' in which China led the fight against Japan, rather than just the Chinese War of Resistance against Japan.[4]

If this heroic version of China's Second World War history has a number of positive aspects, this book will nonetheless take issue with it, in several inter-connected ways. The War of Resistance was never about the defeat of Japan alone. For China was at war not just with Japan but also with itself. For the historian the challenge has been to combine China's resistance to Japanese aggression and the simultaneous revolutionary war between the Nationalists and the Communists into a single account, an account that must be alert to the ways the two impacted on each other as well as to China's fragmented state at the time. Generalissimo Chiang Kaishek was China's wartime leader, rec-ognised as such even by the Communists. However, even as the leader of the Nationalists he was more the convenor of a fractious alliance than the chief of a disciplined and structured organisation working towards a single purpose.

If China's war with Japan resulted from Japan's attempt to establish a Japan-ese empire across east and south-east Asia, the Chinese Civil War was the product of starkly different views within China about deeper questions made acute by the 1911 Revolution.[5] These questions included: who was to have a say, and on what grounds, in political discourse and decision-making; what should China be seen to stand for; how should central and local authority relate to each other; what to preserve of China's traditions; and what was the country's place in the modern world. No mechanism existed to resolve these key consti-tutional issues, or indeed to foster compromises for them, with the result that the republic that emerged in the wake of the 1911 Revolution disintegrated as soon as it confronted its first major crisis, the death in June 1916 of President Yuan Shikai, the strong man of the Revolution.

By the late 1920s, Chiang Kaishek's Nationalists had prevailed in the civil wars that followed, but powerful regional forces, although nominally incorpo-rated into the new order, remained largely independent, and frequently took to the battlefield to challenge Nationalist rule. In addition, a Communist insur-gency took hold in the central China countryside in the early 1930s. In 1934 the Nationalists succeeded in driving the Communists out of their enclaves, but the Communists then undertook the Long March, as their escape to Shaanxi province, an inhospitable part of a poor province in north-west China, became known when the Communist revolution remained the preferred source for tales of heroic daring-do.

If in 1945 it was clear that Japan's gambit to establish its domination over east Asia had failed, the issues that the 1911 Revolution had shaken loose remained unresolved. If the Nationalists had hoped that leading their country to victory and securing international recognition for China as an equal nation state had bestowed on them the mantle of legitimacy, they were to be disappointed. The Communists, and many others, refused to recognise their accession. And if by 1937 the Communists were but one among many opponents to the Nationalists – and not even the strongest one – by 1945 that situation had changed. In 1937, the Communists commanded perhaps some 30,000 inferior troops, with only a small base in a poor province. By 1945, Communist armed forces numbered some 1 million men, stationed in large bases across northern China. One effect of the War of Resistance in China was the radical narrowing of political options. At the time of the Japanese surrender on 9 September 1945, it was clear that it would be either the Nationalists or the Communists who would take charge of China. So it was that civil war continued for another four years, until October 1949, when, standing atop the Gate of Heavenly Peace overlooking Tian'anmen Square, Mao Zedong announced the founding of the People's Republic of China.

It is simply not possible to separate China's civil war from China's war with Japan. To give just one example, the Communist victory required a tightly disciplined party to ensure that its armed forces, Party cells, administrative organs and mass organisations operating across China's vast spaces implemented a coordinated strategy. In the early 1940s, when China faced the gravest situation in its war with Japan, Mao Zedong spent two years building such a party, combining a ruthless purge of his political opponents with a thorough indoctrination campaign, terrifying Communist Party colleagues into accepting his personal dominance. The negative example of Nationalist disorganisation – for which they became increasingly well known during the War of Resistance – no doubt was one reason Mao concluded that this had to be done if the revolution he wanted was to triumph. However, other factors created by the War of Resistance – such as heightened emotions, social dislocation, economic collapse and the fragmentation of military authority – were critical to his success. Similarly, the growth of Communist power impacted on Nationalist strategy. The Nationalists deployed large armies, including some of their best forces, in blockading Communist base areas, inevitably leading to a reduction in their anti-Japanese efforts.

Artificially separating China's War of Resistance from the Nationalist–Communist civil war inevitably leads to histories that are partial at best. A heroic account of China in the Second World War veils the fact that both the Nationalists and the Communists resorted to horrendous strategies, including scorched earth policies, flooding vast tracts of land, urban terror campaigns, murderous purges and the use of starvation as a military tactic. Unpalatable decisions and horrific measures are at times inevitable in war. Nonetheless, if the Chinese have every reason to be proud that their country survived one of the greatest crises of its entire history and to celebrate this as a collective achievement, historians must try to tell it as it was.

The narrative arc for *China at War* is provided by the failure of conventional warfare in China and the emergence of what might be called national liberation war. When Japanese and Nationalist forces began fighting each other in 1937, they were committed to conventional war, with both sides seeing it as a marker of modernity and nationhood. They believed that war was a matter of deploying forces into the battlefield, arming them with industrially produced weapons and coordinating them through a general staff, while government ministries mobilised the materiel and human resources necessary for what was thought of as total war, in which mass was everything. This was the kind of war conceptualised by the great nineteenth-century military thinker Carl von Clausewitz. To Clausewitz, war was fought between opposing but internally cohesive societies, allowing all events to be placed into a dialectical narrative. That model of warfare did not survive the Second World War. What replaced it is difficult to define. At one end of the new range of possibilities was nuclear warfare, which, fortunately, has proved more a possibility than a reality. Somewhere in the middle is the kind of warfare the US waged in Vietnam, which can be thought of as managerial warfare, characterised by the use of tables, graphs, statistics, calculations and the application of modern business practices to war. Asymmetric warfare (typically between standing armies and insurgents) and terrorism are at the other end of the range.[6]

Both China and Japan realised early on in the conflict that the assumptions they had made about conventional warfare were unsound. By the autumn of 1938, the Nationalists accepted that they would not be able to throw the Japanese into the Pacific, as some had initially hoped might be possible, and nor could they sustain the war at the intensity with which they had pursued it until then. Japan drew the conclusion that it was unlikely that it could force a Nationalist surrender. It also was not willing to pay the price of pursuing the Nationalists all the way to Chongqing in western China, where they had by now fled, and judged that, in any case, the Soviet threat in Manchuria was too grave to risk such a diversion of energies.

Though both the Nationalists and the Japanese were searching for a new approach, neither went much beyond the conventional war paradigm. The Japanese placed greater stress on politics, attempting to bring about a federal China made up of a string of regional governments willing to align with Japan. In 1940–41 they also conducted a ferocious strategic bombing campaign – the first of the Second World War – in an attempt to destroy the Nationalist will to fight. In the Nationalist strategy greater emphasis was put on guerrilla warfare and, especially, diplomacy in order to secure outside assistance. The Nationalists withdrew deep into China's vast hinterland, compelling the Japanese to spread out their forces, and kept the war going by launching limited offensives moving from one war zone to another. The Nationalists also turned to traditional methods of mobilising Chinese society, including by farming out recruitment to village leaders, and adopted an urban terror campaign to prevent the Japanese from consolidating their positions in China's cities. The result was not a stalemate – far from it – but a meat grinder of a war that ravaged the country without bringing any solution.

The internationalisation of the fighting following the Japanese attack on Pearl Harbor in December 1941 profoundly altered the context in which China's war with the Japanese took place, allowing the Chinese to offload a part of the fighting on to the USA, the UK, and eventually the USSR, and also ensure that they would be on the side of the victors. The emergence of the Communists as a powerful force was another, and for China ultimately more important, development during this period. Communist power expanded in two distinct timeframes. The first was the first two years of the War of Resistance, from 1937 to 1939, the second in 1944–5. In the first, Communist troops and cadres fanned out from their base at Yan'an in north Shaanxi province, in order to establish base areas behind Japanese lines. They waged small-scale guerrilla operations, avoiding direct contact with the Japanese, because they were too powerful, and with the Nationalists because they could not afford to alienate them at this point. The Communists carefully calibrated their political, military and cultural strategies to achieve these aims in a divided society in which they had a number of enemies and material resources were scarce. The circumstances under which the Communists were fighting rendered impossible a dialectical Clausewitzian approach to war.

The new way in which they went about conducting national liberation war combined the mobilisation of the countryside, at first on a limited scale for guerrilla warfare and for building up base areas and then for large-scale battles, with the creation of a tightly disciplined Party to provide cohesion, the assertion of a powerful ideology to jell together and motivate followers, the evasion of the battlefield until victory was virtually guaranteed, and the politicisation of all areas of life, including education, the village, court rooms, the media and even the family. Contrary to the romanticism with which national liberation war has at times been approached, it was a tough, merciless form of war – unsurprising, given the conditions under which it emerged.

National liberation war had a long-lasting impact, inspiring similar movements in south-east Asia, Africa and South America in the 1950s, 1960s and 1970s, and with a continuing relevance for today. It should come as no surprise that Abu Ubayd al-Qurashi, one of Al-Qaeda's founding strategists, was well versed in Mao.[7] If atomic bombs were one invention to come out of the Second World War that would fundamentally shape the post-war world, national liberation war was another. The war in China may not seem to matter much to perspectives dominated by the rise of the two superpowers or by the emergence of nuclear warfare. But if we take the emergence of national liberation war seriously, then even though in China there were no great technological breakthroughs, what happened there nonetheless begins to matter enormously.

The years that followed the first period of expansion of the Communists were as difficult for them as for the Nationalists. In 1944, the Japanese launched their largest ever operation on land – the Ichigo offensive – in an attempt to create an overland link between south-east Asia and the Japanese homeland via China, and to drive the Nationalists out of the war completely. For the Communists, Ichigo was an opportunity. In their second period of growth, they flooded into the areas in north and central China vacated by the Nationalists and Japanese, who had to concentrate the larger part of their forces in China for this operation. They doubled the size of their armed forces to around 1 million men and, by the summer of 1945, they were in control of much of northern China, governing about a quarter of China's population. This provided them with the springboard, not to seize power straight away (although they did try that) but to move into Manchuria, train their armies in waging large-scale warfare and, finally, to surround the cities from the countryside and so defeat the Nationalists. National liberation war was never just guerrilla war.

China at War uses this framework of modern Clausewitzian warfare between two sides giving way to national liberation war in a setting with a multitude of enemies in order to bring out other key aspects of the narrative. China was a poor agricultural country fighting an industrialised state with superbly trained and equipped armed forces. Consequently, the Chinese had to 'trade place for time', that is, withdraw into the countryside and try to exhaust the Japanese through attrition, but also wait for beneficial changes in the global context. An important consequence was the virtual disappearance from pre-eminence of the large cities of coastal China, with their banks, industries, movie theatres, department stores and universities. That version of China did not survive the war, or rather, it did not re-emerge until well into the 1990s – although when it did, it did so with a vengeance. During the war, the bulk of the population moved into the countryside; it was here that China's future was decided. The transition was accompanied by enormous movements of refugees as people fled the advancing Japanese forces and as the Nationalists adopted devastating scorched earth measures, denuding areas about to fall under occupation of anything that might be useful to the enemy. The withdrawal into the countryside went hand in hand with new understandings of village China, not just among the Chinese Communists, but more broadly. 'The peasant' and 'the peasantry' now became terms of common usage, effacing the complexity of China's village cultures but also providing village China with a political potency it had lacked in the past. Its inhabitants, who had previously been largely ignored, became subjects who needed to be organised, disciplined, cleansed, indoctrinated and mobilised (and discarded after it was all over). *China at War* returns China's Second World War to the countryside.

One challenge I have set for myself is to explore how the war was digested culturally. Two personal histories, one of a young woman who came of age during the war and the other of a middle-ranking, increasingly disillusioned Nationalist official, are interwoven into the analysis. The first, Chi Pang-yuan, has left us a beautifully written memoir of her experiences, while the other, Chen Kewen, maintained a diary in which he carefully recorded his reactions to people and events around him. They were from very different backgrounds. Chi Pang-yuan came from a politically influential family from Manchuria, while Chen was from a poor but educated family from the far south. Their experiences were not representative or typical, of course, but looking at events through their eyes nonetheless draws us intimately into the war. They give us a less ideological perspective than those provided by the Communist and Nationalist apparatchiks whose accounts have dominated the historiography and the memoir literature so far, because they and their families, while close to power, were nonetheless only on the fringes.

China at War will also discuss the shifts in history, culture and ideology at various points during the war. The struggle between the Communists and the Nationalists was decided not only on the battlefield but in the hearts and minds of the people. The Communists were consistently better at this, able to secure the allegiance of the best and brightest, at least of China's youth. Revolution is a young person's game and China's population was still largely made up of young people at this time. To understand the Communist victory, we need to under-stand why their views gained traction. I analyse these aspects, too, in order to focus on the fact that while China may have been poor and backward, it was also a country with rich traditions in literature, art, philosophical and ethical argument, historical analysis and political debate, all of which mattered hugely at the time, precisely because the Japanese invasion threatened their extinction.

In the USA, the UK, France and Germany, as well as increasingly the Soviet Union, wartime generals and political leaders are still well known, often because of the diaries and memoirs they have written. This is not the case in China. However, in recent years, the memoirs and diaries of such figures have appeared, which allow us to peer beneath the basic facts of battles, cam-paigns and strategic decisions. In this book I rely on such writings to give a more human face to some of those who led China at this critical juncture in its history. For personal networks and personal relations were often important in the decisions that were made – inevitably in a country that was so deeply divided and in which the careful management of human relations is accorded special significance.

China at War treats the warfare in which China was involved between 1937 and 1953 as an interlocking series of events. As I have previously mentioned, its main military trend – there were many others – was the dissolution of dialectical Clausewitzian war and the emergence of national liberation war, a process that was driven by leaders thinking and acting; by people hoping, fighting, caring and dying; and by Clausewitzian chance, that is, by events that cannot be predicted or controlled in the clashes of competing armies. It returns village China and its inhabitants to a prominent place in the story, important because during the Second World War the whole world was still overwhelmingly rural, not just China.[8] It stresses the importance of scholarship, art, culture and ideology in understanding China at war. However, this study seeks to take war seriously as war; that is, recover how it was thought about, analyse how it was planned, and examine how it was enacted, rather than just regret its horrors, see it merely as the context in which ideological or political struggles played out, or, important as these things are, use it to construct narratives about the origins of today's world.

In stressing Chinese and east Asian dynamics, I am consciously resisting the homogenisation that the concept of the Second World War often brings with it, an approach which compresses the complex events that took place in various theatres around the world into a single, usually moralised, dichotomous narrative. As the Cambridge historian David Reynolds has demonstrated, the idea that the fighting around the world amounted to a world war is a post-war construction. As he put it, 'only in 1948 did the British government decide that it had just been fighting the "second world war"'.[9] The USA had acted with more speed, but there, too, the term was only officially adopted after Japan's surrender, when Secretary of War Henry Stimson and Secretary of the Navy James Forrestal proposed to President Harry S. Truman to adopt the term 'as a matter of simplicity and to insure uniform terminology'.[10]

With the exception of Germany, during the war none of the contending countries used the term. As we have seen, the Chinese called their war the 'War of Resistance against Japan', while the Japanese termed it, first, the 'China Incident' – a label widely used in the Anglophone press at the time as well – and, after the expansion of the war to include the US in December 1941, the Greater East Asian War, a name ruled out of order in post-war Japan and replaced with the Pacific War and the China War, in a move that gave rise to a bifurcation in scholarship that has lasted to this day.[11] After Britain declared war on Germany in September 1939, the British talked of 'the European War', or just 'the War', while in France it was 'la Guerre' or 'la Grand Guerre'. The Soviets fought the

'Great Patriotic War', a term first used by *Pravda*.[12] The Germans did talk about a *Weltkrieg* but, as Reynolds remarks, along with their unconditional surrender came the loss of naming rights.

On the Allied side, it was President Franklin D. Roosevelt who first used the term systematically, doing so well before Pearl Harbor, in order to 'prod America out of isolationism into belligerency'.[13] Roosevelt had pragmatic as well as idealistic concerns. America would have been difficult to mobilise unless its citizens were convinced that their country was under threat and they were fighting for a moral purpose. Roosevelt was concerned, too, with ensuring that the war would lead, not to the survival of an international system dominated by empires armed to the teeth and looking at each other with suspicion, and, in the case of Japan, hatred, but to a new global order of independent nation states who freely traded with each other and agreed to work cooperatively to maintain peace and foster prosperity. When in August 1941 the British prime minister Winston Churchill travelled to Placentia Bay, Newfoundland, in the hope of convincing the US president to join the war, he failed in that mission and instead found himself being asked to sign the Atlantic Charter, which set out Roosevelt's ideas about the purpose of the war. If there was to be another great conflict in which millions died, then everything possible should be done to make sure that it would be the last one. The term 'world war' was never merely a factual description of a war fought on several continents.

After 1945 the term Second World War proved political useful. In the USA, the desire to 'bring the boys home' was huge. The surrenders of Japan and Germany made it possible to regard their job as finished and therefore to do so. But if the transition to peace was straightforward for the USA, for China it was not. In Asia and elsewhere, the arming of anti-imperialist and revolutionary movements during the war prevented the return of peace. It was only when these struggles had exhausted themselves, as they eventually did in China in 1949, and when the USA and the USSR consolidated their Cold War front lines in east Asia during the Korean War of 1950–53, that a measure of stability returned to the region. The term Second World War suggests a sense of finality to processes that in many places around the world remained ongoing; or, perhaps, a belief (in many cases unfounded) that peace would now return. In east Asia, wars between countries only really ended when the Cold War order descended over the area during the Korean War.

The time has come to disaggregate the Second World War and become attuned to the differences in each of its theatres. That is not to say that no connections existed between them: the Second World War was an alliance war, which the Allies won because they worked together much better than the Axis powers. Alliance members provided troops, ammunition and other aid to each other. America, a land of increasing plenty, supplied not just arms and ammunition but also food to Britain and the USSR.[14] Events in one theatre impacted on others. The war in China made it difficult for Japan to join Germany's war against the Soviet Union, leaving the latter free to concentrate on fighting the Wehrmacht. Had Japan succeeded in forcing a Chinese surrender, then China's resources would have become available to Japan. We can only speculate about the consequences, but they would have been significant. Japan's attack on Pearl Harbor, meant to put the US Pacific Navy out of action so that Japan could occupy south-east Asia, ensured the defeat of Germany in Europe by bringing the USA into the war. No study of any region during the Second World War should be written without considering its global dimensions.

China at War does not set out to ditch the term Second World War completely. Given both its ubiquity and its continuing appeal, any attempt to do so would be foolhardy; but some refiguring of its meaning is, I believe, in order. The idea that it all began with Germany's invasion of Poland in 1939 and came to a definite stop in 1945 is too limiting to capture the complexity of events. The Second World War is, I believe, best seen as the result of Japan's and Germany's desire, at a time when resources around the world were thought to be restricted, to acquire new land in order to secure the agricultural, mineral and industrial resources they felt they needed to survive in a global order made up of competing empires. They also believed that their countries were overpopulated and therefore needed to acquire new territories (such as the Ukraine, the Caucasus, Manchuria) in which to move what they considered to be surplus populations. Both countries made initial forays – Japan in Manchuria, Germany in Austria and Czechoslovakia – which remained limited and hesitant. But full-out war broke out in Asia in 1937 and in Europe in 1939. Both Japan and Germany pursued quick war strategies in the belief that the greater resources their enemies could potentially marshal left them with no other choice.

In placing themselves on a war footing to resist German and Japanese aggression, other countries built up their armed forces, mobilised their societies, turned their industrial capacity to war purposes, and drew food, energy and people from their colonies to sustain their war effort. They also developed an alliance in which such former enemies as the UK and the USSR found ways to work together. The pre-war world of empire blocs disintegrated during these processes as Japan occupied large parts of east and south-east Asia; as the USA opposed their restoration after the war; and, critically, as national liberation movements organised and armed themselves. What emerged instead was a patchwork of arrangements involving global institutions of governance, new states that emerged out of national liberation movements, and the division of the world in two opposing camps, each led by one of the two superpowers that had grown out of the war, the USA and the USSR. *China at War* uses China not least as a case study to illustrate this process.

The book is divided into four parts. Part I, Staking a Nation, follows Chiang Kaishek's rise to power, examines the efforts of the Nationalists to construct a new Chinese nation and prepare their country for war against Japan, and ends with an analysis of the reasons for Chiang Kaishek's decision to go to war in the summer of 1937. If primary responsibility for the War of Resistance must lie with Japan, it is also the case that Chiang Kaishek's response to a crisis in north China set in motion the series of events that saw China and Japan fight each other remorselessly for seven long years.

Part II, Momentous Times, covering the period 1937–42, traces attempts by the Japanese and the Nationalists to prevail in a conventional war using conventional means as well as the initial expansion of the Chinese Communists and the emergence of war communism. These were momentous times in the sense that the zeitgeist changed. At first, although some segments of the population embraced China's war with Japan enthusiastically, large numbers remained detached. That changed as the sacrifices mounted. By the end of 1938, Japan had captured many of China's largest cities, but it also faced a population who would not settle for anything less than the departure of Japanese troops from Chinese soil, and who defined their own time as decisive for the future of their country and their civilisation.

Part III, The Acid Test, and Part IV, The New China, examine China's War of Resistance after it became part of a globalised war, the Chinese civil war that followed the fall of Japan, and the emergence of a new Cold War during the Korean War. Part III focuses on the alliance aspect of China's victory over Japan, emphasising that while militarily China benefitted little, politically it gained hugely, with important consequences for the world in which we live today. Part IV examines the overwhelming demoralisation of the Nationalists after the end of the War of Resistance, the triumph of the Communists, and the military and diplomatic events during the Korean War that led to the east Asian Cold War order that remains largely in place today.

My understanding of war is shaped in profound ways by my own family's history, a history that has convinced me that there is a good deal of truth to the words of Deuteronomy, quoted at the opening of this chapter: it takes at least three or four generations for the ramifications of such a traumatic event as the Second World War to work themselves through before they can be genuinely consigned to the past.

I grew up in the Netherlands with parents who as teenagers had experienced the hunger winter of 1945, in which 22,000 Dutch citizens are estimated to have died of starvation. My mother maintained a basement with many shelves loaded with rows of tinned food well into the 1960s. I had nightmares for weeks after a family dinner at which an uncle talked about a bomb that had dropped through the roof of his family's home into their kitchen. It was a dud but no one dared move for hours in case a slight tremor would make it go off after all. It is not because of this that the issues of food and bombing figure prominently in the narrative, and I know that I cannot know what bombing and hunger really mean – as my parents were in the habit of reminding me. But as a member of the second post-war generation, I do nonetheless have a direct personal connection to the Second World War.

The importance of the wartime past on my generation was brought home to me during the Easter weekend of 2014, when I travelled with two cousins, their partners, my wife and son to Germany in order to retrace the last journey that my maternal grandfather, Marius Jonker Roelants, made sixty-nine years earlier, in the final weeks of the war. Marius was from Schiedam, a typically picturesque small Dutch town with canals near Rotterdam, where Marius was regarded as a man of some standing. He ran a wine import business, while other members of his family managed the local gin distillery, a bookshop and a printing business.

The Germans had tried Marius for hiding weapons and, in order to keep the citizens of Schiedam in line, had kept him in jail, together with some other prominent locals – murdering a few whenever an act of resistance was carried out. Towards the end of the war, the Germans moved Marius to Germany, where they put him to work in an aircraft factory hidden in a mine. As the Allies advanced, the Germans fell back towards Berlin, dragging Marius along with them, forcing him to walk through the harsh winter. Marius managed to escape along with a Dutch compatriot and a German prisoner – no easy divisions along national lines here. In his letters home, Marius had stated again and again that his health was fine and that his diet was tolerable. Once he regained his freedom, he gorged on supplies found in a hastily abandoned military barracks, thus stilling a hunger that had obviously come to dominate his whole being. Marius was found by American forces shortly after, but he did not survive for long: he died of dysentery only days later.

My cousins and I, we discovered, had very different recollections of our grandfather. Marius had no sons but two daughters, my mother and my aunt. While my mother told many stories about Marius, always in an admiring vein, her sister never did so. One continued to live in the war, while the other wanted to move on. My cousin was even surprised when, at a family funeral, I referred to our grandfather as 'Marius'; he had never heard that name used before for my grandfather, even though he had been named after him. Believing that his life had been affected by his mother's silences, her refusals to recollect, he turned after his retirement to investigating Marius's life. We now know where Marius was and what he did right up until the last day or so of his life. We still do not know, though, where he is buried. To that extent, he remains and will likely remain an unburied soul, or, as was traditionally believed in China about people who had not been properly buried, a wandering ghost who might come to harass his or her descendants.

I drew several lessons from this history at the sharp, personal end. Our journey into the past brought home to me the wisdom of the German President Richard von Weizsäcker, when he said in 1985 that no one should expect Germans to 'wear a penitential robe simply because they are Germans'. But he also stressed that 'their forefathers have left them a grave legacy. All of us, whether guilty or not, whether young or old, must accept the past. We are all affected by the consequences and are liable for it.'[15] Chinese ideas about wandering ghosts speak to the same issue of burdens being bestowed by one generation on the next, as did Deuteronomy. In Europe and the USA these days much of the potency of the Second World War has ebbed away: the war is confined to museums, commemorations, documentaries, movies and textbooks; Germany has apologised for its misdeeds and paid compensation; and the country is fully integrated into both the European and the international order. But it is also the case that Germany is not a member of the UN Security Council; that war memories revived quickly in the 1990s in the former Yugoslavia, dividing Serbs and Croats; and that Greece accused Germany of having failed to fulfil its Second World War reparations when the Germans demanded repayment of the Greek debt to the European Union in 2015. My generation of Dutch has turned its gaze, intellectually, culturally and economically, west to the USA, or, for our holidays, south to the Mediterranean, rather than east towards Germany – which was something that came naturally to our parents and we resumed doing only a decade or so ago. Traumatic events take generations to work themselves out.

The second lesson was that different generations live in different eras with different attitudes. My aunt and my mother grew up in what might be called momentous times, which have shaped their rememberings of the Second World War. They construed the war as an apocalyptic fight between good and evil, fought by giants. We live in less eventful times – and long may they last. Our concerns tend to be about the state of our hospitals, the education of our children, the promotions we might or might not be granted and the sturdiness of our pensions. We are less prone to think in black and white terms. If my mother perceived my grandfather as a resistance hero who could do no wrong, I will not hold it against him that he looted from a hotel a silver soup terrine, now in my possession, while Rotterdam burned from Germany's first major aerial bombardment. If, as one historian has argued, he was the victim of a financial entrapment scheme, in which donations were collected in the name of supporting the Dutch resistance only to disappear into someone's personal bank account, I don't think any the worse of him, but nor do I think any the better of the Germans who executed that person.[16] I do, however, think him foolish for hiding weapons in his town house, where he lived with his wife and two teenage daughters, while the local German commander lived next door.

The histories of areas that have been under occupation are inevitably more complex than those that have not been so; the choices that were made were rarely straightforward, frequently unpalatable, at times simply misconceived, and often simply a choice between equally awful evils. Their histories are written not in D major, 'the key of triumph, of Hallelujah, of war cries, or victory rejoicing',[17] but in the key of G minor, used for sadder and angrier music. That perspective has clearly shaped my understanding of China at war.

My attitude has been affected, too, by the fact that although my grandfather gained the status of resistance fighter, and was formally recognised as such by the post-war Dutch government, my father was a veteran of the misguided Dutch campaign to recover control over its Indonesian colony in the four years just after the war. If I have a different attitude towards the Second World War, it is because I am part of a second post-war generation, one that came of age in an occupied area and whose own fathers had fought the wrong wars. If we have no desire to refight old battles, we are still aghast at the horror of it all, in some ways with increasing incomprehension, a sense that probably results from the fact that we now know clearly the consequences of the paths that were taken, as those who took the original decision could not have done, and because the sharp dichotomies produced by the war have faded.

The next generation will develop its own views, and take issue with mine; we still have at least a generation to go, as Deuteronomy said, before the acts of the wartime generation will begin to impact upon us less. It is unlikely that even then we will simply forget or care less, but we will do so differently. 'Lest we forget' is an important admonition, but also a phrase too often abused, certainly in east Asia, to sustain legacies of hatreds.

The final lesson is a straightforward historical one. In our case, because my grandfather ended up in what would become East Germany, we had to wait until after the fall of the Soviet Union before we could gain access to the relevant archives. Local historians and archivists were eager to assist us in reconstructing what happened, digging through paper mountains and, when we travelled through Germany, showing us where this or that building was located, or in which bend of the road Marius's escape took place. The recovery of local histories, less concerned with constructing nationalist narratives or staging politicised acts of remembrance, has barely begun in China, and continues to be constrained by the country's politics. It will take a long time before the wounds caused by the silencing of history begin to heal.

If von Weizsäcker was brave when he declared that Germans, too, should commemorate 8 May – the date when Germany surrendered in 1945 – not as a defeat but as their day of liberation, perhaps it is time for us to acknowledge that the countries that defeated Germany and Japan were not unalloyed paragons of virtue. The British left-wing poet Cecil Day-Lewis, having broken with communism, worked for the Ministry of Information during the Second World War. Discomfited when pressed to defend the Allied cause in the heroic language preferred by British and US propaganda, he wrote: 'That we who lived by honest dreams/Defend the bad against the worse.' Thucydides would have sympathised.

PART I

STAKING A NATION

— ONE —

CHIANG KAISHEK:
SAVING CHINA

Self-control is the chief element in self-respect, and respect of self, in turn, is the chief element in courage.

Thucydides, *History of the Peloponnesian War* (431 BC)[1]

Chiang Kaishek was born in 1887 in Xikou, a town in a lush, mountainous area near the rich cosmopolitan city of Ningbo in Zhejiang province, one of the first Chinese cities to be opened to foreign trade in the nineteenth century and well known for its enterprising merchant culture. Chiang's youth was spent as a scion of an affluent, locally well connected family of salt merchants – which was a financially rewarding occupation at the time. Throughout his life, Chiang would return to Xikou at moments of crisis, for escape and recuperation. For Chiang, Xikou was 'home'.

Chiang came of age as China was falling apart. He was a young boy when in 1895 Japan defeated China both at sea and in Manchuria, an event that resulted in China's loss of Taiwan and which came as a huge shock to all those who believed in China's cultural superiority and in the progress its economy and military had made in the second half of the nineteenth century. The anti-foreigner, anti-Christian Boxer Rebellion of 1900 led to an invasion by eight allied countries, including Britain, France and the USA, and the occupation of Beijing. Five years later, China suffered the indignity of Russian and Japanese troops fighting their war on Chinese soil. And in 1912, the Qing dynasty finally collapsed, having ruled China since 1644. The first incarnation of the Republic of China dissolved within a few years into warlord satrapies. Like many young men of this period, Chiang searched for a way to play his part in reversing China's decline.

He chose a military route, as indeed did many young men at the time, despite the traditional low standing of the military in Chinese culture. In 1906, he enrolled at the Baoding Military Academy, then one of China's premier schools for officers. A year later he transferred to the Preparatory School of the Imperial Japanese Military Academy in Tokyo. Like others of his generation, he was convinced that much could be learned from the first Asian country to have beaten a Western nation. Japan was also geographically close to China.

In Japan, Chiang came into contact with reformers and revolutionaries living in exile. In particular he struck up a friendship with a fellow Zhejiang native, Chen Qimei, who facilitated his admission into the Revolutionary Alliance of Sun Yatsen. The *éminence grise* of China's revolutionaries, best known for his Three People's Principles of nationalism, democracy and the people's welfare, Sun Yatsen is still revered in both China and Taiwan. But at this stage he was living in exile following a botched attempt at revolution in Canton in 1895. During his exile, he spent his time promoting the cause and raising money; in 1905, he established the Revolutionary Alliance, the forerunner of the Nationalist Party (KMT). Chen Qimei and Chiang became so close that Chiang was willing to commit murder for his friend. During the 1911 Revolution, Chen Qimei commanded the Shanghai Army and occupied Hangzhou, the provincial capital of Zhejiang province. Once he learned of the 1911 Revolution, Chiang rushed to Chen Qimei's side. When one of Chen Qimei's rivals, Tao Chenzhang, was on the verge of being appointed military governor of Zhejiang province, Chiang assassinated him to ensure that the post would fall to his blood brother.[2]

As a youth, Chiang was an avid reader of tales about heroic brotherhoods and sacrifices for the nation. A favourite was *The History of My Heart*[3] by Zheng Sixiao, a calligrapher and poet who lived during the transition from the Song Dynasty (960–1279) to the Mongol Yuan Dynasty (1271–1368) and was famous for refusing to have any dealings with the Mongols. The provenance of *The History of My Heart*, full of stories and poems about loyalty, steadfastness and sacrifice is, however, shrouded in mystery. Zheng Sixiao supposedly hid his denunciations of the Mongols in a metal box in a well in a temple, where they were discovered first at the end of the Ming Dynasty (1368–1644) and then, having been lost again, once more at the end of the Qing Dynasty. While a person's youthful reading offers no definitive window into the adult mind, Chiang often wrote about sacrifice in his diary. In 1926, for instance, he announced: 'in ancient times, the wise and the bold sacrificed themselves for the world ... we now want to realise our Nationalist ideology and achieve the independence of China. Neither fame nor death are worth worrying about.'[4]

Chiang lost heart after Yuan Shikai, the first president of the Republic, became increasingly autocratic, suppressing all opposition in 1913. What followed were Chiang's wilderness years, when he spent a lot of time reading, including the influential radical magazine *New Youth*, founded in 1915, which called for the rejection of Chinese traditional thinking and introduced all sorts of new ideas; histories of the revolutions in Germany, France and Russia; books offering explanations and translations of Marxism and Leninism; and even *The Communist Manifesto*.[5] Chiang became a radical: 'businessmen are even worse than politicians, soldiers, and bureaucrats,' he wrote in his diary.[6]

After an attempt to establish a new school at Xikou ran into stubborn resistance from the local elites, he concluded that 'if our country's gentry is not destroyed, the people will not be able to enjoy one happy day in their lives'.[7] Chiang also blamed 'selfish and profiteering large shareholders' for his failure to raise money for the Nationalists on the Shanghai stock market.[8] Revolutionary blood coursed through Chiang's veins.

Chiang also delved into the writings of Zeng Guofan, Hu Linyi and Zuo Zongtang, the Confucian generals who in the middle of the nineteenth century had mobilised their home regions to see off the Taiping rebels, the suppression of whom cost at least 20 million deaths and probably many millions more. He read Wang Yangming, the Ming Dynasty neo-Confucian who had argued that virtue was innate in all of us, rather than something that could only be acquired through years of strenuous self-cultivation and diligent study of the Confucian classics. Historian Yang Tianshi is surely right when he says that Chiang 'read but did not internalise the new learning. When reading the ancients, though, it was as if duckling found water: he used it to define the principles by which to conduct himself and relate to other human beings, as well as a source of models for managing military forces and doing politics.'[9]

Chiang's blood brother, Chen Qimei, was murdered in 1916. Shaken to the core and influenced by the ancient writers he was reading, Chiang began a determined effort to bring under control his bad temper, curb his womanising and live a purposeful, disciplined and worthwhile life. 'I dedicate myself to building my character and strengthening my learning to continue Chen Qimei's revolutionary mission,'[10] he wrote in his diary. In 1919, looking back on his behaviour after the 1911 Revolution, he wrote in self-disgust that he had been 'incredibly dissolute and depraved'. A good friend, Dai Jitao, who was a translator and private secretary to Sun Yatsen, once upbraided Chiang for a particularly vicious outburst. Chiang came close to hitting him, but once he calmed down he acknowledged that Dai 'looks down upon me because of my own terrible character; I must learn to be vigilant'. Bridling his anger and resisting temptation became a lifelong effort for Chiang. 'Now I wish to put my mind straight and cultivate the self, but no matter how hard I work at improving my knowledge and then strive to implement it, I fear it is too late.'[11]

In 1919, China was rocked by a wave of student demonstrations when it became clear that Japan would get its way at the Paris Peace Conference. Japan had joined the First World War on the Allied side and its navy had helped police international shipping lanes. In 1917, China had also joined the war on the Allied side, expecting that at the post-war peace conference the Allies would agree to hand over German possessions in Shandong province to China.[12] When the USA, the UK and France instead agreed to Japan taking them over, student demonstrations erupted across China. These fuelled the May Fourth

Movement, whose more radical wing, in a fit of iconoclastic fervour, called for the destruction of the 'Confucian Shop' – China's traditional culture – so that 'Mr Science' and 'Mr Democracy' could flourish. Chiang rejected the movement's iconoclasm but drew some energy from it: 'this is the first protest movement of the Republic, a real breakthrough. I now see that our spirit is undiminished and that the revival of the Republic will happen one day.'[13]

Another wave of protests a few years later further revitalised Chiang's energies. On 30 May 1925, the Shanghai International Settlement police shot dead two protesters at the Louza police station, where fifteen students involved in organising strikes and protests were being held. During the spring, demonstrations and strikes had taken place regularly in protest against the working conditions and deaths in Japanese factories, as well as the high-handed measures of the foreign Shanghai Municipal Council. The shooting at the Louza police station occurred after protesters had forced their way into the building in order to release the students. The incident triggered a nationwide response, with protests and strikes taking place in most major cities, including Canton, where foreign police in the Shameen Concession killed dozens of Chinese protesters.

These incidents left Chiang furious. 'The stupid British slaves [probably a reference to some Sikh policemen from India] look on Chinese lives like weed, to be rooted out mercilessly. When I learned of these incidents, my guts nearly split apart. I have never been so upset in my life,' he wrote, adding later, 'We must not forget this day of shame.'[14] Having been patronised by drivers and telephonists working for the foreigners, he fumed: 'parasites working in the foreign concessions for municipal governments and foreign companies should all be killed.'[15] Now fully recovered from his post-1911 Revolution despair and both angered and motivated by incidents such as the Louza shooting, Chiang Kaishek was once more ready for action.

Sun Yatsen and Chiang Kaishek

Chiang's search for a purpose in life ended when Sun Yatsen's KMT decided to create an independent military force. Until then, Sun Yatsen had put his faith in the ability of an isolated mutiny or local rebellion to spark a nationwide uprising, as indeed had happened in 1911. Otherwise he relied on the support of a powerful local figure in command of a substantial army. That was the case when Sun Yatsen established a military government in Canton in 1917, only to be driven out two years later. He returned to Canton soon after and once more formed a government, but in 1922 he was turfed out of the province once again, this time by Chen Jiongming, a Qing Dynasty legislator and Revolutionary Alliance member who was at the time the military governor of Guangdong province. Chen Jiongming objected to Sun Yatsen's preparations for a military expedition to unify China by force, for which the resources of Guangdong would have to be used. Chen Jiongming preferred a federal form of government, in which the provinces would be largely autonomous, as opposed to Sun Yatsen's more centralised vision for China.

These experiences led Sun to agree with those of his followers, including Dai Jitao, who argued that the Nationalists needed to have their own armies. Following the repeated failure of Sun's putschist strategy and the success of the Red Army in the Russian civil war after the October Revolution of 1917, Dai Jitao concluded that a party army was 'indispensable for destroying the forces of the old and creating a new world'.[16] Shortly afterwards, Soviet agents arrived in China, seeking to export revolution to Asia after it became clear that the revolutions that had broken out in Europe after the First World War were destined to fail. Having decided that Sun was their best bet, the Soviet representatives offered him advisors, arms and funds, which he accepted with alacrity, agreeing to the Soviets' condition that he work with the Communists. Soon after, a Nationalist–Communist united front was negotiated.

Chiang Kaishek's close friend and lifelong confidant Dai Jitao argued that Sun's ideas were rooted in Confucian thinking, a suggestion obviously congenial to Chiang. As with Chen Qimei, Chiang was willing to go to great lengths to help Dai. For instance, he agreed to raise as his own Dai's illegitimate child, Wei-kuo, born in Japan of a liaison with a Japanese woman. Dai feared that his wife would not accept Wei-kuo, but Chiang was as good as his word and appears not to have revealed the child's parentage even to his wife, Madame Chiang.[17] Loyalty to friends and living up to his promises were important to Chiang.

Sun now turned to Chiang to help build up his party army. Not only was Chiang one of his more knowledgeable followers when it came to military affairs, but he had also proved his loyalty and bravery when, in 1922, he had rushed to Sun Yatsen's side when he had taken refuge on a gunboat to escape the shelling from Chen Jiongming's artillery. In 1923, having succeeded in marshalling enough forces to regain his position in Canton, Sun sent Chiang Kaishek to Moscow to negotiate details of a collaboration agreement with the Soviet Union,[18] a mission Chiang saw as an opportunity 'for a fundamental solution for our country'.[19]

In Moscow, Chiang somewhat overstated the Nationalists' position, arguing that they were in control of three provinces in south China and commanded an army of 60,000 troops; he also claimed that the KMT had powerful backing in Manchuria and in the region of the lower Yangzi river. He tried to convince the Soviets to establish a military base at Ulan Bator in Mongolia and at Urumqi in Xinjiang province in order to train and equip a force of 30,000 men in two years. His idea was that, once ready, it would strike towards Beijing at the same time as the KMT's forces would march north from Guangdong province. When the Soviets advised that the Nationalists should first make propaganda for their cause and establish mass organisations, without which military action would be premature, Chiang countered: 'in Russia, the Communist Party only faced the Tsar's government. China is different: we encounter the resistance of all imperialist countries in the world ... This is why we must develop military action.'[20] Chiang concluded from the Soviets' rejection of his proposal that they wanted to expand their own influence in Mongolia and Xinjiang.[21]

Upon his return to Canton, Chiang became commandant of the Whampoa Military Academy, where Soviet advisors oversaw a training programme of cadets recruited from across China, many of whom would rise to prominent positions in the Communist as well as the Nationalist militaries. The academy's aim was to train for the Nationalists' National Revolutionary Army, a corps of officers educated at least to middle school level who were not only dedicated to the Revolution but were honest, competent and trustworthy. Their training included tactics, rifle practice, logistics, engineering, communications, hygiene and geography. Already, by October 1914, 1,000 cadets were in training. By 1929, 7,399 cadets had graduated from the academy, enough to staff a good number of divisions. All had taken courses in Sun Yatsen's ideas, party discipline, socialism and the ills of imperialism.[22]

A Military Affairs Council, established in June 1925, supervised efforts to incorporate local military forces into the National Revolutionary Army. Many were in actuality 'guest armies', which had decamped from poorer neighbouring provinces to grab a resource base in rich Guangdong province. Some had been invited in by Sun as he faced this or that challenge. The Council attempted to integrate these armies by setting up a central supply office, appointing political commissars to all units and creating a unified staff system. Naturally, few armies, guest or otherwise, welcomed such inroads into their independence. Nor did their aggressive tax-raising efforts endear the Nationalists to Guangdong's merchant classes or indeed to its local population.[23]

Chiang Kaishek found his purpose in life when he joined Sun Yatsen's revolution in Canton. Sun Yatsen put him in a position of serious responsibility and drew him into his inner circle, if still only as a junior member. After Sun Yatsen died of stomach cancer on 12 March 1925, the Nationalists turned him into the great missing figure of the Chinese revolution, using his legacy in many ways, including to justify Nationalist one-party rule. But the close relations many had with him, and the sense of personal gratitude they felt towards him, probably also played a role in the emergence of the Nationalists' Sun Yatsen cult. That gave the struggle to be regarded as the true heir to his legacy a personal, and therefore an especially sharp, edge.

Chiang Kaishek's coup

Sun Yatsen's death became a huge public event. Tens of thousands of people attended the memorial service in Beijing. The hearse carrying a giant portrait of Sun proceeded at a solemn pace along Chang'an Avenue, the boulevard that runs east–west through Beijing, passing south of the Forbidden City and north of Tian'anmen Square. In 1929 a similar portrait to the one on the hearse was fixed to the Gate of Heavenly Peace on the north side of Tian'anmen Square in the place where Mao Zedong's portrait now hangs.[24] Mass memorial events also took place in Canton, of course, and in Hong Kong, where the British police wielded their batons to drive away the workers who had brought the traffic to a halt.[25] In New York, a memorial service at International House was, according to *The New York Times*, attended by some 1,000 people and 'the dead Chinese leader was referred to by one speaker as carrying out the ideals of Jesus, Confucius, and Buddha, and by another as "one of the greatest men of all time"'.[26]

Sun Yatsen's death, however, also raised the obvious question of who was to take over. Its consequence was a succession struggle which left one party elder dead, another preferring exile to staying in China, and Chiang Kaishek leading his Nationalist armies out of Guangdong province on a military expedition to unify the country. At stake was the leadership of a popular party with an armed force. But warlord armies were on the march, students were protesting, and workers were striking against both foreign imperialism and domestic warlordism – and the Soviet bid for exporting revolution to China had upended decades of international cohabitation in China. Change, real change, was in the air.

There were three contenders for power. One was 42-year-old Wang Jingwei, the Nationalists' wunderkind, stylishly handsome, forever youthful, charismatic. A Cantonese like Sun Yatsen, Wang Jingwei had passed the fiendishly competitive civil service examinations and then gone on to study law and politics in Japan, where, like Chiang, he joined the Revolutionary Alliance. He rapidly developed a name for himself as a spellbinding speaker and a stylish essayist. Refusing to accept an arranged marriage, he had married the daughter of a rich Penang merchant who was a revolutionary in her own right. A failed 1910 attempt to assassinate Prince Chun, the regent of the child emperor, led to his arrest, a commuted death sentence and nationwide fame. This was much enhanced by the four beautifully crafted poems he published about his selfless sacrifice for China, in one of which he compared himself to the legendary *jingwei* bird, who spent his life carrying pebbles in his beak to fill the ocean, that is, in selfless sacrifice for the good of all. One line read: 'another day, when tender blossoms bloom/please recognise on them the speckles of my blood'.[27] Wang Jingwei, whose real name was Wang Zhaoming, had taken *jingwei* as his pen name.

Hu Hanmin, who was also from Guangdong province, led the right-wing challenge. Four years older than Wang Jingwei, he too had passed the civil service examinations, although at a higher level than Wang, and had then gone on to study in Japan after the Boxer Rebellion. He also joined the Revolutionary Alliance, becoming the editor of its main organ, *The People's Journal*. After the 1911 Revolution, he served as governor of Guangdong province and then joined the rebellion against President Yuan Shikai, after the failure of which he fled to Japan and helped Sun Yatsen reform the National Revolutionary Party, as the Nationalist Party was then called. He followed Sun Yatsen to Canton when Sun formed a new government there and acted in various senior positions, including as Minister of Transport, General Councillor and Acting Marshal when Sun was away from the city.

The third contender was not Chiang Kaishek but Liao Zhongkai. Born in San Francisco in 1877, where his father worked for the Hong Kong and Shanghai Bank, Liao Zhongkai had been educated in the United States, at Queen's College in Hong Kong and at Waseda University in Japan. Having joined Sun Yatsen's Revolutionary Alliance in the year of its founding, he became its financial expert, using his excellent connections among wealthy Cantonese as well as overseas Chinese to raise funds. In the 1920s, he served as Civil Governor of Guangdong province. He was one of the main architects of the first Communist–Nationalist united front and supported Chiang Kaishek's appointment as commandant of the Whampoa Military Academy. In 1923 Chiang resigned in protest at the origins of some of the funds that supported the academy and at Sun Yatsen's reliance on local militarists. In a stream of letters and telegrams to Chiang Kaishek, now back home in Zhejiang province, Liao Zhongkai beseeched him to retract his resignation, writing on one occasion that 'the finances of the Academy have been arranged and you can announce them upon your return. As to other reforms, these we should plan together. If we fail, it will not be too late to resign together then.'[28] Won over by this show of support, Chiang returned to Canton.

Wang Jingwei soon appeared to have emerged as the winner. He was at Sun Yatsen's side in Beijing as the stomach cancer overwhelmed him. On 11 March he recorded Sun Yatsen's Last Testament, in which Sun entreated his followers to 'arouse the masses and struggle together with all peoples in the whole world who treat us as equals',[29] a phrase that could be interpreted as an injunction to continue to work with the Soviets, as Wang Jingwei preferred. On 1 July, Wang Jingwei was elected chair of the National Political Council of the National Government, which had only just been set up. He also became chair of the Military Affairs Committee and the Central Political Council of the Nationalist Party. On 20 August, Liao Zhongkai was assassinated, an event in which, rumour had it, Hu Hanmin was implicated. Hu was arrested and, in an illustration of the influence the Russians wielded, was sent to the Soviet Union for further investigation. With Liao Zhongkai dead and Hu Hanmin out of the way, Wang Jingwei's position seemed secure.

However, Chiang Kaishek took Liao Zhongkai's assassination as evidence, so he wrote in his diary, of 'the existence of counter-revolutionary plots'.[30] Chiang had not been among the original candidates to succeed Sun Yatsen because he was still relatively young; also, as a mere military man, he lacked the stellar educational qualifications of Wang Jingwei, Liao Zhongkai and Hu Hanmin; and he had only just joined Sun Yatsen's inner circle. However, the growing influence of the Chinese Communists, including at the Whampoa Military Academy, and that of the Soviet advisors made Chiang suspicious about the direction of travel. These deepened when the Russian General N. V. Kubishev, nicknamed Kisanka or Pussycat, declared himself opposed to the Northern Expedition, a military campaign from Guangdong province which aimed to unite China, which Chiang believed had been Sun's cherished aim, and for which Chiang was now working hard to train up a new Nationalist army. The condescension of the Soviet advisors towards Chiang strained their relationship and increased his doubts about their intentions. General Kubishev described Chiang as 'irresolute' and unlikely to be a 'success as leader of troops without the aid of outside instructors'.[31] In 1926, Chiang wrote in his diary about Kubishev and the other Soviet advisors: 'I treat them with sincerity, but they reward me with duplicity. These are not comrades with whom I can work.'[32]

Chiang Kaishek's worries intensified further when Wang Jingwei chipped away at his hold on military power. Not only did Wang relieve Chiang of his posts of commander of the KMT's First Division and Canton garrison commander but he sided with Kubishev on the Northern Expedition and agreed to its cancellation. 'The situation is extremely dangerous,' Chiang concluded, 'No revolution will happen if we do not take drastic action to break through this difficult impasse … I must bear insults and shoulder a heavy burden to protect the party and safeguard the nation.'[33] Chiang became convinced that it was up to him to save the revolution that Sun Yatsen had begun. On 27 February, after a series of sleepless nights, he wrote: 'I must be firm in implementing my final decision, otherwise the damage to the party and the nation will be indescribable.'[34] On 5 March he added, 'my situation now is that of singlehandedly facing merciless enemies on all sides. I am like a lone minister without support at court and people treat me as a bastard son. May the souls of Sun Yatsen and other martyrs protect me so that I do not fail.'[35]

On 20 March, Chiang struck. He placed Canton under martial law, arrested those he believed to have been plotting his downfall, disarmed a Soviet guard platoon and secured the recall of Kubishev. Wang Jingwei fled to France to recuperate from his political wounds. A few months later, in June 1926, Chiang Kaishek led the National Revolutionary Army as commander-in-chief of the Northern Expedition, which two years later marched into Beijing, allowing Chiang to claim that he had completed Sun Yatsen's cherished dream of unifying China, bringing it under KMT control, thereby ending the warlord era. In 1929, Chiang Kaishek's portrait replaced that of Sun Yatsen on the Gate of Heavenly Peace. He had moved the National Government to Nanjing in 1927, making that city his capital, and now he claimed to govern all of China.

Chiang had every reason to feel vindicated when, on 6 July 1928, he led a memorial ceremony for Sun Yatsen, whose body rested awaiting burial in a crystal coffin, which had been donated by the Soviet Union, in the Azure Cloud Temple in the Western Hills just outside Beijing. Surrounded by the highest military leaders and officials on the Nationalist side, including provincial generals who had more or less willingly incorporated their forces in the Nationalist order of battle, Chiang reported to Sun's spirit that 'five times the Party came close to destruction and the forces of revolution faced defeat fifteen times',[36] but in the end they had triumphed and Sun's aim had been achieved.[37] Chiang then broke down and had to be helped away as tears streamed down his face.[38]

Chiang had become China's man of destiny, the saviour of the hallowed task that Sun Yatsen had set his followers – certainly in his own mind, if not everybody else's. The path that led Chiang to his new position of prominence revealed much about the man. He was a revolutionary, fiercely opposed to foreign influence in China, but also furious at the dominance of provincial elites, who held back even such minor forms of progress as new schools. For Chiang the transformation of China into a modern nation and the transformation of the self were two sides of the same coin: constant vigilance, strenuous effort, determination, study and sacrifice were needed for both.

Chiang did not reject China's past; indeed, he was inspired by heroic figures from Chinese history and the writings of Confucian philosophers, finding in them embodiments of qualities such as martyrdom, loyalty, duty, self-sacrifice and the management of human relations. He lived by such strictures in his relationships with Chen Qimei and Dai Jitao. Part of his ethic was that the leader demonstrates his moral suitability for leadership by recognising talent, respecting it and allowing it to do its work. Sun Yatsen had treated Chiang Kaishek with that kind of respect. Wang Jingwei may well have hurt Chiang more than he realised, or intended, when he took his command positions away from him, as by so doing he questioned Chiang's loyalty, reliability and talent.

Chiang Kaishek usually appeared in public in military uniform; a famous portrait has him sitting on horseback like Napoleon. He was willing to take huge risks, though he played his cards very close to his chest. He trusted few people then, and, inevitably, even fewer later. Chiang would always carefully analyse a situation – often using his diary for the purpose – assess the various forces impacting on it, and then, as with the ousting of Wang Jingwei, act suddenly and decisively when he judged the moment propitious and the impact likely to be decisive.

The victorious end to the Northern Expedition did not mean that answers had now been found to the deeper constitutional questions that had arisen out of the 1911 Revolution. Indeed, to these questions were now added a host of new ones. Large armies had emerged that had to be either demobilised or defeated. The Nationalists were deeply divided among themselves. The Communists were organising revolts in various places following their suppression in the White Terror, which the Nationalists had unleashed on the Communists during the Northern Expedition, leaving thousands dead, and thus sowing bitter legacies of hatred and distrust that would never go away. New relations also had to be forged with foreign countries, while foreign threats lurked on China's borders. The problems of Chiang Kaishek and his Nationalist government had only just begun.

— TWO —

NATION BUILDING

A house divided against itself cannot stand.
Abraham Lincoln, speech at Springfield, on accepting the Republican nomination
as senator for Illinois (16 June 1858)

On 18 September 1931, Lieutenant Kawamoto Suemori of the Kuantung Army detonated some sticks of dynamite close to the Japanese-owned South Manchurian Railway, near Shenyang. The act was part of a plot by Colonels Ishiwara Kanji and Doihara Kenji, his commanding officers in the Japanese Imperial Army (of which the Kuantung Army was a part), to create a *casus belli* for Japan's seizure of Manchuria. The next day, having accused the Chinese Nationalists of planting the dynamite, the Kuantung Army went into action. Dreams of imperial glory, anxieties about shortages and overpopulation, and a sense of foreboding that it was falling behind in the competition between armed empire blocs pushed Japan on a path that left devastation in its wake and the consequences of which it would have to live with for generations to come.

'First unity, then resistance' was the phrase Chiang Kaishek used in November 1931 to explain his approach to resisting Japanese aggression. In speeches and articles he insisted that China would be able to fight back against Japan only if the country was unified, its leadership had broad support and it was governed by a strong and effective administration. 'If domestically we are divided in our aims and our policies are uncoordinated ... we will repeat the Ming tragedy of being subjugated.'[1]

Chiang Kaishek was referring here to the fate of the Ming Dynasty, which had been overthrown in April 1644 by Li Zicheng, the leader of a peasants' revolt. When Li Zicheng seized the throne in Beijing, establishing his extremely short-lived Shun Dynasty, the Ming general Wu Sangui had turned to the Manchus for help. They had entered north China in force, defeated Li Zicheng's armies, and established the Qing Dynasty, which proceeded to rule China from 1644 until the 1911 Revolution. The failure of the Chinese to unite was allowing a foreign invader once more to seize a part of China, argued Chiang; and if such disunity continued, then the Republic of China could suffer the same fate as had befallen Li Zicheng. The Ming Syndrome, as this existential fear might be called, would haunt the minds of Chinese leaders, Communist as well as Nationalist, for decades.

Chiang had solid reasons to believe that it would be suicidal to take on the well-trained, well-equipped Kuantung Army. From the moment they took power right up to the Japanese attack in Manchuria, the Nationalists had been fighting one rebellion after the other. They had convened a military demobil-isation conference in Nanjing in 1929 at which the assembled regional military leaders had taken the oath 'We solemnly swear before the grave of Sun Yatsen that we will respectfully obey his last will and commit ourselves to troop demobilisation and saving the country.'[2] The words had hardly passed their lips before the Christian General Feng Yuxiang led a rebellion. This was followed shortly afterwards by an uprising in Guangxi province, south China, of the Guangxi Clique, whose leaders, Generals Li Zongren and Bai Chongxi, drew a powerful army, reckoned to be the second strongest in the country, from this poor province. Having joined the Nationalists during the Northern Exped-ition, they were a major force in their government. In 1930, during the War of the Central Plains, virtually all of the regional military commanders united in a punitive expedition against Chiang, accusing him of 'six crimes' which, they argued, had led him to 'part from the party and the nation and earn the hatred of the people'.[3] The ensuing civil war, which brought a million soldiers into the battlefield, lasted from May until November 1930 – thereby also reinforcing China's international image as a hopeless basket case.

Neither Chiang Kaishek nor his Nanjing government were popular in north China. Indeed, had he sent troops there when the Japanese took over Manchu-ria, not only would they have been defeated but the north Chinese generals would have wreaked their revenge. As in the north, so in the south. When the Japanese went into action in Manchuria, China's southern generals also refused to come to Chiang's aid. Chiang sent emissaries to General Chen Jitang, the chair of the Guangdong provincial government, and General Liu Xiang, who headed the largest army in Sichuan province. They rebuffed him, refusing to make any promises about what they would or would not do if he took action against the Japanese. Meanwhile, in his own backyard in central China, the Communists were building up base areas which Chiang had been unable to suppress. His conclusion was that 'only if we are united can we resist invasion. No country that has been internally divided has ever been victorious over a foreign enemy. We can only succeed if we are united, regardless of whether we use diplomatic or military means to deal with our foreign problems.'[4]

During the Nanjing Decade, as the years before the outbreak of full-out war in 1937 became known, military development was an important driver behind the nation-building efforts of the Nationalists. After it became clear that con-vincing the warlords to demobilise their armies was a non-starter, in order to establish their dominance they focused on building up an elite army, with German assistance. Chiang Kaishek regarded the way in which the German army related to the state and was embedded in its society as an essential element of Germany as a modern nation state, and saw China's divergence from this as an indicator of its backwardness. Chiang had learned about the German model while studying in Japan, of course, but he probably also read about it during the First World War in the Chinese press, which had followed events in Europe closely. One military thinker who had received much attention was General Friedrich von Bernhardi, whose 1911 book *Germany and the Next War* described war positively as a creative and cleansing act which brought the best out of a civilisation and strengthened its vitality – an idea which ran through Chiang's thinking as well.[5] Chiang's admiration for the German model also arose from the fact that even though Germany had been defeated in the First World War, it was managing to rebuild its army effectively and rapidly.

Well aware that military victory alone would never be enough, the Nationalists engaged in a host of other nation-building efforts, including constructing a new transport network, fostering industrialisation, promoting education and building up a modern government apparatus, including modern police forces, a judiciary and a civil service. They promoted the New Life Movement, based on a modernised and essentialised Confucianism, to help define the Chinese nation state as well as its culture. If in 1928 assessments and expectations of the Nationalists by foreign observers were low, a decade later they had been replaced by a grudging but nonetheless genuine admiration.

Military Reform

When the divisions of the National Revolutionary Army, as the Nationalists called their armed forces, entered Beijing, the Northern Expedition was declared triumphant. As so often, it proved much easier to begin than to end a war. The number of provincial troops incorporated into the army was alleged to have reached as many as 2.2 million men.[6] This figure included units under Chiang Kaishek's command, but excluded the Fengtian Army in Manchuria, as well as many other less important units. This was no doubt an overestimate, however. Generals padded their roster with fictional soldiers so as to increase their financial base. Nonetheless, it was still a very large number – a product of the fact that military muscle was an indispensable asset in the struggle for power, and also that in a country as poor as China, even at very low rates of pay, military service was an attractive proposition for many.

The Nanjing government adopted an approach that tried to find a way between furthering its core centralising and unifying agenda and the reality that its power was limited. In February 1928, it established KMT branch political councils in Canton, Wuhan, Kaifeng, Taiyuan and Beijing, which 'in their assigned jurisdictions exercise and supervise supreme local authority'. The main military generals were appointed as chairs of the branch political councils, while they also were given high appointments in the Nanjing government. In return for adopting the KMT nomenclature and accepting these appointments, they continued to enjoy virtual independence in the regions under their control.

Having decided to strengthen his own forces and make a core central army that could dominate all others, Chiang Kaishek turned to his German advisors to assist him. The first German advisor, Max Bauer,[7] an artillery expert who served on the German General Staff, had travelled to China in 1928, but in 1933 Chiang went one better when he induced General Hans von Seeckt, 'the Father of the National Defence Army' in Germany, to come to China. Von Seeckt viewed the army as a symbol of the nation: it manifested the state and ensured its dominance, both domestically and internationally, but was itself apolitical. In a memorandum to Chiang, von Seeckt argued that he should build an elite army of sixty divisions, supported by a highly trained officers corps, paid for out of central funds and with a strict personnel system, a strong logistical organisation and a domestic arms industry. The implementation of this vision for the Nationalist military was left to General Alexander von Falkenhausen, who had served in the German army in Turkey during the First World War and who had travelled widely in Japan and China.

In November 1932, the Nationalists established a covert general staff, the secret National Defence Planning Council, to implement von Seeckt's techno-nationalist vision. It began by collecting a vast amount of information, covering most provinces, about China's natural resources, transport infrastructure, marketing networks, population, agriculture, education, revenue flows, existing military forces and international relations, as well as Japan's armed forces. It drew up detailed plans for: the training of first six and then eighteen elite divisions; the assumption of control by the government over key economic sectors such as the electronics and iron industries; the construction of an industrial base in central China well away from the coast, which was vulnerable to invasion; the building of new transport links; and the training of a new officer corps. The data derived from these investigations formed the basis of a raft of new policies, including for the army, government ministries, various social programmes and culture.

Supported by a trade agreement with Germany, by which Germany provided arms and industrial equipment in return for Chinese commodities and mineral resources, this programme advanced with considerable speed in subsequent years. In 1934, a secret Army Reorganisation Bureau began to weed out the unqualified, ill or elderly from Nanjing's forces and retrain the remaining units. In 1933, the Nationalists promulgated a national military service law, which divided China into sixty recruitment regions, one each for the projected sixty divisions. The plan was that all males between the ages of eighteen and forty-five would become liable to serve either in elite 'reformed' divisions under officers trained at the national military academy or in territorial units. Following active service for two years, they would be obliged to serve for six years in the first reserves and then until the age of forty-five in the second reserves. Some 50,000 men were recruited in this way before the outbreak of war with Japan.[8] A specialist group took charge of the construction of fortifications. Nanjing, as the national capital, was kitted out with anti-aircraft and dual-purpose artillery. Heavy artillery was brought in from Germany to fortify Jiangyin, Zhenjiang and Wuhan along the Yangzi river, as well as coastal cities such as Xiamen, Canton and Ningbo. Defensive positions were prepared at Yellow river crossings and fortified points were also prepared at potential battle sites in north China, including at Xuzhou, where the key battle of the first year of the war would indeed take place.[9]

Detailed strategic plans were formulated with the help of German advisors, with the first national war plan formally issued in 1936. Given Japan's military superiority, China opted for a strategy of attrition which would exploit its vast space and huge population. China's most pre-eminent strategic thinker of the time, the colourful and learned Jiang Baili, argued that no resistance should be offered if Japan attempted to occupy China's coastal provinces and that the Nationalists should simply retreat into the hinterland. Von Falkenhausen disagreed, arguing that any attack should be met head on. The Nationalists also had to show that they were willing to make serious sacrifices to defend their country; the population could not be expected to make their own sacrifices if they did not. Von Falkenhausen's view prevailed.

On the eve of the War of Resistance, Nanjing was militarily in much better shape than it had been before. Its central army units' training and weapons surpassed anything that any domestic adversary could bring to the field. Its military dominance in China was assured, even though the ranks of the regional armies remained swollen. Agreement, too, had been reached among the Nationalist military leadership about what strategy to adopt if it came to war with Japan.

Civil Reconstruction

An important plank of Nanjing's nation-building programme was the New Life Movement, a Confucian moral rearmament campaign that had begun in the military in 1933, and was extended to the civil realm a year later. In conformity with the idea that revolution had to combine the transformation of society and of the self, it was based on the following diagnosis of China's ills:

> In our society today, the general attitude is one of moral laziness and apathy
> ... The bureaucracy is insincere and greedy, the people are disunited and

listless, the youth is degenerate and indulgent, adults are corrupt and muddle-headed, the rich live lives of elaborate but dissolute sophistication, and the poor are base and confused. The result is that the bonds that tie the nation together have been weakened, social order has broken down, we are defenceless in the face of national calamities, internal rebellion has spread widely, and foreign aggression continues unabated.[10]

The New Life Movement promoted 'four cardinal ethical principles' (propriety, righteousness, frugality and modesty) and 'eight virtues' (loyalty, filial duty, humaneness, love, faith, justice, peace and equality), all derived from Confucianism, which aimed at turning China's population into properly dressed, courteous, clean, punctual, honest and patriotic citizens who did not spit, knew when to shake hands and queued in line to wait their turn. A New Life hierarchy, reaching down to the lowest levels of society, especially in the cities, promoted New Life ideas by staging rallies, organising propaganda weeks, conducting theatre performances and dispatching students into teahouses and restaurants to upbraid their patrons for their extravagance. Limits were stipulated for banquets, weddings and official entertainment. Physical education and sports were promoted, with many schools installing running tracks, exercise machinery and playing fields.[11] Whatever else it aimed to achieve, the New Life Movement was to turn China's population into healthy and obedient material for the army.

Although it is easy to lampoon the New Life Movement – as indeed it was at the time – it has had a long influence. Even today many schools and offices in China display 'civility certificates' in the same way that those in the West display hygiene and health and safety certifications. Today, President Xi Jinping's administration has again imposed limits on entertainment allowances and continues to campaign against extravagance. New Life ideals have sufficiently broad appeal that their promotion bolsters the standing of those in power.

Building a national system of primary and secondary schools, as well as universities and research institutions, was a priority project. The aim was to nurture a common national identity around Sun Yatsen's Three People's Principles to 'enable us to achieve national independence, the spread of citizen's rights, and the development of the people's welfare'.[12] In December 1934, the Nationalists promulgated a programme for the gradual implementation of a four-year compulsory education system with the aim of eradicating illiteracy. Training colleges were established to train up the required teachers.[13] The Nationalist government also strengthened China's research culture. It supported the Academia Sinica, the Geological Survey, the Peiping Research Academy and the Nankai Institute of Economics, which were set up partly to increase knowledge of China within China but also to enhance China's international academic status. One of the most astonishing achievements was the archaeological excavation of the ancient Shang capital at Nanyang, until then considered mythical, and adding half a millennium to China's recorded history. It restored belief in the reliability of China's own historical record.

In the decade before war broke out, the Nationalists built 6,000 kilometres of public highways, laid 3,300 kilometres of railway lines, improved ports and opened airports. Along China's rivers and coast, steam and diesel vessels began to replace sailing boats. Bus companies provided motorised transport between cities. The Nationalists also introduced a new national currency. The economy grew at an annual rate of over 8 per cent and industry at an annual rate of 6.7 per cent, while electric power increased at an annual rate of nearly 10 per cent.[14] Vast engineering projects that aimed to tame rivers, build reservoirs and generate massive quantities of hydropower were instigated. The first plans for the Three Gorges Dam were drawn up at this time.[15]

The Nationalists also revitalised the *baojia*, a traditional system by which households were grouped into a nested hierarchy of networks whose members assisted and policed each other. The policy, regarded by Chiang Kaishek as of 'the greatest priority', was implemented in rural areas, especially in those in which Nationalist rule had only recently been established. Officials who neglected the *baojia* faced stiff penalties. The aim of the system was to keep China's farmers firmly in place in order to dampen refugee flows, draw settled societies into fighting banditry and strengthen control over predatory local officials.[16] Although presented in traditional terms, this too was a 'dual use' project. The Minister of War, He Yingqin, noted in a report that, besides its immediate role in restoring order and disciplining local officials, the *baojia* was a useful tool for spreading compulsory military service.[17]

Not everything, of course, was about preparing China for war. Real estate developments sprang up, with Western-style houses for the rich, while factories, department stores, restaurants, cinemas, shops and the demand for hired help pulled the rural poor into the country's burgeoning towns and cities. The number of cities with populations of more than 50,000 expanded from 140 in 1919 to 191 just before the war. The population of Shanghai reached 2.5 million, while those of Beijing, Tianjin and Wuhan grew to more than 1 million.[18] This was the modern world of light, speed, clocks and movement; of the modern girl with her closely cropped hair and sporty outfits; and of self-help books for an anxious audience eager to know how to behave in this new world. Radio stations played jazz as well as Chinese music, magazines reviewed the latest European fashion trends, and journals published experimental modernist writing. The 1930s in China was part of what historian Frank Dikötter has called China's 'age of openness', an openness only relative to what had gone before and would come later, but nonetheless offering genuine opportunities for debate, creativity and enterprise.[19]

Foreign Policy

Military strategy shaped the Nationalists' foreign policy as much as their domestic policy. They made sure that Japan was seen as the aggressor – not a hard thing to do – and that China was perceived as an internationalist state. When Japan seized Manchuria, Nanjing appealed to the League of Nations, which in 1932 sent an investigative team, led by Victor Bulwer-Lytton of Great Britain and including representatives from the USA, France, Germany and Italy. They met both Japanese and Chinese government leaders and visited Manchuria. By this time the Japanese had already inaugurated the new Manchu puppet monarchy of Manzhouguo and flattened parts of a Chinese section of Shanghai, both as a warning to the Nationalists of worse to come if they tried to fight and as a display of strength to the many foreign countries with a presence in Shanghai. Japan also sent forces into Rehe, a Chinese Mongolian province.

The Lytton Report to the League of Nations, published in October 1932, was even-handed to a fault. It described Chinese misrule in Manchuria and stressed that Japan had legitimate treaty-based claims in the region, but also argued that the actions of Japan's Kuantung Army could not be construed as acts of self-defence, denied that Manzhouguo had any popular support, and insisted on the withdrawal of the Kuantung Army into the South Manchurian Railway zone, as prescribed by treaty.[20] Even before the report was made public, the Japanese delegation at the League, led by Ambassador Matsuoka Yosuke, walked out. In March 1933, Japan formally withdrew from the League. Japan may have gained control of Manchuria, but it was now internationally isolated, leaving the field wide open for the Nationalists. The Nationalists also learned that appealing to international institutions gained them sympathy but not concrete assistance. They would have to rely on their own military strength.

In 1934, Chiang Kaishek published anonymously an article with the title 'Friend or Enemy?' in *Foreign Affairs*, a journal of the Foreign Ministry. In it he anticipated 'war between Japan and the USA or the USSR, or even a second world war'.[21] He also warned that, although China wanted peace, war was inevitable if Japan persisted in creating 'second and third Manchurias' by establishing a 'North China Country' and a 'Mongolian Nation'. If Japan wanted an 'East Asia for the Asians', its best course, Chiang advised, was to negotiate with China for the reinstatement of Chinese sovereignty over Manchuria, in return for which China would promote Japan's readmission to the League. He argued that Japan would be unable to conquer all of China: 'more than 100,000 Japanese troops have been unable even to establish or maintain order in so-called Manzhouguo.'[22] And even if Japan seized all of China's major cities and railway lines, that did not mean that they had won; the Nationalists would simply continue to fight from the countryside.

The Nationalists courted the USA. Many of their leaders, although not Chiang, had been educated there and greatly admired the country, especially its anti-colonialism. In 1933 Song Ziwen, Chiang's brother-in-law, who served as China's Finance Minister until October 1933, went to the US. Here he met with President Franklin D. Roosevelt, Secretary of State Cordell Hull and other political leaders, and in his public speeches stressed US–China friendship and cooperation. With the USA mired in depression and American isolationism intensifying, Song took to the airwaves. He mentioned that after the American Revolution, trade with China had been important to the US economy. He praised the USA for not being an imperialist country and, at a gala dinner also attended by the bestselling Pearl Buck, he refuted 'the assertion that Japan had to intervene in north China because there was no central and authoritative government there'.[23] Song secured a US$50 million loan for the purchase of wheat and corn on the open market to reduce shortages in China.

After finishing his meetings in the USA, Song Ziwen moved on to London, where he attended the World Economic Conference. Here, Song stressed that China did not 'exclude Western cooperation in the name of "Asia for the Asiatics"' and rejected 'national or regional isolation'; instead 'we welcome Western capital and skill. We desire to maintain a fiscal policy which will not prevent entry of foreign goods.'[24] Song made no concrete gains from his visit to the UK, seeing his proposals for a new banking consortium as well as for a loan from the British government rejected, but two years later the Treasury despatched Frederick Leith-Ross to assist the Nationalists with currency reforms and draw China into a sterling area. Nationalist diplomacy aimed to make clear to potential allies that China was a reasonable and internationalist country which welcomed trade and investment, while Japan was bent on kicking Western countries out of east Asia.

If the Nationalists received sympathy from the UK and the USA – but little else – until well after Pearl Harbor, the Soviet Union, threatened directly by Japan in Manchuria, would provide critical aid in the first two years of the War of Resistance. The cooperation between the Soviets and the Nationalists was purely pragmatic. The Nationalists had thrown Soviet advisors out of China during the Northern Expedition and executed thousands of Communists. Even so, after Japan's capture of Manchuria, Japan was a common threat. The two sides initiated secret negotiations in Geneva to restore diplomatic relations. In December 1932, Yan Huiqing, the Nationalist negotiator, and Maxim Litvinov, the Soviet negotiator, exchanged public diplomatic notes to announce that diplomatic relations had been resumed. But Chiang wanted an alliance, and sent the diplomatic historian Jiang Tingfu to Moscow to begin discussions to that end. Jiang was profoundly suspicious of Soviet intentions, fearing – rightly – that their policy aimed to entrap Japan in China, but he was also convinced that China needed Soviet aid and that national interest rather than ideology should determine foreign policy. His diplomatic views were shaped by his belief that the Qing Dynasty's less-than-adroit policy towards Britain had been a cause of the First Opium War. Appointed ambassador in August 1936, Jiang Tingfu masterminded negotiations that led a year later to a treaty of non-aggression, under which the Soviets delivered a vast amount of military aid once war broke out and extended China a credit line worth US$100 million.[25]

In the half decade between Japan's occupation of Manchuria and the beginning of large-scale fighting in 1937, the Nationalists followed a coherent policy of preparing their country for confrontation with Japan. They extended Nanjing's authority into provinces that had been virtually independent in 1932; they started building up an elite military force; they improved the economy year on year; and the New Life Movement began to instil a new sense of national identity and prepare the population for the sacrifices to come. They worked hard to position China as a peace-loving internationalist country.

Worldwide, China enjoyed a new respect. *The Times* of London published a positive article about 'progress in China' after Frederick Maze, the head of the Chinese Maritime Customs Service, gave a speech about railway construction, road building, irrigation projects and social and public works.[26] An exhibition of Chinese art organised a year later by the Royal Academy of Arts in London attracted over 400,000 visitors. In the US, newspapers reported on the resumption of international debt payments, the creation of a direct telephone link between the USA and China, and the high number of aeroplane exports to China. The *Washington Post* cheered a radio address by Song Meiling, Chiang Kaishek's wife ('China's Wellesley-educated "First Lady"'), which was broadcast around the world. Madame Chiang announced that 'China's "warlord" era, with its attendant civil strife, is nearing an end because public opinion opposes those who want to settle differences by the sword.'[27] The New China was beginning to command international attention.

Nonetheless, many problems remained, especially in the countryside, where only a minority of the population prospered from the Nationalists' nation-building. While the cities had their shanty towns, rural societies remained desperately poor. China's rural crisis, economists now argue, appears to have become acute in the course of the 1920s, when, estimates suggest, the country's food supply fell short of demand by 5 per cent. This only deepened in the 1930s, as the effects of the worldwide depression set in, warfare continued after the Northern Expedition, and extra local tax levies and rent-seeking by landlords depressed rural incomes still further. Widespread opium cultivation also reduced the production of food crops. The 1933 diary of a research team investigating conditions in the countryside makes for shocking reading:

> Shijiamo has irrigated land; the water comes from a small river. When drought occurs, the stream dries up, and the irrigated land becomes dry land. Opium is cultivated on this irrigated land, and the county administration taxes this land. In March of this year the peasants had to eat grass and bark ... Death from starvation, death from sickness, flight, selling oneself into bondage are common occurrences.
>
> Xiaotang village is much poorer than other villages. The peasants in this village starved to death in the autumn of 1928 ... The gates of the county seat are closed to prevent the peasants from entering.[28]

Drought struck north China in 1928–9. The Sino-Western Relief Organisation reported 20 million casualties, including 6 million deaths, and the Chinese press reported instances of cannibalism. In 1930, the Yellow river burst its dikes in Shandong province, and 1931 saw severe floodings of the Yellow, Yangzi and Pearl rivers, leading to a death toll of 2 million people. The Shandong typhoon of 1935 killed around 50,000 people and may have destroyed 2 million homes.[29] In 1926, Walter Mallory, the Secretary of the China International Famine Relief Commission, wrote his famous book *China: Land of Famine.* In the foreword, President John Finley of the American Geographical Society noted that, although 'every inch of soil is in cultivation, carefully manured, well and professionally tilled', nonetheless 'nearly a fourth of the people of the globe live in a land of famine'.[30] Rural conditions did not improve in the following years. In 1931, Pearl Buck published her Pulitzer Prize-winning novel *The Good Earth,* which tells the story of a rural family who, despite working hard, fail to beat the drought and famine.

The Nationalists developed several programmes to deal with the crisis. The *baojia* system was one. They also supported – or at least did not stand in the way of – local initiatives, such as the rural reconstruction efforts in Shandong province of Liang Shuming, memorably called the 'last Confucian', and at Ding county in Henan province by Princeton-educated Jimmy Yen, who had worked for the YMCA.[31] Both stressed local self-reliance and combined literacy campaigns, collaboration among farmers, health and hygiene improvements and technical advances, such as better-quality seeds, with political measures on security and rent reduction. The Nationalists promulgated laws to reduce rent and taxes and facilitated the purchase of land by those who worked on it. Rural cooperative societies provided credit and fostered the sharing of scarce resources such as tools. Refugees were resettled on fallow land. Perhaps in part because of these developments, but also because of improved climatic conditions and a decrease in warfare, from the mid-1930s rural conditions improved. In 1936, the harvest was up by 45 per cent compared to the average of the three years before.[32]

Nonetheless, the success of these efforts was limited. In 1937, large famines were reported in the provinces of Henan and Sichuan. *The New York Times* revealed that in Sichuan 'near famine conditions existed in wide areas of this province with 55,000,000 inhabitants', with 'two hundred persons dying from starvation daily in Chungking [Chongqing]'.[33] The China International Relief Committee reported that '2,000,000 residents of Western Honan have been stricken by a famine that has created 3,000 square miles of silence'.[34] Smuggling had become such an art that customs officers in Tianjin were issued with gas masks because smugglers used 'gas bombs to render them unconscious'.[35] Day-to-day conditions in China were improving but the country remained ill-prepared to face the might of a modern industrialised army.

THREE

NANJING, NANJING

> During that year Nanjing underwent startling expansion. The city
> government encouraged people to build new, modern, custom-designed
> houses in the remote northern section of the city. Just a few years before,
> the Drum Tower, which now rests in the centre of the city, had been one of
> the northernmost points in the city.
>
> Ye Zhaoyan, *Nanjing 1937: A Love Story* (2004)[1]

Chiang Kaishek's Nationalists chose as their capital Nanjing, a city in Jiangsu
province on the Yangzi river some 300 kilometres to the west of Shanghai.
They had good practical reasons for doing this, including the fact that their
power did not extend much beyond the provinces of Jiangsu and Zhejiang.
They also had good reasons *not* to choose other cities. Beijing was danger-
ously close to Manchuria, which was virtually independent and where Japanese
influence was strong. Beijing had also been the home of, first, the Mongols, and
then the Manchus – alien invaders. One strike against Canton was that Hong
Kong, the British colony, was nearby. Also, although Sun Yatsen had made
the province his base, the tax hikes the Nationalists had implemented there
to finance the Northern Expedition and their suppression of a series of local
rebellions had left a lasting legacy of resentment. The Northern Expedition was
as much an effort to escape Cantonese hostility as to reunify China; virtually
throughout the entire decade before the War of Resistance a rival Nationalist
faction governed Guangdong province.

Nanjing, on the other hand, was eminently suitable to be the Nationalist
capital. It had already served six times as China's first city, including during
the Ming Dynasty. It was also at a healthy distance from centres of foreign
power in China such as Shanghai, Beijing and Tianjin. In addition, many of
Chiang Kaishek's most important supporters, including his most trusted generals, came from the lower Yangzi region.

During the Ming Dynasty, Nanjing had been a sophisticated and prosperous
city, with a population of up to a million people. It was famous for its entertainment quarter, its sophisticated literary life, its commerce in porcelain, silk
and ironware, and for its magnificent sixteenth-century porcelain tower, whose
fame had spread as far as Europe. However, the Taiping Rebellion of 1850–64
had wreaked terrible damage on Nanjing, from which even by the 1920s it had

not recovered. When on 19 July 1864 Qing forces entered the city (which had been the capital of the Taiping Heavenly Kingdom) having laid siege to it for many months, they massacred its inhabitants and razed many of its buildings. During the 1911 Revolution, revolutionaries sacked its Manchu quarters, and in 1913 it once again suffered when forces loyal to President Yuan Shikai torched the city while suppressing the Second Revolution.[2] The growth of China's foreign trade had made Shanghai a global trading centre, from which other cities such as Wuhan, up the river in central China, had benefitted. But this new source of wealth had bypassed Nanjing, which remained closed to foreign trade until the 1890s and never caught up. Parts of Nanjing, especially its northern districts, remained in ruins when the Nationalists made it their capital. Farmers tilled land where once there had been houses and roads, with the occasional bridge sticking out from the weeds the only reminder of a prosperous past.

Nanjing's condition did, however, provide the Nationalists with an excellent opportunity to demonstrate their mettle as China's saviours. They were determined to turn Nanjing into a model capital city, on a par with Paris, Vienna, Washington, Berlin and St Petersburg, and to transform this once great but now derelict metropolis into a new source of national pride, and so make it a symbol of China's regeneration. In 1929 the city government adopted the Capital Plan, drawn up by Chinese urban planners largely trained abroad and assisted by foreign advisors, brought in to ensure that the plans met the most exacting and advanced international standards. The Capital Plan stipulated the construction of a network of wide asphalted boulevards so that motorised traffic could travel freely around the city, an administrative district with imposing government buildings, an airport to welcome foreign visitors, a large central station, a financial district, an industrial zone and designated residential areas. The city was to be clean, with a robust sewage system and fresh water piped into homes; comfortable, because of its parks, public spaces and newly planted plane trees, which would shade the streets during the scorching summer; and interesting, because of its museums, theatres, radio stations and cinemas.[3] A modern police force was to be instituted to regulate traffic and fashion order out of the feisty din that had been normal street life, while street lights were to be installed to make the roads safe to travel at night. The city was to be cleansed of all that its planners associated with backwardness: its smells, its filth, its noises, its narrow alleys and its unruly population, which lived and worked in small, tightly packed neighbourhoods.

Naturally, these hugely ambitious plans ran into resistance from Nanjing's residents, who did not want their houses demolished or their neighbourhoods torn apart. The plans could have been realised in full only if the Nationalists' coffers were overflowing, which they were not. In any case, the military operations against the numerous rebellions they had faced in the first eight years of their rule had taken priority. The floods, droughts and famines of the 1930s were to render lavish spending on the reconstruction of Nanjing both politically unwise and of secondary importance.

At the heart of the new Capital Plan, and hence of the new country that the Nationalists hoped to create, was the Sun Yatsen Mausoleum. This was to be much more than just the building in which Sun Yatsen was interred. The aim was to turn it into the ritual centre of the new nation, which would draw strength from his legacy, presented as uplifting and uniting. The mausoleum was designed as an illustration in stone and marble of the country's origins, its future and its core beliefs. It was to serve as a stage on which to conduct state functions and so fill the void created by the disintegration of imperial China's rich stock of ritual practices.

The Nationalists were not fools to dedicate so much energy to symbolic work. The significance of ritual and symbolism in China was illustrated by the attempt of its first president, Yuan Shikai, to restore monarchical government in 1916. He had made the attempt when the institutions of the early Republic were unable to keep the country together and when he faced Japan's Twenty-One Demands, made during the First World War, which would have virtually turned China into a Japanese colony. President Yuan's monarchical movement, however, triggered widespread opposition, which compelled him to abort his plans. The May Fourth Movement that erupted across the country shortly afterwards not only made clear that the country's future could not be built on a return to the past, but also left China in the throes of a divisive cultural war. The Cultural Revolution of the 1960s illustrates that the question had lost nothing of its acuteness fifty years later; the attempt today to construct national rituals around China's war with Japan is a response to the same issue.

The turn to Sun Yatsen as a source of inspiration for a new national narrative and ritual practices was an obvious move. Sun had a long record as a nationalist revolutionary; his death had been marked by mass outpourings of grief; he had been compared to the greatest figures not just in Chinese but in world history; and in his dress and speech he represented modernity. When Sun Yatsen was interred in his mausoleum, *The New York Times* was dismissive of his record as a politician and thinker, but also remarked that 'it is as a symbol of nationalism, rather than as the founder of the Chinese Republic, that Sun Yatsen bids fair to play a great role in the history of this country'.[4]

The Sun Yatsen Mausoleum

'Bury me on Purple Mountain', Sun Yatsen had said on his deathbed.[5] Purple Mountain is a park with high hills and winding paths located outside the city walls to the east of Nanjing. Its highest peak rises to 450 metres above sea level.

As well as the Sun Yatsen Mausoleum, Purple Mountain is dotted with hundreds of iconic buildings, most famously the Ming Xiaoling. This is the tomb of the first emperor of the Ming Dynasty, its high walls and winding Sacred Way lined with exotic marble animals and guarded by two marble eunuchs. There is also the Linggu Monastery, one of the most famous Buddhist monasteries in China; the tomb of Sun Quan, an emperor of the third century AD; the tombs of two Ming generals, Xu Da and Chang Yuchun; a memorial to foreign airmen, including Russians and Americans, who died in the Second World War; a cherry tree orchard donated by the Japanese which grows over the grave where Wang Jingwei, the man Chiang Kaishek ousted, is buried; and the tomb of the murdered Liao Zhongkai, one of the three men who might have succeeded Sun Yatsen. One can learn a vast amount of Chinese history, both ancient and modern, from walking through this park.

Sun Yatsen chose Purple Mountain because it was in Nanjing that he had established the Republic of China and had been elected its Provisional President – thereby helping change the course of Chinese history. Sun also insisted that 'my body should be permanently preserved using scientific methods',[6] that is, it should be embalmed, as Lenin's and Napoleon's had been, so that his grave would become an enduring symbol of the cause he had led.

The Nationalists established a Preparatory Committee for the Funeral of Sun Yatsen. The Committee decided that Sun's mausoleum should be built on the main southern slope of Purple Mountain, higher up and to the east of the tomb of the first Ming emperor, and that the design should be decided through an international competition. Among the Committee's stipulations was that Sun's sacrificial hall should be open to the public so that all citizens could pay their respects to him. This was a very modern idea: access to imperial mausoleums had previously been restricted to a very few, such as the succeeding emperor, the chief mourner. Sun's mausoleum, however, was going to have enough space to accommodate a mass of up to 50,000 people, for the solemn national ceremonies that the Nationalists intended to conduct there. The revolutionaries, protesters and strikers whose energy had brought forth the upheavals of the 1911 Revolution, the May Fourth Movement of 1919 and the mass protests of 1925 were to be present as obedient citizens in these rituals.[7]

The Capital Plan designed the new Nanjing around Sun's mausoleum. The plan also provided for a new centre of government south of Purple Mountain, directly below the mausoleum, with its ministries arranged along a north–south-running grass mall dissected by a wide boulevard, with new party headquarters at its northern – and hence most important – end, with a rotunda with a fountain directly south of it. Had this mall been built, party and government officials would always have had to look up to Sun Yatsen's mausoleum, and so be reminded of the tasks he had set them. The arrangement conformed with the traditional idea that the ruler looks south and also with the *feng shui* notion that nature's forces roll down a mountain.

Lu Yanzhi, the architect whose design won the competition, stipulated that a retaining wall in a bell shape should form the border of the mammoth 12-hectare site. According to Lu, his choice of shape had been made purely on aesthetic grounds, but the judges of the competition seized upon this feature as uniquely appropriate, illustrating Sun Yatsen's lifelong aim of awakening China.[8] It suggested that Sun's message would continue to echo through China and referenced the Liberty Bell in Philadelphia, thus giving Sun's mausoleum a connection with the American Revolution.

The mausoleum was designed to take mourners and pilgrims on a journey that begins at an oval plaza at the base of the mountain slope, on which stands an archway adorned with the Chinese characters for 'universal love' in Sun Yatsen's own hand. From there a stairway with 392 steps, symbolising China's estimated 392 million citizens at the time of building, ascends through the formal entrance gate of the mausoleum inscribed with the characters for 'all under heaven are one community', again in Sun's own calligraphy. The stairway ends at a large plaza leading to the main sacrificial hall in which sits a statue of Sun, staring ahead with a scroll on his lap, as if patiently giving a lecture. A narrow corridor leads to a round tomb chamber in which is a marble sarcophagus with a marble effigy of Sun Yatsen on its lid. From a balustraded walkway, visitors walk round the sarcophagus, their gaze drawn to Sun's body, before re-entering the sacrificial hall.

The tomb chamber is similar in design to Napoleon's at the Hotel des Invalides in Paris, while the sacrificial hall echoes the Lincoln Memorial in Washington. The Chinese words for democracy, nationalism and the people's livelihood – that is, Sun's Three People's Principles – are inscribed above its entrance. Sun's *Outline for National Construction* as well as his Last Testament, including the famous injunction 'the revolution has not been completed; let all comrades strive to implement it', are engraved into its walls. These texts assert that China was not yet ready for democratic government but needed a period of tutelage by the KMT to awaken it, thus providing a justification for Nationalist rule.[9]

All who made the pilgrimage up the stairway into the sacrificial hall, around Sun's tomb, and then down again would be constantly reminded of Sun's principles and urged, again and again, to direct their lives towards their fulfilment. They would also be reminded in many ways of China's imperial mausoleums. This was a clear attempt to draw strength and legitimacy from the mystique of China's imperial past, but it also indicated a new beginning. Many of its features – the steps in three rows, the large curved roofs, the arches, the marble and columns – would be familiar to pilgrims, but they would also be struck by what was new. The mausoleum's roofs were covered in blue rather than yellow tiles, blue being the colour of the sky and of the KMT, for whom Sun had designed as its flag a white sun in a blue sky. If visitors looked up to the ceiling of the sacrificial hall, they would see the KMT flag painted on it. The suggestion was that the Nationalists were building a New China, but one that accorded with an enduring sense of the country's essence.

The mausoleum was a piece of didactic architecture. It positioned the Nationalists' New China as a country with a distinct and venerable cultural heritage, but also a backward present, with the KMT, as part of a worldwide revolutionary process, leading the country towards a new future of unity, nationalism and democracy. It made Sun into 'the father of the country', portraying him as a kind and sagacious teacher who was concerned for all and who had pointed out the path towards a prosperous, inclusive future, free from foreign oppression.

The mausoleum emphasised certain elements of Sun Yatsen's ideology and neglected others. Sun envisioned the New China as a democratic republic with five branches of government, namely the executive, the judiciary and the legislative as per normal, but also an examination branch to supervise national examinations and a control branch to inspect misbehaviour in office. The republic would be based on Sun's Three People's Principles – as mentioned, democracy, nationalism (including the elimination of all foreign privilege in China) and the people's livelihood (a concept never fully explained, but which referred to the use of a tax on rent to provide housing, clothing, education and transport for all). Sun wrote, lyrically almost, about large infrastructure projects such as a national railway system (which China's current government has now delivered). Though the Nationalists made much of these aspects of Sun Yatsen's legacy, especially his idea of China needing a period of tutelage, they heeded little his advocacy of high levels of local self-government.

Sun's was a message of hope, holding out the prospect of a China with efficient bureaucracies, speedy and efficient transportation systems and a prosperous people who energetically, courteously and happily worked for the common good. Sun's call for 'universal love' and his insistence that 'all under heaven are one community' stressed equality, inclusivity and solidarity. But he also insisted that China's revolution would go through three stages: the violent destruction of the past, to be followed by a period of tutelage before the final transition to constitutional government. Sun's belief in the need for a period of tutelage under Nationalist auspices derived from his assessment that the cause of the implosion of the republic after the 1911 Revolution was that 'the Chinese people are deficient in knowledge', a condition, he said, that had resulted from them 'having been soaked in the poison of absolute monarchy'.[10]

The emplacement of Sun Yatsen's body in his mausoleum on 1 June 1929 was turned into a mass spectacle that involved the entire nation. On 10 May, a train with a giant portrait of Sun Yatsen fixed to its front was sent north to Beijing. Events to draw in the crowds – music, speeches, plays, mimes and martial arts performances – were held at each of the twenty-six stops along the way. The return journey was conducted in a sombre and solemn mode. Representatives of the party, the government, civic organisations and military bands waited at stations decorated with wooden arches and flags. When the train arrived, mourning music was played, heads were uncovered, all bowed – not kowtowed – three times to Sun's coffin and then observed three minutes of silence. Afterwards, phonographs played records of Sun Yatsen's speeches.

After the arrival of Sun Yatsen's remains in Nanjing, they were interred in the mausoleum with intricate ceremony. A catafalque carrying his body processed along a boulevard now named after Sun. The body lay in state at the Presidential Palace, where Sun had announced the establishment of the Republic of China. Mourners were arranged in groups, with the highest party and government officials paying their respects first, followed by representatives of government ministries, the armed forces, provincial governments, overseas Chinese, Tibetans, Mongolians, civic associations, farmers unions and merchant associations.[11] At 5 a.m. on 1 June a large procession set off from the Presidential Palace, preceded by criers, mounted soldiers, infantry and a marching band. The procession passed through twenty ceremonial arches, symbolising each province, the special municipalities and overseas Chinese and arrived four hours later at the mausoleum, where Chiang Kaishek presided over the interment ceremony.

This was a staged affair, intricately put together to achieve a number of objectives. It provided an excellent opportunity for the Nationalists to disseminate far and wide Sun's vision for China as they wished it to be interpreted. The ceremonies instantly turned Sun into one of China's greatest historical figures and so sanctified the activities of those who were now left to implement his will, with Chiang Kaishek leading them. Sun's enshrinement was also a way of ritually saying that the first phase of the revolution, marked by violence, was now over. It initiated a new set of practices, which these rituals, through their repetition, orderliness, awe and spectacle, indicated would anchor the New China.

The Nationalists worked hard to make their message stick. Sun's portrait hung in every party and government office. The KMT flag he designed fluttered from all party and government buildings. Every Monday morning, party members conducted a Sun Yatsen memorial service. This began with attendees standing up and bowing three times to Sun's portrait before observing a minute's silence. The liturgy then required the presiding officer to read Sun's Last Testament, which was followed by a lecture expounding on Sun's ideas or reporting on recent progress towards their fulfilment. The Sun Yatsen suit became the regulation outfit for the new elite. Grey in colour, it consisted of a long jacket with a round collar and trousers, all of whose features were said to symbolise some part of Sun Yatsen's teachings. The five buttons of the jacket, for instance, were supposed to refer to Sun Yatsen's five branches of government.[12] The Nationalists literally wore their Sun Yatsen-ism on their sleeves.

The mausoleum was put to work, too. Before every KMT party congress, executive committee plenum, national conference organised by this or that ministry or national convention of one of the many professional associations, attendees would conduct a pilgrimage to the mausoleum. On the mornings of public holidays, Nationalist leaders conducted a public sacrifice in the sacrificial hall, laying a wreath in front of Sun's statue after performing the proscribed ceremony.

Chen Kewen's and Chi Pang-yuan's Roads to Nanjing

In order to become the true capital of China, Nanjing needed to be more than a centre of government and ritual. It had to bring together a great variety of people from across the country for all kinds of activities. In the course of the 1930s, Nanjing began to evolve into such a place, attracting hordes of people attending the many meetings organised by the KMT, government ministries, the army and professional associations. Its sports stadium hosted national sports meetings. Its universities, including the new Central University which trained government personnel, its military academy and its aeronautical academy recruited students from across the country. Academia Sinica, its prestigious research institute, attracted some of China's most famous scholars. New businesses, such as the electronics firm Panda, founded in 1936, brought in engineers, electricians and businessmen. The roads to Nanjing were many and varied, as will become clear from the circuitous trajectories by which Chen Kewen and Chi Pang-yuan, our guides to a more personal history of wartime China, ended up in the capital.

Chen Kewen was born in 1898 into a family of educators in a small village in south China's Guangxi province at a time when village feuds racked the area. Kewen's family had fallen on hard times after the early death of his father, leaving his mother without a stable source of income, which led to her strangling Kewen's twin brother at birth. That twin's existence would be remembered in the family in that Kewen would become known as Fifth Uncle rather than Fourth Uncle, while he used Number Five in his pen name. Kewen was a child of the May Fourth Movement and, like many youths energised by the movement, he joined his school mates in raids on temples to trash religious icons. At the age of sixteen, he was married to the daughter of a local landowner. Unlike others of his generation, he never rejected this arranged marriage, but he did give his wife a new name, National Resurgence. This may sound strange to Western ears, but the name would not have seemed at all odd to Kewen and his family, as personal names in Chinese are made up of regular words and in modern times have often reflected the values, aspirations and concerns of the age, as here.

The May Fourth Movement created the pathways that landed Chen in Nanjing as a Nationalist official. He attended the Great Renewal School his older brother had founded and then studied at the provincial middle school. In 1919, he passed the entrance examinations of the Guangdong Teachers University in Canton. When the Nationalists made the province their revolutionary base, Chen became an activist. After graduation, he taught at a school he founded with friends, edited the party newspaper *Citizen News* and became Secretary of the Farmers Department of the Central KMT Party Headquarters. Chen joined the Northern Expedition, travelling through the provinces of Jiangxi, Hunan and Hubei. He worked with none other than Mao Zedong in the Peasant Movement Training Institute and helped write the 'Draft Programme for Reform of the Land Ownership System'. Most importantly, he became a close associate of Wang Jingwei. Following Chiang Kaishek's victory in the struggle for power between the two, Chen moved to Hong Kong, where he edited Wang Jingwei's mouthpiece, the *South China Daily*, and published a translation of F. J. C. Hearnshaw's *An Outline Sketch of the Political History of Europe in the Nineteenth Century*, which emphasises the benefits of an elite meritocratic ruling class dedicated to maintaining peace, security and morality in a hierarchical social order.[13]

Japan's seizure of Manchuria in 1932 prompted Chiang Kaishek and Wang Jingwei, whose prestige remained high, to work together in government again, with Chiang in charge of military affairs, which included oversight of civil affairs in the many areas where there were ongoing military operations, and Wang Jingwei heading the Executive Branch. This reconciliation enabled Chen Kewen first simply to visit Nanjing without fear of trouble, as he did in that year, and then, in 1935, to move to the capital full time, where initially he took charge of the General Office of the Executive Branch and then of a section overseeing the affairs of overseas Chinese. Although Chen Kewen suffered the loss of a child at this time, nonetheless he would appear to have entered a prosperous phase in his life. In the spring of 1936, he purchased a plot of land in the Lucerne Garden New Village in the foothills of Purple Mountain, using a loan of 6,500 yuan from the New China Trust and Savings Bank to finance the building of a new home.

Living with his wife and mother, Chen Kewen adopted a modern Chinese lifestyle. He enjoyed watering his plants, weeding his lawn, going on walks, hosting gatherings with his friends, their wives and children at his new home, and watching sunsets. He was glad, too, that he could take his mother to the

Central Hospital where Western-trained doctors alleviated her arthritis and dentists cured her inflamed gums by pulling out most of her teeth. Chen enjoyed meeting the great and the good of Nanjing, including Wang Jingwei himself, of course, but also Liang Shuming, the 'last Confucian sage', then busy working on his rural reconstruction movement in Shandong province,[14] and south China military top brass such as Generals Zhang Fakui and Yu Hanmou. Chen and his wife went to watch movies and theatre performances, including of the great Peking Opera singer Mei Lanfang. At Sun Yatsen memorial ceremonies, he listened to speeches by General Chen Cheng, then masterminding the construction of fortresses in central China; the economist Weng Wenhao, who was pioneering central planning in China; and the Confucian nationalist and Chiang confidant Dai Jitao.

Having taken the views espoused by Hearnshaw as well as the New Life Movement to heart, Chen Kewen was determined to behave as a rational, responsible, dedicated and honest civil servant. He was infuriated when he saw a woman put curlers in her hair at a meeting at the City Hall auditorium, when others were dressed slovenly, and when the proceedings were brought to a halt after twenty minutes for a group photograph. He criticised a speaker at a meeting of the Guangxi Fellows Association for being 'immature, flippant, and exaggerated'. He criticised colleagues for being 'absent on holiday' and not taking their work seriously. He also worried that, at a meeting to commemorate the tenth anniversary of a new city government, he found the rosy speeches difficult to take because 'agriculture is bankrupt and there are natural disasters everywhere'. Despite such criticism and worries, Chen Kewen's diaries of the time reveal a man who believed that China was making a hopeful new beginning.

Chi Pang-yuan was from a younger generation. She was born in 1924 at the opposite end of China, in a village near the town of Tieling in northern Liaoning province, where winters were bitterly cold, with the temperature regularly sinking to –20 to –30 Celsius, and the summers commensurately short. A physician who saved her life after her birth, when all her family except her mother had abandoned hope, named her 'the beauty of the country', a learned reference to the Confucian classic *The Book of Odes*.

Pang-yuan's family had risen from obscurity to become one of the most prominent households in Manchuria. Her grandfather, unwilling to look after the family's farm, had attended the Baoding Military Academy, where Chiang Kaishek had also studied, and after his graduation had joined the Fengtian Army of General Zhang Zuolin. General Zhang did well during the 1911 Revolution and rapidly became the military strongman of Manchuria. Pang-yuan's grandfather rose with him, becoming a brigade commander in General Zhang's army.

Pang-yuan's father, Chi Shiying, was a child of his time just like Chen Kewen. In an important gesture symbolic of his republican sympathies, he cut off his queue, a sign of obedience to the Qing Dynasty, soon after the 1911 Revolution. As a young child, he had travelled with his father and mother, living in the barracks to which his father was assigned, thus gaining a much wider knowledge of the area than most young men of his time. At the age of fifteen, he enrolled in an English missionary secondary school in Tianjin, and so became familiar with all the new Western ideas that were flooding into China at the time. He successfully competed for a government scholarship to study in Japan, where, besides learning English and German, he developed a lifelong interest in philosophy, the subject he studied at Tokyo Imperial University a year later.

After his grandmother died, the family insisted that Chi Shiying, who was by then nineteen years old, should return home to marry a local girl from a wealthy family. When he refused, an uncle was dispatched to fetch him. He agreed to return home and marry on condition that 'there would be no kneeling and kowtowing, they would not wear red bridal clothes … he would ride a horse rather than a sedan chair, and he and his wife would go to study abroad together'. These conditions 'were accepted, but except for allowing him to ride a horse, everything else was done in accordance with old customs'.[15] Chi Shiying was only at home during the summers, spending the rest of his time abroad, leaving his wife to face the hard, lonely life of the traditional daughter-in-law, subject to her mother-in-law's every whim and having to do myriad chores without complaint. She frequently fled to a nearby pasture to cry her heart out.

Chi Shiying moved to Germany after he completed his studies in Tokyo, studying philosophy and sociology first at Berlin and then at Heidelberg University, where he read Karl Marx while being taught by Heinrich Rickert, a philosopher of history, and Alfred Weber, one of the founders of human geography (and Max Weber's younger brother). Chi concluded that 'only true understanding and rational education could begin to save backward and degenerate China'.[16] Returning home in 1924, committed to promoting modern education in Manchuria, he became acquainted with a young, idealistic general in the Fengtian Army, Guo Songling. General Guo, whose thinking had been shaped by the May Fourth Movement, invited Chi Shiying to take charge of a new middle school for Fengtian Army children.

The connection to General Guo Songling changed the fate of the Chi family. In 1925, General Guo, by now convinced that civil war should stop and that General Zhang Zuolin should focus on reconstructing Manchuria, rebelled against General Zhang's attempt to assert his influence in north China. The rebellion soon collapsed. By this time Chi Shiying was serving in General Guo's foreign affairs office. The Chi family feared not just for Chi Shiying's life, but also for that of his father, who was still employed in one of General

Zhang's armies. General Zhang chose to be magnanimous: 'The father is one generation, the son another. The kid is a scoundrel, messed up by his study abroad, but his dad should be spared.'[17] General Guo and his wife were captured and executed, with their bodies left to rot in a Shenyang market for three days before relatives were permitted to bury them. Chi Shiying, with six colleagues whose task it had been to rally foreign support for the uprising, found refuge in the Japanese consulate, where Consul Yoshida Shigeru refused to hand them over to Zhang's men, treating them as political refugees. A few months later he facilitated their escape via Korea and Japan to the Japanese concession in Tianjin. Consul Yoshida will reappear in the last chapter of this book as Japan's first post-war prime minister, agreeing a peace treaty between China and Japan.

By now well known in Manchuria, Chi Shiying was to become useful to the Nationalists, once they won him over. They courted him assiduously, ensuring that he met many prominent figures in the party, including Chiang Kaishek. Chi took his time to make up his mind, reading material published by the Communists as well as the Nationalists, but concluded that Sun Yatsen's Three People's Principles offered China its best hope. When Japanese forces occupied Manchuria in 1931–2, Chi agreed to take on the dangerous task of liaising with anti-Japanese resistance forces in the area and facilitating the move south of Manchurian refugees. After the Japanese routed the Manchurian resistance, Chi went back south, taking up residence in Beijing, near the action in Manchuria and in contact with the Manchurian resistance. His family, for whom staying in Manchuria was also no longer an option, joined him in Beijing. They moved house and changed their name frequently to avoid arrest, with the result that on many a morning Chi Pang-yuan asked her mother, 'Mummy, what is my name today?'[18] When life became too difficult in Beijing, they moved to Nanjing.

Chi Pang-yuan remembered the Nanjing Decade as 'a golden decade for our country, and for my father'.[19] Her family lived in safety, first in a cramped old apartment near Xuanwu Lake in the centre of Nanjing and then in a house in a new development area 'with Nanjing highest mountain, Purple Mountain, visible from the second floor bedroom'.[20] Chi Pang-yuan would look back in nostalgia to this period 'because Mummy was no longer a fragile young woman. She and my father formed a strong bond of affection in this tumultuous period. She felt fortunate to share his many hardships. Her wholehearted acceptance of and dedication to her lot gave me a strong sense of security while I was growing up.'[21] Pang-yuan's father did make more covert trips to Manchuria but, having concluded that little good would come of them, he decided that his efforts would be better spent looking after refugee families, lobbying the Nationalists and ensuring that the youth of Manchuria would get an education.

With financial support from the Nationalists, Chi Shiying established North-east Zhongshan Schools – 'Zhongshan' being Sun Yatsen's personal name as pronounced in standard Chinese when rendered in *pinyin*, and 'the North-east' being the term the Nationalists used for Manchuria, as do the Communists today. Chi first established North-east Zhongshan Schools in Beijing and elsewhere in north China, and then in Nanjing. Pang-yuan was happy at school and made friends, while her parents entertained refugees from the North-east every weekend for dinner. One of these dinners, held just after a New Year, made a deep impression on Pang-yuan. Her brother invited a friend from school, the son of the head of the Shenyang Police Department whom the Japanese had doused in petrol and burned to death in public as punishment for the help he had provided to the Manchurian resistance. The rest of the family had fled and dispersed, leaving this young man essentially an orphan. What impressed Pang-yuan was that 'with all the dignity that an 18-year-old young man could muster to hold back his tears, he told the story of his family's destruction in front of the warm stove in our comfortable home'.[22]

In 1928, enemies of the Nanjing government far outnumbered its friends. Not only were Chiang Kaishek's warlord competitors in China's regions hostile to Nanjing, so were others, including many public intellectuals, such as twentieth-century China's greatest author, Lu Xun. However, especially after the Japanese occupation of Manchuria, a good number of these made their peace with the new order, regarding the Nationalists as offering the best hope for resisting Japanese aggression. Nanjing also gained the not-uncritical support of substantial sections of the urban financial and entrepreneurial elites, overseas Chinese community leaders (especially in south-east Asia) and the growing professional classes of lawyers, Western-trained medical practitioners, architects, engineers and teachers. There were many ways by which people found their place in the new order. Contingency, fate, misfortune, ambition, idealism and money all played their roles.

Nanjing was a Nationalist statement of intent. The city functioned as a showcase of the New China. The ritual practices they initiated, the Sun Yatsen suits in which they dressed and the invented Chinese palace-style architecture in which they built their public buildings were indications of the New China they aspired to establish. In time such initiatives might have taken on a patina of durability, naturalness and inevitability and gained a compelling force of their own. But that point had not been reached when the War of Resistance with Japan began.

FOUR

TO WAR

And you will hear of wars and rumours of wars. See that you are not alarmed, for this must take place, but the end is not yet. For nation will rise against nation, and kingdom against kingdom, and there will be famines and earthquakes in various places.

Matthew 24:6–7

On 27 December 1936, China erupted in jubilation. Two weeks earlier Chiang Kaishek had been taken prisoner by his supposed allies in what became known as the Xi'an Incident and had been at serious risk of being put to death. But he had been released and returned safely to Nanjing. As the news of Chiang's return spread and the implication sank in that another round of civil war had been avoided, 'firecrackers made Shanghai like a battlefield of the Western Front. Hundreds of thousands turned out to celebrate the Generalissimo's release. Similar demonstrations are reported from many important centres throughout the country.'[1] *The New York Times* reporter Hallett Abend, who was no great admirer of Chiang Kaishek, reported a day later that 'many cities are busy sweeping up the debris of the fireworks celebrations, and telegrams congratulating the generalissimo on his safety are filling all wires'. Chiang's popularity, 'at a low ebb eight months ago, now has risen to extraordinary heights'.[2] A coup attempt can do wonders for one's political career – if one survives.

Chiang burnished his new status with a somewhat haughty show of magnanimity, issuing a public statement that told his captors: 'as you no longer try to make any special demands or force me to give any orders, it marks a turning point in the life of the nation ... and as you both admit wrongdoing, you may remain my subordinates.'[3] One of the main coup plotters, General Zhang Xueliang of the Fengtian Army, accompanied Chiang on his flight back to Nanjing. He was to spend much of the rest of his life as Chiang's prisoner, mostly under a loose house arrest. In 1993, at the age of ninety-two, he was allowed to leave Taiwan. The plight of General Yang Hucheng, the second coup leader, was worse: he was executed in 1949, along with his wife and children, just before the Nationalists retreated to Taiwan.

Ever since the Japanese occupation of Manchuria, Chiang had put unification before resistance. When the Marco Polo Bridge Incident, triggered by a

Japanese soldier going missing near Beijing, erupted in July 1937, Chiang Kai-shek's suddenly enhanced status and his judgement that the Japanese did not want a serious war in China at this time led him to see the incident as an opportunity to push back against Japanese encroachment in north China. Even if some Japanese leaders, including members of the top military brass in Tokyo, were hesitant about going to war with the Nationalists at the time, they would not give in. Thus began the Second World War in east Asia.

On a Collision Course: Chinese and Japanese Policies before the Xi'an Incident

In 1936, China's northern provinces hosted a large number of armies: General Yan Xishan in Shanxi province commanded 43,000 troops; General Han Fuju had as many in Shandong province; 28,000 troops served under General Song Zheyuan in the provinces of Hebei and Chahar; and General Yang Hucheng's North-west Army also had 28,000 troops. With 85,000 men in Shaanxi province alone, the Fengtian Army of General Zhang Xueliang was the largest force in the region. In addition, there were the Communists. Following the Long March, they had set up a new base at the town of Yan'an in northern Shaanxi province. The prospects were grim for all: bitterly cold in the winter, the area could not support this many soldiers, and if China came to blows with Japan, then these forces were in the front line, a heroic but risky place to be.

Following on from its occupation of Manchuria, Japan's aim had been to create a series of autonomous authorities all along the Soviet Union's southern flank, from the Gulf of Bohai in the Yellow Sea, through northern China and the Inner Mongolian provinces of Rehe, Chahar and Suiyuan, all the way to Xinjiang province in the far west.[4] Japan's first push came in January 1933, at a time when Nanjing's forces were battling the Chinese Communists in central China. When a skirmish took place at the Shanhaiguan Pass, where the Great Wall of China plunges into the Gulf of Bohai, fighting between Chinese and Japanese units spread to most passes on the Great Wall in northern China. Unwilling, and unable, to mount any sort of campaign against the Japanese, Nanjing decided that its best option was to negotiate. The Tanggu Truce, signed on 31 May 1933, in the city of Tianjin, provided for a demilitarised zone south of the Great Wall and implied a *de facto* Nationalist recognition of Japanese control of Manchuria and Rehe, which the Japanese now occupied.

Contrary to common Western perceptions, Inner Mongolia was not an empty no-man's land. In the 1930s Prince Demchugdongrub was able to bring the Mongolian tribes in Suiyuan province together under his leadership. According to the historian and journalist Owen Lattimore, who had travelled widely through Mongolia, Prince Demchugdongrub was a Mongolian nationalist, who, frustrated by Nanjing's refusal to meet him halfway, had been 'unable to resist the assertion of Japanese control'.[5] In 1933, he established a Mongol federation, which agreed an alliance with the Japanese puppet state of Manzhouguo in Manchuria, triggering a flood of Japanese funds, arms and advisors. In December 1935, Prince Demchugdongrub moved his forces into northern Chahar, annihilating the modestly armed Peace Preservation Force of the Nationalists who were based there. In the following spring, he occupied southern and eastern Chahar, severing the strategically significant Beijing–Suiyuan railway and establishing a Mongolian government at Huade county in south-east Chahar, some 175 kilometres north-west of Beijing.

After the Tanggu Truce, Nanjing and Tokyo both signalled a desire for improved relations. In early 1935, Japan's foreign minister announced that Japan would follow a policy of non-aggression. Wang Jingwei, then China's premier and Minister of Foreign Affairs, assured Japan's ambassador to China, Akira Ariyoshi, that China, too, hoped for 'a relaxation of the present tension'.[6] Wang announced an end to China's boycott of Japanese goods, a boycott that had stymied Japan's economic recovery from the Great Depression. However, in May the chief of staff of Japan's China Garrison Army in north China, Major Hashimoto Guma, took the initiative into his own hands.

After the murder of two Japanese journalists, Guma demanded a KMT withdrawal from Hebei province, including from the cities of Tianjin and Beijing. Units of the Kuantung Army moved south from Manchuria, demands were ramped up and an ultimatum for their acceptance was set for 12 June. As had happened in Manchuria, Tokyo followed where its field commanders led. Still unready and unwilling to fight back against Japanese inroads, Chiang Kaishek again opted to negotiate. The result was the withdrawal of the Nationalists from Hebei province and the creation of the East Hebei Anti-Communist Autonomous Council.

At this time, Chiang's priority was to strengthen Nanjing's position in south China. His success in driving the Communists from central China, which had allowed him to implant his forces in all the provinces through which the Communists had fled, caused the authorities in Guangdong and Guangxi provinces to fear that he was now aiming to surround them. Their attempt to mount a rebellion collapsed as a result of Chiang's growing military strength; the adept use of bribes, which induced several infantry divisions and Guangdong's air force to declare loyalty to Nanjing; and the failure of other provinces to rise up in support. By July, Guangdong's Chen Jitang had retired to Hong Kong, leaving Guangxi isolated. Following several months of negotiations, the leaders of the Guangxi Clique, Generals Li Zongren and Bai Chongxi, accepted appointments as determined by Nanjing and professed their loyalty in return for the promise that any further Japanese inroads would be resisted. The Guangxi Clique had sought to foment support for their rebellion by loudly calling for resistance to Japan – at a very safe distance from any front lines. By avoiding civil war and facing down the Guangdong and Guangxi rebels, Chiang enhanced his prestige considerably.

With the situation in south China much improved, in 1936 Chiang Kaishek turned his attention to the north, focusing initially on Prince Demchugdongrub's Mongolian federation, a move that meant challenging Japan by proxy. In the autumn Chiang travelled to Xi'an and Loyang for parleys with Generals Fu Zuoyi and Yan Xishan about a counter-offensive into Chahar and Suiyuan involving central forces under General Tang Enbo's command disguised in the uniforms of Yan's Shaanxi Army. These combined central–local forces were to 'undertake an offensive to Bailingmiao with a feint toward Shangdu' – key cities under Prince Demchugdongrub's control.[7] They succeeded in capturing both, in victories hailed by Chiang Kaishek as 'the beginning of China's rejuvenation'.[8] US military intelligence agreed, stating that 'Chinese resistance is stiffening and public opinion is rallying behind the resistance'.[9]

Chiang then wanted to push ahead with a follow-up offensive, supported by his air force of seventy aeroplanes. However, he was forced to call off the operation when General Zhang Xueliang refused to implement his order to press ahead with a campaign against the Communists, whose new base at Yan'an, according to Chiang, threatened the rear of the forces fighting Prince Demchugdongrub.[10] He also feared that Prince Demchugdongrub and the Communists would form an alliance.[11] General Zhang's refusal had come as a result of the fact that Chiang Kaishek welched on an earlier promise to allow him to move into Suiyuan.[12] The relationship between the two broke down; discussions ended in shouting matches; Chiang told Zhang that if he disobeyed his orders to suppress the Communists, he would disperse his armed forces to the provinces of Fujian and Anhui, meaning that Zhang would lose them.[13]

General Zhang Xueliang, supported by General Yang Hucheng, whose units were in the majority in the city of Xi'an itself, took Chiang Kaishek prisoner on 12 December, not only because of this rupture in relations, but also because for many months they had been negotiating with the Communists to form an alliance against Chiang under the banner of forcing Chiang Kaishek to resist Japan. In preparation for this uprising, they made contact with other generals in northern China as well as in Sichuan province in western China.[14]

To make the situation even more complicated, Chiang Kaishek too had been in discussion with the Communists. In November 1936, a Nationalist negotiator told his Communist counterpart that Chiang's conditions for settlement and a new Communist–Nationalist united front were a reduction of the Red Army to 3,000 personnel, with the assignment of all its officers to Nationalist army units and the incorporation of its Communist officials into the Nationalist administration.[15] Essentially, in return for ending military action against them, and in accordance with his aim of creating a unified China under a centralised authority, Chiang demanded their submission.[16] When Generals Zhang Xueliang and Yang Hucheng took Chiang Kaishek prisoner, Chiang's gambit to exploit his thrust into north China to bring the Mongolian Federation to heel and to deal with the Communists once and for all appeared to have misfired spectacularly.

The Xi'an Incident

On the morning of 12 December, just as Chiang had completed his morning exercises in his temple residence a few miles outside Xi'an, the sound of gunfire alerted him to the fact that all was not well. His suspicions having already been aroused two days earlier, Chiang concluded that General Zhang Xueliang's Fengtian Army had revolted. He was right. Together with two bodyguards, Chiang climbed over an outside wall into a moat far deeper than he had anticipated, hurting his back to such an extent that he was 'unable to move for three minutes'. Under cover of the morning fog, the three climbed up the hillside north of the temple, with Chiang more crawling than walking because of his injury.[17] They hid in a small cave under some rocks, but were soon discovered. As his captors approached, Chiang told them: 'I am Chiang Kaishek. You have found me, so it is up to you whether you kill me. However, I continue to be your superior officer. Do not humiliate me in any other way.'[18] The soldiers led him away.

The coup quickly petered out. One reason for this was that Stalin believed that the Nationalists were in a better position to rally China against the Japanese than the Communists. He instructed the Communists, who could not afford to alienate him, not to support Zhang Xueliang and to facilitate a quick settlement. Stalin was concerned that if Chiang Kaishek was removed or killed, a different, more pro-Japan faction might take charge of the Nationalists. Moscow quickly made known that it was not behind the plot and that it regarded the coup as 'Japanese-inspired skulduggery, intended to make China easier prey for Japan's next bite'.[19] Following a rapid build-up of Soviet forces, its Far East Command at the time of the Xi'an Rebellion had at its disposal some 250,000 troops, more than 800 aeroplanes and around twenty submarines.[20] Although in a strong position, Moscow was reeling from the shock delivered by the Anti-Comintern Pact, signed only weeks before, on 25 November, by Germany and Japan. In this, Japan and Germany vowed not to sign any treaty with the Soviet Union, to consult each other if the Soviet Union attacked either one of them, and to collaborate in the fight against international communism, while Germany also agreed to extend diplomatic recognition to Manzhouguo. Moscow concluded that Japan and Germany intended to foment trouble in countries bordering the Soviet Union prior to a joint attack. It concluded that 'a united, self-confident China, next to the Soviet's own Red Army, is the strong-est protection the Soviet Union can have against Japanese aggression'.[21]

Stalin threw his weight behind Chiang Kaishek. While deploring 'Chiang's anti-Communist stand',[22] Moscow praised 'his progress in unifying China and his increasing firmness against Japanese demands'. Stalin ordered the Chinese Communists to change their strategy towards the Nationalists. Learn-ing of Chiang's capture the day after it had happened, on 13 December, they were delighted, telling General Zhang Xueliang that 'the whole world rejoices about the arrest of the mother of all criminals' and informing Moscow that 'the elimination of Chiang Kaishek can only have positive results'. They were astounded, no doubt, when Moscow told them that their call for Chiang's dis-missal and trial was 'inappropriate' as it undermined 'a united front to resist Japan'. Moscow ordered the CCP to 'firmly advocate a peaceful settlement'.[23] Their negotiator, Zhou Enlai, the future premier, was dispatched to Xi'an to see that this happened.

Other factors leading to the quick resolution were, first, that Nanjing des-patched its best units, including its air force, on a 'punitive expedition' to Xi'an and, second, that, as in the case of the revolt of the provinces of Guangdong and Guangxi, no other significant regional leader was prepared to come out in support of the coup. Nanjing's forces made rapid progress in their march to Xi'an and a week after the coup had begun were ready to surround the city.[24] Rumours circulated that 'a small but powerful cabal' in Nanjing was pressing ahead with military action, which included bombing raids, not to save Chiang but to get him out of the way so that they could implement a Japan-friendly foreign policy.[25] It is likely that a number of key regional generals had promised support to the coup, but that when push came to shove, they did not do so. One of them, General Han Fuju of Shandong province, even loudly declared that he had become a 'Nanjing ally'.[26] The plotters had become isolated.

During the coup, Chiang gave all the signs of being willing to die a mar-tyr's death. Following Sun Yatsen's example, he drew up a last will in which he wrote: 'my actions have been so misguided that reactionaries have been able to exploit them to incite their forces ... I must sacrifice my life for the party, the country, and the people.'[27] According to his brother-in-law Song Ziwen, who arrived in Xi'an on December 20 and jotted down a set of notes of all that had transpired shortly after the incident was over, Chiang had told him that 'he could not agree to anything under duress, and that the only way is to leave everything to a military solution', of which Chiang Kaishek would likely have become a casualty.[28] General Zhang Xueliang told William Donald, an Australian advisor to the Nationalists who had flown to Xi'an to mediate, that Chiang Kaishek 'wants to be a martyr'.[29] The yearning for martyrdom can be a powerful one.

According to the journalist Hallett Abend, who had a private dinner with Chiang Kaishek and Madame Chiang shortly after their return to Nanjing, Chiang appeared to have a religious experience at Xi'an. 'He had refused food, he refused water, he refused the services of a doctor ... except his one expressed wish, a Bible.' Abend also reported that Chiang told him that 'I confessed my sins and shortcomings, and then I prayed that if God had really chosen me to lead China to her salvation, he would show me a sign.'[30] When Chiang opened his eyes, 'I saw two white hares', which he followed to their hide-out when he tried to escape. Abend commented that 'always since that captivity in December of 1936 the Generalissimo has devoutly believed that he has been chosen to lead China to her eventual salvation'.[31]

It is not the case that joint resistance to Japan by the Nationalists and the Communists had become a certainty. However, there had been discussions. According to Song Ziwen, Chiang had initially agreed to the following four terms: 1) reorganisation of the government; 2) renunciation of the He-Umezu Agreement (made in June 1935, by which Japan took virtual control of Hebei); 3) the launching of a campaign to resist Japan; and 4) the release of seven political prisoners. But then Chiang changed his mind, refusing to agree to anything while he was in captivity. Song had talks with Zhou Enlai and General Zhang Xueliang, while shuttling back and forth between Nanjing and Xi'an by aeroplane. Various verbal promises were made, which boiled down to Communist recognition of Chiang Kaishek as China's national leader, an end to the Communists' anti-Nationalist operations, Nationalist financial support for the Communists if they joined the fighting against Japanese forces, as well as the removal of most pro-Japanese Nationalists from the government.

After these few promises were made, Chiang Kaishek and Zhou Enlai met briefly, and then Chiang, his wife, Song Ziwen and Zhang Xueliang made their way to the airport – in some haste, as they feared that General Yang Hucheng 'might use force to secure the person of Chiang Kaishek'. Instead Yang Hucheng had 'a violent altercation' with Zhang Xueliang, stating that 'you started the coup and without securing anything you are allowing the Generalissimo to go. He will surely cut off our heads.' Zhang Xueliang feared for his life, not just because of his altercation with General Yang, but also because many officers in his own forces were unhappy with him. Upon his arrival in Nanjing, he declared to Chiang that 'I have penitently followed you to Nanking to await punishment befitting my crime.'[32] He was despatched to a villa frequently used by Madame Chiang, in the foothills of – where else – Purple Mountain.

Following up on their verbal promises at Xi'an, the Nationalists and the Communists conducted negotiations for a final agreement.[33] Chiang Kaishek wrote in his diary that his ultimate aim was the abolition of the CCP, the disavowal of communism by its members and incorporation of Communist forces into the Nationalist order of battle.[34] His negotiators promised financial support and supplies, permissions for the Communists to administer a number of counties in Shaanxi province, not as a Soviet but as a Special Region, and retention of a small number of troops. Zhou Enlai, the Communist negotiator, wrote in a paper setting out his negotiation strategy that the Communists were prepared to 'acknowledge the leadership of the KMT in the entire country' and halt anti-KMT activities, but they could not agree to the abolition of the CCP. However, if 'the KMT can reorganise itself as a national revolutionary alliance' (Chiang Kaishek had made noises about this at Xi'an), then the CCP would join as a bloc.[35] Zhou argued that the CCP would not renounce communism but would accept the Three People's Principles of Sun Yatsen as appropriate for China today. No agreement was reached before the outbreak of war.

Even if the Xi'an Incident did not lead to an immediate agreement between the Nationalists and the Communists, three things had changed. The incident had made clear exactly where the Soviet Union stood. Chiang Kaishek was their man in China; Stalin was prepared to order the Communists to support him; and they had done so. Secondly, the incident removed the Fengtian Army as a significant force in north China. Before the Japanese ejected it from Manchuria in 1931–2, it had been a powerful force of 150,000 troops or so, well stocked with arms from the Shenyang arsenal. The Fengtian Army had retreated into north China, but over time dissatisfaction and demoralisation had spread through its ranks. Following the Xi'an Incident, the army was initially transferred to the provinces of Henan and Anhui, then its units were distributed to other commands. Chiang Kaishek had removed the most serious military threat to Nanjing in north China.[36] The third change was that Chiang's stature had increased and that he had come to see himself as carrying the fate of the country on his shoulders.

The Throw of the Dice

Even though Chiang Kaishek returned to Nanjing a national hero, his back was still giving him pain and he remained in poor health for six months. A period of respite to recover from his wounds was extended twice, until the end of May. During this time Chiang frequently went back to his beloved hometown of Xikou. His first, depressing task was to arrange the burial of his older brother, Chiang Jieqing, who had collapsed when he heard that his younger brother had been taken captive. He never recovered and died on 27 December.[37] Jieqing had a significant political career of his own, having served as a district magistrate and as a member of the governing council of Zhejiang province. His death meant that Chiang Kaishek became the pater familias, responsible for managing the affairs of the Chiang family. Chiang also had to bury one of his subordinates, General Zhang Peilun, who died in February 1937. A happier development was the return of his only son Ching-kuo from the Soviet Union. Ching-kuo had gone there to study in 1925 but had been detained as a hostage from 1927, when Chiang Kaishek had dismissed his Soviet advisors. Ching-kuo returned to Xikou with a blonde Russian wife just three days after the interment of his uncle. Ching-kuo, who had denounced his father while in Russia, was given a Chinese tutor and put to work in a remote location, probably to reacquaint him with Chinese customs and to test his loyalties.

Even the best Shanghai doctors were unable to cure Chiang Kaishek's back.[38] Abend reported to the US ambassador, Clarence Gauss, that when he interviewed Chiang in June 1937, he found him 'not in good health', wearing braces for his back and in constant pain.[39] Chiang also suffered from terrible toothache. The treatment for this was straightforward, if radical. In April, over the course of a number of days, Chiang had his remaining eight teeth pulled out in a Shanghai hospital. Once recovered, he felt 'as if a great burden has been lifted', but also had the realization that 'I am beginning to age'.[40] Throughout these months, Chiang complained in his diary of feeling overburdened, indecisive and listless. Only in early July did he regain a sense of equilibrium, writing on 1 July, 'I did not sleep well, but I rose early and gave a lecture for one hour and a half without feeling tired: my strength is back.'[41] By the time he had to face the Marco Polo Bridge Incident, Chiang was beginning to feel both physically and mentally stronger.

Following the Xi'an Incident, Chiang was also optimistic that he could achieve the full reunification of China in 'three to five years'.[42] His focus was on dissolving the Fengtian Army and on bringing the forces of General Liu Xiang in Sichuan province to heel: 'If we are able to unify and reorganise these two large old forces, then although the warlords of other provinces will still have many troops, they will be nothing to worry about.'[43] While 'maintaining the status quo' in northern China, the immediate priority was 'to secure Hunan, settle Sichuan, and consolidate Guangdong'.[44] In terms of foreign affairs, Chiang focused on drawing Britain closer into Chinese affairs, sending his Minister of Finance, Kong Xiangxi, to London to discuss economic, intelligence and military cooperation.[45] But an outbreak of fighting between Chinese and Japanese forces jerked history in a different direction.

The Marco Polo Bridge Incident

In the summer of 1937, Colonel Mutaguchi Renya, commander of the First Infantry Regiment of Japan's China Garrison Army, was training his units as part of a radical military reform programme.[46] First Infantry were stationed in north China by virtue of the Boxer Protocol of 1901, which gave foreign countries the right to station troops at the diplomatic missions in Beijing as well as along the railway line from Beijing to the port city of Tianjin. By 1937, with most foreign embassies having relocated to the new Nationalist capital at Nanjing, there remained little reason for foreign countries to keep troops in northern China, but Japan did. It had some 7,000 troops in the area, armed with artillery, tanks and aircraft.

Colonel Mutaguchi ordered drill after drill for his units, made up of both veterans and raw recruits straight from Japan, so that they would respond rapidly and aggressively to any incident. A recently introduced training manual stressed night-fighting capabilities to ensure that they could bring their skills to bear at a time of day when the enemy was at its most vulnerable. In early July, with the company-level training course completed, Mutaguchi shifted to battalion training, insisting on the use of live ammunition, not only to make the exercises realistic, but also because the local population, wearied by the incessant night-time disruption, had grown hostile. Exhausted by months of night-time training, worn down by the oppressive summer heat and operating among a resentful population, Mutaguchi's units were on edge.

On 7 July, one unit under Mutaguchi's command, Eighth Company, led by Captain Shimizu Setsuro, marched from their barracks with partial field pack (a small concession to the stifling humidity of a north China summer), canteen, ammunition, emergency rations and weapons through territory controlled by General Song Zheyuan's 29th Army to their assigned training ground near Marco Polo Bridge, a twelfth-century bridge known for the beauty of its eleven arches. What happened next remains unclear to this day.

It may well be that 'the trouble started when Chinese troops mistook a sham attack on Marco Polo Bridge for a real one', as *The Times* of London reported.[47] In any case, having heard gunshots, Captain Shimizu conducted a roll call which revealed that Private Shimura Kukujiro was missing. When Captain Shimizu heard more gunfire from the direction of the fortress city of Wanping, which guarded the eastern shore of Marco Polo Bridge, he demanded entrance to the city to conduct a search. As it was late at night, the Chinese duty officer at Wanping declined his request, arguing that such an action was bound to lead to disturbances. The following morning, Captain Shimizu's forces, reinforced by troops from the Japanese legation guard at Beijing and the nearby town of Fengtai, began an assault on Wanping which lasted for five hours and ended, as Hallett Abend reported, when 'the Chinese retreated under machine gun fire, suffering heavy losses. Scores of bodies were reported floating downstream.'[48] Some 200 Chinese and ten Japanese lay dead.

The Marco Polo Bridge Incident became famous because of the chain of events it set in motion rather than because it was a particularly egregious instance of Japanese high-handedness. Although this it was. 'It is no secret,' as *The Times* stated, 'that their military exercises and training proceed as if it were Japanese territory. The river at Marco Polo bridge is used as a target for artillery fire regardless of the farming activities of the Chinese peasant ... Japanese soldiers have summarily arrested Chinese in the streets of Peking and even in their houses, and Chinese and foreign civilians have frequently been manhandled.[49] However, similar incidents had happened before.

Confronted once again with a spot of local difficulty, the Japanese and Chinese commanders on the scene quickly moved to de-escalate the situation and begin negotiations for a settlement. Had they been left alone, containment would likely have won the day. Decisions in Tokyo and Nanjing, however, ensured that the Marco Polo Bridge Incident came to mark the beginning of full-out war between China and Japan, a war that over the next seven years was to cause untold damage to China and, in its last year, to Japan as well.

Powerful voices in both countries clamoured for war. In Japan, two cabinet members, Muto Akira of the General Staff and the chief of the Military Affairs Department, Tanaka Shin'ichi, made the case for war.[50] China, they argued, should be dealt with now, while it remained divided and its military reforms were far from complete. This was so that Japan would not have to worry about its rear when the time came to fight the Soviet Union, which was a far stronger and more dangerous opponent. A war would also have gone down well with considerable segments of the Japanese population, who were smarting from the effects of the 1930s depression, high levels of military expenditure, concentration on investment in heavy industry and disappointing returns from Japan's empire-building plans, not just in Korea, Taiwan and Manchuria, but also in north China.

In China, enthusiasm for war could be found in many places, too. Intellectuals, students, the Communists, civic organisations, the press and even some regional leaders – often generals without much loyalty to the central government in Nanjing – called for armed resistance against Japanese aggression. Many criticised Chiang Kaishek for failing to defend China. Every twist of the Japanese knife had been met with large demonstrations 'to resist Japan and save the country' in cities and towns across China, including Nanjing, Beijing, Shanghai, Canton, Wuhan and Changsha.[51] After the Japanese occupation of Manchuria, 'commercial, political, and patriotic organizations throughout the country swamped government officials at Nanking with telegrams, and newspapers and speakers voiced resentment'.[52] At the second anniversary of the occupation, students across China vowed: 'I swear to avenge national humiliation.'[53] In 1935 Beijing witnessed 'immense student demonstrations' when autonomous governments were inaugurated in Hebei and Chahar in north China and Inner Mongolia, with the protestors shouting slogans such as 'China for the Chinese' and 'Down with Japanese Imperialism'.[54] In 1936, policemen in Tianjin had problems coping with student protests there,[55] while in Chengdu, in the far-away province of Sichuan, Japanese offices were ransacked and some Japanese civilians killed.[56] War was a popular option in China, too.

But there was no real rush to war. In Japan, Premier Konoye Fumimaro, who was a vacillating and worrying sort, had only recently been appointed. In the six months previously, two other administrations had come and gone. The political atmosphere was tense, with Japanese elites still in shock from a military coup by young officers in February 1936 which had led to the deaths of several senior politicians. Premier Konoye wanted stability, not adventure. Parts of Japan's military were also reluctant to go to war at this point because a comprehensive military reform programme had only just begun. Even Colonel Ishiwara Kanji, one of the masterminds behind Japan's seizure of Manchuria, who was now serving at the Tokyo High Command, argued that the policy of building up a string of autonomous regions across north China should be abandoned and that relations with Nanjing should be improved. This would ensure that Japan's rear area would not become a threat if war broke out with the Soviet Union, which had strengthened its Far Eastern front. A revised Japanese war plan called for the avoidance of friction with China and insisted that any incident should be settled quickly and locally.[57] Foreign Minister Sato Naotoko called for a 'new start' in relations with China, jettisoning earlier demands for China to recognise Manzhouguo and collaborate with Japan in the fight against communism.[58]

For the Chinese, if it did come to a full-blown conflict Chiang Kaishek could have no confidence in the outcome. His armies were inferior, the authority of his government in north China remained fragile at best, and some top commanders, government officials and public intellectuals were warning against escalation. George E. Taylor, an American educator who spent a few years in China advising on building up modern universities, spelled out the dangers in a prescient article published in the *Manchester Guardian* in February 1937:

Ordeal by battle, it is urged, would unite the nation. On a very long view this is probably true, but would the Nanking Government survive the ordeal? Those who think that China could resist in the interior provinces forget that the revenues of the National Government, such as Maritime Customs, Salt Administration and Railways, depend on the coastal provinces and big cities – the easiest objects for Japanese conquest. A government driven from the capital and cut off from Shanghai would be little more than a guerrilla band and its large unpaid armies willing material for the Communists ... Millions of peasants have almost nothing to fight for, and these, in the disorder and economic dislocation which would necessarily be part of war, would find the problem of livelihood far more urgent than that of resisting the enemy.[59]

Chiang Kaishek was well aware of the risks. A few months later, he contemplated the possible outcomes of the war that had now begun. He worried that it would lead to a resurgence of the warlordism that racked China after the 1911 Revolution; that the Chinese Communists would 'win over the masses' and 'seize political power'; that Japan and other foreign powers would agree a settlement that would end with China's partition; that the Nationalists would split apart, with one grouping forming a 'bogus government'; and that war would cause economic collapse and economic disintegration so that 'the people will grow to hate the war and turn their backs on it'.[60] Many of these nightmares would be realised.

Escalation to War

Japanese imperialism – that is, Japan's desire to drive Western countries from east and south-east Asia and then colonise these areas – was the deep cause of the Second World War in east Asia. No country, if it had the means, would have tolerated the presence, let alone the high-handed actions, of foreign military units on its own territory. Had Japan's leaders been more thoughtful about the strength of Chinese nationalism, more realistic about the essential weakness of their own position, and less keen to take affront, it might have dawned on them that by far the better response to the Marco Polo Bridge Incident was to forge ahead on evolving a workable settlement with the Chinese Nationalists.

Japan's response to the incident got off to a bad start when Premier Konoye shied away from facing down Army Minister Sugiyama Hajime, who had called for a forceful response, including the despatch of three divisions to north China to beef up Japan's China Garrison Army. On 11 July Konoye adopted the implausible policy of approving Sugiyama's request on the condition that the accepted policy of non-expansion be maintained and that the troops were recalled if the situation changed.[61] Konoye's problem was that Sugiyama, who refused to discuss military affairs in cabinet on the grounds that he could not trust some of its civilian members, could bring down his government by resigning.[62] In the Japanese constitutional system, as interpreted at the time, the army answered to the Emperor alone.

But it is not the case that Chiang Kaishek merely reacted to Japanese provocation, severe as it was. He based his actions on the belief that the Japanese were 'strong on the outside, but brittle inside'.[63] He judged that the Marco Polo Bridge Incident provided him with an opportunity to press Nanjing's claims in northern China. He ordered the Nationalist 21st and 25th Divisions to the area, thinking, as he wrote in his diary, that he could pressure the Japanese into evacuating Fengtai, the town near the March Polo Bridge, abolish the 'bogus East Hebei Autonomous Council'[64] and smash the He-Umezu Agreement.[65] Chiang gambled, as he had done before.

The situation soon span out of control. On 14 July, local Japanese military authorities declared that 'the entry into Hopei [Hebei] Province of troops of the Chinese Central Government will violate the Tanggu Truce of June 1934 and will not be tolerated'.[66] As Japanese forces poured into northern China, on 17 July Chiang Kaishek made his now famous 'The Limit of Our Endurance' speech from Lushan, a resort in the mountains of central China. 'If Marco Polo Bridge is forcibly occupied by a third country, then Beijing, our ancient capital and the political, military and cultural centre of north China, will become a second Shenyang,' he declared, referring to the Shenyang Incident which resulted in the Japanese occupation of Manchuria. 'Hebei and Chahar,' he warned, 'will become like Manchuria ... [and] Nanjing might well suffer the same fate as Shenyang. The outcome of the Marco Polo Bridge Incident therefore is a question for all of China.' He concluded that 'we have reached the limit. If a conflict is unavoidable, then the only option that remains is to fight a war of resistance and be prepared to make the ultimate sacrifice.'[67]

Chiang laid down as his conditions for a settlement that it would not infringe on China's territorial integrity and sovereign rights and that no changes would be made to the existing military and political arrangements in north China.[68] Chiang referred to the Boxer Protocol and the Tanggu Truce as treaties relevant to defining Japanese rights in the area. He could only disown those by rejecting international agreements, which would have undermined Nanjing's internationalist strategy. But he did implicitly reject the He-Umezu Agreement, which was not an official treaty because it consisted merely of an exchange of letters and hence had no standing in international law.

On 16 July, having completed his encirclement of Beijing, General Katsuki, commander-in-chief of Japan's China Garrison Force, handed an ultimatum to General Song Zheyuan, commander-in-chief of the Chinese 29th Army, demanding that units of the 37th Division in Beijing, as well as forces from west and north of Beijing, be withdrawn south 'to guard against a recurrence of incidents'.[69] The Japanese Army Ministry insisted that Nanjing should not stand in the way of a local settlement,[70] something that Chiang Kaishek was unwilling to accept – understandably so, given that he regarded the Marco Polo Bridge Incident not as a local but as a national affair. As *The Times* reported, Nanjing was 'fully committed to the non-recognition of any arrangements made without the approval of the National Government'.[71]

On 17 July the Operations Section of the Japanese Staff Department finalised a battle plan which called for the elimination of General Song Zheyuan's 29th Army and the occupation of the Beijing–Tianjin region. While the hope was to restrict the fighting to north China, it was argued that 'if full-out war breaks out', the 'destruction of the central government' would take no more than three or four months.[72] The Japanese cabinet approved the plan on 20 July.[73]

War fever now gripped Japan. 'Some Diet [parliament] members are demanding that a fundamental solution should now be reached,' the Tokyo correspondent of *The Times* reported, adding, 'Hundreds of women stoop to complete "thousand stitch girdles" for troops at the front', 'groups of young men spent today careering around the City' and '1600 reactionary patriots marched to the Meiji Shrine'.[74] In Shanghai, many too anticipated a new bout of warfare, albeit with less enthusiasm: 'memories of 1932', when during their take-over of Manchuria Japanese bombers flattened parts of Shanghai in order to warn Nanjing off from taking any precipitate action, 'have been recalled by the stream of humble Chinese in every variety of conveyance – rickshaw, taxicab, motor-lorry – with pathetic bundles of possessions coming from Chapei [Zhabei] to the International Settlement during the last 48 hours'.[75] (Zhabei was a Chinese neighbourhood of Shanghai to the west of the International Settlement.)

The Japanese had no trouble dealing with the little resistance they encountered as they moved in: Beijing and Tianjin were in Japanese hands by 29 July. Chiang's response was to beef up resistance by ordering central army units into battle. General Tang Enbo invested Nankou, a town to the north-west of Beijing on the Beijing–Suiyuan railway, which was important to the Japanese if they wanted to advance further into Inner Mongolia. The Japanese, in turn, thrust south to bring central army units at Baoding to battle. The battle for Nankou was intense, with the Japanese throwing artillery, tanks and aeroplanes into the fight. General Tang Enbo was quickly put on the defensive.[76] The town was lost on 15 August, the Chinese forces having suffered a large number of casualties. Despite General Tang Enbo's heroics, the north China generals continued to shun serious battle with the Japanese. A German advisor who investigated the north China front reported: 'the speed of retreat of our armies appears to have exceeded the schedule of the Supreme Command'.[77]

Chiang Kaishek's choice was to accept Japanese control of north China or plunge the country into full-out war. Besides the collapse of resistance in north China, he was also confronted with the dispatch of five army divisions and elements of the Japanese navy to Shanghai. Thirty-two vessels of the Japanese Second and Third Fleets were at the port by 13 August.[78] Chiang Kaishek was defiant, stating after the fall of Beijing that 'from now on there can be no such thing as a "local settlement"' as 'China can only hope to obtain justice and peace after she wins a final victory on the battlefield'.[79]

At 8 p.m. on 7 August, forty-one people took their seats in a meeting room at the Endeavour Society, an officers' club on Sun Yatsen Road, Nanjing. Chiang Kaishek was in the chair. The attendees included the most senior civil and military officials of the Nanjing government, including: Wang Jingwei; the commander of the Shanxi Army, Yan Xishan; the second most senior figure of the Guangxi Clique, General Bai Chongxi ; and General Feng Yuxiang of the North-west Army. The meeting began with an account by Army Minister He

Yingqin of the Marco Polo Bridge Incident and the fighting that had taken place since then. This was followed by a report on the Japanese troop strength and deployments in China. Chiang Kaishek then took the floor. He declared that he wanted a frank exchange of views, but made no bones about his own position, stating that 'this war between China and Japan truly is the key moment which will decide whether our country survives or perishes. If we win, our country and our nation will revive and we will turn danger into safety. If not we shall condemn our country to eternal damnation.'[80] As the time neared 11 p.m., all those in favour of war were asked to stand up. All did so, agreeing that 'in military and diplomatic affairs, we shall obey the instructions and arrangements of the central government'. On 13 August, Chiang ordered the Chinese forces at Shanghai into battle, ensuring that the fighting was now no longer a local northern China issue. Chiang had staked his nation.

PART II

MOMENTOUS TIMES

FIVE

THE BATTLE OF SHANGHAI

The whole Shanghai front is collapsing and the situation in Shanxi is also precarious, but we must resist Japan to the bitter end and not turn our backs on our original resolve. As to the Communists and the warlords, things will be OK if we give them a bit more power and then work on them with our righteousness and justness.

Chang Kaishek, diary entry (25 October 1937)[1]

The Battle of Shanghai is still often described, simplistically, either as a plucky but doomed effort by the Nationalists to stand up to the Japanese (as most foreign journalists described it at a time), or as a botched operation in which Chiang Kaishek persisted for too long in the hope of securing foreign support (as some critics among his own generals argued at the time, as well as some foreign ones later).[2] Running a war, though, is a complex business, especially at a time when the media was becoming increasingly important, and doubly so when Chiang's own side was made up of a diverse range of armies, many of which were actively hostile to one another. In the Battle of Shanghai, the Nationalists not only had to make sure that the right units arrived in the right place at the right time, that they were supplied properly, and that their actions were coordinated for the achievement of a common objective. They also had to make sure that the actions on the ground supported the messages they wanted them to deliver to their supporters, to the general population, to various military forces in the country and to foreign audiences. If the Nationalists were less competent at the first set of tasks, they managed the second with much greater success, helped no end by a Japanese obtuseness when it came to judging how their actions would be perceived.

War plans are tricky documents to interpret, not only because military leaders tend to overemphasise dangers in order to secure enhanced budgets, but also because few survive first contact for long. It is nonetheless worthwhile to review China's and Japan's avowed plans at the outbreak of war. They give insight into how the two countries judged their own strengths and weaknesses, the strategies they anticipated the enemy would adopt, and the ways in which they planned to counter them. Without some knowledge of these war plans, the initial operations of both the Japanese and the Chinese forces are difficult to understand.

Uppermost in Japanese thinking was the threat from the Soviet Union. In 1937 the Japanese General Staff estimated that so far the Soviet Union had deployed sixteen infantry and three mechanised divisions in the Soviet Far East, with a total of 290,000 troops, 1,200 aeroplanes and thirty submarines. The Japanese Kuantung Army in Manzhouguo, by contrast, had no more than 80,000 men under arms and could put just 239 aeroplanes into the air. In 1936, Japan adopted a massive rearmament and military reform programme to meet the Soviet threat and be ready for a world war anticipated to start after 1940. Because Japan lacked the heavy industry and mineral resources to build the necessary number of aeroplanes, tanks, heavy artillery and ships to catch up with the Soviets, Japanese operational doctrine stressed shock, night attack, close combat, high morale and superior firepower at the point of contact.[3] Japan's foreign policy was coordinated with its military strategy. Japan signed the Anti-Comintern Pact with Germany in November 1936 in the hope of trapping the Soviets in a European quagmire, or at least of reducing the Soviet threat on the Manzhouguo–Soviet border.[4]

One option open to Japan was simply to be content with what it already had in Taiwan, Korea and Manzhouguo and not bother about China. Had the war begun before 1935, Japan might well have exercised that option. Its war plans of the time did not regard north China as strategically important. If an incident flared up, Japan would send in troops to protect Japanese lives and property, then withdraw once peace had been restored. But Japan's 1936 war plan did declare north China vital to Japanese national security. Japan had begun to fear the forward policy of the Nationalists in the north which threatened its access to north China's coal, iron ore and food resources. The Xi'an Incident spooked the Japanese as it heralded an end to the 'first unity then resistance' policy of the Nationalists, an enhanced role for the Soviet Union in Chinese affairs, and some reconciliation between the Nationalists and the Communists. Until then the Japanese did not have to worry about any threat to their rear if war was declared with the Soviet Union. Now the chances were that Chinese forces would jump on the opportunity to recover the north, as Chiang Kaishek indeed tried to do even without such a war.

Japan's 1937 plan therefore stipulated that, in case of war with China, Japanese forces were to occupy the five provinces of north China and the lower Yangzi region,[5] the first to secure the Kuantung Army's rear and the second to cut the Nationalists' major supply line and destroy its tax base. These two tasks were to be accomplished in a 'quick victory after a short war' in order to prevent the Soviet Union from mobilising its forces and exploiting the situation.

By contrast, Nationalist war plans called for a protracted war of attrition. Given the disparity in fire power between the armed forces of the two countries, a straight fight between a Japanese and a Chinese division would have been over in days, probably hours. A Japanese division on war footing consisted of some 25,000 men armed with around 10,000 rifles, 300 light machine guns, 100 heavy machine guns, 300 grenade launchers and 100 pieces of artillery. It had one mechanised unit with 40 light military vehicles and 20 armoured cars, some 6,000 horses and around 300 other vehicles, as well as a chemical warfare unit.[6] In early 1937, the Imperial Japanese Army had some 247,000 men under arms, arranged in 17 infantry divisions, 4 tank regiments and 54 air squadrons. Compulsory military service meant that this force could be expanded massively in short order.

The best Chinese divisions, the German-trained Reformed Divisions, of which there were just twenty in 1937, possessed 11,000 troops. Their prescribed armaments consisted of 3,800 rifles, 275 light machine guns, 54 heavy machine guns and 46 pieces of artillery. Chinese armaments, though, were inferior to those of the Japanese. Chinese mortars, for instance, had a maximum range of 1,200 metres, while Japanese ones could hit targets five times that distance. Few even of the Reformed Divisions had been equipped in accordance with the official standard. The Nationalists had just 3,000 vehicles and 10,000 horses and mules in total. The Chinese air force only had 202 serviceable aeroplanes with the 'total number of bombs only sufficient for 22 full strength sorties', according to the British air attaché.[7] Training levels in the Chinese armies were well below those of the Japanese. China had no navy worthy of the name. Logistics were such a shambles that General Chen Cheng, commander-in-chief at the Battle of Shanghai, remarked that 'we do not have the ability to supply our front-line troops.'[8] Even three or four divisions would not have been able to resist one Japanese division for very long.

General Alexander von Falkenhausen, the chief German military advisor, had a major hand in drafting China's war plans. 'War on a national scale is a necessary experience for China and will unify her,' he declared, suggesting that fighting Japan would do for China what the 1870 Franco–Prussian War had done for the unification of Germany by Prussia.[9] The war plans he helped put together provided for two alternative courses of action. The first – and more aggressive of the two – argued for immediate attacks on Japanese troops in north China and preventing Japanese landings in Shandong as well as at Shanghai. If that failed, Plan B called for a withdrawal into the countryside, with a main Nationalist base in Sichuan province in the far west, well protected by high mountains, supported by a productive agriculture and with a large rural population from which troops could be recruited in vast numbers at little cost. Both aimed at keeping the Japanese north of the Great Wall, either straight away or after attrition had weakened the Japanese troops.[10]

To prepare for the implementation of this strategy, supply depots were established across north China with sufficient ammunition for three months of fighting as well as food and fodder for one month.[11] Fortifications were built at Nanjing and Wuhan, at important narrows along the Yangzi river and at port cities such as Canton and Xiamen. China could not possibly match Japan's mighty navy, but fortifications along the coast and the Yangzi were to be constructed to resist Japanese amphibious landings and keep China's lines of communication to the outside world open. Battlefields were prepared in north China and a line of fortifications – China's Hindenburg Line – was erected west of Shanghai, running from the Yangzi south to the sea, in order to isolate the Japanese in the city, if need be, and protect the capital at Nanjing should Shanghai be lost.[12] When war broke out in 1937, only a third of the Nationalist plans to build an elite army of 60 Reformed Divisions had been finished, not all fortifications had been completed, arms industries bought from Germany still had to be installed and much materiel was yet to arrive. But the Nationalists were more ready to put up a fight than ever before.

The Battle

On 13 August 1937, Chiang Kaishek activated the more aggressive of his two war plans when he threw his two best divisions, the 87th and the 88th, against the Japanese Special Naval Landing Force, at Shanghai. Chiang's move was calculated, first, to drive Japanese forces at Shanghai into the sea, and, second, to reduce pressure on Nationalist front lines in north China. After taking Beijing and Tianjin on 28 and 29 July, the Japanese had paused for a week to prepare two follow-up offensives with seven divisions, one to drive west along the Beijing–Suiyuan railway and the other to push 100 kilometres south and bring the Nationalists' main forces to battle at the city of Baoding.[13] For Japan, north China, not Shanghai, remained the main front, until their slow progress at Shanghai became embarrassing.

In Shanghai, tensions had been steadily rising during the weeks before Chiang Kaishek ordered his two best divisions into action. Japanese evacuees from cities up the Yangzi river had swelled the Japanese population of Shanghai to 30,000. The arrival of vessels from Japan's Yangzi Flotilla and its Third Fleet, designed to operate in coastal areas, had deepened Chinese anxieties. On 9 August, two Japanese marines had been ambushed near the Hongqiao air field to the west of Shanghai, leading to a Japanese demand two days later for the complete withdrawal of the Chinese Peace Preservation Force from Little Tokyo, the Japanese section of the Shanghai International Settlement.[14] The British ambassador reported to London that 'hostilities were inevitable' if the Japanese did not make a 'compensating concession'.[15] He floated the idea that the British might take over the policing of Little Tokyo. The suggestion was quashed because 'our troops' would end up having 'to fire on Chinese in defence of the Japanese and so draw the odium on ourselves'.[16] The citizens of

Shanghai knew what was coming: the *North China Daily* reported on 6 August that 'the exodus from Chapei and Hongkew [two Shanghai districts] reached alarming proportions … a conservative estimate put the number of refugees [since 26 July] at 50,000.'[17]

On 14 August, the world woke up to the Battle of Shanghai when China's air campaign went horribly wrong. The Chinese air force had taken to the sky to hit Japanese naval vessels whose guns had been pounding the 87th and 88th Divisions, which had begun their offensive the previous day.[18] Its prime target was the *Izumo*, Japan's flagship moored provocatively off the quay in Shanghai opposite the Japanese consulate. No bomb found its target, but stray bombs that afternoon hit the famous Cathay Hotel on the corner of the Bund and Nanjing Road, the nearby Palace Hotel and the Great World Amusement Centre not far away. The Chinese explanation at the time was that flak from the *Izumo* had hit the bomb carriage of the aeroplanes involved, a way of putting the onus on the Japanese.[19] The US aviator Claire Lee Chennault, famous later as commander of the Flying Tigers, stated in his memoirs that the Chinese pilots, forced to fly in at 1,500 feet because of cloud cover, rather than at 7,500 feet as planned, had failed to adjust their bomb sights.[20]

The kind of precision bombing required to sink a ship right next to hotels, shops, consulates, offices and apartment buildings was well beyond the capacity of any aircraft of the time, and certainly not in the bad weather – a typhoon, no less – that prevailed that day. Chennault had designed the raid himself and hence must share a considerable part of the responsibility for its outcome. It was a catastrophe. The *North China Herald* reported that 'bombing at the Great World cost 1,047 dead and 303 injured, while 120 persons died at the Cathay and Palace hotels'.[21] Foreign journalists spread news of 'Black Saturday' around the world. *The New York Times* called it a 'terrific' slaughter, while *Le Figaro* spoke of 'a tragic day for Shanghai'.[22] *The Times* commented that 'what happened yesterday in Shanghai has, perhaps, never been paralleled anywhere else'.[23]

The *Izumo* was never hit, despite many more attempts, while the 87th and 88th Divisions failed to reach their objectives: the Japanese Marine Headquarters, a fortified building spanning two blocks, and the Japanese Golf Club, which was in the process of being transformed into an air field.[24] The Nationalists had hoped to deliver a decisive blow, an *Entscheidungsslacht*, as their German advisors put it. They failed because of the fire delivered by Japanese naval guns. Meanwhile the Japanese also fought on from previously prepared strong points throughout Little Tokyo. The Nationalists flung ever more troops against these with little or no reconnaissance, making little headway but incurring unsustainable numbers of casualties. Despite their numerical superiority, the Nationalist forces were unable to overwhelm the Japanese in this first attempt.[25]

On 16 August, Chiang Kaishek ordered a second attack, Operation Iron Fist. Designed by Colonel Hans Vetter, one of the German advisors, Iron Fist aimed to cut through Japanese lines in two places and punch towards Shanghai's main river, the Huangpu, and cut Little Tokyo into three separate sections. This time, Japanese strong points were to be skirted around. Some units penetrated as far as the last street before the river, but once more poor intelligence, lack of coordination and limited firepower meant that Operation Iron Fist fell at the last hurdle.[26] The creeping barrage the Nationalist artillery was supposed to lay down in front of its advancing infantry troops was too far forward. The Japanese defenders had ample time to ready their machine guns, mortars and rifles once the barrage had passed overhead. By 19 August Iron Fist had lost its momentum.[27]

Then the tide turned. On 23 August, the 3rd and 11th Divisions of the Imperial Japanese Army began the largest amphibious landing ever attempted to date. Well before sunrise, landing craft ferried the first wave of troops to their designated landing places, exploiting the high tide to deposit their cargoes as high as possible up the five-metre-tall river dike. The 11th Division disembarked at Chuangshakou, a town some 16 kilometres up the Yangzi river from where the Huangpu joins it. The 3rd Division's target was Wusong, a fort at the mouth of the Huangpu river a few kilometres north of Shanghai. By 7 a.m., the Japanese had stabilised beachheads at Shizilin, Chuanshakou and Wusong.[28] Over the next few days they unloaded tanks and artillery, while engineers constructed a pier and some roads. By this time, the Japanese air force had secured control over the skies above Shanghai, not because their aeroplanes were superior to those of the Nationalists but because the Chinese could not afford to sustain further losses and so were forced to withdraw. The 3rd Division was poised to wheel around Shanghai, cutting off Nationalist lines of retreat, while the 11th Division stood ready to strike directly south into Shanghai.

Nonetheless, General Matsui Iwane, the commander-in-chief of the Shanghai Expeditionary Army which had just landed, found he needed until late October to overcome Nationalist defenders in between the beachheads and Shanghai. The region increasingly resembled a First World War battleground, covered in trenches, its dark earth churned up and pockmarked by craters, bodies spread through no-man's land, with the blasts of exploding shells and the whistling of bullets filling the air. As long as the defenders found easy cover among the canals and streams that criss-crossed the area, they hindered the movement of Japanese units. For Japan, supply soon became a difficulty, as cargo first had to be transferred from transports to lighters, then landed at one of the beachheads, and finally moved to the battlefront over waterlogged terrain. Because of shortages, rates of fire were reduced to one fifth of standard daily quotas.[29] Only on 22 September, after the Nationalist stand at Shanghai had lasted for more than two months, did Tokyo approve the despatch of three additional divisions.[30]

The Japanese had to fight hard for each metre gained. The Nationalist front line held until 11 September. Their forces then pulled back in good order to the Wusong creek, midway between the Yangzi river and Shanghai, holding it successfully for nearly a month.[31] The arrival at the front of four Guangxi Army divisions led to an attempt at a counter-offensive on 21 October. Following a barrage at dusk, the 174th and 176th Divisions of the Guangxi Army attacked at night to avoid bombardment by Japanese planes. Initially they made rapid progress, but they lost their momentum and dug in before sunrise, waiting for the Japanese counter-offensive. They tried again the next night, again without success. Then, on 23 October, according to their commander-in-chief, Chen Cheng, the Japanese 'hit the front like a hurricane, resulting in the most horrific losses … the troops were either blown to pieces or buried in their dugouts'.[32]

Following this setback, Nationalist and Guangxi Army forces retreated to their next line of defence at Zoumatang creek. Reinforced and resupplied, General Matsui ordered an offensive using maximum firepower on 25 October to prevent the Chinese forces from consolidating their positions. The Chinese were forced to pull back further to the southern shore of the Suzhou creek. This creek – a river, really – originates in Suzhou, runs along the southern border of the Zhabei district when it enters Shanghai, provides the dividing line between Little Tokyo and the rest of the International Settlement to the south, and then flows into the Huangpu river. Its high banks, which prevent it from flooding Shanghai, offer excellent protection to defenders and make crossings difficult.[33]

On 1 November, Japanese units secured a beachhead on the southern shore of the Suzhou, after which they were able to push large numbers of forces across it.[34] To make matters worse, on 5 November, the Japanese conducted an amphibious landing at Hangzhou Bay to the south of Shanghai, which took the Nationalists, once more let down by intelligence failures, completely by surprise. The single division and three artillery batteries of the Nationalists defending the area were no match for the three divisions of Japanese.[35] General Matsui's forces moved south while the new arrivals moved north, threatening to trap the Chinese forces in Shanghai in a pincer movement.

They narrowly escaped this fate. Nationalist field commanders had urged Chiang to order a retreat for weeks, but he had resisted, hoping that his forces might hold out until a meeting in Brussels of the signatories of the 1922 Nine Power Treaty, which guaranteed Chinese sovereignty and territorial integrity, and which Chiang hoped would condemn Japan and take positive steps to aid China. It had been called in October and began sitting on 3 November. Chiang believed it essential to demonstrate at Shanghai that China was still capable of fighting Japan; there would be little point for any of the Nine Power

Treaty signatories, who included France, Britain and the USA, to aid China if its armies were about to collapse. But on 9 November Chiang had to bow to the inevitable. A failure to order a general withdrawal risked the loss of all remaining forces, some of which were close to collapse and even mutiny.[36] The Battle of Shanghai was over. The best estimate of Japanese losses is 9,115 killed and 31,257 wounded, while Chinese casualties reached a staggering 187,000.[37] The Brussels Conference was adjourned indefinitely on 24 November, declining to endorse intervention.

Bombing

The Japanese triumphed, not just at Shanghai but also in north China, where they occupied Nankou on 25 August and then rapidly thrust westwards, bringing the entire Beijing–Suiyuan railway under their control by early October. They also seized the northern section of the Tianjin–Pukou railway. On 8 November, one day before the Nationalists retreated from Shanghai, the Japanese celebrated victory in the Battle of Taiyuan in Shanxi province, 400 kilometres inland, in north-west China.[38] The Japanese had implemented their war plan almost exactly according to schedule. Their use of bombing, however, undermined successes on the battlefield. In the era of mass war, when public opinion mattered more than before, how a victory was achieved mattered.

Japanese bombing in China played into worldwide fears about mass bombing, much as atomic and nuclear bombs were to do during the Cold War. In the 1930s aerial bombing was still a fairly new weapon. In the First World War, planes had been used largely for reconnaissance purposes, although also for tactical air support. Airships dropped bombs over London, causing little damage though much fright, provided a hint of what was to come. By the Second World War, aeroplanes were much faster and were able to carry large payloads of up to 500 kg, including incendiaries fitted with delay detonators. The Luftwaffe had just given a demonstration of the destruction bombing was able to wreak when it attacked the Basque town of Guernica during the Spanish Civil War in April 1937, which triggered mass protests in cities around Europe. *Guernica*, Pablo Picasso's most famous painting, had only just been unveiled in the Spanish Pavilion of the Paris International Exhibition. Chiang Kaishek chose to make his stand at Shanghai, full of foreign diplomats, bankers, businessmen and journalists, not only for military reasons, nor just to have the war threaten their interests in China, but also 'to make all countries furious with Japan'.[39] The Japanese bombing of Shanghai achieved exactly that.

Foreign journalists vied with each other to produce the most iconic account of the bombardment. Had a prize been on offer, *New York Times* journalist Hallett Abend's description would have been in the running. When he heard what was happening, he rushed back from the north China front, travelling in overcrowded trains and ships to reach the city on 22 August. A chapter in his China memoir entitled 'Terror and Death' recalls how, after his arrival in Shanghai, he went to purchase a pair of binoculars at the Wing On department store. He stayed in his car while his assistant headed into the shop. After lighting a cigarette, Abend looked up and saw a silver streak:

> Then it hit. There was a tremendous sickening lurch of the ground, accompanied by a shattering explosion so close that my eardrums and my windpipe seemed to be affected … The worst part of a bombing experience is that period of utter paralysis which follows the concussion. For as much as four minutes, if the bomb is a big one, nothing moves except swirling smoke and thick dust, and there is no sound except the continued tinkle of falling broken glass and the rumble of crumbling masonry. After about four minutes the wounded begin to moan and shriek and try to drag themselves away; then come the sounds of sirens and ambulances.[40]

Abend's depiction of bombing, with its initial stillness followed by the quiet tinkle of falling glass giving way to growing noise, disorientation and panic, and ending with pandemonium, shaped later depictions of bombing, including in movies. When Abend lunched with Cecil B. DeMille in the autumn of 1942, the legendary Hollywood director quizzed him on 'the immediate after-effects of a bombing'.[41] He was then directing 'a picture based on the Japanese attack on Java' – presumably *The Story of Dr Wassell*, released, coincidentally, on D-Day, which went on to receive an Oscar for its special effects. Its portrayal of bombing would become film cliché.

It was China's air force that was responsible for Black Saturday, as well as for the bomb that nearly did for Abend and his assistant. Yet Japanese intransigence, rather than Chinese incompetence, was held responsible. The Japanese authorities in Shanghai declined a suggestion made by the British consul after the first raid on the *Izumo* in the morning but before the afternoon attack, that the 'Japanese flagship and destroyer at naval buoys be withdrawn'.[42] They also refused other suggestions aimed at reducing the chances of conflict, even those made by the wife of the US President, Eleanor Roosevelt, who was in Shanghai at the time.[43]

Once Japan's naval air force established its air supremacy, it bombed government buildings, bridges, barracks and railway stations in cities such as Shanghai, Nanjing, Tianjin, Canton, Hangzhou and Suzhou, with the inevitable consequences. *Oriental Affairs*, a Shanghai newspaper edited by the British China coast journalist Henry Woodhead, who looked back on the days of the Anglo-Japanese alliance with nostalgia, commented that 'we have ocular evidence of what it means to bring war in its modern form into a city of over three million inhabitants'. He reported an 'appalling list of civilian casualties from aeroplane bombs' and commented that 'the extensive use of aircraft has shown that even where military objectives are aimed at, the toll of non-combatants must reach alarming proportions'.[44] Harold Timperley, a *Manchester Guardian* journalist, reported on hundreds and even thousands of civilian casualties resulting from Japanese raids on Nanjing, Shanghai and Canton.[45] Frank Oliver, a journalist with the news agency Reuters, recorded that a Western diplomat in Nanjing, whom he did not identify, told him that one day 'a hundred planes came over like flights of geese and bombs were dropped in almost every section of Nanking inside the city walls. Possibly the electric light plant was a military objective, possibly a small water pumping station near me (too damned near) was another. But what about the Central Hospital and the Nationalist Health Administration?'[46] H. S. 'Newsreel' Wong, working for Hearst Metrotone News, produced the war's most iconic photograph, of a wailing child sitting in torn clothes covered in soot amidst the wreckage of Shanghai's bombed-out South Station.

For Chi Pang-yuan, too, the bombing brought home the horror of war. At night, as she lay in bed, the sirens warning of a coming raid sounded even more threatening than during the day. 'Not long after the one long and a series of short blasts of the final warning of the air raid siren, I heard the low roar of the approaching airplanes. Then followed the explosions and flames from the bombs. Alone in bed, I heard the creaking of the fastenings of the window screen in the autumn wind. In my mind I saw the debris that had filled the sky fall back to earth, scattering on the endless steps of the Sun Yatsen Mausoleum, on the waves of Xuanwu Lake, on Dongchang Park, on the roses in front of the houses in Fuhou Street, and on the window shutters of the Drum Tower Elementary School. Death was at my window.'[47] The outbreak of war, she wrote, 'ended my youth'.[48]

For Chen Kewen, whose home was in the Nanjing suburbs, the Japanese bombing was initially no more than an inconvenience: his cook, gardener and rickshaw puller decamped for the safety of the countryside.[49] Initially he took pride in the effectiveness of the Nationalist air force and Nanjing's anti-aircraft guns.[50] Because Japanese bombers targeted not just military but also cultural centres and government buildings, he too came to regard the Japanese as 'barbaric'.[51] The Japanese air raid on Canton, whose death toll was underreported in Nationalist newspapers so as not to cause panic, left him 'speechless ... although the whole world criticises the Japanese, they do nothing. We must rely on our own forces if we are to escape the Japanese menace.'[52] Japanese bombing hardened the Chinese will to resist, alone if necessary.

There was similar outrage around the world. Lord Meston, president of the Liberal Party in the UK, 'appealed to Liberals in all constituencies for the fullest support in condemning Japanese outrages'.[53] Prime Minister Neville Chamberlain declared at the Conservative Party conference that autumn that 'non-combatants have been killed and mutilated by aerial weapons which, we are told, were aimed at military objectives, but which, in no case, can be considered instruments of precision. It is a sickening and horrifying spectacle from which the mind revolts.'[54] John Rabe, an employee of the Germany engineering company Siemens, who would at the end of the year establish the Nanjing Safety Zone, was equally appalled.[55] He appealed, without success, to Hitler to put pressure on Japan to stop the carnage. In India, the scholar Gulshan Rai wrote in the *Civil and Military Gazette* that Japanese militarism was a greater threat to India than British colonialism.[56] *The Leader* of Allahabad professed that 'all right thinking men throughout the civilised world will be with China and against the military gangsters in Japan who are seeking to rob it of its valuable territories and convert it to a vassal state'.[57]

These reactions in India, reported by German intelligence to Berlin, worried German Foreign Office officials, who did not want Japan to do anything that would strengthen Britain. One of these, Ernst von Weizsäcker, the father of the future president quoted in the introduction to this book, was deeply critical of Japan, arguing that its actions in China prevented the consolidation of the country under the Nationalists and played into the hands of the Soviet Union and the Chinese Communists.[58] On 5 October, President Franklin Roosevelt famously called for a 'quarantine of the aggressor nations', not mentioned by name but understood to refer to Germany, Japan and Italy. The Soviet Union protested at Japan's 'bombing of Nanking' and warned that Japan 'would be held responsible for any consequences of these illegal acts'.[59]

The Japanese response to an attack in late August by a Japanese aeroplane on British ambassador Hughe Knatchbull-Hugessen reinforced the association of Japan with barbarity, militarism and intransigence. Ambassador Knatchbull-Hugessen had been travelling from Nanjing to Shanghai in a car flying the British flag when a Japanese aeroplane first bombed and then strafed it, leaving the ambassador wounded, reportedly by a bullet that had passed through his chest and damaged his spine. The *North China Herald* published a photograph of Knatchbull-Hugessen slumped in the back of his car with blood spilling over its back seat and on to the floor. The British Foreign Secretary, Anthony Eden, rejected the Japanese excuse that Chiang Kaishek had been the target, although Chiang had indeed been on the road – evidence, as Chen Kewen noted, of the frightening truth that Japan had informants in the Nationalist government.[60] Eden demanded a formal apology, the punishment of the perpetrators and a promise of better behaviour in the future. He called it an 'outrage' when the Japanese replied that 'they may have been the ones who shot and bombed

Knatchbull-Huggessen and therefore expressed their regret'.[61] The famous opponent of appeasement this time judged it best to leave it at that.

The USS *Panay* Incident was to the US what the attack on Knatchbull-Hugessen was to the British. On 12 December, soon after Shanghai had fallen and Nanjing too had been taken, Japanese aircraft sunk the US gunboat even though it was flying the US ensign. The attack resulted in two people dead and ten seriously injured. In an interview with Hallett Abend, General Matsui blamed a Japanese colonel, a 'publicity hound' who was 'ignorant, dangerous, and wants Japan to fight the world right now'.[62] After taking a town on the Yangzi river upstream from Nanjing, this colonel had 'ordered the planes to bomb everything that moved on the Yangtse'.[63] Previously, Abend had been friendly with General Matsui and a touch pro-Japanese, but he changed his attitude during the Battle of Shanghai.[64]

Against this background of Japanese brutality, tales of Chinese heroism became desirable. Once retreat became inevitable, one battalion of the 88th Division was selected to occupy the Four Banks' warehouse in the Zhabei district, right on the edge of the International Settlement, from where foreign journalists could observe and report on the Nationalists' last stand. The battalion held out for four days as the Japanese pushed forwards with artillery and tanks, reinforcing the image of Japanese barbarity. Throughout the siege, the Nationalist flag flew defiantly from the warehouse in a sea of Japanese Rising Sun flags fluttering from the surrounding buildings, thus deflating the claims of a great victory by the Japanese. 'Shanghai gasped with pleasure', or so one jobbing journalist, Roads Farmer, reported from the city.[65] The 'Doomed Battalion', as it was dubbed, was meant to impress not only foreigners. Chen Kewen, who read about it in Chinese newspapers, 'was inspired, and moved to tears'.[66] The British appealed to the Japanese to allow the battalion to withdraw to British lines on the opposite side of the Suzhou creek, but the Japanese refused. Instead they trained their machine guns on groups of soldiers as they dashed at irregular intervals over the bridge into the International Settlement.[67]

China gained much sympathy, but no practical help from France and the UK, let alone the USA, which remained isolationist. Previously, following its acquisition of Manchuria and the attack on Shanghai in 1931–2, Japan remained 'widely seen to have a strong case against China', according to John Simon, the British Foreign Secretary.[68] Many treaty port foreigners believed that a strong dose of Japanese would sort out Chinese disorder and civil war; some diplomats were convinced that cooperation with Japan offered the best hope of stabilising east Asia and protecting their colonial assets.[69] The Battle of Shanghai changed such attitudes. Japan stood condemned in the court of public opinion, while China came to be seen as standing up for adherence to international treaties, international cooperation and open access to markets and standing up to aggression and militarism. The books published in subsequent years by journalists who had witnessed the Battle of Shanghai sustained that reputation.[70] 'China alone has for 25 months fought single-handed and against tremendous odds to uphold the right of a nation to live its free and independent life,' as one put it.[71] In 1941, China officially became one of the Allies.

Adversaries into Allies?

'To fight a foreign force is straightforward but to pacify the interior is difficult.' So Chiang Kaishek worried on 12 August, just before the Battle of Shanghai. He feared that 'the Communists, political opportunists, and the warlords will exploit war with Japan to make threats, issue demands, let their ambition run wild, and activate their plots'.[72] The Nationalist aim at Shanghai was not only to defeat the Japanese but also to use the battle domestically to forge unity out of rivalry. Chiang's deployment of his best forces at Shanghai virtually compelled his domestic rivals, especially those who had long called for resistance to Japan, to make their own contribution and join him.

The Chinese forces at Shanghai formed a rainbow coalition of armies that had beaten chunks out of each other during the previous decade. They became allies – of a sort. The Guangxi Clique, which had the second-strongest force in the country, hedged its bets. When Chiang Kaishek asked for its backing after the Marco Polo Bridge Incident, Li Zongren publicly vowed his support for Chiang but privately declined an invitation to come to Nanjing.[73] His deputy, General Bai Chongxi, did accept Chiang Kaishek's invitation. He was to serve as vice chief of staff of the Nationalist army throughout the war.[74] During the Battle of Shanghai, he regularly visited the front and his suggestions about personnel and tactics were implemented.[75]

Chiang Kaishek's first appointee as commander-in-chief at Shanghai was the Christian General Feng Yuxiang. Following his defeat in the 1930 War of the Central Plains, General Feng had lived in Nanjing, studying, writing and making himself popular with speeches calling for resistance to the Japanese. Chiang Kaishek appointed General Feng to Shanghai to illustrate that bygones were bygones and that the battles in the north and at Shanghai were linked. But Feng proved unpopular at Shanghai with his subordinate field commanders. General Bai Chongxi ridiculed him in his memoirs, saying that Feng's fear of Japanese bombing had led him to place his HQ impossibly far from the front.[76] Whether true or not, it is clear that long-held animosities did not evaporate overnight.

Different armies competed for glory. The counter-offensive by four Guangxi Army divisions towards the end of the battle was in part a genuine attempt to turn the tide in the fighting north of Shanghai; however, it was also designed to show up the Nationalists and enhance the reputation of the Guangxi Clique.

The plan backfired, though, seemingly because, in an effort to seize the lime-light, Bai Chongxi rushed his preparations. One of his subordinates charged him with extreme negligence, arguing that the operation had been planned in a hurry on maps whose scale the general had not understood.[77]

Had the infighting stayed at this level, it would have been containable, but while agreeing to send their armies to Shanghai, the generals of the regional armies also exchanged secret codes among themselves and continued to hatch alliances which excluded the Nationalists.[78] One of these, between the Sichuan and Shandong generals, nearly prevented the Nationalists from being able to enter Sichuan province after the fall of Wuhan.[79] This lack of unity undermined the combat effectiveness of Chinese forces throughout the war.

The inclusion of the Communists proved the most difficult issue. The day after the outbreak of the Marco Polo Incident, they issued a circular telegram, proclaiming: 'Beijing and Tianjin are in danger. North China is in danger. The Chinese nation is in danger. The whole nation must unite.'[80] In a telegram of the same day to Chiang Kaishek, their leader Mao Zedong declared that 'we are ready to sacrifice our lives for the nation under your leadership ... and follow your army to fight the Japanese dwarfs to the bitter end'.[81] Despite the stirring language, deeds did not follow words without some tough negotiations. Only on 23 September, after Chiang Kaishek had bowed to Communist demands, did the two parties announce their new united front.[82]

No Communist unit fought at Shanghai. Throughout the battle Mao Zedong insisted that his forces would not engage in anything but 'autonomous, dis-persed guerrilla warfare behind enemy lines'.[83] The only concession Nationalist negotiators were able to extract from the Communists was an agreement to confine their operations to a limited area of Hebei and Chahar provinces, a concession which the Communists were well aware the Nationalists had no hope of policing. As the historian Yang Kuisong says, 'the two parties were deeply suspicious of each other ... the CCP naturally hoped to wage war in the enemy's rear to achieve independence and autonomy'; they also took good care not to encroach on Nationalist areas so as to avoid clashes with them.[84]

Surviving units of the Fengtian Army – of Xi'an Incident fame – were deployed at Shanghai, not at the front but at China's Hindenburg Line, between Shanghai and Nanjing. The retreat of Chinese divisions from Shanghai turned into a chaotic rout when, according to the *Washington Post*, 'certain Manchu-rian [Fengtian Army] units, regarded as poor fighters, were ordered to defend a relatively safe sector. General Liu, in command of these troops, refused to order his troops to the front, and the Japanese pierced the line in this sector without encountering any resistance.'[85] China's Hindenburg Line collapsed, allowing the Japanese to storm towards their next target, Nanjing.

Although there were clearly limits to the cooperation among China's generals and their armies, despite the discord and the backstabbing, the coalition held – and would do so by and large for the duration of the war. Without the Battle of Shanghai, in which Chiang demonstrated his commitment to resisting Japan, this would not have happened. If the broader story of China at war is that of China evolving a new sense of unity and shared destiny, then the Battle of Shanghai stands as a significant turning point in that story, despite the flaws the fighting pointed up in its military preparedness and wavering levels of enthusiasm for war afterwards.

Rallying the People

In a country where there is no public opinion polling, a true assessment of the public mood is impossible. We can only take soundings. The educated and newspaper-reading youth, who had made their views loud and clear during the protest movements of the previous decade, broadly welcomed the war. However, there were also those who had grave doubts about the course on which Chiang Kaishek had set their country. And great numbers of people living in village China had no idea what was happening.

Historian Parks Coble wrote that 'the Battle for Shanghai was greeted with near euphoria by much of the informed public. They were ready for war.'[86] The *Dagongbao*, or *'L'Impartial'* ' as its masthead would have it in French, was one of the most prestigious newspapers in China. The battle, it proclaimed, signalled 'the first time that the entire nation' had fought together against a common enemy, thus marking the birth of a new age: 'Children of China! We ought to congratulate you. You have been born into this great age!'[87]

One *Dagongbao* staff writer, the Sichuan-born Fan Changjiang, became one of China's most famous war reporters. He rushed first to north China to cover the fighting there, and then to the Shanghai front, combining battle accounts, human interest stories and travelogue into reports that made him famous across China.[88] War euphoria grabbed many young writers and journalists who had joined the National Salvation Movement, established in the aftermath of the loss of Manchuria and which opposed Chiang's 'first unity then resistance' policy. One such writer, Qian Yishi, wrote a month into the Battle for Shanghai that 'before, people said China was the sick man [of Asia]. Now the sick man is well and has taken up arms to resist the enemy.'[89] In an article published on 18 September, the anniversary of Japan's occupation of Manchuria, the Communist Mao Dun, who was also one of twentieth-century China's greatest novelists, proclaimed that 'this year the whole nation has lit the beacon fire of the struggle for our freedom', adding 'the nation's shame of 18 September is forever gone'.[90]

The Shanghai defeat came as a heavy blow to Fan Changjiang. Reporting after the battle, he detailed the city's destruction, the chaos that overwhelmed its normal routines, and the misery felt by its refugees.[91] But Fan remained determined to inspire. He reported, for instance, about a young truck driver he met as they fled Shanghai. The young man battled with mud, bad tyres and breakdowns, but he also spoke excitedly about his desire to become a pilot or a tank driver. China's future, Fan suggested, depended on mobilising the energy of such young people. 'All our compatriots must understand that we have just started our great enterprise. For this to be completed might take three years, five years, or even ten years of struggle,' wrote Wang Yunsheng, another prominent journalist, indicating that no one should give up just because Shanghai was lost.[92] Reporters linked with the Salvationists responded to the defeat by deciding that their duty now was to rally the country. They became propagandists.

The war met with other responses. Peking University historian Wang Qisheng is probably right that 'although the media burst with articles enthusiastic about resisting Japan, privately many favoured peace'. [93] Chen Yinke, one of China's greatest twentieth-century historians, stated just after the outbreak of the war that 'the Chinese lower classes are ignorant and the elites are just pretending ... Neither north China nor the central government really wants to fight. If we resist Japan, we will be destroyed.'[94] Wang Jingwei, the Minister of Finance Kong Xiangxi, and Hu Shi, a liberal public intellectual with a towering reputation, were all peace advocates.[95]

A particularly interesting reaction to the outbreak of war was that of Feng Zikai, a writer, musician and painter, who produced some of China's most famous, and subtle, wartime cartoons. These featured Buddhist temples and school houses destroyed by Japanese bombing; a soldier with his rifle next to him taking a quiet moment to play his *erhu*, or two-stringed fiddle; another soldier admiring a flower; and, harrowingly, a child feeding from its mother's breast although a bomb has already decapitated her. With his cartoons, Feng, a Buddhist, drew attention to the realities of war, to Japanese brutality and Chinese heroism, but also pointed to the existence of another reality in which nature, life, beauty, family, art and peace are treasured. 'To cast down the pen and take up arms', to quote the title of one cartoon featuring a soldier marching proudly with a rifle flung over his shoulder, suggests that the war against Japan was necessary and just, but also that other, better realities should not be forgotten.[96]

Chen Kewen's attitude reflected his May Fourth beliefs. He shared the initial euphoria when the Battle of Shanghai commenced, writing that 'everybody is excited'.[97] On 10 October, the anniversary of the 1911 Revolution, Chen stood in front of his home, sang the KMT party anthem, recited Sun Yatsen's Last Testament and launched into the national anthem. This was an act of defiance. Japanese bombing raids had caused the cancellation of a mass gathering.[98] After Shanghai was lost, he joined a mass rally of up to 20,000 people in commemoration of Sun Yatsen's birthday. As Chen prepared to leave Nanjing in late November, he was downcast, comparing the moment to the Song Dynasty's abandonment of north China to invaders in the twelfth century. Chen's diary suggests a man committed to serving the government that had given him the opportunity to use his talents – a viewpoint which accorded with both traditional concepts of loyalty and duty and notions of modern nationalism.

It is difficult to assess to what extent the war was supported or even known about in rural society. Fan Changjiang reported that he met farmers, even some who were tilling their plots of land in earshot of battles, who had no idea that there was a war going on. When making his way from Shanghai, he travelled through a village in rich Jiangsu province whose schoolmaster and students did not know that China was fighting Japan.[99] In places beyond the reach of radio broadcasts and newspaper distribution networks, this may have been a common reality. Like Wang Yunsheng, Fan Changjiang saw it as his mission, his contribution to the war effort, to take the war to China's broader population.

The Battle of Shanghai did not end with a great Chinese victory; indeed, it pointed up the many ways in which China's armed forces were inferior to Japan's. They were badly equipped, poorly trained, indifferently commanded and followed tactics that had become outmoded by the end of the First World War. Divergent loyalties frequently hindered effective coordination. And yet, the Nationalists made several important gains. Japan's use of bombing may have been effective militarily, destroying Chinese supply lines, putting entire command centres out of action and killing large numbers of troops usually deployed too close together. But it also strengthened anti-Japanese sentiment not just in China but elsewhere, including in India, a development that undermined Japanese appeals to Asian solidarities. Japan stood condemned and internationally isolated – important when no nation could win the war on its own but had to fight as a member of an alliance.

China's stock, on the other hand, had risen. At the turn of the century China had been regarded as important internationally – hence the Allied Expedition at the time of the Boxer Uprising – but by the end of the First World War it had ceased to matter. Its recurrent civil wars and horrendous famines made it seem truly like the Sick Man of Asia. During the Great Depression of the 1930s, few paid much attention to what was happening in China. The Battle of Shanghai suddenly changed all that. Just as importantly, the battle also ensured that the War of Resistance became regarded as a national war. What began as a conflict between the Nationalists and the Japanese became a war between China and Japan.

SIX

TRADING SPACE FOR TIME

The defence has a natural advantage in the employment of those things, which – irrespective of the absolute strength and qualities of the combatant force – influence the tactical as well as the strategic result, namely, the advantage of ground, sudden attack, attack from several directions (converging form of attack), the assistance of the theatre of war, the support of the people, and the utilising of great moral forces.

Carl von Clausewitz, *On War* (1832)[1]

After the Battle of Shanghai, their previous war plans were no longer much help to either the Nationalists or the Japanese. The Japanese had assumed that the war in China could be wound up once they had taken north China and Shanghai, but this now proved not to be the case. In one of their two war plans, the Nationalists had allowed for a long war of attrition, even for a withdrawal all the way to Sichuan province, but only in vague terms. In order to convince their followers, their armed forces, their allies and China's population at large that they were capable of defeating the Japanese, they needed to substantiate their ideas.

War plans are suggestive of a high level of state control over war, featuring rational planning, calculation and preparation. But now the war moved, as Clausewitz would have put it, into 'the realm of probability and chance', in which 'courage and talent' and 'the particular character of the commander and the army' were what would shape events.[2] This was as true for the Japanese, whose field commanders acted with a high degree of autonomy, as for the Chinese, over whom Chiang Kaishek's authority had been reduced following the destruction of some of his own forces.

The year between the fall of Shanghai and the fall of Wuhan in late October 1938, marked by one Japanese massacre, the two battles of Xuzhou and Wuhan and a series of horrific self-inflicted wounds, was one of the most terrible in modern Chinese history. By the end of 1938 the Japanese controlled much of north China and the Yangzi river valley all the way from Shanghai to Wuhan. The retreating Nationalists' scorched earth policy, however, ensured that they held not thriving commercial centres and a productive countryside but piles of rubble and flooded fields.

The human toll was enormous. China's losses during the Battle for Wuhan alone amounted to 250,000 men, while Japan's were 100,000.[3] The official Chinese figure for the victims of the Nanjing Massacre is 300,000.[4] While that number is hotly disputed, there is no doubt that a terrible massacre did take place. One instance of the damage caused by the Nationalists' scorched earth policy, the breaking of dikes on the Yellow river, although hardly reported at the time and mentioned only briefly in most accounts of the war, caused a loss of life which must be counted in the millions.

One consequence of the fighting was that China went on the move. The best estimate is that some 60 million people – a seventh of the population – took flight. Many became refugees for just a short time, but others for much longer. Chi Pang-yuan was one of those caught up in the Nationalist retreat inland; we shall follow her as she makes her way to Chongqing, a journey that would take her more than a year. In narrating the Battles for Nanjing, Xuzhou and Wuhan, Chen Kewen's diary provides us with insight into the atmosphere at China's political centre, first in Nanjing and then in Wuhan.

Nanjing

'Again an important day in my life', Chen Kewen wrote in his diary on 26 November 1937. 'I had to say a temporary goodbye to my beloved Nanjing. Who can say when we will be able to return or whether the city's gorgeous walls and lakes will survive the Japanese jackboot.'[5] His forced departure pained Chen Kewen: 'the prospect that the enemy will seize this ancient city, derelict ten years ago but now modernised: it is as if robbers have seized a beautiful daughter just when she has grown up.'[6] The previous day Chen had a conversation with his mentor, Wang Jingwei. Wang counselled endurance, resolve and unity, despite believing that the future was bleak: 'We are defeated militarily, and internationally too our position is very bad. The Japanese will be free to slaughter the country.'[7] In the case of Nanjing, that assessment proved prophetic.

On the same day that Chen Kewen left Nanjing, Chiang Kaishek travelled to Purple Mountain and climbed up the stairs to the Sun Yatsen Mausoleum to bid farewell to the Father of the Country. At this time, Chiang was wrestling with the question of whether to defend Nanjing: 'Nanjing is not defensible, but we also cannot just walk away from it.'[8] No one believed that the Nationalist military could hold the city, but to abandon the symbolic heart of the new China without a fight would suggest a lack of commitment with unforetold consequences. A reluctance to abandon 'millions of dollars' worth of equipment', such as the anti-aircraft guns and artillery pieces scattered throughout the city and its suburbs, without ever putting them to serious use, may also have affected the decision-making.[9]

In the end Chiang Kaishek concluded that he had to at least make a show of defending 'our capital and Sun Yatsen's resting place'.[10] Ten days before his visit to the Sun Yatsen Mausoleum, the Supreme Defence Council had already ordered the relocation of KMT headquarters and the government to Chongqing, with all offices needed to direct the war moving to Wuhan. The retreat to Chongqing guaranteed, or so the argument went, 'the survival of the government' and hence 'resistance to the end'.[11] But fighting the Japanese at Nanjing still made sense, in Chiang's view, because of the possibility that the Soviets might enter the war. A Nationalist emissary to the Soviet Union reported that they were considering this. Via the Soviet delegation in Nanjing, Marshall K. Y. Voroshilov made it known that if the situation in China reached crisis point, the Soviet Union would intervene.[12] On 30 November, Chiang sent a personal message to Stalin requesting military intervention.[13]

On 5 December, Stalin scotched the idea.[14] Nonetheless, the battle for Nanjing went ahead on the same day. The population had been expecting it. Even before Chen Kewen's departure, 'the city had become desolate as the roads filled with people fleeing danger and seeking safety. Carrying their household goods on their shoulders and with their children in tow, they headed out of the city, not knowing their destination.'[15] In command of the city's defence was General Tang Shengzhi, who 'vowed to live or die with Nanjing'[16] and, to underscore his determination, ordered all transport ships at its port district, Xiaguan, to be withdrawn.

General Tang declined a Japanese demand on 10 December to surrender Nanjing. The next day, Chiang Kaishek instructed him to continue to defend the city, arguing that 'any additional day that Nanjing can be held, the greater the glory of our nation; and if you can fight on for half a month or more, then no doubt great changes will happen in the domestic and international situation.'[17] Already by the next day the situation had become hopeless, Japanese forces having surrounded Nanjing on three sides, leaving only the Yangzi shore to the east of the city open as a possible escape route. As the Japanese troops neared the city's high walls, with only a few gates allowing passage in or out of them, it became impossible for Nanjing's residents and defenders to melt away into the countryside. In addition, Japanese forces were nearing Xiaguan to the east, while the Japanese navy had crashed through barriers on the Yangzi downriver and were about to appear off Nanjing, too.

On 12 December, General Tang concluded that any further resistance was hopeless and ordered his forces to fight their way out through Japanese lines. This retreat turned into chaos when General Tang gave an oral instruction that 'the 87th and 88th Division, the 74th Army, and the Training Regiment may cross the Yangzi river if there is a steamer'.[18] Tens of thousands of troops turned on their heels and headed for Xiaguan. 'Not just cars could not move, even people could not do so … everybody fought to get on board a ship, shouting and firing their rifles. When a boat headed into the river, troops fired at them from the shore, sinking them. Others sank because they were overcrowded.' It is not clear how many people died in the stampede. A 'Third War Zone General Report on the Battle for Nanjing' put the number at over 100,000. Being based on the idea that ten divisions tried to make their way to Xiaguan, this figure is probably an overestimate. Most divisions, and certainly those who had just fought at Shanghai, were under strength, often woefully so. Nonetheless, the number of deaths will have been very great indeed.

General Tang was one of the lucky escapees. Despite his vows, he left Nanjing at 8 p.m. on the night of 12 December, without, so later reports claimed, informing even his own staff.[19] He made his way to Wuhan, apologised to Chiang Kaishek and asked to be punished for his failures. Chiang did not take him up on this, probably because of his own responsibility for the disaster, but General Tang was widely condemned as a coward and an incompetent. The rumour swirled around Wuhan, so Chen Kewen's diary suggests, that after his arrival there General Tang wired 400,000 Chinese dollars to a bank in Hong Kong – a story that implied that it was not nationalism but plain avarice that had led him to take command of the city's defence.[20] He devoted the rest of his life to the study of Buddhism – a way of indicating that he had abandoned all ambition. It is possible that the rumours about General Tang were the result of scapegoating.

The Japanese had not planned to attack the Nationalists' capital. After the Battle of Shanghai, neither the General Staff in Tokyo nor the commander on the ground, General Matsui, favoured the occupation of Nanjing. But General Yanagawa Heisukei, the commander of the 10th Army, which had just landed at Hangzhou Bay, followed his own nose. Trained to exploit any opportunity quickly and decisively, on 15 November he ordered his units to disregard the limits placed on their area of operation and pursue the fleeing Chinese forces. When General Matsui learned that the Nationalists had lost half their troops and that the rest were demoralised, he came round to General Yanagawa's view that the seizure of Nanjing would precipitate their surrender.[21] The General Staff provided retrospective approval for his plans on 1 December. Japanese forces charged forwards, covering over 30 kilometres a day, travelling without rations or supplies because their logistics were unable to support such a fast-moving front. They torched homes, farms and even whole villages in order to thwart possible Chinese ambushes.[22] Having not carried either blankets or winter uniforms, they arrived at Nanjing exhausted, hungry and bitterly cold.

When they approached Nanjing, the Japanese had an excellent opportunity to make a good impression. The Nationalists's scorched earth policy had extended to everywhere within 15 kilometres of the city, including 'whole villages', while within Nanjing 'the torch was applied to districts around South

Gate and in Hsiakwan [Xiaguan]'.[23] Chinese soldiers had also begun looting the city, in part because they had run out of food and water but also because 'the realisation was becoming general that the majority were trapped and must die'.[24] According to *New York Times* reporter Tillman Durdin,

> When the final collapse of the Chinese came in Nanking, so great was the feeling of relief among the populace and such was the bad impression created by the break-up of the Chinese municipal regime and the defence command that the people were ready to welcome the Japanese troops. Indeed scattered bands of civilians actually cheered Japanese columns as they marched in from the South Gate and the West Gate.[25]

The Japanese failed to avail themselves of this opportunity; instead they perpetrated a terrible atrocity.

General Matsui's plan had been to leave most of his forces outside the city and, as a symbolic gesture, enter Nanjing with just the military police and a few battalions of each of the two armies that had encircled it.[26] Instead, because so many Chinese soldiers who had not surrendered remained in the city, 70,000 troops were marched in, many of whom were exhausted, hungry, cold, thirsty and frightened. The orgy of violence that followed focused first on soldiers and suspected soldiers within the city, but it then expanded outwards to the suburbs, involving large numbers of civilians.

Durdin left Nanjing by river on the gunboat USS *Oahu* on 17 December, four days after the Japanese occupation, having born witness to the mass execution of Nationalist soldiers and suspected soldiers. In early January he reported that the Japanese had admitted that 15,000 Chinese had been rounded up 'during the first three days' of the occupation and that they captured another 25,000 Chinese soldiers in hiding throughout the city,[27] who were 'systematically rounded up and executed'.[28] These included thousands of Nationalist soldiers who had fled to the Nanjing Safety Zone, established by foreigners in the city to protect civilians. The Safety Zone was to be a demilitarised zone, but some guards had admitted Nationalist soldiers, who feared for their lives, after they laid down their arms. The Japanese took them away in groups and executed them en masse. Events like these were bound to come to Durdin's knowledge.

Xiaguan was another area where mass executions took place. The Japanese had made no preparations for accommodating prisoners of war and initially were also under pressure to make the city safe for a victory parade in which Prince Asaka, a member of the royal family, was to participate. Lieutenant General Nakajima Kesago, the commander of 16th Division, wrote in his diary of the Nationalist soldiers that 'since our policy is not to take prisoners, we made a point of executing them as soon as we had captured them'.[29] Tasked with clearing the Xiaguan area, his division rounded up '22,550 at eight different locations'.[30] One careful contemporary analysis estimates that the 'number of Chinese prisoners executed by the 16th Division ranges from 4,000 to 12,000'.[31] The Yangzi became 'a river of dead bodies' as corpses were shoved into the water.[32]

At Mufushan Mountain to the north of Nanjing, another regiment was tasked with guarding 20,000 prisoners, housed in a local barracks. They had been ordered to take care of these soldiers, but a fire broke out in the barracks and machine guns were let off. There seem to have been few survivors.[33] Another instance of the mass killing of prisoners of war involved a regiment of the 9th Division. It reported that it had executed '6,700' soldiers during mopping-up operations, a figure 'very close to 7,000, which happened to be the number of rifle and machine gun bullets the regiment reported to have spent', and hence likely to be accurate.[34]

In this first phase of what came to be called the Nanjing Massacre, or Atrocity, the Japanese hunted for Nationalist soldiers who had changed into civilian outfits. They checked the bodies of those they stopped for marks that indicated that a person was a soldier, including looking for bruises on the shoulder left by the recoil of a rifle. Inevitably many civilians were caught in the dragnet. 'A favourite method of execution', according to Durdin, 'was to herd groups of a dozen men at entrances of dugouts and to shoot them so the bodies toppled inside. Dirt then was shovelled in and the men buried.'[35] In actions that could only be counterproductive, the Japanese also targeted firemen and policemen. According to Durdin, 'any person, who through excitement or fear, ran at the approach of the Japanese soldiers was in danger of being shot'.[36]

As well as the large-scale massacres, there were many smaller ones. To take just one example, on 15 December members of a small Japanese unit killed 100 prisoners of war they were escorting after panic broke out when a Japanese soldier either fell or was pushed into a pool of water. His comrades, all fresh recruits, 'being already scared, started stabbing or clubbing the prisoners while crying out cursing words. The prisoners began to flee as the panic spread', upon which the Japanese soldiers turned their rifles on them.[37]

After the first phase, mass executions on this scale became rare, if only because most of the Nationalist troops now lay dead, but Japanese brutality continued. Hallett Abend reported from Shanghai on 24 January that 'the conditions in Nanking one month and ten days after the victorious Japanese Army crashed the gates of China's former capital are so lawless and so scandalous that Japanese authorities continue to refuse permission to any foreigners except diplomatic officials to visit the city'.[38] Looting was rife. 'Nearly every building was entered by the Japanese soldiers, often under the eyes of their officers, and the men took whatever they wanted. The Japanese soldiers often impressed Chinese to carry their loot.'[39]

So was rape. There are many gruesome accounts of rape, which in some cases involved all the women of a family. Survivors have told harrowing stories, and awful photographs have been published. The lowest estimate of the number of rapes is 4,000 to 5,000, while the more common figure is around 20,000. Recounting details of these incidents would be gratuitous. However, it is worth pointing out that rape continued throughout the six weeks that the Nanjing Atrocity is usually considered to have lasted, partly because the Japanese military police were so ineffectual.[40] Underpaid, lacking in discipline and suffering from low morale, they were simply ignored by the soldiers, who certainly did not seem to fear that their actions would be punished.

Abend noted that 'Shanghai observers speculated whether a condition of mutiny existed among the soldiery.' That does not seem to have been the case, given that, for instance, the Shanghai Expeditionary Army gave orders to lower units to dispose of large numbers of prisoners of war. Abend's comment was an indication of the bewilderment caused by Japan's atrocious behaviour in Nanjing.

The figure of 300,000 is etched into the front of the Museum for the Commemoration of the Nanjing Massacre in Nanjing, established in 1985, representing an estimate of the number of victims of the atrocity as endorsed by the Chinese government. This estimate is based on the judgments of the Tokyo and Nanjing War Crimes Tribunals, both of which have been criticised for the way they handled evidence.[41] The figure is essentially a political one, in the sense that the Chinese government has endorsed it and uses it for political purposes. Over the last three decades much research has gone into refining this estimate, for instance by using burial records, although even that is not without its problems. Three hundred thousand would appear to be an overestimate.[42] A recent analysis by a Japanese historian, who initially accepted the Chinese government's estimate of the scale of the atrocity and then rejected it, puts the number of victims at '45,000 to 65,000'.[43] That figure forms the lower end of reasonable estimates.

Focusing on gaining as accurate a figure as possible of the number of victims of the Nanjing Atrocity has brought with it its own problems, not least that it effaces the victims as individuals. It makes them part of a narrative constructed by Beijing, with which some victims – among whom would have been many staunch believers in the Nationalist cause – might not wish to have been associated. The Nanjing Atrocity has become the enduring symbol of Japanese brutality, eliding other Japanese atrocities in China and elsewhere, then and later. The articulating of horror purely in number terms also brings with it the risk of erasing the differences between the many different atrocities that took place across the world during the Second World War.

Massacres can and have been used as instruments of war. In the case of

Nanjing, though, that does not seem to have been the case. Instead, the conditions in Nanjing when Japanese forces entered, the failures of the logistical system of the Imperial Japanese Army, the occupation of the city by troops that had been both brutalised and exhausted by their training and during three months of fighting, the decision to stage a victory march, and the breakdown of discipline in some parts of the Japanese army seem to have been its main causes. Whatever its origin, Japan will have to live with the reality of that terrible atrocity for generations to come.

From the perspective purely of military history, the Nanjing Atrocity was emblematic of the fact that surrender became rare in the Second World War. In earlier times, when a battle lasted no more than a few days, if that, and took place on a circumscribed battlefield, an individual commander could decide that the battle was lost and that further bloodshed was meaningless. With war spread out in time and space, no commander had sufficient oversight to make that call. Indeed, to continue to fight to the death of all could make sense from an overall strategic point of view. Chiang Kaishek clearly thought so in the case of Nanjing.

Xuzhou

Chen Kewen arrived in Wuhan on 28 November in a British steamer, travelling, rather to his embarrassment, as a privileged official 'safely and exceedingly comfortably'.[44] His family made the journey separately, largely in overcrowded trains and vessels. In Wuhan, Chen and his government colleagues took over buildings in the Japanese concession vacated when the Japanese evacuated to Shanghai. He found the mood in the city a weird mix of defiance, despair, optimism, anger and decadence. One of Chen's colleagues, who had been offered a job in a bank and hence no longer cared about what he said, parted with the words: 'to reform the political system, it's best to ask Mao Zedong to take over as head of the government and Zhu De [the Communist commander-in-chief] as chief of the army.'[45] Reports about military casualties, refugees, clogged-up transport networks and collapsing order filled Chen Kewen's meetings with a deep pessimism: 'they inevitably ended with mutterings about "it's nonsense to say that China cannot lose"'.[46] To Chen's anger, some colleagues dined, drank, sang and visited prostitutes as if there was no tomorrow.[47] 'Sister, I love you' was a popular song on the ships that carried government personnel to Wuhan.[48]

Morale improved in subsequent months. Chen Kewen's spirits were lifted when he heard marching soldiers bellow 'The March of the Volunteers', a patriotic song composed in 1935, which became widely popular and is now the PRC's national anthem.[49] He was impressed with Chiang Kaishek's determined attitude. Looking tired but resolute, Chiang kept an audience of a thousand people spellbound at a Sun Yatsen memorial meeting, insisting that the fight would continue and that no compromise with Japan was possible: 'such a supreme commander will lift the spirit of the broad masses,' Chen wrote.[50] A New Year's Day lecture by Chiang in the city's auditorium brought tears to his eyes.[51] Theatres staged patriotic plays such as 'Night Light Cup', a story about a son who wishes to join the war but whose mother wants him to work to pay off the family debts. In cinemas, newsreels reported on Japanese bombing attacks before showing feature films such as the movie version of Pearl Buck's *The Good Earth*.[52] The radio broadcasted 'war reports and heroic marches'.[53] Chen's resolve to do his best for his government and country strengthened: 'if we organise ourselves,' he wrote, referring to the thousands of people like himself in government jobs who had to make the system work, 'then after a hundred defeats we shall be able to gain the final victory.'[54] He spent his days doing his job, going to dinners, playing cards and reading, including Darwin, H. G. Wells's *The Shape of Things to Come* and *Marriage Destinies to Awaken the World,* a seventeenth-century novel by Pu Songling critical of the corruption of his time and pessimistic about the future. The Bible, according to Chen, was selling briskly.[55]

Chiang reached for his inner Brutus to toughen military spines. He convened a meeting of senior officers of the First and Fifth War Zones of north China on 11 January 1938. He talked at length about the lack of discipline, the looting by China's own soldiers, the failure of divisional commanders to coordinate their actions and the general disregard for central orders. Chiang singled out for criticism the military governor of Shandong province, General Han Fuju, who had simply withdrawn when a few 'second-rate' Japanese divisions entered his province. That move endangered the Fifth War Zone, in between north China and the Yangzi delta and a forward defence for Wuhan. When the meeting drew to a close, General Han was arrested.[56] He was charged with disobedience and sent to Wuhan, where he was condemned to death by a court martial on which sat generals Li Zongren and Bai Chongxi of the Guangxi Clique, generals Chen Cheng and Hu Zongnan for the Nationalists, and his former patron, General Feng Yuxiang. The trial was meant to symbolise the unanimity of Chiang Kaishek and his allies and drive home their determination to fight the Japanese. General Han Fuju was executed with a bullet to the back of his head.

Chiang Kaishek also wanted to make an example of General Liu Xiang of Sichuan province. The Nationalists had long planned to retreat there, but now they needed to be sure they could do so. Ill in hospital in Wuhan, General Liu was confronted with evidence that he had conspired with General Han Fuju and died shortly afterwards.[57] Anyone in Sichuan thinking about resisting the Nationalists had been put on notice. Chen Kewen believed that the deaths of generals Han Fuju and Liu Xiang would meet with popular approval. General Liu Xiang, he stated, had died 'at the right time and in the right place', with some of his forces at the front and he himself in Wuhan at the centre of resistance.[58]

On 15 January 1938, Japanese prime minister Konoye Fumimaro declared that 'the Imperial Government will not deal with the National Government hereafter'.[59] Japan's decision to end intense back-door negotiations must go down in history as one of the greatest foreign policy blunders of any Axis power. By assigning the Nationalists to the dust heap of history while significant Nationalist figures wanted to sue for peace, Konoye ensured that the best option for many became to stick with Chiang Kaishek. All those who depended on the Nationalists, including China's financial elites, also had solid reason to continue to support the Nationalists. Their holdings of Nationalist currency would lose their value if the Nationalists were just cast aside.

The Guangxi Clique and the Communists provided invaluable help in stiffening morale. General Li Zongren spoke with determination at press meetings, pushed his subordinates hard and brought a large part of his Guangxi Army to the Fifth War Zone. In Wuhan, General Bai Chongxi stated in a lecture to KMT party workers that '300,000 deaths is nothing. In the European War no country lost less than thirty plus million men', thus preparing them for the sacrifices that would be demanded of them.[60]

At this time the Communists followed the policy 'Everything for the united front'. Some of their most prominent figures were in Wuhan, including Wang Ming, the Party secretary at the time, and Zhou Enlai. They published the *New China Daily*, which proclaimed Communist support for the Nationalists and the war. They joined mass rallies where they praised their Nationalist colleagues and insisted that Wuhan had to be defended as Madrid had been in the Spanish Civil War.[61] *Diary of an Army Enlistee* by the famous left-wing author Xie Bingying circulated in Wuhan, as did she herself, speaking at many rallies. The famous Communist author, intellectual and archaeologist Guo Moruo rushed to Wuhan from Japan, where he had been living with his Japanese wife and children. In Wuhan he published poems and essays, spoke at public gatherings and joined rallies.[62]

The presence of many eminent foreigners buttressed morale, too. The writers Christopher Isherwood and W. H. Auden, the journalists Edgar Snow, George Taylor, Jack Belden and Michael Lindsay, German advisors such as Alexander von Falkenhausen, photographers such as Robert Capa and V. Rogov, and the activist and journalist Agnes Smedley were all there. 'History, grown weary of Shanghai, bored with Barcelona, has fixed her capricious interests upon Hankow,' wrote Auden and Isherwood.[63] (Hankow is part of Wuhan, which is in fact made up of three cities.) With the eyes of the world fixed on Wuhan, and with world sympathy on China's side, suing for peace became difficult.

A significant victory buoyed spirits. Following the falls of Shanghai and

Nanjing, the defence of Wuhan became the focus of Nationalist strategy. Forces were deployed in the outer approaches to Wuhan in north and south China, barriers were constructed at three strategic points along the Yangzi river and several rings of fortified defences were thrown up around the city.[64] General Li Zongren, commanding the Fifth War Zone, blocked Japanese approach routes from north China and Shandong province. After the decision was made in early January 1938 to try to stop the Japanese from moving on Wuhan through Shandong, troop numbers there were increased from 80,000 to 300,000.[65]

As had happened after the Battle of Shanghai, Japanese action on the ground undermined General Staff orders 'not to be dragged into expanding operational areas and becoming trapped'.[66] Claiming that they needed to pursue fleeing Nationalist forces in order to pacify occupied areas, Japanese ground forces swung into action, aiming to clear the Tianjin–Nanjing railway, converge at Xuzhou and cut all lines of retreat for Nationalist forces in the Fifth War Zone. The advance of General Hata Shunroku's 13th Division from the south was stopped at the broad Huai river, which cuts through the north China plain from west to east. In the north, General Itagaki Seishiro's 5th Division was brought to a halt at Linyi in south Shandong province. The Nationalists poured reinforcements into the Fifth War Zone, including General Tang Enbo's four powerful German-trained divisions. Japan's 10th Division, led by General Isogai Rensuke, overconfident from a series of quick victories in Shandong, advanced from the north-west towards Xuzhou, hoping to unlock the battle-field. But they became trapped at Taierzhuang, 60 kilometres north-east of Xuzhou, between defenders in the town itself and General Tang Enbo's forces to their rear and on their flank. On 7 April, the units having lost contact with each other and having incurred between 10,000 and 20,000 casualties between them, General Isogai ordered a retreat.[67]

Wuhan erupted. 'A million and a half Chinese in this temporary capital tonight jubilantly celebrated China's first decisive victory,' reported the *Washington Post*.[68] The city 'has gone wild with excitement', according to *The Times*.[69] Chinese newspapers had been hailing the exploits of the Fifth War Zone for days; they issued special editions on the day of the victory. When Chen Kewen learned of it, he 'ecstatically embraced' a friend. Hundreds of thousands of people joined a victory parade that evening, while General Feng Yuxiang published a poem in which he called the Japanese 'soft-shelled turtles in a jar' and predicted that all Japanese forces would be driven from China 'before the spring wheat turns yellow'.[70] In his memoir, General Chen Cheng, now the commander-in-chief of the Wuhan Garrison Command, compared the Taierzhuang victory to the Battle of Tannenberg, the famous August 1914 battle in which the German commander, Field Marshal Paul von Hindenburg, and his deputy, Erich Ludendorff, trapped and destroyed an advancing Russian army.[71]

The victory could not have come at a better time for the Nationalists. A KMT emergency conference opened on 29 March to rally supporters, convince the general population that they had a plan for the future and to broaden the base for the war. The conference adopted a provisional constitution that linked war to national redemption. 'The Three People's Principles and the Last Testament of Sun Yatsen are our guides in fighting Japanese aggression and remaking the country,' it declared.[72] The constitution presented China's war with Japan as part of a global 'fight for peace and justice in the world'. It also established a National Political Consultative Conference to 'unite all forces in the country',[73] and promised 'full safeguards for freedom of speech, publication, assembly and association'. The conference appointed Chiang Kaishek as Director General of the KMT, adding the party portfolio to the army and government ones he already possessed.[74] The Chinese press welcomed the constitution as 'substantially in agreement with wishes expressed in various quarters over the last half year'.[75] The Communist Party instructed its members to 'adopt an attitude of active support'.[76]

The first meeting of the National Political Consultative Conference, presented in the foreign press as China's national assembly, took place in July. It had a 200-person membership, made up of eighty-eight provincial representatives selected for their local stature, as well as important non-KMT intellectuals, politicians, artists and entrepreneurs. These included Communist luminaries such as Mao Zedong, Wang Ming and Deng Yingchao, Zhou Enlai's wife; well-known leaders of smaller parties; the last Confucian, Liang Shuming; Jiang Baili, the strategist who had first called for a war of attrition; the Malay Straits entrepreneur Chen Jiageng (Tan Kah Kee), representing overseas Chinese; and the political scientist Qian Duansheng. It formed, one commentator argued, 'the best group of people China has had'.[77] The conference met four times a year to review both domestic and international policies, call ministers to account and conduct investigations through its committees.[78] Although some ridiculed its proceedings as 'endless meetings, few decisions, and even less action',[79] Chen Kewen's response was that 'at least it provides an education in democratic politics'.[80]

Following the Taierzhuang victory, Nationalist forces counter-attacked. 'Generalissimo Chiang's armies, estimated at 500,000 men, were on the offensive at both ends of the Long–Hai railroad', reported the *Washington Post*,[81] referring to the east–west-running railway in northern China. However, the Japanese General Staff decided that the Taierzhuang victory would not be allowed to stand. Abandoning plans not to expand operational areas in 1938, it poured reinforcements into Xuzhou, bringing the number of Japanese troops deployed there to 400,000.[82] New staff officers were dispatched to China to ensure proper coordination. Japanese commanders began to talk about doing to the Chinese what Hannibal had done to the Romans at the Battle of Cannae: encircling and destroying them after a minor tactical setback.[83]

They did not succeed. Although hard-pressed by Chiang Kaishek to go on the offensive, on 15 May General Li Zongren ordered a retreat before the Japanese could finish the encirclement, telling Chiang, 'I fear the complete defeat of the enemy will be impossible.'[84] Most Fifth War Zone forces retreated from Xuzhou in good order. Li Zongren's ability to ignore Chiang Kaishek's orders illustrates a phenomenon described by the historian Stephen MacKinnon: Chiang Kaishek increasingly had to share power over military operations with an older, more established generation of generals who regarded him as a bit of an upstart. These men shared a common background in having studied at China's military academy at Baoding after the 1911 Revolution; they knew each other well; they had solid local support; and they had vast battlefield experience – although often very little knowledge of recent innovations in equipment, tactics and strategy.[85] This development fits with Clausewitz's observation that chance and the commander becomes more important as war slips from state control.

Wuhan

This brutal phase of the War of Resistance had yet to reach its climax. On 18 June 1938, Tokyo approved a plan to take Wuhan and occupy Canton that summer and autumn.[86] Some 400,000 troops, deployed in two armies, amassed for the assault on Wuhan. They faced 800,000 Chinese troops in two war zones, the Fifth War Zone under General Li Zongren as before and the Ninth, south of the Yangzi river, under General Chen Cheng. While Japanese ground forces advanced along four lines of approach, its navy, making use of the high levels of the Yangzi during the summer months, also joined the fray.

The Battle of Wuhan began on 14 June, when the Japanese seized the city of Anqing, about 100 kilometres upriver from Nanjing, after just one day of fighting. Next was the Madang barrier, also on the Yangzi, which the German advisors who had helped in its construction had vouched would hold for three months. It fell within days because the Japanese attacked it from the rear, having landed units upstream. The Nationalist commander charged with defending the area where the Japanese landed was executed after having repeatedly failed to obey orders to attack. Resistance in the Ninth War Zone was tougher, but by the end of July the last major opposition before Wuhan south of the Yangzi had been crushed. In the Fifth War Zone, the Japanese also had to work harder, in September having to battle three weeks in order to advance just 10 kilometres. However, by the end of that month they overcame the last Yangzi river barrier at Tianjiazhen, some 150 kilometres downstream from Wuhan. By this time, in central China another Japanese force had advanced along the Huai river and cut the Beijing–Wuhan railway. Japanese forces could now move on Wuhan from the north, the east and the south, making any further resistance pointless.

Already by late June, Wuhan had begun to empty out, with some of Chen Kewen's colleagues deciding to return to Beijing and Shanghai.[87] They were done with fighting for the Nationalists. If the restaurants of Wuhan had been busy in the first months of the city's defence, by July they were empty, as beggars and refugees crowded its streets. On 17 July, government personnel were instructed to be prepared to leave the city on ten days' notice. Following a policy decided the previous December, Chen Kewen's main task in Wuhan was to facilitate the movement of people, offices, industries, equipment, archives and materiel to Chongqing.[88] The Nationalists fought so hard at Xuzhou and defended Wuhan with so many troops that they bought enough time to complete the transfer of people and goods to 'the rear', in south-west China.

Chen Kewen left Wuhan on 1 August, his task complete. By this time, the great excitements of the spring had dissipated. In early summer, Mao Zedong published his pamphlet *On War of Attrition*, in which he argued that both those who maintained that China could prevail over Japan quickly and those who believed that China had no chance of doing so were wrong; China would win, but only after a very long time, and only if it fought according to the principles he espoused. In Chongqing, Chen Kewen found the atmosphere different to that in Wuhan. In Wuhan 'men and women found it easy to meet and to be together. Chats in coffee shops, conversations in restaurants and cinemas: none of that is possible here.'[89] In Chongqing, Chen Kewen soon realised, he would have to live a more Spartan and dangerous life, with no likelihood of a resumption of his Nanjing life any time soon. His May Fourth yearnings would have to be put on hold for the time being.

Scorched Earth

On 21 August, Chiang Kaishek and his wife Chiang Meiling set off to Cockerel Mountain, a resort north of Wuhan. Here they prayed and recited the fifth book of Jeremiah's *Lamentations*, which grieve for God's destruction of Jerusalem and bewail his anger with his followers.[90] It begins with 'Remember, O Lord, what is come upon us: consider, and behold our reproach. Our inheritance is turned to strangers, our houses to aliens. We are orphans and fatherless' and ends with 'But thou hast utterly rejected us; thou art very wroth against us.' As the pair pondered the wreckage of war, a question that might well have pressed on their minds was whether God's wrath had been provoked by the destruction caused by Japan's armed forces or the Nationalists' own scorched earth policy.

The scorched earth policy was deliberate. As historian Yang Weizhen has pointed out, well before the War of Resistance began, Chinese strategists and commentators had seized upon Russia's defeat of Napoleon in 1812, when the Russians burned Moscow to the ground, as well as Britain's use of the policy during the Boer War in South Africa, as promising precedents.[91] Antecedents can also be found in Chinese warfare. 'Clearing the countryside and erecting high walls' – moving food and people inside walled settlement and destroying the surrounding countryside – was a standard practice in the Chinese military tradition. Already in a speech of April 1936, later published as a pamphlet, General Li Zongren advocated: 'resist Japan by scorching the earth.' According to Yang Weizhen, by the time of the Battle of Wuhan, 'resistance of Japan through a scorched earth policy … had become policy'.[92]

It had been first enacted in Shanghai. As Hallett Abend reported on 9 November 1937, when the Nationalists withdrew, 'the Chinese set fire to the large Japanese-owned Toyoda cotton mills … several factories, scores of houses, and two large coal yards were set ablaze'.[93] The next day 'civilian refugees … with fires at their backs set by retreating troops, stormed the bridges and river bank of the French Concession in search of safety'.[94] 'Foreign military observers,' according to Abend, 'are amazed by the extent of the Chinese destruction of everything within the zones they still control. Most of this destruction is said to be purposeless.'[95] At the same time that Shanghai was being set ablaze, in Qingdao, the port city in Shandong province, 'Chinese military mobs … destroyed during the past 24 hours a large part of the Japanese mill area of this great German-built port city.'[96]

The policy was not only applied to cities. A December 1937 battle plan formulated by the Military Affairs Committee ordered that 'roads in each war zone must be immediately destroyed (up to 30 kilometres from front lines and 100 from rear areas) to slow the enemy' and 'all walls surrounding cities and towns must be dismantled. They are no use in resisting the enemy, while the enemy might use them to resist our attacks.'[97] It is not clear to what extent this part of the policy was implemented.

During the Battle of Xuzhou, Chinese defenders burned the provincial capital of Shandong, Ji'nan, to the ground. When the Japanese finally entered Xuzhou itself, they found a flattened city, where 'two tremendous fires, apparently started in munitions storehouses, blotted the city out from the air under a blanket of smoke and shot flames hundreds of metres in the air'.[98] Zhengzhou, to the west of Xuzhou, was also razed.[99]

The Yellow river carries the nickname 'China's sorrow'. For vast stretches, the riverbed runs well above the surrounding countryside, with the result that devastating floods occur if its dikes are not maintained. Following the Battle of Xuzhou, Japanese forces pursued retreating Chinese units, prompting Chiang Kaishek to unleash the Yellow river against them. The logic was as impeccable as it was merciless. As one local commander wrote in a message to Chiang:

Xuzhou has fallen and the enemy's main force has gone deep into eastern Henan and western Shandong. Unless we break the cauldrons and sink the ships to show our determination, the Central Plain cannot be defended. We intend to divert the Yellow River's waters to submerge the enemy. It is clearly well known that the sacrifice will be heavy, but with the urgent need to save the nation the pain must be endured.[100]

This commander would not have written in such a way unless he knew that Chiang agreed.

Chiang Kaishek's order to break the Yellow river dikes was all the more tragic because it was based on a fear of what the Japanese might do next rather than what they actually did.[101] Chiang anticipated that after the capture of the railway junction at Zhengzhou, the Japanese armies would use the Beijing–Wuhan railway to attack Wuhan before the Nationalist retreat into Sichuan province was complete. However, both the General Staff in Tokyo, the Japanese Central China Area Army at Xuzhou and the local commanders had issued orders to these forward units to halt their advance. The historian Ma Zhonglian, a researcher with the Chinese Military History Museum, concludes from his review of the evidence that 'Japanese forces stopped their westward advance of their own volition. There is no evidence to show that breaking the dikes at Huayuankou caused them to halt their advance.'[102]

The floodwaters advanced at an average rate of 16 kilometres per day, inundating everything in their way.[103] The Yellow river changed its course, no longer flowing north-east to Shandong province, but south-west, overflowing into vast stretches of productive agricultural land in Henan, Anhui and Jiangsu provinces, before adding its waters to the Huai river and the great lakes of north Jiangsu. The best estimate is that 800,000 people, who were given no warning, were killed outright and 4 million became refugees.[104] The floods wrecked the harvest of that year and many subsequent years. Their impact was long-lasting because they deposited large quantities of silt over the area and because emergency dikes thrown up across the region further disturbed an already fragile drainage system. The degradation of the environment, the destruction of farming communities and the weakening of human bodies contributed to the great Henan Famine of 1942 and 1943, when perhaps as many as 2 million people starved to death and another 2–3 million became refugees.[105] The dike at Huayuankou was not repaired until 1947, as a project of the United Nations Relief and Rehabilitation Agency.

Wuhan, too, suffered much damage. When the Japanese marched into the city through its Baoyang Gate, according to the *Washington Post*, 'near panic prevailed because "destruction units" had begun dynamiting strategic buildings'.[106] The next day 'explosions still rocked the three Wuhan cities ... and flames stabbed the sky as unchecked fires spread a trail of ruin and ashes for the invader to seize.'[107] Chiang Kaishek regretted that the destruction had not been more thorough. The local commander, he moaned, 'had retreated early without authorisation so that not all plans were implemented'.[108]

The city of Changsha was not so lucky. After the Battle for Wuhan, the Nationalists thought that the Japanese's next target would be Changsha, the capital of Hunan province. According to the recollection of General Zhang Zhizhong, the provincial chairman, he received a message from Chiang Kaishek on 12 November stating that 'if Changsha falls to the enemy, the city must be destroyed. Make all necessary preparations beforehand.'[109] Together with local security forces, Zhang Zhizhong organised a hundred teams equipped with kerosene and firewood and instructed them to set the city ablaze if the alarm was given. That happened, it appears, as a result of a false report that the Japanese had crossed a nearby river. They had not, but 10,000 people died as a result and a further 300,000 became homeless following the Great Fire of Changsha.[110] Once again no public warning was issued.

Hallett Abend visited Canton in the spring of 1939. This metropolis of 1.5 million people, once full of noise, light, and life, had, he said, become 'a dead city'. Less than half a million people remained, mostly as employees of the Japanese. True, the Japanese had hit the city hard, bombing it from the air, as Abend had seen for himself when he visited it the year before. But 'The greatest havoc and loss, fully ten times that occasioned by Japanese aerial raids,' he concluded from his 1939 visit, 'was caused by the Chinese dynamiting and setting fire to the city at the time of evacuation.'[111]

The crisis, so Chiang Kaishek appears to have thought, justified extreme measures. For a country facing an overwhelmingly superior enemy, a scorched earth policy was one of the few genuinely effective methods of resistance. In war, the most horrible things might need to be done, as General William Sherman insisted when during the US Civil War he made the south feel 'the hard hand of war' by leaving a trail of destruction, an ocean of chimneyvilles, in his wake. Yet General Sun Yuanliang, who had been the commander of the 88th Division at Shanghai which had led the attack on the Japanese Special Naval Landing Forces, had a point when, in his retirement in Taiwan, he told an interviewer:

When we implemented the scorched earth policy in the beginning of the War of Resistance, we encouraged the population to move inland and disperse. But we did not make any appropriate arrangements for our loyal compatriots, we extended no helping hand to refugees with no place to go; we just let them scatter like rats, to survive or die. This probably was the beginning of us losing the trust of the people in the mainland.[112]

That was said with the benefit of hindsight. The historian Wang Qisheng has argued that, while a good deal of support existed for a settlement with Japan after the Battles of Shanghai and Nanjing, a year later, after the fall of Wuhan and Canton, that was no longer true. The great liberal intellectual Hu Shi, for one, stated that 'in 1937, peace was possible at any time, but this is no longer the case. Then to advocate war was damaging to our country. But to surrender now would be much worse.'[113] The enormous sacrifices may in reality have had a somewhat paradoxical effect, on the one hand strengthening the national will to resist Japan come what may, but also undermining the legitimacy of the Nationalists.

Another historian, Lei Haizong, believed that China had entered a new, inspiring epoch. Having been educated at Qinghua and Chicago universities, Lei had taught at Central University in Nanjing and had moved inland with the Nationalists, first to Wuhan and then to Kunming in south-west China, where he spent the war teaching at Southwest Associated University. He had become famous before the war for a series of articles, written in an accessible no-holds-barred style, in which he excoriated his colleagues for shoehorning Chinese history into a Western scheme of periodisation, with a classical, medieval and modern period. Instead, he argued, China was a civilisation that, uniquely, had gone through two cycles of growth and decline, the first ending in the fourth century AD and the second in his own time. If the influx of talent and energy from south China at the end of the first cycle had enabled that second flowering of Chinese civilisation, Lei's depressing conclusion was that his own day was one of fatal decline. But in December 1938 Lei Haizong wrote another essay, entitled 'National Reconstruction: Anticipating a Third Cycle'.[114] The strength of China's resistance, he now argued, showed that he had overlooked something important: China's vitality.

Lei concluded from China's refusal to give up and to keep fighting that it would revive once more, not quickly, but in a process that would take decades, perhaps centuries.[115] He urged all to embrace this unique historical moment: no matter how much suffering there would be, and no matter how much pain the war was bound to cause, 'to resist the enemy and revive the country', and so speed up China's third revival, constituted 'an unprecedented privilege'.[116] 'We now often talk about living in "momentous times",' he noted, 'this is its real meaning.'[117] Not everybody agreed, as shown by Wang Jingwei's departure from Chongjing, which I will return to later. But the failure of his peace campaign to gain broad traction suggests that Lei's judgement, that these were 'momentous times', had become broadly shared. There was a widespread determination to resist Japan.

That does not mean, though, that Sun Yuanling did not have a point. Morale on the Nationalist side collapsed quickly and comprehensively when the

Nationalists went on the offensive against the Communists after 1945. Conditions then were of course different, but the sacrifices that people had been asked to make and, especially, the little that the Nationalists had been able to do to support those affected by the war may well have been remembered, and fuelled the forces of disenchantment with their cause.

Flight

Japanese ground offensives, the scorched earth policy and bombing explain why the first two years of the war saw the greatest number of refugees.[118] For some, their refugee existence was short: they moved out of the way as the Japanese tsunamied their way through their neighbourhoods and then returned. For others, becoming a refugee was traumatic, but often involved leaving the towns and cities in which they had been working to return to the places where they had grown up and where their families offered support. This was the case for Chen Kewen's family. His position meant that duty required him to stay with the government. Before leaving Nanjing, he sent his mother, wife and children back to his home province of Guangxi. Immediately upon his arrival in Wuhan, he was able to call his wife Zhenjie, who assured him that all were safe.[119] For others, flight meant exhaustion, fear, hunger and death.

So it was for Chi Pang-yuan. In the middle of October, Pang-yuan's family, including her ill mother, were evacuated from Nanjing, together with more than 1,000 students from her father's Sun Yatsen High School. They travelled in groups, first by train to either Wuhu or Anqing (75 and over 200 kilometres respectively up the Yangzi from Nanjing) and then by ship to Wuhan. Pang-yuan's father, Chi Shiying, had secured a hundred rifles; older students were trained in their use in order to protect the groups as they made their way inland.

Refugee life was a crowded experience. Even the roof of the train in which Pang-yuan travelled was packed with people. 'When we went through a tunnel, someone on the roof shouted, "People have been swiped off, they have been swiped off!" but no one in the carriage helped them.'[120] Because of the Japanese bombing, travel on the Yangzi was dangerous. Pang-yuan boarded her ship in the dark of night at a dock where all lights had been extinguished. As crowds fought to get on board, people fell in the water and drowned. When the ship pulled away, people continued to try to climb on board. 'The cries for help of those fallen in the water, the screaming of the drowning, the shouting by those on board for their sons and daughters in that dangerous and terrifying night mixed with the cries of those knocked from the roof of my train carriage during the day has stuck with me throughout my life.'[121] Pang-yuan's ship only sailed at night. During the day it moored under overhanging branches of trees along the shore to hide from Japanese aircraft.

Pang-yuan's mother was already ill when she left Nanjing and her condition deteriorated during the voyage. Upon their arrival in Wuhan, she was rushed to a hospital run by the Catholic Church. Pang-yuan's sister, still breastfeeding, had also fallen ill and was diagnosed with acute gastroenteritis. She did not recover. After doctors told her uncle that there was little hope, either, for Pang-yuan's mother, he bought one small coffin, made a reservation for an adult one and purchased mourning clothes for Pang-yuan and her brother. But her mother did pull through. Her father arrived in Wuhan on 7 December, having stayed in Nanjing with Chiang Kaishek until Chiang's departure. He was thin, filthy and exhausted. 'Truly, the country is wrecked and the people are ruined,' Pang-yuan recollected her father having said when they met up in Wuhan.[122]

When Zhang Dafei, the young man whose father had been the Shenyang police chief and who the Chi family had taken under its wings, heard that Pang-yuan's mother was critically ill, he rushed to the hospital. There he gave Pang-yuan a Bible and told her that he had joined the Chinese air force, telling her that, despite his pacifist instincts, it was his duty to fight Japanese brutality.[123] He too had concluded that these were momentous times during which the Japanese evil had to be fought.

When the Nationalists ordered Wuhan's evacuation, Pang-yuan's father arranged for his students and family to move to a large memorial hall in Yongfeng, a remote town 500 kilometres away in Hunan province. This time the group had to walk, although they had one car which carried Pang-yuan's mother and two other women. Along the way, the students slept in the class rooms or on the sport fields of local schools, with local military forces providing their meals and bedding. As they travelled, they sang 'At the Songhua River', whose first line runs 'My home is at the Songhua in the Northeast'[124] and concludes with 'September 18, September 18, since that miserable day/I've left my homeland, discarded the endless treasure/roam, roam the whole day I roam inside the Great Wall/When can I go home?'[125] 'September 18' refers to the date in 1931 on which the Japanese began their occupation of Manchuria. In Wuhan, Pang-yuan's father had told her mother that he had found a safe home for their baby daughter; only now was she told the truth. Pang-yuan, her family and the students stayed at Yongfeng until October 1938. Although the local dialect was strange to her, the beauty of the town's lush, hilly surroundings, the warmth of its climate and the fecundity of the local agriculture made a deep impression on Pang-yuan.[126]

In October 1938, the Sun Yatsen High School once again had to pack up, first moving to Guilin, a city in north-east Guangxi province by now jam-packed with refugees, where Pang-yuan attended a local school for about a month. During air raids, its population scattered to the countryside, where Pang-yuan witnessed the downing of a Japanese aeroplane, welcomed with applause by the spectators.[127] Soon, though, they were on the move again, this time all the way to Chongqing, travelling some 600 kilometres, once again largely on foot,[128] though Pang-yuan rode on a luggage car, tied to cases stuffed with textbooks, chemistry sets and other school equipment to prevent her from falling off.[129] Having made their way through narrow mountain passes alongside throngs of other people making their escape, Pang-yuan and her companions arrived in Sichuan a whole year after they had set off from Nanjing. While Pang-yuan attended the famous Nankai Middle School, which had moved from Tianjin to Chongqing, the Sun Yatsen High School was accommodated at the Jingning Temple in central Sichuan.

For Pang-yuan, the journey was an education in itself, during which she came to admire the great beauty of south China's countryside but also saw much suffering. What impressed her most was the dedication of her teachers, who travelled with their students – children still – from Manchuria, for whose survival they were responsible. They taught classes wherever and whenever there was an opportunity: 'I came to feel that they represented the hopes and faith of China's intellectuals.'[130] By this she meant Chinese civilisation and its values, which her teachers saw it as their task to embody and transmit, especially in such troubled times. 'Besides their classes, they passed on devotion and love, especially self-respect and self-belief.'[131]

By the end of 1938, Japan and China had both run out of stamina. The Japanese had incurred huge losses, spent a vast amount of money, called up reservists and put their country on a war footing.[132] But the Nationalists had not caved in, although they now faced the gargantuan task of bringing order to the areas they had occupied. Despite enormous sacrifices, the Nationalists had been compelled to retreat all the way to south-west China, many of their strongest forces had lost their combat-worthiness, government offices and armies were scattered all around, and millions of people had to be found a place to live and work. Both sides needed a period to regroup and decide what to do next.

On 25 November 1938, Chiang Kaishek convened a meeting of 200 senior officers for a three-day conference at Nanyue in Hunan province. The main purpose of the conference was to announce the outlines of a new approach to the war, by which the Japanese occupation would be contested from various war zones, in which guerrillas would play a prominent role and for which the Nationalists would train up new armies. Chiang defended his 'trade space for time' strategy, maintaining that he had wanted to avoid fighting the Japanese in north China but instead had aimed to lure them deep into the hinterland of central China and take them on there.[133] He did acknowledge some mistakes, however, including the failure to anticipate the Japanese landings at Hangzhou Bay near Shanghai and at Canton, and the mismanagement of the defence of

Nanjing. Nevertheless he maintained that the overall strategy in what he called the first phase of the war had worked: the Japanese were over-stretched and China could now begin to fight back.

Chiang Kaishek chose Nanyue as the meeting place for this conference for its historical resonance. 'We are meeting at Nanyue ... the place where seventy years ago Zeng Guofan trained soldiers after he had led his Hunan Army to its first major defeat in a battle with Taiping forces.'[134] Zeng Guofan was a Confucian general who had masterminded the ultimately victorious campaign against the armies of the Taiping during the Taiping Rebellion. He had twice attempted suicide after military setbacks such as at Nanyue, but ultimately defeated the rebellion and saved Confucian civilisation. By holding the meeting here, Chiang made the point to his top generals that no matter how bleak the situation, hope should not be abandoned and that, like Zeng Guofan, they were fighting for a great and just cause.

SEVEN

REGIME CHANGE

Force does not work the way its advocates seem to think it does. It does not, for instance, reveal to the victim the strength of his adversary. On the contrary, it reveals the weakness, even the panic of his adversary and this revelation invests the victim with patience.

James Baldwin, *No Name in the Street* (1972)[1]

On 3 November 1938, Japanese prime minister Fumimaro Konoye spoke on the radio to deliver a message meant largely for consumption in China. In the full flush of Japan's victory at Wuhan, and retreating from the declaration made ten months earlier, on 15 January, that Japan did not regard the Nationalists as acceptable negotiation partners, he announced that his government was willing to begin talks with the Nationalist government if it 'abandoned past policies, changed its personnel, seized rich new possibilities, and joined in the construction of a new order' in east Asia.[2] If China failed to embrace the opportunity, he warned, then he would treat the Nationalists as just another local government as Japan created a new political order in China – and crush them if they stood in his way. Thus began Japan's campaign for regime change in China. Still fearful of the Soviets and unwilling to spend the resources required to pursue the Nationalists all the way to Chongqing, the Japanese abandoned their hopes for a decisive victory and instead pursued a limited victory and a negotiated settlement.

In his memoirs, Lieutenant Colonel Horiba Kazuo, chief of the War Direction Section of the Imperial General Staff, explained that Konoye's November 1938 China declaration was an attempt to draw a line under controversy about Japan's China policy. A group of hardliners insisted that the Nationalists should be forced to surrender and that Chiang Kaishek should be excluded from any negotiations. Others, Lieutenant Colonel Horiba vocally among them, protested that the likely consequence of this approach was the disintegration of China, leaving a patchwork of local governments much like the warlord satrapies that had emerged after the 1911 Revolution. As then, some were likely to have close relations with Western countries, thus undermining Japan's strategy in China.[3] Some sort of central government had to remain in place for Japan to work with.

Prime Minister Konoye attempted to frame a new positive narrative for

Japan's actions. In this, Japan's new order would emerge from an alliance between the Japanese empire (including Taiwan and Korea), Manzhouguo and a China organised along federal lines. That alliance would have the manpower, the economic resources and the space to enable Japan, as the head of the empire, to triumph in a new global conflict and end Western imperialism in east Asia. The new order was presented as based on the principles of 'good neighbourliness, the common defence against communism and economic cooperation'[4] in order to foster solidarities and restore east Asia to its rightful place in the world. This narrative, Konoye hoped, would replace alternatives such as that of the Nationalists, who talked of China being on the path towards becoming a unified modern nation state independent of both the Western empires and Japan; that of the Communists, who saw China as part of a global revolutionary process leading to a Communist world order; and the constructions of liberal Western-oriented elites who envisaged China's future as a modern state organised along Western lines.

Japan had set to work to establish regional governments immediately after the fall of Nanjing. On 14 December 1937, a Provisional Government for the Republic of China was inaugurated in Beijing's Zhongnanhai, a beautiful garden complex west of the Forbidden City, now the home of the PRC leadership. Its leader was Wang Kemin, who had studied in Japan, served several times as Minister of Finance, and was no friend of the Nationalists. Indeed, they had issued a warrant for his arrest after they came to power. Formally Wang was the chair of the executive council of the Provisional Government. The presidency had been left deliberately vacant as an enticement to figures of greater national stature. In March 1938, a Reformed Government was established for the provinces of the lower Yangzi region, headed by Liang Hongzhi, who, like Wang, had served in various pre-Nationalist governments, including as premier. In Mongolia, Prince Demchugdongrub established a Mongolian Alliance in Zhangjiakou in November 1937. Made up of various Mongolian leagues, in the Japanese scheme of things this constituted a third regional government.

Even before their forces had taken Wuhan, the Japanese established a 'joint committee' of the representatives of these three governments in preparation for the creation of 'a truly new central government'.[5] According to the principles the committee adopted, each region would be 'broadly self-governing' with respect to 'transport, communications, postal affairs, finance, the Maritime Customs Service, the consolidated tax, the salt tax, education and ideology'. Only 'foreign affairs' would be a central government prerogative.[6] After the Battle of Wuhan, Japan's political strategy was to inject life into this new federal structure for China and induce, or compel, the integration of the Nationalists within it.

North China, as we have seen, had an important place in Japanese thinking. The Japanese thought the region critical to the safety of the rear of the Kuantung Army in Manchuria after the Nationalists began to consolidate their rule. They also believed that access to its natural resources would finally deliver the material benefits of empire-building that had so far proved illusory to them, and so guarantee the economic health of the Japanese empire. They planned to import iron ore, coal and raw cotton from north China and export cotton textiles, sugar and rayon to it.[7] The industrial economy, the sound infrastructure and the excellent health and educational facilities to be created there would also showcase the advantages of being part of the Japanese empire to the rest of China.[8]

Behind this ambitious vision to remould China lay Japan's acute need to reduce its military operations there in order to free up resources to prepare for war with the Soviet Union. For military purposes, China was divided into several secured areas and one combat region. In the former, Japanese forces were to garrison major cities and lines of communication. Japanese forces would undertake further offensives only in central China, and then only to the extent necessary to prevent the resurgence of Nationalist military power and in a clearly delimited area of operation. This new strategy, it was hoped, would allow Japan to reduce troop numbers. The savings made would free up resources for a military build-up that would see the country have sixty regular and thirty temporary divisions and an air force of 250 squadrons by late 1939 or early 1940.

One can see why Japan could convince itself that reshaping China politically was a feasible undertaking. A provincial self-government movement had enjoyed widespread support as a solution to warlordism in the 1920s. The rebellions against the Nationalist government in the 1930s illustrated that the Nationalists were far from widely admired, even if they had begun to stabilise their rule after 1935. In China, regional differences are strong and regional loyalties are powerful. Federalism was not an illogical option for the country, nor one that lacked an intellectual or historical basis.

Foreign intervention was unlikely. In September 1938, Britain and France infamously acquiesced to Hitler's annexation of Sudetenland in Czechoslovakia when they signed the Munich Agreement. If they were this weak-kneed in their own backyard, it was unlikely that they would act with greater firmness in east Asia, where they had already accepted Japan's creation of Manzhouguo. Japan had left foreign concessions in China well alone, and nor had it taken over the Maritime Customs Service, which collected 50 per cent of Nationalist revenue, crucial to China's foreign debt, which was held mostly by Western countries. Stanley Hornbeck, the most influential State Department official supervising China policy, did not believe that Japanese aggression was a serious threat to US economic interests.[9] Germany had recalled its military mission to China and had recognised Manzhouguo.

The Soviet Union also declined to become directly involved in the war in China, although it did provide a good deal of assistance to the Nationalists. The Soviets delivered 348 bombers, 542 fighters, 82 tanks, 2,118 vehicles, 1,140 artillery pieces, 9,720 machine guns and 50,000 rifles, paid for by Nationalist deliveries of raw materials during the first few years of the war.[10] If Japan hoped to trap the Soviet Union in a European quagmire, Stalin tried to do the same to Japan in China, with much greater success. But his refusal to despatch forces into China even as the Japanese marched on Wuhan indicated that he had no desire to involve ground forces in China's war with Japan.

The politics of regime change dominated events in China from the Battle of Wuhan until the outbreak of the Pacific War. It gained a major boost when Wang Jingwei, whose hopes to succeed Sun Yatsen after his death had been destroyed by Chiang Kaishek's 1926 coup, began a peace campaign in December 1938, just after the end of the Battle of Wuhan. Both the Nationalists and the Japanese spent much energy and effort on dealing with this development, the former to minimise its consequences and the latter to support it, including through a strategic bombing campaign, which was at its most intensive during the summers of 1940 and 1941.

Puppetry

On 20 December 1938, following a two-day delay caused by bad weather,[11] Chiang Kaishek flew to Xi'an to bolster morale in a war zone responsible for defending the northern approaches to Sichuan province and thereby preserving Nationalist control over a region important for its wheat and cotton production and for containing the Communists. Unsurprisingly, the Xi'an Incident of two years before weighed on his mind.[12] The next day he learned that Wang Jingwei had flown to Kunming, the capital of Yunnan province. General Long Yun, the strongman of Yunnan province, informed him that Wang 'has an agreement with the enemy and is travelling to Hong Kong to negotiate a peace deal'.[13] Chiang Kaishek was shocked to his core: 'This shameless renegade is the cause of all misfortune of the party and the country.'[14] Xi'an was not to hold many happy memories for Chiang.

Wang Jingwei's departure from Chongqing was a huge blow to the Nationalists. After Chiang and Wang reconciled their differences following Japan's seizure of Manchuria, Wang had become head of the Executive Branch, which made him China's premier. In effect, he fronted the 'first unification, then resistance' policy, while Chiang Kaishek focused on military affairs. In the second half of the 1930s, a personality cult developed around Wang Jingwei. Three collections of his essays about revolution were translated into English, as was a poetry collection, which presented him as the 'foremost man in the Nationalist Government ... known in his own country also as a distinguished scholar and a classical poet of high merit'.[15] The cover of the 18 March 1935 issue of *Time* magazine carried a drawn portrait of 'Premier Wang Chingwei'.

In the weeks before Wang Jingwei's departure from Chongqing, his associates had worked out the contours of a deal with Japanese officials in Shanghai. In return for the recognition of Manzhouguo, permission to station Japanese troops in Inner Mongolia and the granting of most favoured nation rights to Japan in the economic exploitation of north China, the Japanese agreed to the withdrawal of their forces from areas occupied since the Marco Polo Bridge Incident, recognition of China as an equal, respect for its sovereignty, the abolition of extra-territoriality and the eventual return of its concessions.[16] While Prime Minister Konoye was aware of the negotiations in Shanghai, the agreement did not reflect settled Japanese government opinion, but was more in the nature of a kite-flying exercise, launched by officials working on their own initiative in the hope that it might lead to something, but easy to disown if it did not.[17]

On 22 December, four days after Wang Jingwei left Chongqing, Konoye made a further statement about Japan's China policy at a press conference hastily convened when Wang Jingwei's departure from Chongqing was confirmed. Wang had gone to Hanoi in Vietnam rather than to Hong Kong, in contrast to what General Long Yun had told Chiang Kaishek. Presumably Wang had provided false information to General Long to keep his real destination secret for as long as possible and to throw any would-be assassins off his tail. Konoye declared that Japan was willing to work with 'far-sighted Chinese' on the basis of equality to foster economic cooperation and jointly defend themselves against communism.[18] Fearing a domestic backlash and caught between two camps in Tokyo, Konoye had been reluctant to go public, but Wang Jingwei's move had forced his hand.[19] For the same reason, he omitted a commitment to troop withdrawal from his statement as had been agreed by Japanese negotiators, thus greatly weakening Wang's case.[20]

Rather than turn back, Wang Jingwei ploughed on. On 30 December, he published a telegram he had sent to Chiang Kaishek the previous day in the *South China Daily*, Wang's main mouthpiece, published in Hong Kong. Presenting himself as a loyal KMT member making the case for a new direction in policy, he argued that Konoye's statements indicated that Japan would respect China's sovereignty, return 'north China and all occupied areas' and refrain from 'intervention in domestic military and political affairs'. He went on: 'the goal of the War of Resistance is our country's survival and independence'. His agreement with Japan promised that, and hence, he submitted, now was the time to begin negotiations. Wang stressed that no deal should be signed unless it included an unambiguous commitment to troop withdrawal.[21]

Wang Jingwei's agreement with the Japanese grew out of discussions begun soon after the Marco Polo Bridge Incident. Before the outbreak of war, he had expressed publicly, including in radio broadcasts, his doubts about the wisdom of going to war with Japan, which he feared would cause massive destruction and most likely end with the Communists as the main beneficiaries. When push came to shove he had voted in favour of war,[22] standing up when Chiang Kaishek asked all those in favour to do so when they met back in August 1937 in Nanjing, just before the Battle of Shanghai. But he also joined the Low Key Club, which had a branch in Hong Kong for back-channel discussions with the Japanese.[23] As one member put it, the aim was to make sure that 'the war should end at the right point'.[24] Members included Zhou Fohai, the KMT's deputy propaganda director,[25] and Gao Zongwu, the head of the Asia Desk of the Foreign Ministry. In early 1938, after resigning from his post, Gao shuttled back and forth between Shanghai, Hong Kong, Wuhan and Tokyo, meeting Japanese businessmen and officials keen to end the war, including advisors to Prime Minister Konoye.

Besides disagreeing with Chiang Kaishek that China would outlast Japan 'by some fluke' in a war of attrition,[26] Wang Jingwei wanted an end to the war because he was horrified by Chiang's scorched earth strategy. After he learned that Canton had been abandoned without much of a fight but nonetheless had been turned to ruins, he commented that 'not to fight and yet to implement a scorched earth policy will do the Japanese no harm but incur us the hatred of our people.'[27] After the Battle of Wuhan, Chiang Kaishek stated that Japan 'will only find scorched earth and empty cities'. Wang criticised him, saying that such an approach had 'few advantages and many disadvantages', including forfeiting popular support for operations in the enemy's rear.[28] Following the Great Fire of Changsha, he went public, asking in an article in the *Central Daily News*, 'how can we fight if we destroy everything in places near battle zones?'

Wang Jingwei began his peace campaign in the anticipation that leading political and public figures and some of the main generals of southern China would rally to his side, either as public supporters of the campaign or, as some accounts have it, as members of a new administration to be established in the region.[29] Before leaving, Wang had been in contact with many of them, including generals Long Yun, Xue Yue, Chen Jitang, He Jian and Yun Hanmou. General Long Yun had apparently assured Wang: 'I am prepared to follow you to save us from disaster.'[30] But only a handful of officials and not one general, not even Long Yun, followed Wang.[31] Wang Jingwei asked China's ambassador to the UK, Guo Taiqi, to circulate a message rallying support among China's diplomatic missions. Guo's response was to implore him to retire to France.[32] The ambassador to the USA, Hu Shi, told Wang, '[Y]ou know very well that I opposed war for six years [since the occupation of Manchuria]; I now oppose

peace talks as against the long-term interest of the country.'[33] After praising
Wang at length, Minister of Finance Kong Xiangxi, who was himself involved
in peace negotiations, declared his opposition: 'your sudden departure has per-
plexed all colleagues in the party and the government. We fear that the enemy
will exploit it to sow dissension.'[34]

Several reasons besides Konoye's failure to mention troop withdrawals
explain the cool reception to Wang Jingwei's démarche. Rumours circulated
in Chongqing that punitive expeditions had been drawn up ready to strike
out against any rebel.[35] The fall of the Konoye government just at this critical
moment was also unfortunate for Wang Jingwei.[36] An announcement of an
American credit agreement for $25 million suggested that Western powers
were beginning to come down from the fence on which they had been sitting
for so long.[37]

It mattered, too, that the difference between Wang and Chiang was not
really, as Wang was implying, between continuing the war come what may
and a more or less honourable peace. Chiang Kaishek had been negotiating,
too. Another deal was on the table, one that also included a provision for troop
withdrawals, but did not demand recognition of Manzhouguo and did not
stipulate an indemnity payment to Japan.[38] While Wang was willing to accept
vague Japanese promises which Konoye then omitted to mention, Chiang
steadfastly held to the position that Japan first had to complete the withdrawal
of troops from all areas conquered since the Marco Polo Incident before he
would even begin formal negotiations.[39] Chiang appeared the more realistic
and hard-headed of the two. In any case, given Japanese actions so far in China,
Konoye's proposals would have seemed to many more a veiled demand for submission than a genuine statement of intent.

Chen Kewen's response indicates that even an acolyte saw Wang Jingwei's
move as a failure of judgement. Chen was not part of Wang's inner circle, but
he was a regular visitor to his home and a frequent contributor to the *South
China Daily*. Chen felt an intense sense of betrayal when Wang suddenly left
Chongqing without having told him what he was planning. He wrote Wang
Jingwei a long letter, asking him why he had faith in Japanese intentions and
questioning his timing: 'morale is low and people have not been prepared for
peace negotiations. The sudden appearance of your telegram might cause the
disintegration of our fronts and the collapse of the rear.'[40] Later, in his diary,
he quoted verbatim a 'perceptive' attack on Wang Jingwei in the press. This
ridiculed Wang as 'a traditional man of letters', in the grip of emotions, with
an enormous self-regard, 'unsuited for politics', lacking in rationality and easily
excited;[41] missing, in other words, the cool, masculine determination needed to
see China through these momentous times.

If Konoye's refusal to make a public commitment to a Japanese withdrawal from China crippled Wang Jingwei's campaign from the outset, an attempt by Chiang Kaishek to assassinate him, on 21 March, closed the door on both Wang Jingwei's return to Chongqing and on his disappearance into exile, ensuring that Wang's campaign would continue to cast a spell over events. So far, Wang Jingwei had not actually defected. The bullets shot by Chiang's would-be assassins missed him but killed his confidential secretary and close friend Zeng Zhongming,[42] who had been with Wang since before the 1911 Revolution.[43]

A few days later, Wang Jingwei published an article entitled 'Just an Example' in the *South China Daily*, claiming that he had declined a French offer for protection and had been waiting for Chongqing's response to his proposals, but that his honour now required him to push ahead with the cause for which his friend had given his life.[44] He revealed, too, that before the fall of Nanjing, Chiang Kaishek had rejected the unanimous recommendation of the Supreme Defence Council to accept a settlement that had limited Japanese demands to a demilitarised zone along the Great Wall, an expanded demilitarised zone in Shanghai and self-government for Inner Mongolia, implying that it was just Chiang's obstinacy that was to blame for the terrible damage done to China since the fall of Shanghai.[45] Shortly afterwards, Wang sailed from Hanoi to Shanghai to live there under Japanese protection.[46]

In Shanghai, Wang insisted to the Japanese that, to demonstrate they were serious about peace, they should recognise a new central government established by him and conclude a peace treaty with it. Wang insisted that the Provisional and Reformed Governments should be incorporated into his government and that it should retain all the laws, symbols and institutions of the Nationalists. His Japanese interlocutors decided to go along with him, waiting to see what would happen. The negotiations dragged on for a year, all the while making Wang appear ever more like just another puppet.[47]

Final negotiations for a deal began on 1 November 1939, on Yuyuan Road in Shanghai. The conditions to which Wang Jingwei's negotiators were asked to agree included the acceptance of advisors at all levels, the virtual separation of north China, the continued presence of Japanese troops in many areas of the country, the payment of indemnities, the granting of special economic rights to Japan and the acceptance of Japanese monopolies.[48] Such monopolies were to be established in north China for electricity generation, the railway industry, air transport, cotton production and the cement industry,[49] illustrating that shortages were compelling Japan to treat north China not as a model area, as was avowed initially, but as a place from which to extract desperately needed resources to enhance Japanese war-making capabilities, as had always been the aim. Wang's representatives fought hard, but with little negotiating power, they were unable to force the Japanese to improve their offer; they accepted demands which treated China like a colony.[50]

This outcome illustrates that Japan's version of a negotiated settlement essentially amounted to a Chinese surrender. In part, the Japanese government had to be seen to be the victor in order to mollify the Japanese public. They had made huge sacrifices, and the press had made much of Japanese victories and promised great benefits from Japan's empire-building exploits. As much as Premier Konoye and others wanted to extricate Japan from the war in China, the Japanese public was unlikely to have accepted a settlement that could not be presented as a triumph.

Two of Wang Jingwei's followers who had left Chongqing with him jumped ship once Japan's conditions for a settlement became clear. One was Gao Zongwu, the man whose shuttle diplomacy had paved the way for their departure from Chongqing; the other was the historian, commentator and theoretician Tao Xisheng. The two fled to Hong Kong, where they published a draft of the agreement, triggering widespread condemnation, and ensuring that, as *The New York Times* reported, 'Japan's whole costly scheme for a puppet central government ... is likely ruined upon the eve of its installation.'[51] Chiang Kaishek wasted no time in declaring that the conditions Wang had accepted were worse than the infamous Twenty-one Demands Japan had attempted to impose on China in 1915 during the First World War.[52] A Chongqing radio broadcast denounced Wang Jingwei as a traitor.[53]

The inauguration of Wang's administration, presented as the return of the Nationalist government to Nanjing, embodied the impossible position in which he now found himself. The ceremony took place in a Nanjing where major avenues had been renamed after Japanese generals, including General Matsui Iwane; where the Japanese had massacred the local population; and where Japanese guards stood to attention at the Sun Yatsen Mausoleum scarred by Japanese bullets.[54] To compound Wang's embarrassment, a Japanese foreign office spokesperson stated at a press conference that Wang's government was as independent as Manzhouguo.[55] Worse, Japan took another year to recognise it, hesitant to do so because it was continuing to pursue negotiations with Chiang Kaishek (thus indicating Japan's estimate of the relative significance of the two). When a treaty between Wang's government and Japan was finally signed on 30 November 1940, it was more a sign of Japan having given up hope of a deal with the Nationalists than fulsome support for Wang. Wang stood in front of the Sun Yatsen Mausoleum, waiting for Japan's representatives, so one report has it, 'as if in a daze, staring ahead at the white clouds that billowed over Purple Mountain, tears flowing copiously down his face'.[56] By now it was beyond doubt that the peace campaign was doomed.

This tearful end to the peace movement was a significant moment in the War of Resistance. No major politician or general had followed Wang Jingwei's lead and thrown in his lot with the Japanese. The Nationalists had sustained huge losses during the first two years of the War of Resistance. Many of their best forces had been crushed and many cities and large stretches of the countryside destroyed. Nonetheless, when the opportunity arose to abandon Chiang Kaishek to his fate, few did so.

This episode shows no one – not Konoye, not Wang Jingwei, not Chiang Kaishek – at their best. Had Prime Minister Konoye responded with greater courage and decisiveness to Wang's overtures, the war could have ended then, which would have allowed Japan to extricate itself from an ever-worsening disaster and avoid all the horrors that followed. Appalled by the destruction the war had caused, yearning for the role of saviour, and unwilling to continue to play second fiddle to a man he thought less talented and certainly less cultivated than himself, Wang persisted in his cause long after it was clear that it was hopeless. It is understandable that Chiang Kaishek put a very high price – death – on betrayal. But in doing so he precipitated Wang's defection, ensuring that Wang's peace campaign would continue far longer than would otherwise have been the case. With men such as these in charge, peace never had a chance.

Strategic bombing

From the spring of 1939, Japan threw its naval and army air squadrons – it did not have a separate air division – against the Nationalist rear, bombing its cities, industries and salt fields for two and a half years. The thinking was clear: bombing was meant to convince the Nationalists to accept Japan's peace conditions or cause the disintegration of their government, in a way that avoided the enormous financial and human cost of a land campaign plus its attendant risk of embarrassing failure. This was the hard element of Japan's push for regime change in China.[57]

Until the Battle of Wuhan, the Japanese army and navy had used air power in ground support operations and to interdict Nationalist supply lines. After Wuhan, such operations continued. Bombing missions targeted the Hanoi–Yunnan rail line and the 'munitions highway' through Gansu province to the Soviet Union.[58] There were also symbolic actions: a raid conducted on 12 December 1939, the third anniversary of the Xi'an Incident, destroyed Chiang Kaishek's family home in Xikou and killed his former wife, who continued to live there, in an obvious bid to bring the war home to him personally.[59] But the main focus was on attacking cities in unoccupied areas, especially Chongqing, the wartime capital, and Chengdu, Sichuan's provincial capital, as well as places, usually with air fields, such as Yichang, Changsha, Guilin, Chijiang, Enshi, Huiyang and Xiangyang.[60]

Chongqing suffered its first air raid on 26 December 1938. Coming just after Chiang Kaishek's arrival in the city and Wang Jingwei's departure, this was a symbolic action designed to impress on officials, businessmen, professionals and the general population that supporting Chiang was the more dangerous option.[61] The first wave of Japanese planes took off from Wuhan at 10.30 a.m. and arrived above Chongqing three hours later, but they had to turn back because cloud cover prevented the navigators from locating their targets. The second wave found clear skies above Chongqing, with the result that 'from the docks to the residential districts, buildings were gutted, bombed into hollow wrecks ... Even hours later, as darkness fell, the city was filled with the sounds of moaning and screams for help.'[62] Further raids followed on 2, 10 and 15 January. The last one 'was the first raid in which the heavily built-up districts within the walls were attacked'.[63] The city emptied out: '30,000 Chinese civilians are fleeing daily from Chungking,' reported *The New York Times*.[64]

These had been test raids to judge capabilities and assess potential impact. A review in March 1940 revealed deficiencies in the skills of the Japanese pilots in night- and foul-weather flying, in logistics and communications, and in the design of heavy bombers, whose fuel tanks were not self-sealing,[65] that is with a sealant filling the hole if the tank was hit. The decision was made to switch the emphasis of the air campaign to north China and attack the air fields there. Lanzhou was the main target as it was a nodal point in the supply line from the Soviet Union.

Only in the early summer of 1940 did the Japanese become technologically able to conduct real terror bombing campaigns, that is, capable of sustaining large air raids on urban populations over a long period of time. Crucial to this was the introduction of the sleek Mitsubishi A6M Zero carrier fighter and the Mitsubishi G4M long-range bomber,[66] nicknamed the Type One Cigarette Lighter by the crews because of its propensity to burst into flames after a hit.[67] Before 1940, no fighter had sufficient range to protect Japanese bombers during the 800-kilometre run from Wuhan to Chongqing. But the Zero's range was nearly 5,000 kilometres, it had a maximum speed of 530 kilometres per hour, and it carried two 7.7mm machine guns spitting 500 rounds per minute as well as two 20mm cannon with 60 rounds each. The Zeros were so good that Allied pilots shunned dogfights with them until 1943.

Two other developments fed into the Japanese decision to carry out a campaign of terror bombing. Firstly, Hitler's Blitzkrieg in May 1940 led them to conclude that a new world war would soon break out and therefore that the fighting in China had to end. The prompt capitulation of the Dutch after the German bombing of Rotterdam may have convinced the Japanese that bombing campaigns against cities could bear fruit. The second development was the occupation of Yichang in June 1940. Yichang is located on the Yangzi river on the border of Sichuan province. Being able to stage air raids from there would cut flight times to Chongqing almost in half.

Operation 101, Japan's first strategic bombing offensive, lasted through the summer of 1940. The plan was to make use of the good weather during the summer to hit Chongqing at least thirty times with 100 aeroplanes in each sortie and assault Chengdu at least twenty times. According to Japanese statistics, 27,000 bombs with a total weight of 2,957 tons were dropped on Chongqing. Their assessment was that 20 per cent of Chongqing had been irreparably damaged, its economy had collapsed and inflation was skyrocketing.[68] Japanese losses stood at 107 aircraft and 89 crew. These figures suggest that pilot error, equipment failure and bad weather were more responsible for Japanese losses than Nationalist defences. In the summer of 1941, Operation 102 repeated the exercise at even greater intensity.

The Nationalists did their best to protect the population of Chongqing and other key cities. Anti-aircraft guns were acquired, populations were dispersed and planes from the Soviet Union, 160 of which were stationed at Chongqing, were put into the air.[69] Early warning systems were also put in place, dependent on 'a network of observation towers, intelligence outposts, and ground and radio communication lines'.[70] One large red ball, lit at night, was raised on tall platforms or nearby hills and one long and one short blast of air raid sirens were sounded when an attack was expected. When Japanese planes approached to within a certain distance, a second round red ball was hoisted up and the sirens sounded one long and six short blasts.[71] In Chongqing, more than a thousand air raid shelters were dug each year from 1939, so that by 1944 half a million people could be accommodated in them.[72]

Operations 101 and 102 failed in weakening the Nationalists' resolve,[73] but they caused terrible damage. When the bombing of Chongqing intensified, Chi Pang-yuan, her mother and her two sisters were among those ordered to evacuate the city.[74] They stayed at the barracks of General Li Mi, the father of a school friend of Pang-yuan's, some 15 kilometres outside Chongqing. For Pang-yuan and her friend, the summer of 1939 was a jarring time. As the Japanese air raids continued over Chongqing, Pang-yuan learned to ride, a skill she was proud to acquire and which made her think of her relatives back in the north. 'Every morning we galloped over dirt paths lined by trees, the cool breeze blowing through the short cropped hair I had when young.'[75] During term time she was relatively safe at her residential school. Nonetheless, the air raid siren 'which made me jump out of bed after waking from my dreams in moonlit nights ... cut deep, deep wounds into my heart which will never heal'.[76] It also deepened her anger: 'to lack a feeling of safety while roving through one's own country and when even clear skies mean violence, how can I forget that?'[77]

After Pang-yuan entered the sixth form, she lived with her parents. Day after day she took refuge in the small air raid shelter of *Tide and Times*, the journal her father edited. One day in the summer of 1941, they emerged to find half of their home gone. 'That evening, during torrential rain, we crammed into one room which still had half a roof, partly sitting and partly lying down. Mother was ill again ... Father sat at the end of her bed, shielding her head from the rain with a large umbrella. So we waited for daybreak.'[78] However, the Japanese carpet bombing did not turn Chongqing's population against the Nationalists. 'Not only did the bombing generate in me a strong determination not to be cowed, but also of wanting to howl in anger.'[79] Bombing also stiffened Chen Kewen's resolve. Even though corpses were decaying in the street, he wrote, 'everybody gritted their teeth, determined to construct a great future out of this misery'.[80] Bombing, he added contemptuously, was a method used by 'a nation which bullies the weak but fears the strong'.[81]

The Nationalists used Japan's bombing campaign to claim for themselves the role of protectors of defenceless victims. After one raid in May 1940, Chiang declared 'the government has been working night and day to devise efficient and permanent measures for safeguarding the people against danger from the air'.[82] That, though, came with its own dangers, as a disaster on 5 June 1941 showed. On that day an estimated 10,000 people were trampled to death or died from suffocation when the exits from a large tunnel became blocked, not just because of the bombing but also because of government bungling.[83] The outcry was enormous.

Admiral Harry E. Yarnell, in a public address made just after his retirement from the post of commander of the US Asiatic fleet, evaluated Japan's terror bombing as 'perfectly stupid as a military performance' because it had done more than anything else 'to unify China'.[84] It would take a long time for that assessment of the impact of terror bombing campaigns on local populations to become generally accepted.

The Winter Offensive (December 1939–January 1940)

At the Nanyue Military Conference on 25 November 1938, Chiang declared that in the first phase of the war, up to the Battle of Wuhan, Japan had been 'lured deep into a battle area advantageous for decisive campaign by our forces'.[85] Now, he stated, 'we will shift from defence to offence and turn defeat into victory'.[86] A nationwide offensive in the winter of 1939–40 aimed to put that thought into action.

On the twenty-eighth anniversary of the outbreak of the 1911 Revolution, 10 October 1939, the Nationalist Military Affairs Commission adopted a 'War Plan for the Winter Offensive of the National Army'.[87] The maximum objective was the reconquest of, most importantly, Wuhan, but also of Kaifeng and Jiujiang.[88] If that proved unattainable, then large numbers of enemy troops were to be eliminated and a substantial amount of territory liberated. The offensive's operational strategy was straightforward: the Yangzi river was to be blocked to deprive the Imperial Japanese Army's 11th Army at Wuhan of supplies and reinforcements; troops in the Wuhan region would then attack the 11th Army, while all other forces across China, including Nationalist guerrilla forces, would cut railway lines as well as highways and harass the Japanese to prevent relief forces from being able to make their way to Wuhan. Like so many military campaigns, the winter offensive had political as well as purely military objectives. Coming in the aftermath of Wang Jingwei's defection and in the run-up to the inauguration of Wang's government, it was meant to serve as a clear demonstration of the continued ability of the Nationalists to mobilise forces across the country.

Following the Nanyue conference, the Nationalists rearranged their forces in eight war zones and two large guerrilla zones. The two most important war zones, the Fifth War Zone in north Hubei, west Anhui and south Henan province, and the Ninth War Zone in the provinces of Hunan and Jiangxi, were to surround the 11th Army. The Tenth War Zone in Shaanxi province protected the cotton and wheat-producing region, defended the Tongguan Pass critical to the security of north-west China, and kept an eye on the Communist base area of Yan'an to the north. The Eighth War Zone operated in the region bordering Mongolia, with its complex ethnic make-up. General Yan Xishan's Second War Zone invested the Zhongtiao mountains in south Shanxi province. South China was only lightly defended because it was thought, erroneously as it turned out, that the Japanese were unlikely to attack this area because that risked premature conflict with Western empires.

The distribution of Nationalist forces in far-flung war zones across China compelled the Japanese to spread their nearly 1 million troops across the country and ensured that no single Japanese offensive could deliver a decisive blow. War zones were located in agriculturally productive areas with large populations to simplify supply and help with recruitment. Generals with strong local ties served as local commanders, while the central forces, which were invariably better armed, were led by generals loyal to Chiang Kaishek.

Two events that happened during the summer of 1939 suggest that the Japanese were vulnerable. Firstly, the Soviet General Georgy Zhukov, later the hero of the Battle of Stalingrad, inflicted an embarrassing defeat on the Kuantung Army at the Battle of Nomonhan, a border war fought on the Mongolia–Manchuria border involving hundreds of aeroplanes and tanks. But Germany's decision to sign a non-aggression treaty with Japan's main enemy, the Soviet Union, on 23 August, came as an utter shock to Japan. The failure of 11th Army units to capture Changsha that autumn was a further disaster. In 1939 shortages also compelled Japan to introduce rationing.[89] Chiang, always on the look-out for the fortuitous moment that might radically alter a situation, had good reason to think that a counter-offensive might stand a chance.

Initially, the Winter Offensive scored some stunning successes. Suddenly, all across China, from Shaanxi in the north-west all the way to Guangdong and Guangxi in the south, Japanese officials and soldiers lay dead, Japanese buildings were burning and Japanese military units were under fire. General Okamura Yasuji, commander-in-chief of the 11th Army, was shocked: 'We have never seen the Chinese army undertake such a large-scale and determined attack.'[90] On 20 December, the Chinese ambassador to the USA told President Roosevelt that China had begun 'a widespread offensive against the Japanese on all fronts' and that he 'was confident we may hear of some victory soon'.[91]

Unlike the 1968 Tet Offensive – the surprise nationwide attack on South Vietnamese and US positions during the Vietnam War – the Winter Offensive made no lasting impact. The performance of Third War Zone forces was woeful. They stopped their attempt to block the Yangzi river after only three days, despite facing just one Japanese division in dispersed formation along a 25-kilometre front and despite also having been supplied with extra heavy artillery and being supported by diversionary attacks on the cities of Nanchang and Hangzhou.[92] Also, the main supply line of the 11th Army in the Wuhan region was not severed, a major setback.

Clashes between forces under General Yan Xishan, who had controlled Shanxi province since the 1911 Revolution, and the Communists, who had used the War of Resistance to build up their strength in the area, blunted the efforts of the Second War Zone, tasked with clearing the Zhongtiao mountains. The plan called for a main offensive led by General Wei Lihuang with three armies, supported by Communist forces led by General Zhu De, who were to block two mountain passes into Shanxi and prevent Japanese relief forces from entering the province. This operation fell apart when General Yan Xishan and the Communist forces came to blows.[93]

The fatal blow was a surprise invasion of Guangxi province in the south by the Imperial Japanese Army's 5th Division. Its aim was to sever the Hanoi–Kunming railway by which military materiel was transported to the Nationalists. The Japanese landed at Pakhoi on the south China coast on 15 November. A week later, they captured the provincial capital of Nanning, from where they advanced north to the Kunlun Pass, threatening General Long Yun's Yunnan province. A political objective of the Japanese invasion was to put pressure on generals in south China, such as Long Yun, and suggest to them that joining Wang Jingwei might be a better option for them.

Chiang Kaishek ordered south no fewer than nineteen divisions from the Ninth War Zone, including General Du Lüming's 200th Division, China's only fully mechanised division, thus upending the Ninth War Zone's plans for attacking the 11th Army. The battle for the Kunlun Pass raged for the next few weeks. The Nationalists were victorious there, but failed in their drive towards Nanning. On 26 December, Nationalist spokesmen 'conceded' Japanese claims that their hold over Nanning was secure.[94] It was clear that Japan's invasion of Guangxi province had spiked the Winter Offensive.[95]

Despite the disappointing denouement, the Winter Offensive had one positive result for Chiang Kaishek. General Li Zongren of the Guangxi Clique had become a national hero in the first year of the war, feted for the Taierzhuang victory. The disaster in Guangxi diminished the stature of the Guangxi Clique and reduced its war-making potential.

The Winter Offensive had been a bold attempt to go on the attack, embarrass the Japanese and seize the strategic initiative. It came after two-thirds of Nationalist forces had been retrained and re-equipped. After it failed, the prospects of a second Nationalist military build-up were remote. Shortages were beginning to be felt everywhere. Japanese bombing had destroyed much of Sichuan's small industrial base. The KMT was demoralised and widely derided as ineffectual, a criticism which Chiang Kaishek wholeheartedly and frequently endorsed and which had led him to found a new party, the Youth Party, intended as an alternative to the Chinese Communist Party for China's youth. Importing weapons and ammunition had also become impossible. The Japanese blockaded the coast. In the summer of 1940, Britain, afraid of angering the Japanese as it struggled to survive German attacks, even closed the Burma Road. The Soviet Union, having pocketed an armistice with Japan, reduced its support for the Nationalists. The Nationalists had few options left other than to keep going and hope for positive changes in the international situation.

Nightmare visions of scarcity in land and resources had driven Japan to seek the occupation of first Manchuria and then north China. But rather than solving such perceived shortages, Japan's occupation of ever more territory intensified them. In essence, Japan ended up becoming responsible for the feeding of an extra 100 million people living in areas that depended on food imports. While most Nationalist forces were stationed in food surplus regions, Japan itself, Manchuria, north China, the lower Yangzi and Canton regions and Wuhan were all net food-importing regions. Already in 1939, shortages in north China led to calls for imports from Japan, the opposite of what had been intended. That year Japan shipped in 6 million bags of rice from Australia. By 1941, rations in Japan were reduced to 330 grams of cereal per day.[96]

In the face of the reality that China was not proving to be the solution to Japan's resource problems and that the Nationalists had not submitted and nor were they likely to, Japan had two options: go after Chiang Kaishek and utterly defeat him, which required a massive increase in troop numbers and a denuding of the Kuantung Army facing the Soviets in Manchuria, or withdraw. The latter option was difficult because the Japanese population had been fed stories of great victories and a bright new Japanese-style future spreading all over east Asia.[97] The Japanese government was faced with a difficult choice.

The Imperial Japanese Army's Yichang Operation of spring 1940 underlined the problem. Tokyo decided on a temporary troop surge to degrade National-ist combat capacity before beginning a draw-down to 500,000 troops at the end of the year, and a further reduction by 100,000 persons each of the fol-lowing two years. Two additional divisions were allocated to the 11th Army, which was ordered to clean out the Fifth War Zone and seize Yichang. On 1 May, three Japanese divisions thrust into northern Hubei, seeking out the 31st Army Group commanded by General Tang Enbo, the general loyal to Chiang Kaishek and a key contributor to the Nationalist victories at Taierzhuang in the spring of 1938 and at the Kunlun Pass the previous year. General Tang adopted a tactic, whose usefulness had been proven several times before, of falling back until the Japanese reached their objectives and began to return to their jumping-off points, then to fall on their flanks. General Zhang Zizhong, one of the heroes of the Shanghai campaign, led his forces into the battle area from the east, tempting two Japanese divisions away from General Tang's forces. General Tang mauled the remaining one, causing 4,000 casualties.

The Japanese regrouped and inflicted heavy defeats on Fifth War Zone forces, but controversy then erupted among 11th Army commanders about whether to return to Wuhan or continue on to Yichang. The expansionists won the day and on 12 June Yichang fell into Japanese hands. Five days later, they departed as planned after having tipped tons of food and captured weapons into the Yangzi river, only to be ordered back again after Hitler's triumphs in Europe convinced Imperial General Headquarters to order the permanent occupation of Yichang.[98]

This level of prevarication underscored the fact that Japan had begun to act opportunistically rather than in line with a considered long-range plan. A Communist offensive, the largest of the war, which lasted through the autumn, illustrated that even if the Nationalists could somehow be forced to the negoti-ating table, Japan's problems in China would still be far from over. In what was called the Hundred Regiments Offensive, a large number of small Communist units attacked Japanese forces all over north China between 20 August and 5 December, fighting back against Japanese pacification campaigns and con-vincing Chiang Kaishek that they were serious about resisting Japan.[99] Once Japan tried and failed to bomb the Nationalists to the negotiating table for the second time, in the summer of 1941, it had become clear that regime change had run its course. Japan was stuck.

Momentous times create heroes. General Zhang Zizhong died on the after-noon of 16 May 1940, in north Hubei, while resisting the Japanese push to Yichang. When the news reached Chiang Kaishek in Chongqing, he was, his diary records, 'deeply distressed' and immediately ordered General Li Zongren to recover General Zhang's body and move it to Chongqing. Further reports declared that when Zhang died he had been leading an attack, had suffered wounds to his arms and chest but had refused to be taken behind the lines, instead insisting that his forces move on 'for the country, for our people, for our commander-in-chief. My conscience is now at peace. Kill the enemy to revenge their evil.'[100] When the Japanese discovered who they had killed – the most senior Chinese general to die during the Second World War – they gave him a respectful burial. When Nationalist units recovered his bodily remains, they were treated with herbs, dressed in a new uniform, placed in a hardwood coffin and transported to Chongqing, first in a truck and then on a steamer up the Yangzi.[101] As the news spread, people came out in their hundreds and even thousands, so reports claim, bowing, setting off firecrackers and offering incense, flowers and fruit, with one woman preparing a bowl of noodles 'to make General Zhang a good northern meal'.[102]

Chiang Kaishek, surrounded by his highest officials, welcomed the general's coffin at one of Chongqing's gates. It was transported to the north Chongqing suburb of Beipei, where a temporary tomb was being prepared to serve as General Zhang's resting place until such time as his home town was recovered and he could be buried there. Soon he was being compared to China's most famous hero of the past, General Yue Fei, who in the twelfth century had battled to 'win back our lakes and mountains, our streams and plains' from northern invaders, only to be murdered on the orders of a peace-mongering official of the Song Dynasty, Qin Hui. Zhang Zizhong's Chongqing tomb became the site for annual sacrifices, his story became the subject of popular songs, one of China's most famous authors produced a play about his heroics, memorial tablets to him were placed in shrines across the country, and a suburb of Yichang and even a whole county were renamed after him.[103]

The founder of the Chinese Communist Party, Chen Duxiu, now living in exile in Chongqing having been expelled from the Party, produced a memorial scroll with the line 'it is after winter's cold that we know the pine tree and the cypress', in a reference to Confucius's *Analects*, China's most important classical text, meaning that a person's true character stands revealed only after facing the hardest test, just as pine trees and cypresses will not shed their green even after the severest winter cold. This was apposite because General Zhang Zizhong, who was one of the north China generals, had fled from Tianjin when the Japanese approached the city, even though he was its mayor. But he redeemed himself, first at the Battle of Taierzhuang and then during the Yichang Operation, in both cases cooperating with Chiang loyalist General Tang Enbo. The contrast with the behaviour of Wang Jingwei and Yan Xishan was clear, which is no doubt why Chiang decided to foster a Zhang Zizhong cult.

Momentous times also create villains. Wang Jingwei died in a hospital in Nagoya in Japan on 10 November 1944 and was buried on Purple Mountain in a concrete grave with a view of Sun Yatsen. His mourners knew what would happen, and it did. Upon their return to Nanjing the following year, the Nationalists blasted open his tomb, dug up his body and dumped it in the Yangzi river.[104] Any vestige of Wang's existence was eradicated. When I visited in 2005, there was a sculpture of Wang and his wife, Chen Bijun, at his gravesite. It had the Wangs kneeling, head bowed in shame in the direction of the Sun Yatsen Mausoleum, arms tied together behind their backs, with a fence around it, just like the statues of Qin Hui and his wife outside the temple dedicated to Yue Fei in Hangzhou. Wang was to stand condemned as the Qin Hui of his time.

The statues of the Wangs are no more, I am told, because Nanjing citizens destroyed them repeatedly and local officials became tired of having to repair them. In their place stands a cherry orchard donated by the Japanese. Wang's poetry remains officially unpublished in China, although it does circulate and is admired for its beauty and sophistication. His poetry earned much praise at the time and was read as suggesting Wang's essentially honest intentions. One admirer compared his peace campaign to 'the example of the Buddha feeding his body to a hungry tiger'.[105] Had Wang lived to see the end of the war, the Nationalists in Sichuan, who by then were in an extremely weak position, would likely have offered him a deal to facilitate their return to Nanjing. Consequently his reputation would have been different, as it would be for Indonesia's Soekarno, the Philippines's Manuel Roxas, India's Subhas Chandre Bose and Burma's Aung San, all of whom worked with the Japanese occupiers.[106] Timing is everything.

EIGHT

WAR COMMUNISM

Even anger against injustice
Makes the voice grow harsh. Alas, we
Who wished to lay the foundation of kindness
Could not ourselves be kind.

Bertolt Brecht, 'To Posterity' (1939)[1]

'One of the most barren, chronologically depressed, and sparsely populated regions in China.' Thus has the historian Lyman Van Slyke described Yan'an, the wartime home of the Chinese Communists.[2] When the journalist Edgar Snow made his way there to meet Mao Zedong in 1936, for an interview that would lead to his classic book *Red Star over China,* which made Mao famous in the West and in China, he described the region as 'one of the poorest parts of China I had seen ... the crops grown are strictly limited by the steep gradients, both in quantity and quality. There are few genuine mountains, only endless broken hills, hills as interminable as a sentence by James Joyce.'[3]

At the beginning of the twentieth century a member of the North China Famine Relief Commission characterised the area as a 'nest of plunderers lost in the wilderness'.[4] Since then, things had only become worse. When Otto Braun, a military advisor to the Communists, arrived in Yan'an in October 1935, he found the region a 'poor calcified land' racked by 'years of warlord campaigns, horrific banditry, and terrible harvests and epidemics'.[5] He also noted that there were few children under ten still alive. With a population of just 1.4 million people in 1937, Yan'an nonetheless became the cradle of the Chinese Communist revolution.

Only a master technician of violence – Mao Zedong – could have forged in this poor region a force that would triumph in the 1945–9 Chinese Civil War. Luck also played an important part. In 1934, the Nationalists drove the Communists from bases in central China, forcing them on to the 9,000-kilometre trek from central China to the barren wastelands of north Shaanxi province that became known as the Long March. During that time leadership splits became so bad that two central committees claimed supremacy. The survival of the group led by Mao came down to coincidence. In September 1935, according to Mao biographer Alexander Pantsov, 'Mao and his comrades learned to their surprise' that a Communist base existed in north Shaanxi just 350 kilometres away. So Mao took the forces loyal to him there.[6] The other group, initially larger and stronger, was mauled by Muslim forces in north-west China.

Context was critical. In 1972, when Japanese prime minister Tanaka Kakuei visited China in advance of the normalisation of relations between China and Japan, he met with Mao Zedong in Mao's study in Zhongnanhai, the leadership compound next to the Forbidden City. During his visit before the meeting, Prime Minister Tanaka had repeatedly apologised for Japan's invasion of China. Mao's personal physician recalls in his memoirs that when Tanaka was about to do so again in the meeting, Mao stopped him, saying that 'the "help" of the Japanese invasion' had made the Communist victory possible.[7] Mao had made similar statements to previous Japanese visitors. In 1956 he told Lieutenant General Endo Saburo, a vice chief of staff of the Kuantung Army, 'We must thank you. Precisely because you fought this war, you taught the Chinese people, who had been like a sheet of loose sand, to unite.'[8] Without the Japanese invasion, the Chinese Communists would have withered away in the barren north-west.

But more than luck and circumstance were needed. In China, there is the notion that there were two Maos, the good Mao who led the Communist revolution before 1949 and restored China's pride, and the bad Mao, who was responsible for the purges of the early 1950s, the crushing of dissent in the late 1950s, the terrible famine that followed and the Cultural Revolution. That is too simple. Mao Zedong was never a cuddly liberal or a huggable Communist; he was always a tough revolutionary, who was determined to destroy what he saw as the iniquitous, cruel and diseased China of his day. He was inspirational, charismatic and idealistic, and knew how to speak to village China, but he was also committed to the use of violence, and perfected its use as he learned from experience, not just for the sake of the revolution and the creation of the New China – although that was most certainly true – but to enhance his own personal power.

The Rustification of Communism

Marxism–Leninism came to China as a hyper-urban ideology. In Marxism, urban industrial workers are the social group that drives historical change. Karl Marx could hardly have been more scathing about peasants, dismissing them as 'the class that represents barbarism in civilisation',[9] or, famously, 'a sack of potatoes' forming a millstone around the neck of revolution.[10] Revolutions took place in cities rather than in the countryside. The October Revolution began in Petrograd, in 1871 the French Communards took over Paris, and the 1848 revolutions erupted in cities such as Vienna, Paris and Berlin. In 1921, when the Chinese Communist Party was founded, its members were convinced that in China, too, the revolution would begin in the cities, manned by trained industrial workers mobilised by full-time revolutionaries, not by village hood-lums. The big events of recent times in China, including the 1911 Revolution and the May Fourth Movement, had also taken place in urban centres. History happened in the city, not the countryside.

But the Chinese Communists would grow strong not in the cities, but in village China. This was partly, once again, as a result of circumstance. The Nationalists forced the Communists out of China's cities, first in 1927, when thousands of Communists died in the White Terror that followed the Nation-alist victory in the Northern Expedition, and then in the early 1930s, when the Nationalists rolled up Communist secret service organisations, making it impossible for Communist operatives to stay in the cities. The Chinese Communists were forced into the countryside, where they had to make the best of things.

But the rural flavour of Chinese communism was also the result of a growing realisation among intellectuals, scholars and activists in the 1920s and 1930s that the fundamental problems holding China back lay in the countryside, tortured as it was by poverty, famine, drought and epidemics. The anthropolo-gist Fei Xiaotong, who had studied with the great anthropologist Bronislaw Malinowski at the London School of Economics, outlined the patterns of human relations structured around family and religion in the Chinese coun-tryside. Like the Confucian sage Liang Shuming, the US-educated Christian reformer Jimmy Yen initiated a rural revival movement, promoting tax and rent reform as well as education across north China. They wanted to turn back-ward peasants into modern citizens. The husband of Pearl Buck, the author of *The Good Earth*, was the rural economist John Buck, who lived in China from 1915 until 1944. After surveying landholding and rural productivity, he concluded that technological backwardness, not landlordism, was responsible for rural poverty. The left-wing 'moral economist' R. H. Tawney, who spent a year in China, argued that overpopulation and absentee landlordism had severed customary partnership relations between owner and cultivator. In 1931 he concluded, presciently, that 'the revolution of 1911 was a bourgeois affair. The revolution of the peasants has still to come ... it is likely to be unpleasant. It will not, perhaps, be undeserved.'[11]

In 1937 Deng Tuo, who later became the editor of the Communists' most important newspaper the *People's Daily*, published the 500-page *History of Famine Relief in China*, which remains fundamental reading for the study of the subject. Deng Tuo trawled though China's vast storehouse of histor-ical writing to produce a history, ranging from ancient times to the present, about instances of famine, the thinking about the causes of famine and the approaches various governments had adopted to providing famine relief. He studied economics and joined the Communist Party in 1933 when he was just twenty-one years old. As a Marxist, he inevitably rejected the idea that famine was somehow a natural phenomenon and instead argued that relations of production were its fundamental cause.[12]

But the countryside was not seen just as a problem.[13] Chi Pang-yuan's memoirs turn elegiac when describing her place of birth in Manchuria, where she found support in close and supportive family and village relations. While retelling her life as a refugee, she paints the countryside as a place of astounding beauty offering refuge, human warmth and even laughter. Chen Kewen loved Nanjing, but he sent his family back home to the Guangxi countryside when the war broke out. His sense of duty compelled him to travel with the government to wherever it relocated – Nanjing, Wuhan, Chongqing – but his diary is full of lament about the corruption, carpet-bagging, womanising, self-indulgence and wastefulness he found in these cities. Chiang Kaishek returned to his home town of Xikou, or some place like it, whenever his troubles overwhelmed him. Many writings by Lu Xun, still widely regarded as China's greatest modern author, are about the alienation from the countryside of a newly urbanised elite who associate their rural home towns with safety, honesty, simplicity and happiness, and urban China with the opposite. Chinese communism drew on such understandings of urban and rural China, and aimed to restore the lost solidarities of village China, not through education but through revolution.

Mao's epiphany came in early 1927, after the Northern Expedition reached Wuhan and the Nationalists had split into a left-wing faction there and a right-wing faction under Chiang Kaishek in Nanjing. Mao was born in 1893 into a prosperous farming family in Shaoshan, Hunan province.[14] As with Chen Kewen and Chi Pang-yuan, modern schools and universities provided the pathways for Mao to move away from Shaoshan, first to the provincial capital of Changsha and then to Beijing and Shanghai. Like Chen Kewen, Mao was swept up by the May Fourth Movement, talking, reading, writing, walking and experimenting with new organisations and new modes of life. He shared the movement's national self-loathing: '[W]e Chinese simply have no idea how to handle a coherent undertaking.'[15] Mao represented Hunan at the founding of the Chinese Communist Party in 1921, turned professional revolutionary after Soviet financial aid provided stipends to China's Communists, and until 1925 worked in Hunan to build up the Party's presence there. When a warrant was issued for his arrest, he was compelled to flee to Canton, where he found a patron in, of all people, Wang Jingwei, who arranged for him to work in the KMT's propaganda department and at the Peasant Movement Training Institute.[16]

A month-long tour of the Hunan countryside in January 1927 convinced Mao that the CCP's rural policy was wrong. That policy was minimalist, calling only for rent reductions rather than land redistribution, so as not to alienate the Nationalists, many of whose members (including officers in the National Revolutionary Army) had substantial interests in the countryside. The CCP's strategy at this time, when the Nationalists and the Communists were ostensibly working as a united front, focused on seeking to take over the Nationalist Party from within. The Communists therefore restricted their activities to distributing propaganda primarily among urban workers, although they also established peasant associations in Guangdong province. At the same time, they built up their influence in the Nationalist party, the Nationalist government established after the death of Sun Yatsen, and the armed forces being trained by Chiang Kaishek. This policy became increasingly untenable as relations soured between the Nationalists and the Communists, especially after Chiang Kaishek's coup.

In March 1927, Mao wrote the now celebrated 'Report on an Investigation of the Peasant Movement in Hunan'. Entirely on their own initiative, Mao exalted, the Hunan peasantry were implementing revolution. Peasants were overthrowing 'local bullies, the bad gentry and the lawless landlords, and in passing they also hit out against patriarchal ideas and institutions of all kinds'.[17] They were eradicating the old China's vices of gambling, opium-smoking, vulgar opera performances, superstition, excessive feasting and banditry. 'Extreme force' was being used, Mao admitted, but he defended it, suggesting that revolution was 'not like inviting people to dinner, or writing an essay, or painting a picture'; it was 'an act of violence by which one class overthrows another'.[18] Mao had been convinced of the need for violence from the time he had joined the Party. He declared in a debate with those who put their faith in education that 'we simply must have a reign of terror' because the opponents of change, such as warlords, rich businessmen and landlords, would use the forces available to them, including local militias, to crack down before education could do its magic.[19] The lesson Mao learned in Hunan was that the violence he believed necessary to bring about revolution could be found most easily in the countryside. He did not want to turn farmers into citizens but peasants into revolutionaries.

Over the next few years, Mao recruited a military force first in the Jinggang mountains of west Hunan province and then in south Jiangxi province. But he combined militarisation with building rural bases and transforming power structures by redistributing land, constructing new administrative organisations and drawing poor peasants, the youth and women into mass organisations. Some of his fellow Communists objected to building such bases, preferring dispersed guerrilla warfare, but Mao was adamant: 'People cannot always walk or stand. They must have a place to sit. Bases are the buttocks of the Red Army.'[20] Determined to prevent his forces from degenerating into yet another bandit gang, he laid down a set of simple rules to make his soldiers aspire to higher standards of behaviour. These were the 'Three Rules of Discipline' (obedience to orders, no confiscations of peasant property and the prompt surrender to higher authority of all things taken from landlords) and 'Eight Points of Attention' (politeness, honesty, courtesy to women and so on). This was a kind of New Life movement for beginners. To secure Party control of the Red Army, Mao appointed political commissars right down to platoon level. These commissars were responsible for pastoral care of the troops as well as compliance with Party directives. Given that the Communists survived on sacking towns, confiscating property and demanding ransoms, these principles were acknowledged more in the breach than in the observance.

In his report on the Hunan peasant movement, Mao worried about wealthy families and gentry infiltrating and undermining peasant associations. In 1930, after the Red Army had grown to 60,000 troops, that fear – plus conflicts with Party members with strong local ties, differences with the Shanghai leaders about military strategy and organisation, and his own paranoia about a Nationalist underground network of agents – resulted in Mao ordering a witch-hunt in which thousands of Party and government officials and Red Army officers were executed.[21] In this violent period of China's history, during which one's enemies were legion if sometimes imagined, Mao was not alone in using violence to defend his position, settle scores and purify his ranks of dissenters. As he would put it later: 'revolutionary war is an antitoxin that not only eliminates the enemy's poison but also purges us of our own filth.'[22] Throughout his career, Mao regularly adopted violent means to purge the Communist Party, especially prior to major military campaigns, as he did in the 1940s and again several times later. He did so, of course, well before Stalin adopted the systematic use of violence to conduct his purges in the Soviet Union.

In the aftermath of this particular purge, Mao lost much of his power, not only because of its excesses, but also because the CCP leaders, unable to continue operating from Shanghai due to Nationalist suppression, arrived in Jiangxi with grandiose visions of using the Red Army to seize large cities and even whole provinces. Mao believed that the priority should be to consolidate the Jiangxi base area, an attitude his opponents condemned as 'extreme right opportunism', 'kulak deviation' and 'guerrillaism'.[23] For several years Mao became marginalised. He whiled away the time living with his family in temples on mountain tops, practising the flute and writing poetry. He later recalled: 'at this time not only a single person, but not even a single devil dared to cross the threshold of my house. All that was left for me was to eat, sleep, and shit. At least they didn't cut off my head.'[24]

Mao's talents as a guerrilla leader could not be denied. In 1930, the Nationalists began the first of five operations to drive the Communists out of Jiangxi and other central China provinces. While CCP leaders called for meeting the

Nationalist advance head on, Mao insisted on 'luring the enemy in deep', initially by using guerrilla warfare to slow it down and then by concentrating an overwhelming number of fighters on hitting exposed Nationalist units on the flanks and in the rear. Mao summarised this tactic as 'the enemy advances, we retreat; the enemy camps, we harass; the enemy tires, we attack; the enemy retreats, we pursue.'[25] Such tactics worked four times, but on the fifth, in 1934, the Nationalists deployed 1 million troops to ring the Jiangxi Soviet with a string of concrete blockhouses, building new ones as they advanced, thus squeezing the trapped Communists ever more until escape became the only option. The Nationalists succeeded in clearing the Communists from central China and forcing them on the Long March.

When the surviving Long Marchers, morose, tired and defeatist, arrived at the town of Zunyi in Guizhou province in January 1935, Mao seized his chance. With the support of backers talked round during the previous months, he charged that the surrender of the Jiangxi base area was the result not of overwhelming Nationalist forces but of mistaken military strategy. Mao focused his criticism on Otto Braun, a tall, blond Soviet agent of German descent who proved an easy target not only because he was a foreigner but because he did not speak Chinese. The meeting concluded by restoring Mao's membership of both the Party's political and military leadership organs. Elated, he told his wife, He Zizhen, that 'the meeting figured that a Buddha like me might still prove useful'.[26] Heavily pregnant with their fifth child, a month later she had to abandon her newborn baby to a local family: children were not allowed on the Long March.

This was the revolutionary school of hard knocks, bound to wash away any last smidgen of sentimentality. Raising a guerrilla force was not difficult in China's countryside, where weapons were plentiful and for which, to people living close to famine, just a bowl of rice and a few vegetables formed an acceptable offer. Disciplining that force and lashing it to revolution was a different proposition, especially since the local enemies of revolution were fighting over the long term. These years of living in the countryside, in the midst of poverty, constant warfare and factional infighting, taught Mao Zedong and his colleagues much about harnessing the grievances of village China. But they were also aware that they had suffered a near-fatal defeat. The question remained how to translate rural unrest into a powerful force capable of taking power.

Theorising Guerrilla War

When Mao arrived in Yan'an in 1935, he was just one of several CCP leaders. He had established himself a reputation as a guerrilla commander, but otherwise he was considered unextraordinary. He was even regarded as rather peasant-like and boorish. Visitors to Yan'an at the time depicted Mao as busy – hearing reports, issuing orders, attending meetings, hosting visitors and giving lectures – but relaxed. Edgar Snow described him as having 'the simplicity and natural-ness of the Chinese peasant, with a lively sense of humour and a love of rustic laughter' and combining 'curious qualities of naiveté with the most incisive wit and worldly sophistication'.[27] A year later, the British journalist James Bertram marvelled at Mao's natural charisma: 'I waited for the oratorical tricks of the demagogue, but … Mao spoke in his homely dialect and with continual lively play of peasant humour, in direct and concrete terms.'[28]

In his first few years in Yan'an, Mao had time to play cards, smoke, drink and eat, as well as to seek out the company of a pretty Shanghai actress, Lily Wu, who had travelled there to join the Communists. Mao's tryst with Lily Wu earned him a beating from his wife, who in a fit of rage hit him 'with a long handled flashlight … until she was out of breath'.[29] He Zizhen left Mao, who married, not Lily Wu but another Shanghai actress who had come to Yan'an, Lan Ping, better known to history as Jiang Qing.

Mao's calm, confident, boisterous exterior hid a man grappling with the fundamental issue of how to transform the Red Army's ragtag units, a divided Communist Party and its poor rural base in Yan'an into a serious revolutionary force. That meant first of all establishing that he was not just a guerrilla com-mander. At Zunyi, one of Mao's critics had charged 'your methods of warfare are not particularly clever; they are based on just two books, *The Romance of the Three Kingdoms* [a Robin Hood-type novel] and Sunzi's *The Art of War*.' Mao admitted later that at the time of the Zunyi Conference he had not actu-ally even read the latter.[30]

Mao read up on his Marxism–Leninism and with the aid of a Marxist–Leninist brains trust produced a series of theoretical essays, including 'On Practice', 'On Contradiction' and 'On the New Stage', making major state-ments on philosophical, social, economic and cultural issues.[31] These articles insisted that revolution in China must follow its own path, rather than mimic the course of revolution in the Soviet Union. The Chinese Communists there-fore had to develop their own revolutionary practice, one in which, according to Mao, the countryside and the military had a uniquely important place. If the revolutionaries in Europe had succeeded by seizing political power in a capital, then in a China that was overwhelming rural and where political and military power was dispersed rather than controlled by a centralised state bureaucracy, that was not possible. In articles such as these, Mao set out his strategy for revolution in China, in the process suggesting that he not only understood Marxism–Leninism but could enrich it. He was determined never to be pat-ronised again by those with greater knowledge of Marxism–Leninism, as had happened in the past.

Mao Zedong's most important military work was *On Protracted War*, a long pamphlet published on 1 July 1938. Although influenced by the Soviet army's *Field Training Manual*, Sunzi's *The Art of War* and Erich Ludendorff's *Der Totale Krieg*, Mao engaged most fully with Clausewitz's *On War*. He repeatedly quoted Clausewitz's famous aphorism 'war is the continuation of politics'.[32] Mao wrote *On Protracted War* while Clausewitz was being translated into Chinese on his orders, chapter by chapter, with Mao discussing completed chapters with a select group in weekly seminars which often lasted deep into the night.[33] *On Protracted War* reflected *On War* in its dialectical style of reasoning, its emphasis on the importance of rational calculation by commanders, and the significance of the will of the people. Like Clausewitz, Mao stressed that 'war is bloodshed', meaning that it was merciless, that there was nothing pretty about it, and that the only role for the enemy on the battlefield was his destruction. For a man who declared that a reign of terror was necessary, that revolution is not a dinner party and that power comes out of the barrel of a gun, Clausewitz confirmed much of what Mao had long thought.[34]

On Protracted War was written and published after China's defeat at the Battle of Xuzhou. Part of its purpose was to counter the defeatist atmosphere that had descended on the country and to reassure Mao's readers that victory would be China's, even if it would be slow in coming.[35] Following Clausewitz's description of a defensive strategy, Mao suggested that the War of Resistance would go through three phases, beginning with a retreat (which had not yet ended), followed by a long period of stalemate and then a counter-offensive in which China would prevail. Mao then reassured his audience that the future was theirs even if much hardship would have to be endured.

On Protracted War was not just a propaganda piece aimed at boosting morale, but also an attempt by Mao to demonstrate his credentials as a military theorist, who had learned from but had also added to Clausewitz. In Clausewitz, guerrilla war was ancillary, a tactic of last resort. For Mao, 'protracted guerrilla war ... knocks on the gate of strategy', and so had become 'quite new in the entire history of war'.[36] Guerrilla war could have strategic significance in China's war with Japan because China was a large and populous country, only a small part of which the Japanese could occupy. That opened up Japan's rear as the place to develop base areas from which to mobilise the population and conduct guerrilla warfare. Mao never thought that the use of guerrilla war alone would secure revolutionary victory. 'The outcome of the war depends mainly on regular warfare, especially in its mobile form, and guerrilla warfare cannot shoulder the main responsibility for deciding the outcome.'[37] The Communists went on to the offensive in the Civil War only after they had trained up a large army which was well armed and able to sustain large-scale battles.

Building base areas was critical to Mao's plans. He said little about base building in *On Protracted War*, which circulated publicly, because he did not want to alienate the Nationalists by revealing that he wanted to gain territory. However, he did discuss base areas extensively in a draft essay he abandoned before composing *On Protracted War*. Base areas in the enemy's rear were 'essential because of the protracted nature and ruthlessness of the war'; [38] they were also what distinguished national liberation war from 'peasant wars of the "roving rebel" type'.[39] In base areas, the Communists could 'arouse the masses for struggle against Japan'.[40] 'We must arm the people, i.e. organise self-defence forces and guerrilla units; we must organise the workers, peasants, youth, women, children, merchants and professional people.'[41] Mao found plenty in Clausewitz to confirm his belief in the importance of popular support in war.[42]

The general pattern in base building was for Communist forces and officials to move into an area, presenting themselves as legitimate military and civilian authority, and make contact with local administrators, military groups, secret societies and religious groups.[43] Influence was slowly built up through persuasion, infiltration and education. The next step was to build up a three-tiered military structure, an administrative hierarchy and mass organisations. Once an area was sufficiently secure, Communist cadres would promote rent- and interest-reduction campaigns and press for the cancellation of surcharges and extra levies, steps defensible as implementing Sun Yatsen's 'land to the tiller' programme.[44] Campaigns against collaborators and abusive landlords would follow. Mao insisted that base areas, usually but not always constructed in poor hilly regions, should not be overburdened. 'In every base area, the total number of those not actively engaged in production (including those serving in party, government, army, popular organizations, and schools) should constitute no more than 3% of the population.'[45] During the War of Resistance the Communists largely stuck to that formula, but not later during the Civil War when they readied themselves to wage large set-piece battles.

The Communists developed a set of economic, social and political policies, which the historian Mark Selden has baptised the Yan'an Way as a means of attracting popular support. Direct elections for local assemblies up to county level and mass organisations of all kinds drew base area populations into politics far more widely and deeply than ever before, thus giving them an unprecedented, and hence for them electrifying, role in public life. Campaigns were organised to promote literacy, enhance hygiene, improve the lives of women, strengthen public health and fight what was depicted as superstition. Base area life was full of meetings at which both leaders and led discussed national and local affairs. Selden was wrong to believe that the Yan'an Way alone made the base areas viable. Opium cultivation was the foundation of Communist finance.[46] Moscow's emissary, Peter Vladimirov, quoted one high-ranking Communist as having stated laconically that 'with the money we earn from opium exports to the Nationalists, we buy their arms, which we will use to overthrow them'.[47] But the Yan'an Way was important in suggesting that the Communists would be radically different to the Nationalists in garnering popular support.

Mao and Clausewitz are rarely put together. But it is not so strange that, in his search for a successful military strategy, Mao should turn to the most widely celebrated military thinker of modern times. In *On War*, Mao found many ideas that confirmed his own thinking, including about the brutal nature of war, the importance of popular support and the key role of commanders. Clausewitz recognised that not all wars are about crushing the enemy and that victories might be relative and lead to compromise, but in his discussions of absolute war, he stressed that a crushing victory on the battlefield was necessary to impose one's will on the enemy. Mao would pursue just such a victory in the last years of the Civil War. Mao was likely thinking about this, too, when he sent young cadres for military training in the Soviet Union during the War of Resistance.

The Japanese Rescue Chinese Communism

Yan'an became the cradle of Chinese communism, but, as Mao admitted, the Japanese invasion provided the conditions that allowed the Communists to break out from their confines, spread out across north China and lay the foundations for their eventual triumph. However, if Japan's invasion offered salvation, initially at least, after the December 1936 Xi'an Incident which led to Chiang Kaishek calling off his campaign of annihilation, and then provided the opportunities for the Communists to grow, it was also full of danger. The Japanese, the Wang Jingwei government and the Nationalists all had their reasons to strike against the Communists either separately or jointly, with the Communists' own actions during the War of Resistance having the potential to make that more or less likely. A carefully calibrated policy was required, which could also be adjusted in the face of developments.

In the negotiations about a new united front that followed the Xi'an Incident, the Communists clung to three basic conditions, the most important of which was a single independent headquarters for all their military forces. They feared that if their forces were divided, the Nationalists would deploy them in different regions and then feed them one by one into the jaws of the advancing Japanese armies. The two other demands were autonomy in Yan'an and the continued existence of the Communist Party.[48] Chiang Kaishek's hope was a single command for all military forces in China and a single governmental system in which regions had a considerable amount of autonomy as long as they acknowledged the ultimate authority of the central Nationalist government.

The post-Xi'an negotiations dragged on without resolution until the Marco Polo Bridge Incident and even the Battle of Shanghai. They were fully concluded only on 22 September 1937, when the new united front was formally announced.[49] The agreement provided that the Communist forces in Yan'an were renamed the Eighth Route Army of the National Army, while the units that had remained in central China became known as the New Fourth Army. Yan'an became a Special Administrative Region. The Communists issued a public statement declaring that 'the Three People's Principles of Mr Sun Yatsen are what is required for China today; we will struggle for their full realization. We will stop all violent policies aimed at overthrowing the Nationalist administration as well as all movements to spread communism, while we also annul policies for the violent confiscation of land.'[50] But they had retained full independence of command and they remained in full control of Yan'an. With Chiang Kaishek needing Communist collaboration in order to claim that China fought as a united country, he had blinked first.

Nationalist and Communist commanders were all smiles and politeness when together they defended Shanxi province against the Japanese invaders. Having taken Beijing, units of Japan's 5th Division marched west, reaching the province in the middle of September 1937. Eighth Route Army headquarters ordered three Communist divisions into Shanxi from bordering Yan'an. The three divisions were: 115th Division led by General Lin Biao, who moved into central Shanxi; 120th Division under General He Long, who took up positions at the Yanmen Pass north of the provincial capital of Taiyuan; and 129th Division under General Liu Bocheng, which deployed to the east of Taiyuan. The three cooperated with General Yan Xishan's Shanxi Army, as well as National Army units commanded by General Wei Lihuang. General Yan Xishan vouched to Chiang Kaishek that his new Communist collaborators were 'honest in their support for you and they are truly enthusiastic about resisting the enemy'.[51] A Communist commander was heard to say that 'wherever the Eighth Route Army goes, that's where the central government goes and where the KMT goes'.[52]

All this friendliness led to a victory in late September when, in collaboration with the Shanxi Army, two regiments of General Lin Biao's 115th Division ambushed a supply column of the 5th Division of the Imperial Japanese Army in a narrow defile at Pingxingguan Pass. While Communist propaganda celebrated the event as a giant Communist success, as it continues to do today, General Lin Biao reported that a lack of reliable communications equipment had made coordination impossible between his own forces, the Shanxi Army units and Nationalist forces, with the consequence that units did not arrive on time, if at all. His battle report made clear that the Communist forces were not ready for this kind of warfare:

We never encountered such a strong foe in the Northern Expedition and the Soviet Period. Their infantry are able to deploy themselves with individual initiative in combat situations. Although wounded, they refuse to give up their arms … Our army's military skill and training still leave a great deal to be desired. In the past half year, our troops have had a chance to rest and regroup, and their discipline, morale, and regularization have progressed greatly; but in combat training we still have a long way to go.[53]

To persist in fighting in this way risked wasting all the Communists' forces in no time.

Mao Zedong had insisted from the beginning of the United Front that Communist forces should only fight guerrilla warfare in mountainous areas on the flanks or to the rear of the Japanese.[54] Only after the middle of November, when the Battle of Shanxi was over, was he able to convince his colleagues that the Eighth Route Army was not ready for positional warfare. Having prevailed, Mao was then able to force through a new policy, built around his view of the importance of building base areas behind enemy lines. He issued an instruction in the name of the Party insisting that 'primary importance should be given to creating base areas and mobilising the masses, and we must disperse our forces, rather than laying emphasis on concentrating them for combat'.[55] He ordered General Lin Biao's 115th Division into the mountainous regions in northern Shanxi, while General He Long's 120th Division moved to northwest Shanxi and General Liu Bocheng's 129th Division marched to the Taihang mountains in the south-east of the province. Each set about building a new base area. It was not just the Japanese invasion but this policy of building base areas that allowed the Communists to grow so rapidly during the War of Resistance.

By February 1938, it became clear that the next battle would be for Xuzhou, the railway junction that lay between the north China and central China fronts. Mao saw his opportunity, telling his front-line commanders: 'the enemy … must suffer from a severe lack of forces in the whole of Hebei, Shandong, and northern Jiangsu.'[56] The Communists should move into these areas, he insisted. Building bases behind Japanese lines was also necessary because the Japanese were in control of most of Shanxi province. Their next step might be an invasion of Shaanxi, which could lead to the occupation of Xi'an and an offensive against Yan'an.[57] Having bases elsewhere provided for the possibility that Yan'an might fall and would allow the CCP leadership to move elsewhere.

Mao Zedong ordered 115th Division, commanded by General Nie Rongzhen, who had replaced the wounded General Lin Biao, to north Hebei province with the instruction to advance east into Shandong province and south into the provinces of Henan and Jiangsu.[58] In January 1938, General Nie Rongzhen inaugurated the Shanxi–Chahar–Hebei Border Region.[59] Communist forces in the Taihang mountains were ordered to expand into the provinces of Hebei and Henan.[60] Some units marched to Shandong province, where they set about building a further base area in a mountainous region on the province's south coast.[61]

Base building worked. From 1937 to 1940, Party membership grew from 40,000 to 800,000, while the Eighth Route and New Fourth Armies expanded to 500,000 troops.[62] The Japanese invasion proved a godsend for the Chinese Communists. Without it they would not have expanded so quickly or so widely. This was of course not just the work of Mao Zedong, but also of many Party officials, activists, commanders, soldiers and Party members, all determined to exploit the opportunities the war with Japan provided.

War within War

Rapid Communist expansion inevitably provoked Nationalist suspicions about the Communist commitment to fighting Japan. Such suspicions were strengthened by a public warning issued by a founding member of the Party, Zhang Guotao, in May 1938. Zhang had been in charge of his own base area before the Long March and had been the chair of a central committee rival to Mao's. He had made it to Yan'an, but without his forces, and was first humiliated by Mao and then purged from his leadership positions. He published his warning letter having fled Yan'an for Wuhan. In it he said that the 'real objectives' of the Communists 'are to preserve effective forces and maintain the special status of the border governments and some guerrilla zones to boost the development of its own forces' and that 'the CCP is insincere about unity in the War of Resistance'.[63] In April 1940, a New Fourth Army defector claimed that Mao had stated at a farewell rally when his unit had set out from Yan'an in September 1937 that 'the War of Resistance is a great opportunity for us to develop. Our policy is to focus 70% on expansion, 20% on dealing with the KMT, and 10% on resisting Japan.'[64] That report was seized upon then, as it still is now, by those who argue that the Communists were never serious about resisting Japan and that their aim was to let the Nationalists do all the fighting.[65]

Until the fall of Wuhan, Chiang Kaishek had ignored warnings like these. In January 1939, though, he wrote in his diary that 'perhaps they think their time has come. Alas. The greatest danger is not the Japanese, but most of all Communist expansion everywhere.'[66] By this time, the Communist Eighth Route Army had already grown to 160,000 troops.[67] The KMT Central Executive Committee decided in the same month to adopt a set of measures to contain the Communists. It ordered that any organisation not registered with the KMT or the national government would be treated as a criminal entity. Several associations were placed under supervision, including the Youth National Salvation Association and the Wartime Rural Work Promotion Association.[68] Offices and businesses suspected of being Communist fronts were closed down.[69] The Nationalists also dispatched their own guerrilla forces into the provinces of Shandong and Hebei to counter Communist expansion. Some counties ended up with three different magistrates: a Nationalist, a Communist and a Japanese one.[70] By the end of 1939, the Nationalists had deployed 400,000 troops to blockade Yan'an in an attempt to prevent the movement of Communist officials and soldiers in and out of their main base area and to undermine its economy.[71]

These measures were unable to prevent further Communist growth.[72] Moreover, the Japanese targeted mopping-up operations against the Nationalists. In Shandong, these 'caused the destruction of Nationalist administration below the provincial level'.[73] Once the Japanese withdrew, Mao ordered the Communists in Shandong to grab local government control, grow the armed forces to 250,000 troops, expand into the provinces of Jiangsu and Anhui and recruit another 150,000 troops there.[74] The Communists in Shandong grew strong enough to introduce a system of progressive taxes, which they collected in grain.[75] Later they even issued their own currency.

North China became a powder keg. Not just the Nationalists and the Communists, but also the Japanese, the Wang Jingwei government and the Guangxi Clique, whose leader, General Li Zongren, was commander-in-chief of the Fifth War Zone, had interests to protect there. As one advisor to Chiang Kaishek put it in early 1940, 'the Japanese, the traitor Wang Jingwei, and the Communists are all our enemies. The Japanese and Wang Jingwei are absolute enemies. The Communists are dispersed between their units and ours. They are even more difficult to deal with.'[76] He feared that Communist expansion in this complex situation would lead to armed clashes from which only the Japanese and Wang Jingwei would benefit.

The Nationalists decided that the best option was to assign Nationalist and Communist forces their own areas of operation, rather than try to fight alongside each another. Nationalist negotiators proposed that the Communists confined their operations to the area north of the old bed of the Yellow river, while their own would stay south of it. Given that at the start of the War of Resistance the Communists had been assigned a campaign area of a mere twenty or so counties, this was a significant Nationalist concession. The Communists initially demanded that they should be allocated all five provinces of north China – Shandong, Hebei, Henan, Anhui and Jiangsu – but in the end they accepted the proposal. Detailed preparations were made for a staged withdrawal of the entire New Fourth Army, first to northern Jiangsu and then to the area north of the Yellow river.

This attempt to separate Communist and Nationalist forces led directly to the New Fourth Army Incident of January 1941, the most violent clash between the two during the War of Resistance, in which 10,000 Communist troops were killed, including, as said, political commissar Xiang Ying. The incident took place when the Japanese were conducting mopping-up operations in central China in preparation for the inauguration of the Wang Jingwei government. Discussions taking place between the Japanese and the Nationalists triggered Communist fears that Chiang Kaishek was preparing to cut a deal with the Japanese and Wang Jingwei. If all the Communist forces were concentrated in one place, they would offer an easy target for Nationalist and Japanese attacks, coordinated or not. Adding to the febrile atmosphere were internal Communist and Nationalist divisions. On the Communist side, Mao Zedong and Xiang Ying were deeply suspicious of each other. On the Nationalist side, General Li Pinxian of the Guangxi Army, General Yu Xuezhong of the Shandong Army and General Han Deqin of the central Nationalist forces did not see eye to eye either.

The first conflict occurred at Huangqiao in Jiangsu province in October 1940. In the spring of that year, Mao Zedong had ordered Communist forces in Shandong and Jiangsu to put pressure on the position of General Han Deqin, who had masterminded the expansion of Nationalist guerrilla operations in Jiangsu province. If the Communists feared Nationalist collusion with the Japanese and the Wang Jingwei government, the Nationalists were concerned that the Communists were preparing to establish a new base area in the region. The danger for the Nationalists was that the Communists could then operate in a continuous zone from north China to the Yangzi delta. General Han Deqin stood firm at Huangqiao, but he lost thousands of troops.[77]

Preferring to preserve the united front, both sides downplayed the incident. But the Nationalists became determined to force the New Fourth Army to move northwards. PRC historian Yang Kuisong, who has had unique access to Communist archives, has shown that the two sides were in daily contact as the Nationalists cleared two corridors through their ranks for the New Fourth Army. They placed supplies, including ammunition, at various stages to be picked up by New Fourth Army units as they made their way north. The New Fourth Army did begin to move, but it all went wrong when one of its divisions moved in an unexpected direction, surprising Chongqing, Yan'an and Nationalist front-line commanders, all of whom were in telegraphic contact. In the fighting that followed, a whole Communist division of 10,000 troops was destroyed in a battle that lasted three days.[78] Its commander, Ye Ting, was arrested, while political commissar Xiang Ying was killed.

From his examination of the telegraphic traffic, Yang Kuisong concludes that Chiang Kaishek did not issue the order to shoot and that Yan'an too had no influence over what was happening on the ground. The failure of communication equipment was no doubt an important factor and there may well have

been the desire on both sides to avoid serious clashes, but a deep mutual suspicion resulting from a decade of civil war meant that something like the New
Fourth Army Incident was bound to happen sooner or later. The Communists used the incident to unleash a propaganda storm against the Nationalists
which undermined their domestic as well as their international reputation. The
united front survived because neither side was willing to risk the consequences
of a complete rupture, but relations never recovered. The Nationalists stopped
their subsidies to Yan'an and the Communists refused to attend meetings of
the Political Consultative Conference.

Disciplining the Party

Rapid expansion in the early years of the War of Resistance caused problems
for the Chinese Communist Party, as it had in Jiangxi. Mao Zedong noted in
a telegram to General Peng Dehuai that 90 per cent of its 800,000 members
had joined after the War of Resistance had started.[79] Most of these were urban
youths, leading Mao to call for 'a struggle between proletarian and petit-bour-
geois ideologies' in order to baptise the new arrivals into communism and
acquaint them with rural conditions.[80] But the campaign was also designed
to root out 'agents provocateur and internal treachery'.[81] Mao, though, did not
want a repeat of the 1930 orgy of killing in the Jiangxi Soviet. He designed the
Rectification Campaign, as it came to be called, as a controlled exercise containing specific stages. Mao was learning from experience how to use violence
as an instrument of power. He did not use violence for violence's sake. He
applied it in a considered and calculated way, in the same way that he used his
charisma and his ability to inspire to drive the revolution in the direction he
believed was the correct one.

The Rectification Campaign began on 1 February 1942, when Mao addressed
a gathering of 1,000 cadres in Yan'an. He stressed Party control of the movement and insisted that 'no one must be killed and only a few arrested'.[82] The
campaign targeted what Mao called three diseases – subjectivism, sectarianism and Party formalism – to be cured by the collective study of twenty-two
documents, five of which were written by Mao himself. Subjectivism was the
reliance on one's subjective understanding resulting from the failure to apply
the general truths of Marxism–Leninism to Chinese conditions. Sectarianism
referred to protecting one's own faction and ignoring orders from a higher
authority. Party formalism was the habit of Party officials to produce writings
full of empty clichés and generalisations, compared by Mao to 'the lazy old
woman's long, foul-smelling foot bindings which should be thrown into the
privy at once'.[83]

Rectification began at the top of the Party and over the next two years moved
down its hierarchy,[84] with participants required to keep diaries and produce

self-criticisms, said by Mao to be 'a great weapon in the thought struggle'.[85] In their diaries and self-criticisms, Party members reflected on when, where, how and with whom they had fallen into error, not just in their behaviour but also in their thinking. This was shock therapy: 'the first step is ... to give the patient a good jolt: yell at him "you are sick"', as Mao put it.[86] Because self-criticisms were preserved in the personnel files of each Party member, for the rest of their lives each had to live with the idea that the Party could punish them for something to which they had already confessed – an excellent way to ensure subordination to the will of the Party.

Already by 8 June over 17,000 people were enrolled in the campaign. One man had assumed that, because he had not studied, did not have any close friends or relatives and did not write, he could not possibly be suffering from any of the three diseases of subjectivism, sectarianism and formalism. Study, though, convinced him that he was in fact suffering from all three.[87] Another was pulled up for forgetting the importance of politics in deciding who to marry. He had joked that in looking for a spouse his conditions were that 'first, it must be a human being, second, it must be alive, and third, female', adding that he would prefer his wife to stay at home.[88] He was criticised, not for misogyny, but for forgetting his politics. Beginning with the rectification of such individual attitudes, the small groups in which the texts were studied moved on to reflect on the work styles of their work units. Like the Nationalists, the Communists regarded revolution not just as a force for change in social and political relations, but also of the self. Self-criticism was meant to transform the individual.

The study of documents and collective self-criticism were designed to forge an individual link with a transcendental revolutionary truth, including a correct understanding of the history of the Chinese Communist Party. In 1941, Mao Zedong ordered the compilation of two volumes of Party resolutions, reports, minutes and key articles by its leaders from the Party's founding until 1941.[89] The collections were meant to illustrate two things. Firstly, only the Chinese Communist Party could be the agency of China's redemption, a cause for which it had battled warlords, imperialists and the Nationalists, who had begun as true revolutionaries under Sun Yatsen but had abandoned the revolution after they had come to power and now served the interests of imperialists, large landlords, capitalists and warlords. The second was a depiction of the history of the CCP as the overcoming of two deviations, one that was leftist and had cost the Party dearly by calling for uprisings when they were impossible, and the other that was rightist and which had shied away from revolution. Because he had been able to apply the universal truths of Marxism–Leninism to the specific conditions confronted by revolution in China, the suggestion was that Mao had been able to formulate the correct line, as it was called, the right revolutionary strategy to deliver the country from its troubles and bring about the New China.

Mao was determined to use the Rectification Campaign to stamp his authority on the Party. He compelled competitors to submit self-criticisms and acknowledge in public their acceptance of the correctness of his views. Party leaders who had worked and studied in the Soviet Union came in for special attention. Most did not put up much of a fight, but an exception was Wang Ming, who had stayed in Moscow from 1931 as head of China's delegation to the Communist International and had been sent back to China to enforce a more fulsome Communist commitment to the united front. In March 1940, Wang Ming republished 'Fighting for the Further Bolshevisation of the Chinese Communist Party', which he had written in the early 1930s, as a defence of his views. Wang Ming held out until 1944, suffering a good deal for his pains, including being refused medical treatment when he was seriously ill.[90] But in 1944 he produced a letter stating that he agreed with a Party resolution on the history of the CCP which affirmed the Maoist interpretation of its past.[91] Mao was triumphant a year later when Mao Zedong Thought was enshrined in the Party constitution.

Mao used the campaign to drive home the cost of criticism against him. Wang Shiwei, educated at Peking University and working for *Liberation Daily* in Yan'an, published a series of satirical pieces criticising aspects of Yan'an life under the title *Wild Lilies*. In the introduction he describes a young woman, Li Fen, a fellow Peking University student who was executed after having been arrested in Hunan province in 1928. Before her execution, she had put on three levels of clothing and sown them together to protect herself from rape. 'For the nation's sake, we really do not want to go over old scores from the class struggle. We really are truly impartial and magnanimous, so much so that we are using all of our strength to recruit representatives to walk with us on the same road towards the light. But, in the process of recruitment, old China's dirt and filth contaminate us, spreading germs and infecting us with disease.'[92] This was a not-so-veiled criticism of Mao Zedong and his cavorting with Shanghai actresses. Wang was condemned as a Trotskyist, placed under arrest and executed in 1947.

In 1943 the Rectification Campaign span out of control, despite Mao's original intentions. This was as a consequence of developments that have not yet been made fully clear. In August, the Central Committee issued a directive stating that in Yan'an the Nationalists 'have a huge network of spies' and that the Japanese had 'many Chinese working as spies'. Party officials were there-fore ordered to 'eliminate counter-revolutionaries hidden in the Party'.[93] Kang Sheng, the Party's security chief, took charge of the campaign. Determined to root out 'counter-revolutionary ideological poison', he justified his purge as saving the Chinese-ness of his victims:

Why does the Communist Party make so much effort to rescue you? Simply because it wants you to be Chinese, and not be cheated into serving the enemy. Those of you who have lost your way, be conscious, take a firm decision, repent to the party, and cast off the special agent's garb ... and put on Chinese clothes ...[94]

As had happened in Jiangxi province in the early 1930s, torture was used to secure confessions and many people were executed after Kang Sheng claimed that in Yan'an alone there were 1,400 spies.[95] Mao apologised three times after he reined in the campaign, at one time stating 'during cadre investigation, the whole of Yan'an has made mistakes. Who is responsible? Me, because I issued the orders.'[96]

None of this would have made much sense unless Mao Zedong articulated a new vision for China's future. He addressed the question 'Whither China?' in 1940 in 'On New Democracy'.[97] In this famous tract he traced the history of China's revolution back to the Opium War, arguing that China had become a semi-feudal and semi-colonial country in which the bourgeoisie was too small to lead the revolution, as had been demonstrated by the failure of the 1911 Revolution to give rise to a stable republic and by the abandonment of revolution by the Nationalists. As Marxist doctrine demanded, Mao argued that China would have to pass through a democratic and a socialist revolution, but because of the weakness of its bourgeoisie, the Communists would have to shoulder the leadership in both phases and they would need to establish a democracy 'of a special type – new democracy' ruled by a government that represented the peasants, the workers, the petty bourgeoisie and the national bourgeoisie.

In this way, Mao could suggest that only a few – compradors working for foreigners, large landlords – would have anything to fear from the Communists. The state, Mao declared, would only take over 'large banks, industries, and businesses'.[98] He insisted that, under the CCP, the state would look after 'over 90% of the toiling masses of workers and peasants throughout the nation',[99] providing them with education, protecting them from imperialism and enhancing their prosperity. Mao stressed that the CCP would support business and protect China's industry against foreign competition. To counter accusations that the CCP would make China subservient to Moscow, he stressed the importance of nationalism. The CCP would restore 'the dignity and independence of the Chinese nation'.[100]

In Yan'an, Mao Zedong did more than branch out from the military sphere into the civilian realm. He wrote on a broad range of cultural, economic and social issues, setting out a different vision for the New China, as he had done in 'On New Democracy', and highlighting the differences between the Communists and the Nationalists. Mao was turning into a cosmocrat. Not only was he a competent executive, a charismatic guerrilla leader, a shrewd strategist and an innovator of Marxism–Leninism; now he was a sage and saviour, who understood the past, had deduced its direction, had seen the future and had discerned the path towards it. Had Mao remained just a military leader, he would never have been able to dominate the CCP. That would be true, too, if he had merely been a political leader expert in Marxism–Leninism. In the Chinese tradition, political achievement is more highly esteemed than military glory, although the highest praise goes to those who excel both militarily and politically. Mao claimed unique expertise in both realms.

Mao Zedong underscored his uniqueness not just by dominating meetings, addressing large rallies and having all Party members imbibe his most important articles. He did so through the way he dressed and went about his daily life and in his use of language, setting him apart not only from other Communist leaders but also from Chiang Kaishek. Whereas Chiang wore military uniforms, Mao wore patched peasant clothing; whereas Chiang was stiff, upright, distant and controlled, Mao was relaxed, talkative and entertaining. If Chiang went to bed early and rose at the crack of dawn to do his exercises and pray, Mao slept during the day, smoked endlessly, ate sloppily and cracked jokes, often off-colour ones. Whereas Chiang continued to write in a semi-classical style, Mao – a perfectly good classical poet – wrote in a simple, direct and colloquial way and addressed people by their personal names. None of this was incidental, of course, but was used by Mao to stress the difference between the old, hierarchical, Nationalist order and the new vibrant, open, energetic and egalitarian Communist one. Yan'an became the radical new rural alternative to Nationalist urban backwardness, exploitation and corruption.

Mao Zedong and Chiang Kaishek both confronted the question with which Sun Yatsen had first struggled: how to transform a China which was like a sheet of loose sand, as Sun Yatsen put it, into a cohesive and unified nation able to resist imperialism. The histories of both the Nationalists and the Communists provided ample examples of the dangers of disunion. Factionalism had split the CCP even during the Long March, with nearly disastrous consequences. Nationalist divisions had almost led to the defeat of the Northern Expedition, while now, in the War of Resistance, there were two National governments, one in Nanjing under Wang Jingwei and the other in Chongqing under Chiang Kaishek. Chiang Kaishek's Nationalists themselves were more a coterie of different factions than a unified government, which undermined both their political and military effectiveness. The Nationalist Party, the Guomindang, was widely vilified as ineffectual; it certainly had done nothing to unify China's various armed forces and transform them into a cohesive fighting force.

Mao paid so much attention to disciplining his party and carrying out a rectification campaign in the midst of war because he saw a disciplined, unified, effective and energetic party as the answer to the Sun Yatsen question of how to bind China together. He cast the Party as a web over all organisations, including the army, governmental offices and mass organisations, in order to coordinate all the varied activities of the Communists on the battlefield, in the villages, in the media, on the stage, in schools and in universities across all regions of China.

In Yan'an, Mao Zedong became the undisputed leader of the Party, towering over other Chinese Communists. He not only reorganised the Chinese Communist Party through a distinct revolutionary strategy, but also expounded a new understanding of China's past, present and future. The rebirth of the Communists and the growth of Mao's power during the War of Resistance meant that between him and Chiang Kaishek China now had two saviours, each with a powerful base, each promising China's redemption and each convinced of his own unique value. That could only spell trouble.

PART III

THE ACID TEST

NINE

THE ALLIES AT WAR

Governments may think and say as they like, but force cannot be eliminated, and it is the only real and unanswerable power. We are told that the pen is mightier than the sword, but I know which of these weapons I would choose.

General Sir Adrian Carton de Wiart, *Happy Odyssey* (1950)[1]

The New Fourth Army Incident of January 1941 showed that the Communists had become a force to be reckoned with. However, the consequences of the revival of the Communists would unfurl only in the last year of the war. Japan's decision in December 1941 to invade colonies of the USA, Britain and the Netherlands in what we now refer to as south-east Asia administered a far more immediate impact. It yanked the War of Resistance in China in an entirely new direction.

British prime minister Winston Churchill learned of the new development on the evening of 7 December, while he was entertaining the American ambassador John Winant and US Special Envoy Averell Harriman at Chequers. Having spent the evening commiserating with his American guests, that night, according to Churchill, he 'slept the sleep of the saved and thankful'.[2] This was an over-simplification: Churchill remained anxious that the USA would not join in the war against Germany right up to the moment that Hitler declared war on the US four days later, on 11 December. Churchill was also worried that 'we are going to be heavily attacked in Malaya and throughout the Far East'.[3] But once it was clear that the USA, with its massive industrial capacity and agricultural resources, had joined the war, Churchill was right to believe, as he wrote, that 'Britain would live'.

In Chongqing, Chiang Kaishek also had cause to breathe a sigh of relief. On 5 December, the journalist Owen Lattimore, who was now an advisor on China policy to President Roosevelt, informed him that a last ditch effort by US Secretary of State Cordell Hull to secure peace with Japan was dead in the water. Chiang declared in his diary that 'this is our greatest diplomatic triumph'.[4] Although prone to writing in overly dramatic language in his diary, this time he had reason to do so.

At a meeting held on 22 November in Washington, Hull had told representatives of the UK, the Netherlands and China that the USA was not yet prepared for a two-ocean war. To secure a delay, so he told them, he had proposed to Japan's ambassador to the US, Nomura Kichisaburo, that, in return for Japan's agreement not to invade south-east Asia and reduce its troops in southern Annam (Vietnam), the USA would relax its oil embargo. This had been imposed on 26 July after Japan deployed 50,000 troops into southern Annam. Japan being completely dependent on oil imports, the embargo posed a devastating threat to its war-making capacity: an aircraft carrier without fuel is just a huge metal box clogging up a harbour. When pressed by the Chinese ambassador, Hu Shi, to say whether a Japanese undertaking not to attack Yunnan was part of the agreement, Hull declined to say.[5] Holding Ambassador Hu back after the conclusion of the meeting, Hull assured him that the delay would be only 'for a short period of transition'.

The Nationalists went into overdrive to put pressure on Hull. Had Hull's deal gone through, it would have come at an awkward time for the Nationalists. General Yan Xishan in Shanxi province had negotiated a compromise with Japan, the Wang Jingwei government had only recently been inaugurated and the Chinese economy was in free fall. Yunnan province was ruled by General Long Yun, who was no friend of Chiang Kaishek; he probably would have cut a deal with the Japanese rather than fight them. Nationalist resistance might well have disintegrated had Hull had his way and the US had concluded a deal with the Japanese.

Chiang Kaishek instructed Ambassador Hu and Lattimore to lobby the State Department and the Oval Office to stick to US demands, made when negotiations had begun back in February, for a Japanese withdrawal from China.[6] A message from Lattimore to Laughlin Currie, Roosevelt's economic advisor, read: 'Generalissimo has shown me Chinese ambassador's summary of America's suggestions ... He is shocked by suggestion that an agreement would be no worse than Britain's closing Burma Road. He wishes President to understand that fundamental question is not wording of terms but departure of principle involving sacrifice China, callousness of which impossible to hide.'[7]

At his press conference on 4 December, which made the front pages across the USA, Hull 'charged Japan', so the *Washington Post* put it, with pursuing a policy of conquest. Hull had come to the conclusion that 'seven months of negotiation have done nothing to bridge the broad gap between the Japanese position and that of the United States'.[8] As Lattimore told Chiang Kaishek, that meant that Hull had abandoned any hopes of an acceptable peace deal. Denied US acquiescence in their ambitions in China, the Japanese began Nanshin, the conquest of south-east Asia otherwise known as the Southern Expansion Doctrine, of which the assault on the US Pacific Fleet at Pearl Harbor was part. If Japanese intransigence was as responsible as the Nationalists' diplomatic push for sinking Hull's peace gambit, given the huge consequences that flowed from this, the importance of the Nationalists' efforts should not be underestimated.

Britain and China both benefitted from the USA's participation in the Second World War, but each also paid a price. In terms of military aid, Britain benefitted hugely but China did not. China received only US$2 billion of the US$50 billions-worth of supplies which the US made available to its allies during the war under the Lend–Lease programme of 1941, under which the president was authorised by Congress to transfer war material without payment to any state whose defence was considered vital to US interests.[9] Most of that aid only arrived in China towards the end of the War of Resistance. By contrast, Britain obtained US military assistance on a cornucopian scale. But politically, the reverse was the case; China benefitted hugely and Britain less so. Because of Roosevelt's support, the Nationalists were not only able to secure the abolition of unequal treaties and the return to China of foreign concession areas, they also gained recognition of China as one of the Big Four countries in the world, with a commensurate role in international affairs. In contrast, Roosevelt's actions did much to set in motion a process of decolonisation that would lead to the end of a world order dominated by militarised empires, such as Britain's, to which Churchill remained deeply attached.

Europe versus Asia

The moment the news of Pearl Harbor reached him, Chiang Kaishek fired off telegrams to Roosevelt, Churchill and Stalin to propose a military alliance. To coordinate the defence against Japan's Nanshin, Chiang proposed a joint command for the USA, the Soviet Union, the UK and China, with a US commander taking the lead.[10] Chiang was especially keen on an immediate Soviet declaration of war on Japan; only the Soviets could make a significant difference in China. As desperate as Chiang was for foreign assistance in his war with Japan, he would not join an alliance on any condition. He wrote in his diary that China should insist on: 1) Recognition by the Soviet Union and the UK of Chinese claims over Tibet, Xinjiang and Outer Mongolia; 2) Acceptance by all of Chinese sovereignty over Manchuria; and 3) The return to Chinese control of all foreign settlements and concessions in the country and the abolition of all foreign special legal privileges.[11] Resistance against Japanese aggression stood in the service of bringing about the Nationalist version of the New China.

Chiang Kaishek called for an 'Asia first' strategy. Because Japan was the weaker opponent, he argued, it would be best to defeat it first so that all resources could then be concentrated on defeating Germany. The cold water was not long in coming. Stalin informed Chiang a week after Pearl Harbor that the USSR would not take up arms against Japan until after the defeat of Germany. He also warned Chiang that China should resist joining the USA and the UK in their war against Japan in south-east Asia so as 'not to be sold out by them'.[12] The USA and the UK also rejected an Asia-first strategy. Two weeks after Pearl Harbor, Churchill sailed to Washington, where he gave a rousing speech at a joint session of Congress. He and Roosevelt presided over a series of meetings involving senior military and political leaders, named the Arcadia Conference, which made decisions that would shape Allied strategy for the next two years. These included the affirmation of a Europe-first strategy, the creation of a Combined Chiefs of Staff organisation as well as a joint Munitions Allocation Board; and the decision that their first joint effort would be Operation Torch, the invasion of French North Africa.

The Europe-first strategy was not unambiguously popular in the USA. Immediately after Pearl Harbor, surveys suggested that 60 per cent of the US population favoured focusing the war on Germany, but after the Japanese made gains in the Pacific, especially the Philippines (which was still a US colony), that changed.[13] For a large number of Americans, Japan was Enemy Number One and China 'the favourite ally'.[14] But well before Pearl Harbor the consensus in the US military was, as its Plan Dog memorandum of November 1940 put it, 'if Britain wins decisively against Germany we could win everywhere; but ... if she loses the problem confronting us would be very great; and, while we might not lose everywhere, we might, possibly, not win anywhere.'[15] Plan Dog therefore defined US strategy as 'an eventual strong offensive in the Atlantic as an ally of the British and defensive of the Pacific'.[16]

Between January and March 1941, at the same time that diplomatic talks were being held in Washington between the US and Japan about avoiding war, American and British military staff members were engaged in secret discussions, known as the American-British Conversations (ABC). Fusing the key features of Plan Dog and British strategy, the report that resulted from these meetings defined the Atlantic Ocean and Europe as the decisive theatres of war. The main US effort should therefore occur there. The priority was the safeguarding of sea communications between the UK and the USA so that forces could be gathered together in the UK for an eventual offensive against Germany. American and British military planners agreed that Italy should be eliminated from the war early on and that Germany should be subjected to a sustained air offensive. In case Japan joined the war, the defence of the British Commonwealth would be the UK's and the USA's first objective.[17] The ABC agreements did not constitute a military alliance and nor did they commit the US irrevocably to joining the war, but they formed important steps towards both. They had a profound impact on the decisions Churchill and Roosevelt reached in Washington at the Arcadia Conference, at which it was resolved to adopt a defensive strategy towards Japan: the UK would take responsibility for holding Singapore, while the USA would defend the Philippines and Australia.[18]

By contrast with the discussions in Washington, those in Chongqing involving China, the UK, the US and the Netherlands ended in acrimony.[19] The Nationalists were offended when General Archibald Wavell, the British commander-in-chief, India, declined a Nationalist offer of military assistance in Burma, fearing that they would overburden Burma's disintegrating infrastructure. An indignant Chiang Kaishek told Wavell that he should not think of Chinese forces like another native army from the British Empire, only good 'for railroad protection duties and digging trenches'.[20] The British looked down upon China's military capabilities, and they let it show.

The exclusion of the Nationalists not just from the Combined Chiefs of Staff and the Munitions Allocation Board but also from ABDA (America, British, Dutch and Australia) Command to coordinate the defence against Japan injured Nationalist pride. The creation of a separate China Theatre, in which Chiang had command of 'all Allied forces now or in the future in China' – essentially his own – did nothing to assuage his hurt feelings. He told a US diplomat that 'China is regarded as an ally only in name'.[21] It is possible that concerns about the security of Chinese secret military codes shaped the British and American attitude, but it is also the case that China was simply not seen as an important theatre of war. China did not figure large in either the ABC or the Arcadia agreements.

From the American perspective, the adoption of a Europe-first strategy made sense. An Asia-first strategy would have been sensible only if the USSR was willing to join an attack on Japan, if the USA had completed its military build-up, and if Britain had not decided to focus on the defence of the Middle East rather than its colonies and dominions in the Far East.[22] The USSR was still reeling from the German onslaught, Operation Barbarossa, which had begun only half a year earlier. Shoring up the defence against Hitler, on both Germany's eastern and western flanks, was crucial to prevent the nightmare scenario outlined in Plan Dog from becoming a reality. Reports from China made it clear that Nationalist forces had lost much of their fighting ability, and so would be unlikely to help sustain a major campaign against Japan.[23] Britain's air and naval forces were concentrated in Europe and the Middle East, counting on Japanese awe of British imperial might and US aid to defend its Far Eastern colonies. It made sense to give priority to reinforcing the Allied position in Europe, not in the least to prevent a Soviet collapse.

The Europe-first strategy was never as one-sided as the term suggests. Once it became clear that the US Pacific Fleet was not damaged as much by Pearl Harbor as the Japanese had hoped – no carriers had been sunk, and the Pacific War was going to be a carrier war – steps were undertaken first to shore up the Allied position in the Pacific, including by strengthening the defences of Australia. By the summer of 1942 the US navy was fighting back against the Japanese at New Guinea and Guadalcanal.

However, there was a problem. The embracement of China as an ally served the UK and the USA well in suggesting that they were not fighting a race war and had been serious in August 1941 when they had issued the Atlantic Charter, with its promise of self-determination. But they had little faith in China's military capacity and they were not prepared to deploy substantial military assets to China. The US tried to square this circle by staging dramatic actions that required few resources but would illustrate its commitment to China, partly to boost China's flagging morale but also because they would generate uplifting reports in the US press about American forces taking on the Japanese in Asia and winning. The Doolittle Raid of 18 April 1941 was an example.

That day, Lieutenant Colonel James Doolittle took off with sixteen B-25 medium bombers, each loaded with four 500-pound bombs, from the aircraft carrier USS *Hornet* in the western Pacific Ocean. His aim was to carry out an air raid on Japan. The raid inflicted little damage, but on 19 May President Roosevelt was to be photographed pinning the Medal of Honor on to the chest of the recently promoted Brigadier General Doolittle at a ceremony at the White House. He praised Doolittle for 'a highly destructive raid on the Japanese mainland'.[24]

Symbolic stunts to bolster domestic morale are part and parcel of modern warfare. However, the collateral damage inflicted by the Doolittle Raid on China was substantial. The B-25s had been stripped of all but essential equipment to make them light enough to take off from the USS *Hornet*. Their wingspan required that they take off with their port wing over the side so that their starboard wing did not hit the carrier island. A line was drawn on the *Hornet*'s flight deck to make this possible and prevent the planes from crashing into the Pacific. Their engines had to be throttled at maximum power with the breaks on to permit a short take-off run. Too heavy to re-land on the *Hornet*, the plan was that, after the raid, the B-25s should make their way to Nationalist air fields along the east coast of China.

Having been compelled to take off early, because the Japanese had spotted the flotilla, the planes ran out of fuel before reaching their destination. Three ditched at sea, one flew to Vladivostok and the rest crash-landed in the provinces of Zhejiang and Jiangxi. Two Japanese columns of 50,000 troops each swept through northern Zhejiang to destroy Nationalist air bases and then thrust into Jiangxi province to do the same there.[25] The devastation was enormous, not only because of the Japanese actions, but also because the Nationalists continued their scorched earth policy.[26] President Roosevelt and chief of staff General George Marshall had ignored Chiang Kaishek's warning that the Doolittle Raid would trigger Japanese reprisals.[27]

The US involvement in the Allied defence of Burma was similarly conducted to show support for China, by taking on the Japanese somewhere on land while minimising expenditure of military assets. In February 1942 General Joseph Stilwell was sent to China as chief of staff to Chiang Kaishek in his capacity as Allied commander of the China Theatre. The headlines that greeted Americans as they opened their newspapers that spring ran along the lines of 'Chinese Cavalry Routs Jap Panzers in Burma' [28] and 'Stilwell's Chinese Army Hurls Back Foe in Burma'.[29] The US press widely quoted Stilwell as saying that 'America means business in this war and the happiest day of our lives will be when Chinese and American troops together enter Tokyo'.[30] Such headlines were music to the ears of US political and military leaders, who did not take for granted their fellow citizens' 'willingness to make the wholehearted commitment' that the war required and 'accept the inevitable costs that full-scale war required and entailed'.[31]

Behind sunshine tales of Allied harmony and vigour lay a different reality. Burma was an accidental battlefield. The Japanese had planned to move no further north than Moulmein at the mouth of the Salween river in south-east Burma, in order to neutralise a British air base there. However, Nanshin made more rapid progress than expected. That made it attractive for Japan first to move north-west from Moulmein to cross the Sittang river and take the port city of Rangoon, the only remaining substantial port through which Allied supplies could be shipped to China, and then to head north for the Yenangyaung oil fields, which produced 4 million barrels a year. Occupying the hugely fertile rice fields in the valleys of the Irrawady, Sittang and Salween rivers was a further attraction.[32] The Japanese forces faced little opposition. Burma's population was generally hostile to British rule and initially only some 10,000 British, Burma Army and India Army troops stood in their way.[33]

The Japanese routed the Allies. On 22 January, the 55th Division of the Imperial Japanese Army crossed from Thailand into Burma. Moulmein was in Japanese hands just over a week later, on 31 January. Attempts over the next few weeks by 17th India Division, 1st Burmese Division and British units to conduct a fighting withdrawal towards Rangoon descended into chaos, especially after a tough five-day battle, from 19 to 23 February, for control of the Sittang river bridge ended in a decisive Japanese victory. While the British had initially declined Nationalist assistance, they now welcomed it. On 3 March, at staff talks at Lashio, the largest town in north Burma's Shan state, the Nationalists pressed the British to hold Rangoon while they concentrated their 5th Army at Toungoo, 200 kilometres north of Rangoon, to begin a counter-offensive from there.[34] That plan ceased to make sense after the British decided that Rangoon could not be defended and evacuated the city on 7 March. The torching of 5,000 tyres, the destruction of 900 trucks and the wrecking of 1,000 machine guns, all destined for China, by the retreating British troops annoyed the Nationalists.[35] With Rangoon in Japanese hands, the British and the Nationalists concluded that their best option was to attempt to defend the Yenangyaung oil fields and the city of Mandalay in Upper Burma.

General Joseph Stilwell only arrived in Burma after the event, when a Japanese victory there was virtually assured. He had been chosen to lead the American war effort in the region and to assist Chiang in part because of his knowledge of China. He had served three tours of duty there, the last as Military Attaché from 1935 to 1939. General Marshall had initially offered the position to General Hugh Drum, who had declined when he learned that no ground, air or naval forces would be made available to him, which had led him to conclude that he would be sent as 'just another empty gesture of good will'.[36] Stilwell, however, accepted that the US would not commit significant resources to Burma. His formal role was to act as chief of staff to Chiang Kaishek, and to be the commander of all US forces in the theatre and supervisor of supplies sent to China.[37] He had to take the long road to Chongqing, travelling there via Europe, the Middle East, India and Burma. He reported to Chiang Kaishek for the first time on 6 March, just after the British had begun torching Rangoon.

General Stilwell had served under General Marshall while the latter carried out the 'Benning Revolution' at Fort Benning, the USA's premier infantry school. To avoid costly man-wasting static battles like those of the First World War, Marshall instilled offensive tactics in his trainees, aiming to snatch quick victories in operations directed by commanding officers willing and able to take the initiative at the front. As Marshall put it, 'a democracy cannot afford a Seven Years War'.[38] When discussing operational plans with Stilwell on 9 March, Chiang Kaishek stated that, given what had just happened, the best option for the Allies was to focus on the defence of Mandalay in Upper Burma. Wedded to the offensive, General Stilwell would have none of it, arguing that 'our best option is to begin an offensive at Toungoo … we shall score a huge victory.'

General Stilwell's orientalist disdain for most things Chinese prevented him from taking Chiang Kaishek seriously. According to him, the Nationalist leader was 'a stubborn, ignorant, prejudiced, and conceited despot' who 'wants to be a moral potentate, a religious leader, a philosopher, but has no education. If he had four years of college education, he might understand conditions in the modern world.'[39] Stilwell characterised discussions with Chiang about next steps in Burma as 'a session of amateur tactics by Chiang Kaishek … I showed him the solution, but the stooge jumped in … I let them rant.'[40] The 'stooge' was one of Chiang's most senior staff officers. In holding out for an immediate counter-attack, Stilwell was following the example of his mentor, General Marshall. It took Churchill in high bulldog mode to persuade Marshall that an invasion of France in the spring of 1942 could only result in a bloodbath, a judgement borne out by the failed Allied raid on Dieppe in August and then by the difficulties US and British forces encountered when they invaded French North Africa. If Marshall could not ignore Churchill, Stilwell was not going to let a mere Chinaman stand in his way.

Stilwell returned to Burma on 11 March, after Chiang had assigned command of his Fifth and Sixth Armies to him. Chiang Kaishek had done so primarily because he did not want a British officer in charge of his forces but also to draw the US into China's war with Japan. Stilwell promptly ordered two Nationalist divisions, 55th Division and 22nd Division, to move south to Toungoo, where the 200th Division, the one that was fully mechanised, had already taken up position. They were to prepare for an immediate counter-offensive on Rangoon. Four days later, 200th Division was encircled and withdrew into the city. As a mechanised force, its strength lay in operating in the open field. The 200th Division fought hard, but it failed to destroy a bridge that gave access to the road network leading to Lashio, not far from the Chinese border, 200 kilometres north-east of Mandalay. Once they had this bridge in their possession, the Japanese decided on an immediate advance towards Lashio to separate British and Nationalist forces and capture a key Nationalist logistical and command centre. The Japanese took Lashio on 29 April, rendering any further resistance hopeless.

As the disaster unfolded, Stilwell, aware of the extent to which he had been built up in the press as an American hero, became worried: 'What a sucker I'll look if the Japs run me out of Burma.'[41] His loss of Burma, however, was reported not as a defeat worsened by misconceived tactics, but as an impressive effort by 'outnumbered forces who gave the best they had against a foe with more equipment'.[42] His retreat, largely made by vehicle and in front of what he referred to as the 'deluge' of Nationalist 'hordes',[43] was turned into an awe-inspiring tale of selfless leadership, with Stilwell said to have preferred to stay with his men as they marched through unforgiving jungle and over high mountain ridges rather than accepting an offer of being flown out.[44] He was portrayed as the prototypical straight-talking all-American hero, preferring action to flowery words, in contrast to the politicians in Washington and London. *The New York Times* thundered that Roosevelt and Churchill 'could learn something from General Stilwell, who is no orator but has been in the thick of battle. As for the lesser officialdom, it could sit at Stilwell's feet and learn from him some salutary rules both as to diction and as to policy.'[45]

It would be unfair to place the blame for the Burma disaster on Stilwell. He arrived too late to make any real difference. Japanese superiority at sea and in the air, and the fact that the Japanese forces were more accustomed to jungle warfare, were the decisive factors. However, Stilwell's attempt to begin a counter-offensive in contradiction of Chiang Kaishek's orders cost the Nationalists some of their best troops. Chiang Kaishek fumed in his diary: 'the responsibility for the enormous sacrifice of our forces in Burma lies entirely with Stilwell's command failures. Rather than admitting his own mistakes, he just blames our senior commanders. When we began to lose, he was all in a fluster and only thought about fleeing to India, having no concern for our forces.[46] In reality, only two Chinese squads of eighteen soldiers accompanied Stilwell.[47] He had asked Washington, but not Chongqing, for permission to head to India rather than China. Allied cooperation in east Asia could hardly have begun in a worse way.

Bad Blood

The place of China in the Allied strategy for the defeat of the Axis powers was never satisfactorily resolved. China could not simply be abandoned, partly for military and partly for political reasons. At least half a million Japanese troops were tied down there and China's manpower and resources would become available to Japan if China fell or surrendered. The inclusion of an Asian country as a full member of the alliance was important for symbolic reasons. But that did not answer the strategic question of China's function in the defeat of Japan.

All too real logistical difficulties impacted answers to that question. Supplies to China coming from the USA first had to round Cape Horn off southern Africa, then sail to Karachi on the west coast of India. From there they had to be transported by rail to Assam in eastern India and flown over the Himalayas, a dangerous route, to the city of Kunming in Yunnan province. Even then they would still be hundreds of kilometres away from the Chinese fronts. This journey took about four months.[48] Convoys from the US to the UK took just a couple of weeks, meaning that much more could be achieved in a much shorter time by giving primacy to Europe.

The differing views of the two most senior US commanders in China about optimum use of the limited supplies that reached China turned the China Theatre into a site of acrimony. Even if General Stilwell managed to escape to India with two Nationalist divisions without Chiang Kaishek's authorisation, the arrival of Nationalist forces there offered a practical way for the US to assist China at little cost. In early March, when Stilwell met Chiang in Chongqing, he had stated that the US was ready to train and equip thirty Nationalist divisions and that 800 US officers would arrive soon to assist with this programme.[49] With the Burma supply line cut, the USA had no way to ferry the required supplies to China. However, 8,000 Nationalist soldiers were now in India and military supplies meant for China were accumulating there. The army training programme could therefore be implemented in India. The British were prevailed upon to provide housing, food and pay for the Nationalist forces and to allocate barracks at Ramgarh, 300 kilometres west of Calcutta, to the programme.[50] The attractiveness of the project for the Nationalists was obvious; it allowed them to outsource the training of a large modern force. Additional troops were selected from various war zones in China. From October 1942, American transports began delivering 400 Chinese troops to Ramgarh per day; by the end of the year 32,000 troops were undergoing training there, a figure that would nearly double over the next two years.[51]

The question became what to do with this force, known as X Force. For Stilwell, the point was to drive the Japanese from north Burma in order to open up a supply line to China large enough to equip a new army in Yunnan province, which became known as Y Force. Once that army was ready, according to Stilwell, it should drive to the China coast to open a port there, and then take on the Japanese. Stilwell was convinced that the Japanese had to be defeated in China.[52]

That was not General Marshall's view. In a memorandum to the USA's Joint Chiefs of Staff dated 25 August 1942, he argued for 'the re-opening of the Burma Road', partly on the grounds that it would 'keep China in the war'[53] and prevent the 'total collapse of Chinese resistance'.[54] Boosting Chinese morale and demonstrating that the US stood with China were key objectives. A longer-range aim was to use the Ledo Road, from Assam to Kunming, as a supply line for US air bases in China from which the Americans could undertake bombing campaigns against Japan.[55] The Ledo Road would be fitted out with an oil pipeline. Marshall did not believe that Japan needed to be defeated in China.

Stilwell's view not only differed from that of his commanding officer, but also from the maverick, quarrelsome and flamboyant Claire Chennault, the man who had had a hand in designing the ill-fated attack on the Japanese flagship, the *Izumo*. Chennault had spent much of his youth hunting and fishing in north-west Louisiana. 'Beyond the fringes of cleared cotton fields,' he wrote in his memoirs, 'I stayed out for weeks at the time', happy in the presence of 'wolves, bears, deer, wild turkey, occasionally panthers, and many smaller species of wild game'.[56] He learned to fly in the Army Air Service in the First World War and became chief of the Pursuit Section of the Air Corps Tactical School, joining its aerial acrobatics team. He resigned his commission as captain in April 1937 because of ill health but also because of conflicts with his superiors about air tactics. Chennault disagreed with the prevailing view that bombers would dominate air warfare in the future and that they did not need fighter protection.[57]

Chennault went to China in 1937 on the invitation of Chiang Kaishek to knock the Nationalist air force into shape. The offer was attractive to him, not just because of the high salary that came with the job, but also because it provided an opportunity to prove his theories. Precisely because China was a peripheral theatre, it attracted a motley crew of people like Chennault, out of sorts and out of favour in their home countries. They included the Communist Agnes Smedley, a troubled denizen of Missouri who found her calling as a journalist, became the lover of an Indian independence movement leader and a supporter of the Chinese Communists, developing an obsession with General Zhu De, their commander-in-chief. Herbert Yardley was another one, a cryptanalyst who had established the USA's MI-8, the Black Chamber dedicated to breaking enemy codes, in the First World War and had been hired by Chiang Kaishek to help break Japanese codes. Yardley's memoirs of his days in China, full of gambling, drink and womanising, are highly readable, if short on information.[58]

General Adrian Carton de Wiart stood out even among this group of eccentrics. A British officer born of a Catholic aristocratic Belgian family, Carton de Wiart had fought in both the Boer War and the First World War, during which he had been awarded the Victoria Cross. He regarded as his happiest days those spent shooting and hunting 'in feudal splendour' after the First World War on a Polish estate, which had been given to him.[59] During the Second World War, he served in Norway, Yugoslavia and Italy, where he was imprisoned, including for four months in the Villa Medici in Rome, getting on well with some of his equally aristocratic wardens. Although shot in the stomach, arm, face, ankle, leg and ear, he declared in his memoirs that 'frankly, I had enjoyed war'.[60] To Carton de Wiart war was sport, jolly good sport. After being repatriated in 1943, Churchill sent him off, eye-patch and all, to Chongqing as his personal representative to Chiang Kaishek. It is often in peripheral theatres that one finds mavericks, attracted there for their own reasons or sent there because they are either not wanted or not appreciated at home.

Unconventional ideas can also find their chance in such places. Colonel Orde Wingate's long-range penetration tactics, in which units were deployed far behind enemy lines and relied on resupply by air, were tested in Burma. Similarly General Chennault was able to try out his innovative air war tactics in China. Two ideas were central. The first was the importance of reliable intelligence so that fighters could be fed accurate information about the flight path of incoming bombers. Chennault developed a 'spider net of people, radios, telephones, and telegraph lines that covered all of free China'. This provided warning of Japanese raids but also 'located and directed friendly planes'.[61] The second was that he trained his air crews to fly in pairs to slash through a formation of enemy bombers, 'using speed and diving powers to make a pass ... with one plane always protecting the other's tail'.[62] After one attack, they would ascend once more and then dive again, repeating the manoeuvre as often as possible.

Between 1938 and 1940, when Soviet pilots were active in China, Chennault was kept out of sight, having been tasked with training Chinese pilots at Kunming. In 1940, Chiang Kaishek sent him to the USA to recruit pilots for a volunteer air force, an idea to which Roosevelt had given his blessing. Chennault's Flying Tigers, as they were called by the Nationalists,[63] first went into action two weeks after Pearl Harbor, with Chennault feeding squadrons in rotation into Burma. Having too few aeroplanes and with pilots still undergoing training, the Flying Tigers could not stem the Japanese advance, which was supported by some 500 planes.[64]

Like Stilwell's exploits, Chennault's provided welcome copy in the US. A US army newsreel, 'The Flying Tigers Strike Back', shows the Flying Tigers downing Japanese fighters. The voiceover states that they were 'making the Japanese pay dearly' for Pearl Harbor.[65] On 16 April, Chennault was re-inducted into the US Army with the rank of Brigadier General. He had already become 'the famed commander of those fabulous "Flying Tigers"'.[66] His portrait adorned the cover of *Time* magazine in December 1943.

General Chennault's view of the role of China in the Second World War was radically different from Stilwell's. In November 1942, Chennault wrote to President Roosevelt (who had asked him to correspond with him directly) that with a small air command of 105 fighters, 30 medium bombers and 12 heavy bombers he would be able to establish air supremacy in China, after which he could attack Japanese shipping lanes and so reduce Japanese pressure on the US Pacific Fleet and support General Douglas MacArthur's planned offensive in the southern Pacific.[67] Stilwell disagreed, arguing that air bases in China needed the protection of ground forces. Japan's flattening of Zhejiang province after the Doolittle Raid illustrated the problem.[68]

The personal animosity between the two generals undermined US operations in China and Burma. Marshall tried to keep the peace between them, advising Stilwell, for instance, 'would it not be wise in the light of your success to give Chennault his chance?'[69] However, the disagreement between the two became so severe that one soldier lamented 'the opinion of most of us is that if the different commands would stop fighting, we might get somewhere.'[70] The conflict came to a head in the spring of 1943 when both men were called to Washington to make their respective cases in front of Roosevelt and Churchill.

Stilwell's performance was a disaster. He 'shut up like a clam', 'muttered about China not fighting', criticised Chiang Kaishek at length and insisted that Japan had to be defeated in China. Chennault, on the other hand, set out his case cogently and promised early successes against the Japanese.[71] When Roosevelt asked Chennault's opinion of Chiang Kaishek, Chennault replied that he had always kept his word with him and was holding China together.[72] Roosevelt ruled that Chennault's plan should be given the green light. He had received reports about Stilwell's 'open rudeness' to Chiang Kaishek and had had several requests for Stilwell to be relieved of his duties, including one from the British.[73] Stilwell was kept in place because Chennault's closeness to Chiang Kaishek made him unsuitable for the top command in China. The result was the entirely unsatisfactory situation that Stilwell was senior to a man who not only had upstaged him in Washington in front of his own wheelchair-bound commander-in-chief (ungraciously dubbed 'rubberlegs' by Stilwell),[74] but now had to implement a strategy with which he fundamentally disagreed to help a subordinate he loathed.

The trouble between Chiang Kaishek and Stilwell, the fights between Stilwell and Chennault, and all the other difficulties in relations between the National-ists and their allies should not obscure the fact that US support for China did boost morale in China no end. The death of President Roosevelt on 14 April 1945, so Chi Pang-yuan remembers, 'shocked all of China deeply'. One of her teachers, Zhu Guangqian, who had studied in Britain and France and was a close friend of the cartoonist Feng Zikai, interrupted a class when the news broke. He read out Walt Whitman's poem 'Oh Captain! My Captain!' as an act of commemoration.[75] Its first stanza reads:

Oh Captain! My Captain! our fearful trip is done
The ship has weather'd every rack, the prize we sought is won
The port is near, the bells I hear, the people all exulting
While follow eyes the steady keel, the vessel grim and daring
But oh heart! heart! heart!
Oh the bleeding drops of red,
Where on the deck my Captain lies,
Fallen cold and dead.[76]

Similarly, when Claire Chennault was set to return to the USA in August 1945 just before Japan's surrender, Chongqing residents turned out in their thousands to bid him farewell.[77] American support revitalised Nationalist resistance.

China in the Planning for Victory
The tide of war turned in the Allies' favour during the spring of 1943. In early February the surviving units of the Wehrmacht's 6th Army finally surrendered at Stalingrad, marking the end of the beginning of Germany's invasion of the Soviet Union. Australian and US ground forces defeated Japanese army units at Buna-Gona on the northern coast of Papua New Guinea in a campaign that lasted from November 1942 until 22 January 1943. By February 1943, US forces secured Guadalcanal at the same time after a battle that had lasted half a year. British and American armies forced the surrender of the Germans and Italians in north Africa in mid-May.

In Allied strategy, the war in China remained very much secondary to these operations. At a meeting in August 1943, Roosevelt and Churchill agreed that 'the main effort' with respect to China should be 'establishing land communications and improving and securing the air route' from India to China, but they made 'no decision … on actual operations'.[78] They did, however, create South East Asia Command (SEAC), which included Burma and Thailand, under the command of Lord Louis Mountbatten. If one motivation was to shake up a command that had so far produced little, another was to spike Nationalist claims of sovereignty over north Burma.[79] An American quip circulating at the time had it that SEAC stood for 'Save England's Asian Colonies'.

During a visit to Chongqing in October, Mountbatten told Chiang Kaishek that Roosevelt and Churchill supported a campaign in Burma, but when Chiang asked whether his allies were prepared to provide naval and air support, Mountbatten's evasive answer was that 'he had not yet been assured by telegram on this point'.[80] From the first moment that an operation to reconquer Burma was mooted, Chiang had insisted that in return for the deployment of large numbers of Chinese troops, the US should make three of its own divisions available, the UK should assist with naval forces and that sufficient air power should be put into place to establish air supremacy.[81]

In November 1943, Churchill, Roosevelt and Chiang Kaishek met at Cairo. Discussions about operations in Burma, the only place where the Allies could conceivably fight together in east and south-east Asia at this juncture, were largely for show. This was the only Allied conference where the Nationalists were present. Sir Alan Brooke, the British Chief of the Imperial General Staff, sought to lever the Americans into taking the blame for doing nothing in Burma by insisting that the operation could only go ahead if the invasion of Europe was postponed, knowing full well that General Marshall was determined to press ahead with that campaign.[82] Chiang Kaishek, who needed 'joint warfare by the Chinese, British and American forces' for domestic political reasons,[83] agreed to the deployment of US-trained Nationalist forces at Ramgarh as well as in Yunnan, but once more reiterated his demand that US ground and British naval forces be deployed as well as enough aircraft to drive the Japanese from the skies above Burma. General Marshall made clear that he would not make US ground forces or any additional aircraft available. Roosevelt ruled in favour of an amphibious landing on the Andaman Islands off the Burma coast, an action that required the deployment of a British naval task force in the Bay of Bengal but not the involvement of US ground forces. When pressed by Chiang Kaishek, Churchill promised UK naval support, but only in a vague way.

After Cairo, Churchill and Roosevelt flew to Tehran to meet Stalin. With the Soviet–Japanese Non-Aggression Pact still in force, the Russian leader had been unable to come to the Cairo meetings, where he would have had to meet with Chiang Kaishek. Stalin made an offer Roosevelt and Churchill could not refuse: if Roosevelt and Churchill committed to the invasion of France in the spring of 1944, he would launch a counter-offensive against the Wehrmacht on the eastern front and join the war against Japan three months after the defeat of Germany. Now, finally, a clear strategy for the defeat of both Germany and Japan was in place – one that reduced yet further the strategic significance of China.

To give the D-Day landings on the coast of Normandy every chance of success, the decision was made to transfer the landing craft designated for the assault on the Andaman Islands back to Europe, a decision which President Roosevelt was left to communicate to Chiang Kaishek.[84] Coming so soon after promises of significant support for China, this was a slap in the face for Chiang. Although it would have to be conducted largely with Chinese forces, the operation in north Burma was nonetheless allowed to continue. The justification was the construction of an overland supply line to China. This was to assist China, of course, but it would also be helpful in relieving the logistical difficulties in supplying 20th Bomber Command, the USA's strategic bombing force controlled from Washington. This was designed to attack Japan with the B-29 Superfortress bombers, something that at this point in the war could only be done from bases in China.[85]

Chiang Kaishek agreed to the continuation of the invasion of north Burma; his options were either to do so or not to have the USA and the UK on side at all. Only Chiang Kaishek seemed to grasp that the assumption that the Japanese would simply wait while the Allies defeated Germany before turning their attention to China was built on quicksand. On 1 January 1944, his telegram to Roosevelt warned:

From the declaration of the Tehran Conference, Japan will rightly deduce that practically the entire weight of the UN forces will be applied to the European Front, thus abandoning the China Theatre to the mercy of Japanese mechanized land and air forces. It would be strategic on Japan's part to liquidate the China affair in the coming year. It may therefore be expected that before long Japan will launch an all-out offensive against China so as to remove the threat to their rear.[86]

Chiang's words would prove prophetic.

Diplomatic Success
The Nationalists gained little militarily from being one of the Allies, but diplomatically they achieved a tremendous amount. When the War of Resistance broke out, China was a country with no say in the international corridors of

power. By the end of the Second World War, the humiliating unequal treaties imposed on China after the 1838–42 Opium War were finally abolished. By 1944, China was regarded not just as a state of international standing; formally it was treated as one of the Big Four, a position translated after the war into a permanent seat on the UN Security Council. Roosevelt's support for China, and his use of China to curtail the British Empire, were important to these successes.

After Pearl Harbor, Churchill rushed off to Washington, but Chiang Kaishek went to India, the jewel in the British imperial crown, to cement an intensifying relationship with leaders of the Indian independence movement. Accompanied by his wife, Song Meiling, Chiang arrived in New Delhi on 9 February 1942. They faced a delicate situation. Britain was China's ally but anger towards the British was widespread in India and some sympathy existed for Japan. Chiang's visit took place just before a British mission, led by War Cabinet member Stafford Cripps, travelled to India to negotiate with Indian leaders. Its failure would lead to the Quit India Movement that began in August. The Axis powers were actively courting Indian National Congress Party members, including Subhas Chandra Bose, who was then in Berlin and who in 1943 formed the Indian National Army from India Army soldiers taken prisoner by the Japanese during the Battle of Singapore. Chiang was instinctively sympathetic to India's independence campaign, but he could not easily turn his back on an ally either, and he feared that the Japanese would find a way to exploit anti-British disorder in India. An India in Japanese hands had implications for China that were too frightening to consider.

In India, Chiang held many meetings with Jawaharlal Nehru, the Congress Party leader who would become India's first prime minister after independence. Nehru had pursued close relations with China since the outbreak of war. For instance, he held a China Day in 1938 and wrote about China and India as ancient civilisations, both threatened by Japan and struggling to 'secure freedom' from British imperialism.[87] 'Behind the war and inhumanity and violence … a new China is rising, rooted in her culture, but shedding the lethargy and weakness of the past, strong and united, modern, and with a human outlook.'[88] On a personal level, however, the two leaders were not natural bedfellows. In August 1939, Nehru visited China. During a Japanese raid, he and Chiang Kiashek sheltered together in a bomb shelter at Chiang's residence in the Huangshan mountains just outside Chongqing, during which Chiang became increasingly annoyed with Nehru's loquaciousness.[89]

The British had attempted to dissuade Chiang from his visit to India. Churchill had even sent a personal appeal,[90] but Chiang had rejected it. The British insisted that, if he had to go, he should meet the Governor-General, Lord Linlithgow, before seeing anybody else. In his meeting with Lord Linlithgow,

Chiang urged Britain to grant India dominion status, while in discussions with Nehru he suggested that India should follow China's example and seek a gradual path to independence. Nehru's response was that a real transfer of power had to take place before he could support India's participation in the war.[91]

Following his return to Chongqing, Chiang sent a telegraph to President Roosevelt, urging him to put pressure on Churchill because 'if the Indian political problem is not immediately and urgently solved, the danger will be increasing daily … If the Japanese should know the real situation and attack India, they would be virtually unopposed.'[92] Fully aware of Churchill's sensitivity about India, Roosevelt forwarded Chiang Kaishek's message as an indirect way of pressuring the British prime minister on the issue. Churchill's predictable response was that Allies should not interfere in each other's domestic affairs.[93] That nothing came of Chiang Kaishek diplomatic démarche is unsurprising; that he assumed a position of equality with his allies with the right to advise them, and that he did so with US support, was a new development. In Whitehall, eyebrows shot up in alarm.

According to Roosevelt's son, Elliott, when Churchill and his father met in August 1941 to draw up the Atlantic Charter, with its promise of self-determination for all people, Roosevelt had admonished Churchill about wanting to preserve the British Empire, saying, 'I can't believe that we can fight a war against fascist slavery, and at the same time not work to free people all over the world from a backward colonial policy.'[94] Churchill had attempted to confine the applicability of the charter just to Europe, but Roosevelt believed that it should be applied worldwide. Supporting China in seeking recognition as an equal partner in the alliance offered the US president a way of pursuing his understanding of the Atlantic Charter.[95]

In the spring of 1942, Washington started to consider placing relations with China on an equal footing to its other allies. Maxwell Hamilton, the Chief of the Division of Far Eastern Affairs of the US State Department, wrote a brief arguing that this step would give substance to the assertion that 'the present war is a people's war' in which the Allies 'are fighting not only for self-preservation but also for human rights and decencies and greater equalities'.[96] Secret discussions began with Britain. The British response was that it accepted the case in principle but that going ahead at present 'would be constructed as the fruit of a sense of weakness',[97] and ran the risk of fanning the flames of unrest in India.

For the Nationalists, abolishing the unequal treaties was important in and of itself. But the matter had become urgent because Japan and the Wang Jingwei government were in discussion about returning all foreign concessions to Chinese control, leaving Wang on the brink of a huge propaganda coup.

Chiang Kaishek instructed Guo Taiqi, the Nationalist ambassador to the UK, to broach the subject of ending the unequal treaties while Guo was in Washington, on his way back to China via the USA.[98] Guo's meetings with Secretary of State Cordell Hull culminated in an exchange of diplomatic notes.[99]

Under pressure from Hull, the British went along with the idea of concluding new treaties on the basis of equality with the Nationalists. They had indicated at the outbreak of war that they were willing to negotiate such a treaty, but in 1942 they hesitated, fearing the impact it might have on the situation in India. Hull wanted a short treaty achieved after short negotiations, and dealing with issues of principle only, but the British insisted on a more detailed treaty, settling such issues as the right to trade, to own property, to reside anywhere in China and to navigate in coastal and inland waters. British interests in China were far larger and went far deeper than American ones. The negotiations dragged on longer than Hull wanted, but by the thirty-first anniversary of the 1911 Revolution, they were sufficiently advanced for Chongqing, Washington and London to be able to announce that they were in talks about ending the unequal treaties. In a nice flourish, 'V' for victory was tapped out on the Liberty Bell in Philadelphia's Independence Hall to commemorate the event.[100] In a message of thanks to President Roosevelt, Chiang Kaishek declared that its chimes 'resounded in the hearts of all our people'.[101] The new treaties, ensuring China's equality, were signed on 11 January 1943 – as it so happens, one day after the Wang Jingwei government and the Japanese did the same.

A non-official but highly visible way of building up China's status in the world was by giving prominence to the glamorous Madame Chiang Kaishek. She visited the United States from 27 November 1942 to 4 July 1943. While Churchill had gained respectful plaudits for his oratory in the USA, Madame Chiang's fame was more like that of a Hollywood star, pulling in vast crowds wherever she went and bringing traffic to a halt. She was presented as China's pro-American Asian other: modern, articulate, Christian, progressive and democratic, yet also Asian, slightly mysterious, feminine and vulnerable. Her vulnerability was for real: she was in the USA for medical treatment.

Madame Chiang was entirely comfortable in an American setting. She was born in China, but had spent her teenage years in Macon, Georgia, and had earned a degree at Wellesley College, Boston, ensuring that she spoke fluent English with an American accent. During her American visit, she addressed a joint session of Congress, during which she praised US armed forces and US democracy, left the race issue alone, called for US leadership in the war and talked at length about Japan's 'sadistic fury' and 'military might'.[102] These were the kinds of messages the Americans were eager to hear and the Roosevelt administration was keen to promote.

Madame Chiang toured the length and breadth of the USA, travelling to

Boston, New York, Chicago, San Francisco, Atlanta and Los Angeles. In New York, 'she disappointed none of the thousands who waited for sight of her, first at Pennsylvania Station, then at City Hall, and finally in the heart of China-town', where 50,000 people jammed the streets.[103] The finale of her US tour at the Hollywood Bowl attracted 30,000 people and became 'a spectacular, star-studded pageant', as could be expected from its organiser, *Gone with the Wind* producer David Selznick. Its highlight was a 45-minute address by Madame Chiang.[104] If Churchill was a symbol of the USA's links with its British heritage, Madame Chiang signposted a new future in international relations.

Such events were of course multi-directional. Madame Chiang's visit was useful to President Roosevelt, but it also helped the Nationalists' efforts to woo the USA. In 1940, the Nationalists asked the painter Chang Shu-chi to produce a painting, *Messengers of Peace*, as a gift to President Roosevelt to mark his third inauguration. Chang completed the work, consisting of a hundred doves, in Chongqing. The painting, which carried an inscription by Chiang Kaishek, was formally presented to US Ambassador Nelson Johnson just before Christmas 1940. A letter from the ambassador to Roosevelt made clear that the painting was meant to be 'symbolic of the position which the President of the United States holds in the present world'.[105]

At the Cairo Conference, Roosevelt once more used Chiang Kaishek to advance his project of creating a new non-imperialist post-war order. In the preceding months, Cordell Hull had worked hard to gain recognition of China as one of the Big Four at meetings of the Allied foreign ministers in Moscow. Churchill was incandescent, believing it 'an absolute farce' that China should be recognised in such a way.[106] He told Foreign Secretary Anthony Eden that China would simply be a 'faggot vote' for the US in any Four Power organisa-tion.[107] At Cairo, Roosevelt sidelined Churchill and pulled out the stops to build up Chiang Kaishek as a world leader, something telegraphed to the world by newsreels and photographs of Churchill, Chiang Kaishek and Roosevelt, sitting together in a row in the garden of the residence of the US ambassador, with Roosevelt in the middle, Churchill to one side, cigar in his hand, and Roosevelt and Chiang Kaishek turned to one another, sharing a joke. Madame Chiang, who had been translating for her husband, was seated next to Churchill. She was often cropped out or erased from the photograph, despite being one of the most powerful women supporting the Allied cause.

The Nationalists had prepared carefully for Cairo. They were not content with serving as Asian decoration to a meeting dominated by Churchill and Roosevelt, nor was it their aim just to relegate a century of humiliation to the past. At the conference, Chiang insisted on the return to China of sovereignty over Manchuria, Taiwan and Penghu, demands that made it into the Cairo Communiqué. In order to spare British blushes, he decided not to be the first

1. Chi Pang-yuan.

2. Chen Kewen in his study as a young man.

3. The Sun Yatsen Mausoleum in Nanjing, March 1934.

4. A relieved Chiang Kaishek and his wife, Song Meiling, return to Nanjing after Chiang Kaishek's capture in Xi'an, December 1936.

5. Wang Jingwei, the Nationalist Number Two known for his handsomeness and his oratorical skills, in a white Changpao (Long Gown) at an outdoor rally. Date unclear, probably 1930s.

6. The famous Great World Amusement Centre in Shanghai was destroyed
by a stray Nationalist bomb on Shanghai's 'Bloody Saturday' – 14 August
1937. Images like this drove home the consequences of aerial bombardment
around the world before it was used to such devastation. Japan, not China,
was blamed around the world for unleashing this kind of destruction.

7. Chinese refugees waiting by a steel gate to gain
access to Shanghai International Settlement during the
Battle of Shanghai, August–November 1937.

8. Japanese soldiers during the Battle
of Shanghai, summer or fall 1937.

9. In early June 1938, the Nationalists decided to break the Yellow River dikes near Zhengzhou in an attempt to stop the Japanese advance into central China. Large areas of land were inundated. Hundreds of thousands of people died and many more were forced from their homes. This photograph by Robert Capa was taken near Zhengzhou in June or July 1938.

10. A Presbyterian Mission orphanage in an unoccupied area of Guangdong Province, 1941. These 300 orphans were under the care of the missionaries who ran this orphanage.

11. The Nanjing Atrocity: bodies washed up on the shore of the Yangzi River, December 1937.

12. This young Nanjing boy lost all his family during the Nanjing Atrocity. He was taken in at Jinling Women's College in the city. Under the leadership of Acting Principal Minnie Vautrin, the College offered sanctuary to thousands of victims. Date unclear, probably December 1937 or winter 1938.

13. The Japanese advance toward Wuhan, 1938.

14. Children being evacuated in orderly fashion from Wuhan, summer 1938. The Battle of Wuhan took place during the summer and early fall of 1938. The Nationalists did not want a repeat of the Nanjing Atrocity and did not stage a fight to the death for the city.

15/16. Harrison Forman was a journalist and photographer, working for *The New York Times* and *National Geographic*. He took these photographs of refugees from the Henan Famine in 1942 or 1943.

17. Henan Famine: Families like this took to the roads with all their belongings in search of survival.

18. The Henan Famine: A woman refugee. Note the contrast between her emaciated face and the chubby baby behind her: families tried to look after their children as best they could.

19. Sha Fei – 'Flying Sand' – was a left-wing photojournalist who joined the Communists in Yan'an. Influenced by Robert Capa and Cartier-Bresson, he became famous for the thousands of action photos he took of the Communists at war as well as his portraits of Communist leaders.

20. Sha Fei's portrayal of a Communist guerrilla hiding in a crop field.

21. The aftermath of bombing in Chongqing, November 1941.

22. A street scene in ravaged Chongqing. The most basic things were very hard work.

23. Photojournalist Harrison Forman visited Yan'an in 1944.
This is a his portrait of a militiaman holding a landmine.

24. Song Meiling, Madame Chiang Kaishek, at the Hollywood Bowl, June
1943. This pageant, meant to showcase America's favourite Asian other,
was organised by David Selznick of *Gone with the Wind* fame.

25. Japan's surrender to China, Nanjing, 9 September, 1945. General Okamura Yasuji affixes his seal to the surrender document.

26. The Communist entrance into Beijing, February 1949. The sign on the army truck reads 'Congratulations on the Liberation of Beijing'. Note the portrait of Mao Zedong on top of the truck.

27. Japanese propaganda poster of around 1938 entitled 'Look. Look. The Cruel Slaughter by the Communist Party'. Cheered on by people waving Japanese flags, the Japanese army roots out the communist devil, masquerading as peace, and communist armed forces ransacking the countryside. The soldiers holds a moneybag on which is written 'Military funds received from the Red Russians'.

28. Poster by Xu Ling, circa 1950. The text reads 'The Chinese People Absolutely Cannot Condone Foreign Aggression and Cannot Allow Any Imperialist to Inflict Brutal Aggression on Their Own Neighbour'. General Douglas MacArthur kills a Korean person cradling a child while the US air force bombs Chinese cities.

to raise the issue of Hong Kong. However, if Churchill raised it himself, Chiang Kaishek planned to state China's claim to the colony in a matter-of-fact way.[108] Chiang also demanded the transfer to China of 'all public and private property acquired by Japan in China since 1931' and 'ownership of most Japanese military equipment, naval vessels, merchant ships and aircraft remaining after the war'.[109] However, 'the key requirements of national defence' were the most fundamental drivers of Nationalist aims at Cairo. Being a 'continental country', Chiang wrote, China should adopt 'the defensive' in the Pacific and 'cooperate with the USA to avoid a tendency toward military competition with it'. Securing China's north-west border region with the Soviet Union was 'the main basis of national security'.[110]

On 23 November, Chiang Kaishek had a four-hour conversation with President Roosevelt, in which he sought US support for the dismantling of the British Empire in east and south-east Asia. He told Roosevelt that 'while your policies toward Soviet Communism have begun to bear fruit, only if your policies toward British imperialism also are successful and the oppressed people of the world are liberated will the USA's contributions to this world war find appropriate reward'.[111] He knew he was preaching to the converted. In line with the policy of having the USA take the lead in the Pacific, Chiang proposed that Liuqiu (Okinawa in Japanese) should be governed by the USA and China jointly under the mandate of a new international organisation. This proposal made sense because until 1874, when it had come under Japanese jurisdiction, Liuqiu, based on the island chain that stretches from Japan's southernmost island, Kyushu, to Taiwan, had been an independent kingdom with tributary relations with the Qing Dynasty.

Chiang Kaishek 'proposed that the USA should carry the main responsibility' in the occupation of Japan for the same reason. Roosevelt opposed that idea. According to Chiang, he 'firmly held fast to the idea that China should be the main player'.[112] Chiang also solicited Roosevelt's support in promoting the independence of Korea. At Cairo, the Nationalists pursued a strategy of drawing the USA into a prominent role in post-war east Asia while securing recognition of a China that included Taiwan and Manchuria.

Although the Cairo Communiqué was not a treaty but a simple press release, it nonetheless would become a key building block of the post-war order. Referring to the USA, the UK and China as 'the Three Great Allies', it declared that 'all the territories Japan has stolen from the Chinese, such as Manchuria, Formosa [Taiwan], and the Pescadores [Penghu], shall be restored to the Republic of China'. It also declared that the three countries were determined to see an independent Korea. No mention was made of French Indochina, nor of Hong Kong, in accordance with Churchill's wishes. Churchill had wanted no mention of Korea or Manchuria, either,[113] but he had given way on these two.

Cairo marked the moment that Churchill had to face up to the rise of US power in the world, both diplomatically and militarily. He had conspicuously failed in his attempt to 'persuade Chiang and his wife to go and see the Pyramids' while he and Roosevelt settled matters.[114] The Cairo Communiqué skirted the issue of the future of the British and French empires, but China's recognition as a great power and President Roosevelt's insistence that China take the lead in the occupation of Japan indicated that Roosevelt was serious about dismantling European imperialism in east Asia.

In the months before the Cairo Conference, Churchill dreamt of a post-war world order run by English-speaking democracies, that is, the US and Britain above all, plus the white dominions.[115] By aligning closely with China, Roosevelt declined to give succour to that idea, as he had to British imperialism in India. Roosevelt did not want a post-war order made up of empires and nor did he want one dominated by English-speaking democracies. He did not believe it realistic that US forces could occupy either Germany or Japan for any length of time. Instead he envisaged a new world order made up of independent states, but with the major power in each region of the world carrying responsibility for maintaining security in its own area. In this scheme, China was to fulfil that role in east Asia.

The implications of Cairo for the future of imperialism in east and southeast Asia were well understood in London. One British Colonial Office official picked up on a statement made by Roosevelt in his 1943 Christmas Eve radio broadcast, in which the US president stated that Cairo had recognised not only 'the restoration of stolen property to its rightful owners' (a reference to the communiqué's declared restoration of Manchuria and Taiwan to China), but also 'the recognition of the rights of millions of people in the Far East to build up their own forms of self-government without molestation'. The official worried that 'the Chinese evidently think Roosevelt's second principle can be invoked for claiming independence for "Indo-China". But this line of argument can be applied just as well to Hong Kong, Burma and Malaya.'[116] Indeed.

The internationalisation of the War of Resistance did not deliver to the Nationalists the military benefits they had hoped for. Militarily they were treated as a minor ally of whom much was expected but to whom little was owed. Politically and diplomatically, on the other hand, becoming one of the Allies did wonders for China. The unequal treaties were abolished and the Allies accepted that territories lost to Japan after the first Sino-Japanese War of 1894–5 would be restored to Chinese sovereignty. China was also formally recognised as a Great Power, a future pillar of the new post-war world order. As 1944 dawned, the Nationalists were well positioned to be the beneficiaries of these developments.

— TEN —

THE TURNING POINT

The two great tyrants of the Earth: Time and Chance
Johann Gottfried Herder, *Outlines of a Philosophy of
History of Man* (1803)[1]

Three military campaigns in 1944 would have a profound impact on the world order that emerged after 1945. On 6 June the Allies implemented Operation Overlord, landing 130,000 troops in three waves on the Normandy coast. Two weeks later, the Soviet Union launched Operation Bagration, by which the Russians inflicted the largest defeat on German forces of the entire war, destroying the Wehrmacht's Army Group Central. By August, both operations had succeeded. The drives into Germany from the west and the east that then followed would bring the Nazis to their knees. A Europe divided into a Soviet-dominated eastern zone and a democratic west had its origins in these developments.

These were Allied successes. The third major campaign of 1944, Japan's Operation Ichigo, marked an overwhelming defeat. For Ichigo, Japan mobilised no fewer than 500,000 troops, 100,000 horses, 1,500 pieces of artillery, 800 tanks, 15,000 mechanised vehicles and a large number of aeroplanes,[2] making it Japan's largest campaign on land of the Second World War. Ichigo's forces slashed through Nationalist armies as if they did not exist, clearing them from the provinces of Henan, Hunan and Guangxi. By October 1944, Sichuan was the only large Chinese province still in Nationalist hands. A Chinese collapse appeared a distinct possibility.

The worst did not come to pass. However, Ichigo inflicted serious damage not just to the military forces of the Nationalists but also on their domestic and international reputation. In 1943, Chiang Kaishek had been riding high, having secured an end to the unequal treaties and having been feted at Cairo as a world leader. He had also felt strong enough to publish a statement of his vision of China's past and future, *China's Destiny*, and so claim to transcendent authority. In China's post-monarchical political culture, such statements have become a key aspect of leadership legitimation. Mao Zedong Thought was written into the constitution first of the Communist Party and then of the People's Republic. Each leader since has published collections of articles intended to suggest he has formulated a distinct political vision uniquely appropriate to his times, a vision usually summarised by a catchy phrase, such as Deng Xiaoping's 'the Four Modernisations' or Jiang Zemin's rather less successful 'the Three Represents'.

'The unequal treaties', Chiang Kaishek charged, had divided his country, enfeebled its people and destroyed its economy, thus causing its humiliating decline in the nineteenth century.[3] Even though no less a person than Sun Yatsen had led the 1911 Revolution, the Republic had been shipwrecked by war-lordism and the fact that most Chinese were uneducated. Now, however, a new China was being forged in the heat of battle under Chiang's leadership, a China that was comfortable with modernity but also with its political and cultural traditions, especially Confucianism. In Destiny, Chiang promised that after the war he would implement constitutional rule and democracy. Now that China had rid itself of the yoke of imperialism and was a leading member of a military alliance whose victory had become a clear prospect, Chiang challenged all his countrymen to rally behind him. If that happened, China would survive the 'acid test' of war with Japan,[4] the greatest crisis in its history, which would decide 'China's destiny of independence or slavery, glory or humiliation, survival or extinction'.[5] If not, China would remain a poor, backward and divided country. The implicit message to the Communists was that they should see the error of their ways and fall into line.

A year is a long time in history. Chen Kewen recorded in his diary in November 1944 that 'these days, when among friends, we can only talk about the war and everybody is in despair'.[6] Rumours about coups against Chiang Kaishek swirled through Chongqing. A group of southern generals who were considering their own declaration of independence approached US diplomats to assess the likely response.[7] Even Sun Yatsen's son, Sun Ke, was making moves to oust Chiang.[8] At the beginning of the war, when Chiang spoke in public, he had appeared to Chen Kewen as determined, confident and strong; now he seemed flat, dull and unconvincing.[9] Gossips leered about an illicit affair, tarnishing the reputation for high morals that Chiang put at the centre of his claim to be the right person to rule China, and prompting him to convene a press conference to deny the rumours – which inevitably only made matters worse.[10]

But if Chiang's domestic reputation suffered serious damage, internationally he had become an irrelevance. In July 1945, when Roosevelt, Churchill and Stalin drafted the Potsdam Declaration, which demanded Japan's unconditional surrender, they did not even consult him. The US Ambassador to China, Patrick Hurley, handed a copy of the text to Chiang Kaishek a few hours before it was published. The only change that Chiang could make was to suggest that China should at least be included as one of the countries issuing the demand (which was not the case in the draft).[11] To Chiang, Cairo must have seemed a very long time ago.

Ichigo was as beneficial to the Communists as it was disastrous to the Nationalists. Having flooded into the areas vacated by the Nationalists and the Japanese, they had grown so strong that they made an attempt at seizing power straight after Japan's surrender. There were, of course, other factors at play in their ultimate victory, but Ichigo set the ball rolling. To that extent, it can be considered as important to the new world order as Overlord and Bagration.

The Ichigo Campaign (April 1944–February 1945)

So why did the Japanese mount this vast operation? The Fundamental Guidelines for the Ichigo Battle, endorsed by Emperor Hirohito on 24 January 1944, restricted the operation's objective to the neutralisation of US air bases in China, especially the air fields of 20th Bomber Command at Chengdu, the capital of Sichuan province, which, Marshall hoped, would carry out the strategic bombing of Japan. In reality, Ichigo's aims were broader.

It originated in plans drawn up in February 1943 by the Operations Section of the Imperial General Staff after Japan's defeat at Guadalcanal for the eventuality that they lost control of the western Pacific. These plans required Japan's armed forces to establish an overland corridor to south-east Asia, in part by using railways running from Peiping via Wuhan to Canton and from Yunnan province to Hanoi. Once an overland route was in place, Japan would use the resources of south-east Asia and China – oil, rubber, tin, rice, coal, and mineral ores – to rebuild Japan's navy and strengthen its armed forces. Anticipating that this would take two years, the plans provided for a Japanese counter-offensive in the Pacific beginning in 1946 and staged from the Philippines.[12]

But the Japanese commanders in China, as always, pursued their own objectives. In charge of the 620,000 troops of Japan's China Expeditionary Army was General Hata Shunroku. He judged that the strategy pursued after the fall of Wuhan, namely to keep Nationalist armed forces down while building up regional administrations to foster the emergence of a decentralised China, had failed. He believed that Ichigo should go for the jugular and take Chongqing. The operational plans developed by Japanese planners in China for Ichigo provided for: 1) the destruction of enemy air bases; 2) the clearing of a railroad corridor through China to south-east Asia; and 3) the crushing of the Nationalists.[13] During Ichigo, Japanese forces time and again sought out the Nationalists' main forces with the aim of annihilating them. The campaign as it unfolded on the ground was never about destroying US air bases alone.

Official documents can only tell us so much; the archives rarely reveal the whole truth. The historian Edward Drea has suggested that the likely overall aim of Ichigo was to force the Allies to the negotiating table by scoring a clear victory. This is because a negotiated peace would have been easier to accept for

Japan and might have allowed it to retain some of its wartime gains. According to Drea, from 1942 Emperor Hirohito hoped for 'a military or naval victory that would lead to a negotiated settlement … The chimera of the decisive battle, be it on land or sea, became not only the Emperor's mantra, but also that of the court, the bureaucracy, and ultimately the die-hard military itself.'[14]

The Japanese would not get their decisive victory, but, with Ichigo, they came close. They could not have known that the Allies were serious about unconditional surrender. And, in truth, Japan's surrender was not entirely unconditional: only after it was made clear that Emperor Hirohito would not necessarily have to vacate his throne did the Japanese lay down their arms.

The Battle of Henan (25 April–25 May)

Ichigo caught the Nationalists wholly unprepared. After Pearl Harbor, the Japanese wound down their operations in China. Faced with growing shortages of everything, but especially food, cotton and salt, Chiang Kaishek instructed his war zone commanders to become self-sufficient. At a military conference in Xi'an in September 1942, he told them that it would be impossible to mount a general counter-offensive in the foreseeable future and that they should grow their own grain and raise their own livestock.[15] They did more than that, smuggling goods to and from Japanese-controlled areas, managing their own businesses and even operating their own mines and industries.[16]

The Nationalist commanders also deliberately kept their units under strength so that they could claim payment for many more soldiers than they actually had. General Tang Enbo, the hero of the Battle of Taierzhuang and vice commander-in-chief of the First War Zone, admitted publicly that his divisions had only 6–7,000 troops, meaning that they were 30–40 per cent under strength. In good Chinese fashion, he listed 'six excesses' undermining the combat capacity of his forces. These were 'excesses in vacancies, of inferior soldiers, of hangers-on, of outside businesses and of family dependents'. He also mentioned 'three shortcomings and three confusions', that is, 'shortcomings in training, discipline and spirit' and 'confusion in the personnel department, in management and in issuing rewards and punishment'.[17] General Tang was referring here not to local but to supposedly elite Nationalist forces.

With their transport networks having broken down and inflation skyrocketing, it was understandable that the Nationalists forces became entrepreneurial, but abuse was inevitable. A Henan Provincial Consultative Council charged General Tang with having provoked popular anger because, in addition to running a large smuggling operation, he had established monopolies for coal mines, cigarette factories and tanneries.[18] The armed forces even took over the collection of the land tax after the Nationalists, forced by inflation, switched to collecting it in grain rather than in money. Only households with surplus grains were supposed to pay the tax, but inevitably they passed on the cost to their tenants and the powerless poor.[19]

Henan's population turned against local Nationalist forces. General Jiang Dingwen, commander-in-chief of the First War Zone, noted in a post-battle report that 'people in the hills of west Henan attacked our units, taking our guns and ammo, and even mortars and telephone poles. They surrounded and killed our troops. Village heads disappeared wherever we went. They sacked our barracks and cleared the fields so some units went without food for days.'[20] Henan was the area which Chiang Kaishek had flooded in 1938 after the Battle of Xuzhou.

From 1942, China was in the throes of a horrendous famine. 'About 20,000,000 are affected. More than a third are near death from hunger. Those remaining are subsisting on grass, roots, leaves, and bark', so *The New York Times* reported in October 1942.[21] It was after the main newspaper in Chong-qing reported on the famine in February 1943 that *Time* magazine reporter Theodore White travelled to Henan to investigate. On 22 March, *Time* published his angry report, which, although toned down on the insistence of the censors, laid the facts in front of the US public,[22] for whom the dustbowls of the 1930s were a fresh memory. To position large numbers of armed forces in Henan was madness. Claire Chennault wrote in his memoirs that General Tang Enbo's forces had 'decayed during four years of inactivity into a poorly disciplined mob, hated by the Chinese peasants whose food they confiscated'.[23] Unsurprisingly, they crumbled in the face of the Japanese tanks and aeroplanes and their well-equipped, hard-hitting infantry.

The Chinese economy had held up well until 1941. But then it imploded, as a result, to a degree, of adverse weather conditions, but also – and more import-antly – because the Nationalists continued to maintain a high level of military recruitment of about 1.5 million men per year. China had for centuries been a food-importing country. Following 1941, a strengthened Japanese embargo cut it off from what remained of the international grain markets. The Japanese also drove Nationalist currency from the areas they occupied, leading to an oversupply that accelerated an inflationary spiral whose fundamental origin lay in the Nationalists reliance on the printing press to finance their war.[24] And so, Ichigo made manifest the consequences of a decline that had begun much earlier. In other words, while China could absorb the Nationalists' strategy of attrition for a long time, it could not do so indefinitely, and by 1942 its limits had been reached.

It did not help that the Nationalists misjudged their intelligence informa-tion. Already in early February they knew that the Japanese had begun to repair a key bridge over the Yellow river and that Wang Jingwei government troops had begun to clear air fields along the Yangzi. The Nationalists assumed that the bridge would not be functional until late May. The Military Operations Ministry judged that Japanese moves in north China were a feint to distract attention from a much larger operation in the south.[25]

Ichigo's forces began to move on 17 April. By the end of the next day, they had destroyed a Nationalist defensive position fortified with tank traps, trenches and bunkers. Descending along the Beijing–Wuhan railway line they took Xuchang, an important rail and waterway junction, a week later. The key battle was for Loyang, where General Tang Enbo's headquarters were located. Prepared defences exploited the hills, cliffs and ravines of the area surrounding the city. Sufficient food and ammunition had been stored for a defence lasting several weeks. Chiang Kaishek's plan was to use Loyang to trap the Japanese. He intended to throw his reserves against the Japanese flanks once their forces tired and their supplies were running down.[26] That tactic had worked in the past, including during three successful operations to defeat Japanese attempts to take Changsha, the capital of Hunan province.

Not this time. On 14 May, the Japanese completed their encirclement of Loyang and, via the Buddhist monks of the famous White Horse Temple, asked General Tang to surrender. Chiang Kaishek refused to give his assent to such a surrender, insisting that Loyang could be defended for at least ten days. Before pushing home their advantage on 23 May, which just about gave Chiang Kaishek his wish, the Japanese made sure to block any escape routes so that they could 'destroy the forces of the First War Zone and then take Loyang'.[27] Japanese artillery pulverised the city walls and their tanks piled in. Two days later, all resistance had been overcome and the Japanese were in possession of the city.[28] Chen Kewen's reaction to the news that Loyang had fallen was to say that 'the situation in the War of Resistance will now become even worse and inevitably victory will be yet further postponed'.[29] Together with their forces from Wuhan, Japanese forces descending from the north cleared the Beijing–Wuhan railway, thus potentially giving their logistical capacity a major boost, and ensuring that later operations to the south of the Yangzi river could be conducted without any fear of an attack on their rear echelons.[30]

Following the fall of Loyang, the Japanese pursued General Tang Enbo into western Henan. For a while, it appeared as if the Japanese might be planning to break through the Tongguan Pass and enter Shaanxi province, important for its cotton and food production, and drive all the way to Xi'an. They could then have attacked General Hu Zongnan's forces blockading the Communists, while also threatening Sichuan from the north. Generals Hu Zongnan and Tang Enbo dug in east of the Tongguan Pass to stem the Japanese surge. But the Japanese did not break through the pass – probably not because they could not do so but because that was not the aim of Ichigo.[31] Destroying meaningful Nationalist resistance in the First War Zone was.

By the end of May, slightly more than a month after it had all begun, the first phase of Ichigo was over. Chiang Kaishek was furious, fuming in his diary that General Tang Enbo was 'courageous but unthinking' and had 'failed to concentrate single-mindedly on military affairs because he is preoccupied with smuggling'.[32] General Jiang Dingwen was an 'incompetent idiot'.[33] Chiang believed that Jiang had avoided battle and had been lying in his reports.[34] The reality was, as the Ministry of Operations acknowledged, that the quality of Nationalist forces had plummeted. This was not only because they were living off the land in a famine region. Chiang Kaishek insisted on having around 5 million men under arms, a level of mobilisation that was simply unsustainable.[35]

The Battle for Hunan Province (27 May–8 August)

Ichigo's next target was Changsha, 350 kilometres south of Wuhan, along the Xiang river and the Wuhan–Canton railway. The Yuelu Academy, located on hills that rise above the western shore of the Xiang, was one of the most famous in China, promoting a version of Confucianism that combined meditation and self-cultivation with a strong commitment to efficient and honest government in the public interest. Hunan province had produced more than its fair share of political, intellectual and military leaders – not just Mao Zedong, whose years in Changsha were formative, but also the leading reformers of the late nineteenth century and the Confucian generals who had led the fight against the Taiping Rebellion.[36]

Changsha had a rough war. Besides enduring the Great Changsha Fire of 1938, the city and its surrounding area had suffered the effects of three previous Japanese attempts to take it. General Xue Yue, commander-in-chief of the Ninth War Zone, defending, had adopted tactics that were as ruthless as they were effective. Each time, he cleared the countryside of anything that might be useful to the Japanese, conducted a fighting withdrawal until the Japanese were at Changsha, and then hit back. He adopted the same strategy this time.

At a meeting of the Military Affairs Council of 29 May, two days after 200,000 Japanese troops had begun to move south from Wuhan, the majority opinion was that Changsha could not be defended. General Bai Chongxi, the deputy chief of general staff, argued that the Nationalists should abandon the Wuhan–Canton railway and instead focus on protecting the city of Guilin in the north-east of Guangxi province, the home base of General Bai's Guangxi Clique. General Xu Yongchang, the head of the Military Operations Ministry, angrily tore into General Bai, arguing that abandoning US air bases in Hunan without a fight endangered China's relations with the USA, which had become strained, and that further retreat might trigger a total collapse.[37] Chiang Kaishek agreed.[38] The defence of Changsha was on.

This time, the Japanese advanced with three columns on a 150-kilometre-wide front, rather than with just a single column. They reached Changsha in ten days, with plentiful supplies,[39] and assaulted the city with two divisions, one of which was practised in street fighting. Changsha fell after just three days of fighting. Only three, woefully understrength Nationalist divisions defended Changsha, two of which were deployed in the city and one on the heights of Yuelu Mountain, where the artillery had been concentrated. Japanese bombers and artillery pounded Yuelu Mountain, while their infantry circled around the city to attack it from the south. The defence of Changsha, led by General Zhang Deneng, descended into chaos when General Zhang ordered re-enforcements to be brought up from the city to Yuelu Mountain. Nationalist staff officers were unable to organise the crossing of these units over the Xiang river, which lay between the city and the mountain. Many units were left stranded, thus becoming easy targets for the Japanese. Instructions had been unclear, with the result that many troops assumed that the order to retreat had been given. On 18 June, the Nationalists withdrew from Yuelu Mountain. Only two companies were left in the city for yet another of Chiang Kaishek's defences to the death.[40]

In contrast, the Battle of Hengyang lasted no less than forty-seven days, from 22 June to 8 August. Hengyang was a city 190 kilometres south of Changsha, on the Wuhan–Canton railway. A major US air base was located nearby, two tributaries of the Xiang river joined it there, and a railway ran from the city to Guangxi province. Hengyang was a key node in south China's transport network. Rivers to the east and north, hills to the south, and flooded paddy fields and canals to the west nullified Japanese armour. The 18,000 defenders, including a US-trained and armed regiment, were holed up in concrete fortifications. They were well armed with field and mountain artillery and anti-tank guns, and had ample supplies of food, salt and ammunition. Two large forces lay in reserve to pounce on the Japanese flanks, while a relief force from Guangdong province was also on its way. Afterwards the Japanese evaluated Hengyang's defences as the best they had encountered in China during the entire war.[41] Chiang Kaishek was optimistic: 'We will hold Hengyang.'[42]

After taking the US air base on 25 June, the Imperial Japanese Army's 68th and 116th Divisions assaulted the city from the south and the west. Losses on both sides were heavy, but the defenders held their lines. Because their supplies were running low, the Japanese temporarily stopped ground operations. However, they were able to resupply their forces at the front once they had brought in more air power to establish air superiority and, on 11 July, following five days of heavy fighting, a new Japanese offensive was able to drive the Nationalists back to a second defensive line. Once more, though, the Japanese advance stalled. Both Chiang Kaishek and General Bai Chongxi believed that they would now withdraw. General Bai Chongxi even prepared a victory parade.[43]

They were wrong. The Japanese prime minister, General Tojo Hideki, who had fired the starting gun on Nanshin, needed a victory to prevent the fall of his cabinet. He reinforced the Hengyang front with one full division and several brigades. While the Japanese air force continued to pummel Hengyang, ground forces away from the city attacked Nationalist reserves, hoping that their destruction would demoralise the defenders of Hengyang. By the end of July, thousands lay dead, disease was rampant in Hengyang and rations were running low.[44] The commander of the Hengyang defence forces, General Fang Xianjue, reported to Chiang Kaishek that 'most houses in Hengyang have been destroyed … our troops have nothing to eat'.[45]

On 3 August, five Japanese divisions, supported by 100 artillery pieces and Japanese air units, launched their third offensive. General Fang's messages were becoming desperate, but Chiang told him to hang on; a relief force was just days away.[46] On 7 August, the Japanese breached the northern city wall and by early the next morning they were in control of the city.[47] The Nationalists had hoped that Hengyang would be China's Stalingrad; it was not even China's Dunkirk.

After this moral-sapping defeat, Chiang ordered the publication of what was supposed to have been General Fang's final message to his leader: 'this will be my last telegram; we will meet again in the afterlife.'[48] In truth, Fang had surrendered.[49] The Japanese treated General Fang with courtesy, imprisoning him in a Catholic church outside Hengyang, but, unsurprisingly, lampooned his supposed last message in their propaganda. Unconvinced, Chiang ordered the compilation of a biographical sketch meant to illustrate his heroism. However, General Fang turned up alive and well in Chongqing at the end of the year. Some argued that he should be punished, but Chiang ruled that he had shown greater courage and determination than anyone else; he was treated to a hero's welcome and restored to his command.[50]

The loss of Hunan, known as the land of the hibiscus, denied the Nationalists a crucial source of resources. They failed in Hunan for many of the same reasons that they failed in Henan. But, in addition, they were distracted by Soviet bombing of Nationalist forces in Xinjiang and Outer Mongolia, 'the first step in asserting Soviet influence in East Asia', as General Chennault wrote to President Roosevelt.[51] There was also the fighting in Burma, which meant that the best Nationalist divisions were not where they were most needed. Japan's control of the air allowed them to resupply their forces and pound Nationalist positions.[52] Most units of General Chennault's 14th Air Force had been assigned to protect the air fields of 20th Bomber Command and assist General Stilwell in Burma.[53] According to Chennault, that and the denial to him of supplies such as kerosene, was the reason for his inability to support the Nationalist forces at Hengyang.

The Battle for Guangxi and Guizhou Provinces (August–December)

The Hengyang defeat caused demoralisation, panic, protest and paralysis among the Nationalists. As in the first two years of the war, the sad sight of columns of refugees retreating in front of advancing Japanese forces reappeared. In September, Chen Kewen worried about tens of thousands of refugees;[54] in early October he learned that no fewer than 300,000 were making their way to the rear along the railway line from Hunan to Guangxi.[55] Hundreds of thousands of others were fleeing elsewhere. Chen Kewen was present at deeply depressing meetings, which had been tasked to find ways of helping the refugees, but which concluded that they could do nothing.[56]

Not just refugees faced difficult conditions. One of Chen Kewen's responsibilities was to improve the welfare of civil servants. He attended a meeting where the desperate situation in Henan was discussed. 'Because of the crop failure last year, no grains could be issued to provincial civil servants, so they were issued money. However, doing so just this one time required 1.7 to 1.8 billion, roughly the same as half of the province's entire annual budget. But, Fabi [the Nationalist currency] cannot be exchanged for rice so how are they to get rice? The problem is impossible to solve.'[57] Not just Henan province was affected. *The Times* reported in February 1944 that 'since last summer 1,000,000 Chinese have died in the province of Kuangtung [Guangdong] in one of the worst famines in the history of China, according to Mr George Adams, acting chairman of the Kwangtung International Relief Committee'.[58] Chen concluded that 'the government has become marooned in a harbour without an outlet. The domestic, international and military situations are all hopeless. Inflation is especially bad. Nothing seems to work.' He personally was depending on dwindling financial reserves to make ends meet. He could treat his own children to just one watermelon per year.[59]

By this time, Chi Pang-yuan was a student at Wuhan University, which had relocated to Sichuan. One day its president called faculty members and students together at a Confucian temple. He announced that 'because the war is going badly and the Japanese might invade Sichuan, the Ministry of Education has ordered all universities to be ready to withdraw to a safe place in case it is needed'.[60] A chemistry professor, wearing a traditional scholar's gown, remarked, 'We have already passed through eight hard years without ever giving up ... not until the final day will the singer and instrument fall silent', a reference to a phrase in one of the Chinese classics meaning that education would continue come what may.[61] Chi Pang-yuan wrote to her parents, asking how she would find her way back to them if she indeed had to evacuate. Her father answered, '[O]ur fronts are overextended ... but in the Pacific and in Europe, the situation is improving. My child, you will be safe if you stay with your school; no matter what will happen with the war, in the years that remain to me, I will find you.' That last sentence left Chi Pang-yuan, she said, with 'a feeling of unease'.[62]

Storms of criticisms erupted out of universities and schools,[63] while foreign papers predicted a Nationalist collapse. *The New York Times* reported on 30 October that 'the political fabric of China, never very strong, has been ripping; schisms have occurred between various local leaders; "war-lordism" has increased.'[64] US military personnel were evacuated from the city of Guilin and 550 barrels of gasoline there were set on fire to prevent them from falling into Japanese hands.[65] The US consulate in Guilin advised US citizens in south-west China to leave because 'the Japanese are believed to have the strongest concentration of troops ever gathered in China'.[66]

Ichigo's advance into Guangxi province went virtually unopposed. An attempt to stop the Japanese at prepared positions at the border failed miserably, with the execution, on Chiang Kaishek's orders, of the commanding general doing little to improve military morale.[67] Although Chiang Kaishek ordered that Guilin and Liuzhou be defended, General Bai believed that this would be futile. By this time, Chiang Kaishek's orders were implemented only to the extent that the leaders of the Guangxi Clique approved of them. Guilin and Liuzhou were abandoned,[68] but not before the usual scorched earth policy was implemented.

Once in possession of the main cities of Guangxi province, the Japanese struck north-west into Guizhou province, thus threatening to break into Sichuan itself. General Albert Wedemeyer replaced General Stilwell as Chiang Kaishek's chief of staff on 27 October. He judged that 'the Japanese were in a position not only to open their inland corridor to the south, but also to drive west, capturing the key cities of Kun-ming, Chung-ch'ing, and Hsi-an [Kunming, Chongqing, and Xi'an]. Inflation was rampant, economic collapse seemed close, and public confidence in the Generalissimo was at a low ebb.'[69] He was appalled that 'Chinese soldiers were starving in their hundreds' but high-ranking Nationalists were 'asking to facilitate their evacuation to America'.[70] He counselled Chiang to prepare to evacuate Chongqing and concentrate on defending Kunming, the terminus of the supply line from India.[71] Chiang told him that he could not accept that advice. Time and again he had insisted that Chinese cities should be defended to the death and the generals who failed to do so would be executed; he could not now just walk away from Chongqing and hope that his already-tarnished reputation would survive. Wedemeyer responded by stating that he would stay at Chiang Kaishek's side come what may.[72]

To prevent the Japanese from breaking into Sichuan, General Wedemeyer moved two Nationalists divisions from Burma to Guizhou. Together with Nationalist forces brought in from other war zones, including several divisions led by General Tang Enbo, they formed a block in Ichigo's path. On 18 December, on Wedemeyer's request,[73] 20th Bomber Command firebombed Wuhan, Japan's command and logistics centre in China, flattening the city. While the Japanese commander in charge of Ichigo, General Okamura Yasuji, continued to favour an attack on Chongqing,[74] the Imperial General Staff decided against this, perhaps because of the bombing or perhaps because by this time the US was firmly in control of the Mariana Islands and had begun bombing Japan from there. The Imperial General Staff decreed a new strategy, instructing Japanese forces in China to redeploy along the Yangzi river and near Shanghai.

Ichigo was finally over.

The Stilwell affair

The Stilwell Affair – that is, the recall of General Stilwell from China in October 1944 – formed a cathartic episode in the USA's relationship with the Nationalists, one that would have a long afterlife. When Senator Joseph McCarthy began to hunt for Communists in the US State Department in 1950, his targets included some people who had served in China, many of whom had been involved with Stilwell. In the 1960s and 1970s, the opponents of McCarthyism used Stilwell – a Republican – to demonstrate that the criticism of these State Department officials made by the Nationalists at the time had been correct and that, had they been listened to, the USA would not have ended up supporting a moribund militarist regime. Because of the politically charged nature of the debate, and the sharp divisions it created in the USA, it became difficult even in US academic circles to discuss the Nationalists during the Second World War other than from a perspective determined by the Stilwell Affair.[75] Criticising Stilwell became an academic taboo.

The Stilwell Affair gained an enduring significance in part because of its post-war role in the USA. At the time, Stilwell's recall marked the moment when China changed from being the USA's favourite ally to a constant source of problems, worry and disappointment. It did not help that General Stilwell was a difficult man. With the exception of General Marshall, he held everybody in contempt, not just Chiang Kaishek ('the Peanut') or the Nationalist commander-in-chief He Yingqin ('graced by no distinction in combat command'),[76] but also, on the British side, General Archibald Wavell ('a tired, depressed man pretty well beaten down');[77] General Alexander ('astonished to find ME – mere me, a goddam American – in command of Chinese troops. Extrawdinery! Looked me over as if I had just crawled from under a rock');[78] and Mountbatten (one of the 'Kandy Kids', that is, someone enjoying life at the splendorous headquarters of South East Asia Command at Kandy on Sri Lanka).[79] His fellow Americans fared no better. Stilwell could not stand General Chennault, of course, but he had as little regard for his successor,

General Wedemeyer: 'Good God – to be ousted in favour of Wedemeyer – that would be a disgrace.'[80]

Throughout his time in China, General Stilwell clung to his view that Upper Burma had to be recovered so that an overland supply line could be laid between Assam in India and Yunnan in China. He was determined to show that his view was correct, and that, perforce, Chiang Kaishek and Chennault were wrong. Once X Force, the two Chinese divisions Stilwell had trained at Ramgarh, had begun to move into northern Burma in December 1943, he was at the front with them, rather than at his headquarters in Chongqing, giving rise to the jibe that General Stilwell was 'the best three star company commander in the US Army'.[81] Out of the strategic loop, Stilwell was largely ignorant of how Ichigo was unfolding in China.

Defeat may be an orphan, but misfortune always has company. At the same time that the Japanese forces were besieging Hengyang, Stilwell's X Force was advancing through northern Burma before it became stuck at Myitkyina, in the centre of Upper Burma, unable to force its way into the city for three months. Before the Burma campaign began, the Nationalists had agreed to the deployment of Y Force, armed and trained by the US in Yunnan, for the Burma campaign, but only on condition that the US would make ground forces available and that the British would supply naval support.[82] Neither had done so. Because of this and because of Ichigo, but also in order to put pressure on Washington to increase supplies to China, Chiang Kaishek declined to order Y Force to advance. Needing to relieve the pressure on X Force, Stilwell asked Washington to put pressure on Chiang Kaishek, who reversed his position after Roosevelt warned that US aid might be withdrawn if Y Force did not move.[83] The first units began to advance in May, but they advanced very slowly.[84]

Faced with a deteriorating situation in China and a stalled offensive in Burma, General Marshall then conceived the idea of putting Stilwell in charge of Chinese forces not just in Burma but in the whole of China. Confronted by the possibility of a Nationalist collapse and fearful that the Japanese might continue the war from China even if Japan itself was occupied,[85] the appointment of Stilwell as commander of all forces in China opened the door to arming the Communists, whose help would be needed if the USA were to successfully land troops on the north China coast. In July 1944, a US Army Observation Group – the 'Dixie Mission' – arrived in Yan'an to scout out possibilities.[86] Besides military officers, journalists and State Department officials formed part of the group. They filed enthusiastic reports about what they found, contrasting the corruption and despondency of Chongqing with a well-ordered, clean and confident Yan'an, where 'morale is very high'.[87] In December 1944, after Stilwell had been dismissed but before this policy had been abandoned, *The New York Times* asserted that Communist forces had 'contained a large part of the Japanese army and have to a great extent prevented the Japanese from exploiting the agricultural resources of the occupied areas'.[88] But the Communists lacked weapons. 'All that is required to change the whole system in North and Central China is a reasonable supply of small arms ammunition and some easily portable weapons capable of breaching Japanese forts.'[89]

On 6 July, President Roosevelt wrote to Chiang Kaishek for the first time to suggest that he hand over command of his forces to General Stilwell.[90] Chiang Kaishek was shocked, because of the implied insult, because he had no faith in General Stilwell, because it implicitly reduced China's status to that of a US colony, and because he did not want US military supplies to reach the Communists. Chiang's response was that he agreed in principle, but insisted that authority over the distribution of US supplies be assigned to China.[91]

Messages went back and forth until 16 September, when Roosevelt sent Chiang a telegram, drafted by General Marshall, which could not have been blunter:

> I have urged time and again in recent months that you take drastic action to resist the disaster which has been moving closer to China and to you … I am certain that the only thing you can now do to prevent the Jap from achieving his objectives in China is to reinforce your Salween armies immediately and press their offensive, while at once placing General Stilwell in unrestricted command of all your forces.[92]

Stilwell also received this message, presumably because it was sent by Marshall, and rushed to Chiang Kaishek's residence. He declined an offer by Ambassador Gauss, who was there, too, to convey the message verbally so as to soften its tone. The general insisted on handing it to Chiang personally. As he wrote in his diary, he 'handed this bundle of paprika to the Peanut and then sank back with a sigh. The harpoon hit the little bugger right in the solar plexus.'[93] He composed a little piece of victory doggerel afterwards, the first stanza of which read:

> I've waited long for vengeance
> At last I've had my chance
> I've looked the Peanut in the eye
> And kicked him in the pants.[94]

In an aide memoire to Roosevelt of 9 October, Chiang recounted that he had consistently disagreed with Stilwell about the significance of the Burma campaign, that at Cairo the USA had made promises it had failed to live up to, and that he had agreed to deploy Y Force units into Burma only after General

Stilwell had threatened to withhold US supplies. He then stated that while in China the Nationalists had faced Japanese forces six times larger than those faced by the Allies in Burma, operations there 'had drained off most of the properly trained and equipped reserves in China'. The only aid the Nationalists had received, he said, were '60 mountain guns, 320 anti-aircraft guns, and 506 Bazookas'. Chiang concluded by noting that 'we have taken Myitkyina but lost all of East China'.[95] Having said his piece, he agreed to place Nationalist forces under US command, on the one condition that the US commander was anyone but Stilwell.

Marshall urged President Roosevelt to insist on Stilwell, but Roosevelt changed tack. The year 1944 was an election year, with the conduct of the war inevitably an important issue and the polls suggesting a 'photo finish' between Roosevelt and the Republican nominee, Thomas Dewey. Gallup predicted a 'very close race' and highlighted several factors favourable to Dewey.[96] In October, support for Roosevelt slipped. For the USA to be held accountable for the crisis in China would have been a boon to Dewey's campaign.

Much better to have Chiang Kaishek take the blame. President Roosevelt decided, as he told Chiang, that 'the US Government should not assume the responsibility in placing an American officer in command of your ground forces'.[97] If China did fall, it would be with Chiang Kaishek as commander-in-chief, not with an American in charge. As Ambassador Hurley was to tell President Harry S. Truman, Roosevelt 'definitely refused to appoint an American commander when the situation in China appeared to be approaching collapse'. Roosevelt warned Chiang that 'a full and open explanation of the reasons for General Stilwell's recall will have to be made. The American people will be shocked and confused by this action.[98] I regret the inevitable harm it will do to the sympathetic attitude of the American people toward China.'[99] Until Stilwell's recall, the US press, which was censored during the war, had reported the disaster unfolding in China only vaguely. Roosevelt made sure this was about to change.

The president personally approved the publication of a report on the front page of *The New York Times* on Tuesday 31 October, a week before the elections. This declared that General Stilwell's recall was due to the 'political triumph of a moribund anti-democratic regime', which was not committed to fighting the Japanese, had become 'increasingly unpopular and distrusted in China, that maintains three secret police services and concentration camps for political prisoners, that stifles free speech and resists democratic forces' and which was led by a man 'bewildered and alarmed by the rapidity with which China is falling apart'.[100] The article justified the decision not to appoint a new US chief of staff to Chiang because it would have 'the effect of making us acquiesce in an unenlightened cold-hearted autocratic regime'.[101] Roosevelt was re-elected, although not, of course, simply because of this exercise in the use of the political dark arts – even if this election was, as he himself acknowledged, 'the dirtiest in history'.[102] He had not wanted to take the risk.

Although personality clashes, politics and racial prejudice all played their roles in the Stilwell Affair, the most important drivers were, firstly, a shortage of resources and, secondly, China's minimal value to US and UK conceptions of how to win the war. America's industrial productivity was phenomenal, but it was not unlimited and hence choices had to be made. The US and the UK reneged on promises to Chiang Kaishek because they judged that their resources could be deployed more usefully elsewhere. The conflicts between Stilwell, Chennault and Chiang Kaishek were at bottom the struggle for control over US supplies to China. Because China was not considered strategically important, until the last year of the war it was not provided with adequate supplies, meaning that the fight for what was available was intense. This prevented the solution Roosevelt used elsewhere with commanders who were at loggerheads with each other, namely to give all of them all they said they needed.

This way of solving difficulties, only possible because of the USA's abundant productive capacity, buried a problem that in the Korean War would come to haunt America. Its overseas commanders were able to pursue their own strategy without sufficient oversight and control from Washington. The Joint Chiefs of Staff did not maintain an effective balance between giving full play to personal initiatives on the ground and exercising effective oversight over what was going on. That was less a personal than an institutional issue, resulting from the fact that the USA was only in the process of becoming a world power.

The USA's Withdrawal from China's War with Japan

When General Wedemeyer arrived in China in November 1944, he was told that 'your primary mission as to US combat forces is to carry out air operations from China. In addition, you will continue to assist the Chinese air and ground forces in operations, training, and logistical support.'[103] The priority remained to support Operation Matterhorn, Marshall's strategic bombing offensive on Japan from China by 20th Bomber Command. The Combined Chiefs of Staff of the US and the UK had already decided in August that supporting such an offensive on Japan from China by ferrying supplies from India to China would be impossible. Once the Marianas had been secured, defending and supplying air bases there would be far easier. However, in September Roosevelt ordered that Operation Matterhorn proceed because he wanted to give the Chinese war effort a boost and because he wanted the bombing of Japan to begin as early as possible. The Marianas campaign did not end until 27 November.

Resource constraints meant that other operations in China had to make do with either less or nothing at all. In May 1944 Marshall made clear to Stilwell that he should abandon his notion of fighting Japan in China, telling him that 'Japan should be defeated without undertaking a major campaign against her on the mainland of Asia.'[104] This meant, Marshall insisted, 'that priority be given during the next several months to a build-up of our air effort in China' – Matterhorn. Marshall ordained that 200 of the 500 aircraft of General Chennault's 14th Air Force be used to defend the Chengdu air fields and 150 to assist Stilwell in Burma, leaving only another 150 to support Nationalist ground forces.[105] At the time of the Battle of Hengyang, Stilwell had declined an appeal by Chiang Kaishek to allocate supplies destined for the Superfortresses to General Chennault's 14th Air Force – a decision in which personal animosities no doubt played a role, but which also conformed to the USA's overall military strategy in China.

Twentieth Bomber Command, led by General Curtis LeMay, initiated operations in June 1944, flying raids over Singapore, Rangoon, Hanoi, Taiwan, Manchuria and Kyushu, the most south-westerly of Japan's main islands, largely from bases in China and India.[106] This experimental phase in 20th Bomber Command's operations came to an end on 15 December. 'As a result of six months of pioneering by 20th Bomber Command, Superfortresses here and in the Pacific can now get down to a steady, efficient smashing of Japan's war potential,' its headquarters announced that day.[107] Three days later, on 18 December, ninety-six Superfortress bombers took off from the Chengdu air fields on their first large-scale strategic bombing raid. Their target was not some city in Japan but, as mentioned, Wuhan. Five hundred tons of bombs, filled with a new incendiary made of phosphorus and napalm invented by Harvard scientists, were dropped on the city,[108] causing a firestorm which lasted several days and left tens of thousands of people dead.[109] Following the raid, General Robert McLure, now the US Army's chief of staff in China, 'served notice on the Japanese that the concentrated bombing of Hankow [Wuhan] on December 18 was only the beginning of such heavy air strikes against their installations in China'.[110] US censorship ensured that, while the actions of the Superfortresses were celebrated in heroic terms, few details of their consequences on the ground reached the American public. After the war, Curtis LeMay, who had personally commanded the raid on Wuhan, was frank: 'enemy cities were pulverized or fried to a crisp.'[111]

The bombing of Japanese cities began in earnest after the raid on Wuhan, using the same technique that had been 'perfected' in China. However, the Combined Chiefs of Staff had been right. Even after the Allies had secured north Burma, built a road and laid an oil pipeline, not enough supplies were getting through to China. The first barrels of fuel reached China, via what became known as the Stilwell Road, only in May 1945. Mud slides and flooding regularly forced its closure.[112] The whole plan of staging a strategic bombing campaign against Japan in China had been built on quicksand. After the destruction of Wuhan, the Superfortresses were withdrawn from China and the air raids on Japan were conducted from air fields in the Marianas.

For the Americans, China lost all remaining military value. But they could not simply walk away. Besides assisting in Operation Matterhorn, Wedemeyer's orders had called for him to make sure that the USA stayed out of 'civil strife, unless to protect lives' and prevent a complete Nationalist collapse. In order to stabilise the situation, Wedemeyer did what he could to prevent Ichigo from reaching Sichuan. He then reorganised his headquarters, improved the living standards of Nationalist soldiers and, once the Japanese forces engaged in Ichigo had begun to withdraw, started to plan a counter-offensive by Chinese forces in China.

This was Operation Carbonado. With the amount of materiel reaching China expected to increase to 100,000 tons monthly, Wedemeyer began 'the training of an army of 36 divisions and 20 commando groups with US liaison, supervision, training, and equipment'.[113] Chennault's 14th Air Force, together with the 10th Air Force, which was scheduled to redeploy from India to China in July 1945, were to establish control of the skies. Carbonado's forces were to strike towards a port on the south China coast to give 'the Generalissimo the opportunity, in time and resources, to create Chinese land forces that can and will carry the burden of at least a proportionate share of the fighting'. A not entirely secondary aim was 'to strengthen the American position at the peace table' by excluding the European powers from China.[114]

After Wedemeyer had been in China for several months, his views about the Nationalists, and in particular Chiang Kaishek, changed. He wrote to Marshall in April 1945 that 'one finds an embryonic nation, a great political entity about to be born. Previously China consisted of a group of feudal dynasties which through the years resorted forcibly or voluntarily to political amalgamation', but true unity was now emerging. 'China at war does not mean large scale modern warfare, but means a stoic amorphous resistance', which nonetheless was holding out. As to Chiang Kaishek, he 'has refused attractive surrender terms on several occasions. This, I think, has been most fortunate for us.'[115]

Some of Wedemeyer's reports about the situation under Stilwell must have set cheeks blushing in Washington. He told the celebrated strategist Stanley Embick that 'my predecessor had neither the character nor the ability to be a good regimental commander ... he spent so much time in the jungles of Upper Burma commanding a few battalions and acquiring a great deal of publicity so that he neglected sorely the responsibilities inherent in his position.'[116] One of Wedemeyer's first acts was to recommend that Frank Dorn, Stilwell's Number Two who had been in charge of Y Force, was not just recalled but demoted, a recommendation that in the end was not accepted. He described Dorn in an efficiency report as of 'questionable loyalty, uncooperative, extremely selfish, of immature judgment, and not dependable'.[117]

If the US press carried numerous reports about Nationalist smuggling, it kept quiet about American involvement in it. Wedemeyer worked hard to force through the publication of an article in *Roundup*, a weekly magazine for US armed forces in China, Burma and India, which revealed that the Criminal Investigation Department of the US Army had uncovered a 'smuggling ring that has been operating over the Hump [the air route from India to China], taking an estimated sum of more that US$ 4 million'. The article went on to explain that 'the list of items smuggled across the towering Hump and disposed of in China reads like an export index. There were arms, ammunition, clothing, military supplies and equipment, drugs, foreign currency, gems, and sundry PX supplies [military gear].' One US Air Force pilot had parachuted from his plane with $10,000 in gold bars, never to be seen again. Eighty-seven major cases were brought before military tribunals and a number of offenders ended up serving stiff sentences at the US Army prison at Fort Leavenworth.[118]

Carbonado's units went into action to defend the Zhijiang air base in Hunan province in April 1945. Despite their success, Wedemeyer decided not to press home the advantage the Nationalist forces had gained because 'we did not believe that a counter-offensive would be wise. Supply remained critical ... in place of an attack, we began building ground and air force stockpiles to give adequate logistical support to a successful offensive ... to Fort Bayard [Beihai].'[119] Japan surrendered before Carbonado could be implemented. US naval aircraft on their way to Fort Bayard, on the Liuzhou peninsula in south Guangxi province, were diverted to Shanghai when the news broke of the end of the war.[120]

Following Japan's surrender, US policy became to 'bring the boys home' with all possible speed. Wedemeyer reported to Chiang Kaishek that President Harry S. Truman, who had succeeded Roosevelt after the latter's sudden death on 12 April 1945, 'emphasized that US forces in the China Theater must be inactivated as early as possible'. Secretary of State James Byrnes stressed that 'Americans must not be employed to facilitate Central Government operations against dissident groups'.[121] On 16 August, the day after Japan's surrender, Wedemeyer removed 'liaison personnel from Chinese units' so that 'US forces will not, rpt [repeat] not, become engaged in fratricidal war'.[122] General Marshall ordered the occupation of ports like Shanghai so that Japanese troops in China could be concentrated there and repatriated 'in an orderly fashion' in the shortest possible time.[123] Once the repatriation was complete, with all Japanese forces disarmed and securely back in Japan under US supervision, thus precluding any possibility of a revival of Japanese militarism in China, the USA would be free to leave the competing parties in China to fight it out.

The Communist Response

The greatest beneficiaries of Operation Ichigo were the Communists. The Japanese concentrated 80 per cent of their forces in Ichigo, that is, 500,000 out of 650,000 troops outside Manchuria, leaving just 150,000 to garrison the rest of the country – an impossibility. The Japanese therefore had to turn to puppet armies, local militia and the police to maintain their positions.[124] Ichigo also brought an end to the ferocious campaign of suppression by Japanese troops against the Communists, popularly referred to as the 'Three All' – burn all, kill all, loot all – campaign. Ichigo also removed any danger of a Nationalist attack on Communist areas. In 1943, General Hu Zongnan in Xi'an had prepared a Blitzkrieg on Yan'an, which was called off only after a Communist sleeper agent on his staff alerted Yan'an.[125] The Communists began a propaganda blitz which convinced the Nationalists that proceeding would cause too much damage to their reputation. In history, sometimes things that are not done are just as important as things that are done. Soon after the Nationalists bottled out of this opportunity to strike a blow against the Communists, Ichigo allowed the Communists to stage a break-out from the areas to which the Japanese and the Nationalists had confined them.

Following their first rush of expansion at the beginning of the war, neither the Communist Party nor the Communist armed forces had expanded. Mao insisted that no area of the organisation should expand beyond that which its population could sustain. Recruitment into the army was made merely to replace casualties. In the summer of 1944, as Japanese forces plunged into Hunan, the Communists abandoned this policy. Over the next year, the Chinese Communist Party and the Eighth Route Army and New Fourth Army all doubled in size, the Party to 1.2 million members and its armed forces to 1 million troops.[126]

As before, Mao Zedong was relatively cautious. He believed that Communist forces should focus on attacking, or winning over, puppet forces, militias and bandit gangs. He did not want to trigger civil war at this point, and nor did he want to take on the superior Japanese forces. However, he did agree to Communist forces being deployed in strategic locations in the south. His thinking was that 'those who arrive first will be rulers, those who come later will be subordinates'.[127] In August 1944, after Hengyang had fallen, one Eighth Route Army brigade, consisting of 3,000 soldiers and 750 Communist officials, marched to Hubei and crossed the Yangzi river into Hunan province. They collaborated with local Communists army units and Party members in Hunan, Hubei and Henan to 'build a dike' between areas controlled by the Nationalists in south-west China and China's seaboard provinces, in order to make it hard for the Nationalists to return to their heartland after the fall of Japan. Ren Bishi, a member of the three-man Central Committee Secretariat, told these forces to be ready to 'occupy Wuhan and Changsha'.[128]

In the autumn, the New Fourth Army, which had grown to 300,000 troops, established an operational base in the lower Yangzi region between Shanghai, Ningbo, Wusong and Nanjing. Its forces stood poised 'to seize Hangzhou, Shanghai, Suzhou, and Nanjing'.[129] A 'Jiangsu–Zhejiang Military Region' was established in January 1945 to ensure that the Communists would 'be able to destroy the enemy, take over Nanjing, enter Shanghai, and cooperate with an Allied landing so that we will be in a strategically advantageous position at the time of Japan's collapse'.[130] The Eighth Route Army and New Fourth Army deployments were designed to leave the Communists in as advantageous a position as possible as it became clear that US forces advancing through the Pacific meant the Japanese were doomed, while the Nationalists were near breaking point.

The change in the military balance of power had serious political repercussions; it allowed the Communists to mount a political offensive. The United Front had virtually ceased to function after the New Fourth Army Incident, but, facing Japanese attacks and an increasingly serious economic situation, in January 1944 Mao Zedong asked the Nationalist liaison office in Yan'an to relay to Chiang Kaishek a proposal to resume negotiations, to be conducted in Chongqing. Chiang Kaishek agreed, instructing his negotiators 'to be accommodating with respect to political issues, but to be strict with regard to military ones'.[131] He believed that an opportunity existed for the genuine integration of Communist forces into the Nationalist order of battle and for Communist acceptance of Nationalist military command authority. If the price was having to allow the Communists a high level of autonomy locally, then that was a price worth paying.

A first meeting between Zhang Zhizhong and Wang Shijie, the Nationalist negotiators, and Lin Boqu, the Communist negotiator, took place in Xi'an rather than Chongqing. The Communists demanded approval of an increased size of their armed forces, and hence in funding, in return for agreeing to incorporate Yan'an in the Nationalist administrative system, the withdrawal of Communist forces after the defeat of Japan to north of the Yellow river, and permission for KMT party organisations to operate in Communist base areas.[132]

The Communists raised their demands as Ichigo's forces drove the Nationalists back. Already by the second half of May, after Henan's villagers had turned their hoes – they did not have pitchforks – against the Nationalist forces, Communist demands had undergone a metamorphosis. They called for: 1) the implementation of democracy and freedom of speech, publication and assembly; 2) the legal recognition of the CCP and all other patriotic parties; 3) the implementation of local self-rule; 4) the recognition of Communist base areas in eastern and northern China; and 5) a substantial expansion of Communist armies. Not the least significant of the CCP's negotiating stances was that it was now working on behalf of other political groups, not just itself.[133]

The Communists further stepped up their demands after the Nationalists lost Hunan province. After the fall of Hengyang, the Nationalists offered 'the beginning of constitutional government within one year after Japan's surrender, with all parties enjoying a position of equality'.[134] In September, the Communists announced that they wanted the immediate convocation of a joint government: 'we hope that the KMT immediately ends one party government and that the National Government calls a meeting of representatives of all anti-Japanese political parties, factions, armed forces, local governments, and civil organizations to organize an anti-Japanese joint government.'[135] The Communists were asserting their political equivalence with the Nationalists while also suggesting that the political failures of the Nationalists had contributed to the disastrous turn that the war had taken. It was probably not coincidental that the USA was expressing similar arguments and demanding similar changes at this time.

On 10 October, the thirty-third anniversary of the 1911 Revolution, Zhou Enlai published an article in *Liberation Daily* just as Ichigo was beginning to threaten Sichuan. In this article he repeated his demand that the Nationalists should agree to a joint government immediately, and added that said government should have authority over military affairs.[136] The Communists knew full well that Chiang would never agree to the latter. The article was simply a provocation, intended to make the Nationalists appear like a reactionary dictatorship trying to cling on to power rather than doing what was best for China. Again not uncoincidentally, US journalists were writing in the same vein at the same time.

Subverting Chiang Kaishek's *China's Destiny* was part of the strategy of the Communists. In 1944 Guo Moruo, the historian, archaeologist and writer who had rushed to Wuhan in 1938 having lived in Japan for a decade, published 'In Commemoration of the 300th Anniversary of 1644'. Guo Moruo was a Communist Party member, famous for romantic poems such as 'The Goddess', although also the subject of controversy, including for being excessively subservient to China's political masters after 1949. Guo lived in Chongqing during the war. Sichuan was his home province.

The year 1644 was, as Guo's readers would have known, the year in which the Ming Dynasty fell to a peasant rebellion led by Li Zicheng. Li Zicheng assumed the title of 'The Charging King', but he would hold Beijing only for a few weeks. The combined forces of the Ming General Wu Sangui and the Manchus defeated him at the Shanhaiguan Pass, the gateway into China from Manchuria. Having fled Beijing, Li died the next year at the hands of the pursuing Manchu forces.

To criticise the present through historical analogy is a common device in Chinese historical and political argument. No one would have missed that Guo Moruo meant to compare 1644 with 1944, with the last Chongzhen Emperor of the Ming Dynasty standing for Chiang Kaishek, Li Zicheng for Mao Zedong, Wu Sangui for Wang Jingwei and the Manchus for the Japanese. The thrust of Guo's argument was that Chiang Kaishek's Nationalists were doomed and that Mao would rise to power on the back of the peasant rebellion he had led in north China. Any doubts anyone might have had about Guo's intentions would have been dispelled by the fact that, while the first instalment of his article was published on the anniversary of the day that the Ming Emperor had committed suicide in Beijing, Guo had finished the manuscript on 10 March, as he noted at the end of the article. That date coincided with the first anniversary of the publication of Chiang Kaishek's *China's Destiny*. This was altogether too much of a coincidence.

Guo Moruo's '1644' challenged the version of China's history which Chiang had articulated in *China's Destiny*. No, Chiang Kaishek was not China's saviour, he was the Chongzhen Emperor. Upon ascending to the throne, the Chongzhen Emperor had acted with skill and decisiveness in removing corrupt officials, Guo wrote, but he had then become rather erratic, spraying contradictory edicts around and causing endless confusion and injustice. The Chongzhen Emperor had been personally frugal, and he had issued edicts in which he declared his concern for his subjects, humbly blaming himself for the hardships they suffered, as all virtuous rulers should. The Chongzhen Emperor had berated his officials, but he had failed to act on advice to force wealthy landowners and merchants to open up their grain stores to relieve famine, instead accepting the case that civil order would break down if the starving were allowed to take what they needed. The Chongzhen Emperor had said the right things, but he had not acted upon them, and when his treasuries were opened after his death, huge amounts of wealth were discovered – wealth that could have been used to alleviate the suffering of the rural poor.[137]

Guo Moruo did not elaborate on the parallels between the Chongzhen Emperor and Chiang Kaishek, but he did not need to. Chiang too had acted with decisiveness after he rose to power. But, like the Chongzhen Emperor, he had developed a habit of constantly castigating his officials, he too had sprayed personal orders around, ignored established military and civilian hierarchies, failed to relieve the suffering in the countryside, even sending his armies there to keep order. Guo's '1644' amounted to a stinging denunciation of Chiang Kaishek.

The piece caused a storm. The day after the final instalment appeared, Tao Xisheng, the editor of the Nationalists' *Central Daily News* and widely thought to have ghostwritten *China's Destiny*, attacked Guo. He argued that Li's peasant rebellion, based in north China, had succeeded in overthrowing the Ming Dynasty, but that it had been conducted 'at a time of extreme foreign threat', resulting in China being 'ruled by an alien dynasty for 260 years'.[138] The debate about '1644' carried on for months. In Yan'an, Mao ordered Guo's piece to be read by all Party members.[139] In subsequent months he regularly criticised the Nationalists and held up the Communists as a competent, fair and democratic alternative. As a political attack piece, '1644' did its job brilliantly. It undermined Chiang's *China's Destiny* with great effectiveness.

Nationalist fortunes reached their greatest height during 1943. China was recognised as one of the Big Four, the Wang Jingwei government was no longer a significant concern, serious negotiations with the Communists were taking place, front lines were holding, and Japan and Germany were on the defensive. The year 1944 was the stark opposite. The pressures that had been building since 1941 not only cracked a façade of stubborn resistance, but came close to engulfing the Nationalists. Operation Ichigo threw their forces out of most of the areas they had controlled since the Battle of Wuhan in 1938, the United States turned sour on them, party morale collapsed, and the Communists spread out across much of the country north of the Yangzi river.

In Chongqing, Chiang Kaishek cut a beleaguered figure. He continued to pray, read the Bible and study Confucian works such as Huang Zongxi's *Ming Confucianism*, a seventeenth-century work which traced the development of Neo-Confucianism in the Ming Dynasty.[140] The Taiwan historian Ch'en Yung-fa is no doubt correct in his suggestion that Chiang clung to the idea that a ruler draws support as much through his virtue as through his political and military strength. But that stance now only added to Chiang's vulnerability. He had been haranguing his commanders and officials from the first day of the War of Resistance. After eight years, such diatribes, besides annoying his audience, could only serve to underscore his failures. Both the famine in Henan and the millions of refugees who had taken to the road undermined Chiang Kaishek's attempt to project himself as a Confucian general in the mould of Zeng Guofan, the famously meditative suppressor of the Taiping Rebellion. Guo Moruo's '1644' had been precisely targeted to undercut that image.

By the spring of 1945, the situation had begun to stabilise. The Japanese were retreating and General Wedemeyer was assisting the Nationalists in building up a new army with thirty-six divisions – although the Japanese would surrender before that rebuilding programme could be completed. The question was whether it would be the Communists or the Nationalists who would make best use of Japan's demise.

ELEVEN

JAPAN'S SURRENDER
IN CHINA

What do we mean by the defeat of the enemy? Simply the destruction of his forces, whether by death, injury, or any other means.

Carl von Clausewitz, *On War* (1832)[1]

After the battle, many new ghosts cry,
The solitary old man worries and grieves.
Ragged clouds are low amid the dusk,
Snow dances quickly in the whirling wind.
The ladle's cast aside, the cup not green,
The stove still looks as if a fiery red.
To many places, communications are broken,
I sit, but cannot read my books for grief.

Du Fu, *Facing Snow* (755–7)[2]

At the stroke of 9 a.m. on 9 September 1945, the slightly stooped figure of the commander-in-chief of Japan's forces in China, General Okamura Yasuji, walked into the auditorium of the Central Military Academy on Huangpu Road in Nanjing. The building had served as the Japanese military headquarters in China during the Second World War and only the previous week had been rechristened as China's supreme headquarters. General Okamura's purpose on this bright and sunny day was to surrender Japan's forces in China to General He Yingqin, commander-in-chief of the Nationalist forces.

When the bespectacled General Okamura entered the auditorium, he and his colleagues removed their swords at its entrance and left them there. General Douglas MacArthur, Supreme Allied Commander in Japan, had ordained that no Japanese should be allowed to wear his sword again after the formal surrender ceremony.[3] By being allowed to take off their swords in the entrance hall, Japan's most senior officers were spared the embarrassment of having to do so in public, a delicate gesture that had the practical advantage of avoiding the horror of General Okamura, or any other Japanese representative, committing *seppuku* – ritual suicide by plunging a sword into one's stomach – after the completion of the ceremony. Accompanying General Okamura were the senior military representatives of Japanese forces in Formosa, Japan's China Fleet, the Japanese Imperial Headquarters, and Japan's 38th Army in French Indochina. Thus, all areas over which China was to assume control as per the Allied decision (which included French Indochina north of the 18th parallel) were represented.

The Japanese delegation was led single file to a small rectangular table. General He Yingqing and other senior Chinese officers were already in place, sitting behind a larger rectangular table on a raised platform. The hundred or so Allied dignitaries, including US, British, Canadian and Dutch military and civil representatives, were also already in their seats, separated from the main actors in the ceremony by a low wooden fence. As the flashlights of the press photographers went off, General Okamura and his colleagues bowed to General He Yingqin and sat down.

General He Yingqin ordered General Okamura to present his credentials; these were handed over by the Japanese chief of staff, General Saburo Kobayashi. General He looked at them briefly before putting them to his side.[4] He then handed General Saburo two copies of the surrender document. General Saburo presented these to General Okamura, who stood up and received them into both hands with arms outstretched, as courtesy required. He sat down, signed them, drew a round seal from his pocket, imprinted it on the document and then nodded his head just once, as if to underscore the finality of the moment. General Saburo took the documents to General He, also courteously presenting them in both hands with outstretched arms. General He Yingqin received them in the same way, signed them in turn, and then had one copy passed back to General Okamura.

The final act was for General Okamura to be presented with Order Number 1 by Chiang Kaishek in the latter's capacity as Supreme Allied Commander of the China Theatre. After having received this, again in the appropriate way, General Okamura and the other Japanese representatives stood up and were led away. The whole ceremony took no more than twenty minutes. The only unscripted moment came when General He Yingqin received the signed and sealed surrender document: he was supposed to have remained seated while doing so, but he could not help himself and stood up out of politeness.[5]

The timing of the ceremony was anything but coincidental. In Chinese the word for the number nine is pronounced the same as the word for 'long-lasting' or 'enduring'. The number nine also has a religious significance, especially in Buddhism. By holding the surrender of Japanese forces in China on the ninth hour of the ninth day of the ninth month, the suggestion was that now a new era of peace would begin and last 'forever, forever, and forever more'. The date also referenced the eleventh hour of the eleventh day of the eleventh month, the time the guns fell silent over the battlefields of the First World War back in 1918.

This carefully choreographed exercise in state theatre had two main object-ives. The first was to make Chiang Kaishek appear the benevolent victor, desirous of peace, magnanimous towards the vanquished and with the good of his country foremost in his mind. Following the 15 August broadcast of Emperor Hirohito in which he announced Japan's acceptance of the surrender terms of the Allies, Chiang Kaishek too had taken to the airwaves to address his nation. He stated that he wished China to be guided by the Christian impera-tives of 'Do unto others as you would have them do unto you' and 'Love thy enemy'.[6] He announced that China's policy was not to seek revenge but 'to treat Japan with generosity and magnanimity', a policy popularised later with the phrase 'Let us repay evil with kindness'.

The second, veiled purpose was to convince the Japanese to collaborate with him in keeping the Communists at bay. Bottled up in Sichuan, with most of his troops weak and demoralised, deep grievances against his regime entrenched across China and his government in disarray, Chiang Kaishek needed the help of the Japanese if his government were to survive the transition to peace. The Nationalists had won the war, but without the help of their mortal enemy, their return to the large cities and fertile plains of China proper would be difficult. To be at the mercy of one's enemy is not what Clausewitz would have regarded as a useful victory.

At his headquarters in Nanjing, General Okamura listened to Chiang's broadcast and took note of its tone.[7] In the days before 15 August, he had received conflicting information. On 10 August, his intelligence organisation had picked up messages from Europe and Chongqing indicating that Japan was preparing to accept the Allied conditions for surrender, with the position of Emperor Hirohito the only remaining stumbling block. However, on 12 August, Japan's Imperial High Command had ordered him to 'protect our ter-ritory and safeguard our Emperor'. He had issued a general order to the forces under his command that they should not 'be misled by enemy rumours about peace' and he had wired Tokyo that he was in agreement with the policy of continuing the war. The next day he was told to transfer two of his divisions to Manchuria to assist Japanese forces fighting Operation August Storm, the Soviet invasion of Manchuria, which had begun on 9 August, the day the USA exploded its second atom bomb.

As late as 14 August, Instruction 1380 of the Imperial High Command, received at 12.30 p.m., Tokyo time, told General Okamura to 'destroy all enemy forces who might attack and fight a war of attrition against the Soviets, the Americans and the Chinese in support of the battle waged by the army on the homeland of the Empire'.[8] General Okamura, in a message copied to subor-dinate headquarters, replied that he remained fully prepared to continue the war. It was only at 5.20 p.m. that afternoon, when he received the message that 'the worst has come to pass', that General Okamura accepted that the war was over.[9] He received confirmation the next morning at 10.10 a.m., and at noon he listened to Emperor Hirohito's first ever radio broadcast, in the company of his headquarters staff, who assembled outside bowing reverentially east towards the Emperor. Their mood is difficult to imagine, not only because a military effort that had begun eight years earlier had ended in disaster, but also because Emperor Hirohito was considered divine. It was as if a deity had decided to speak out. Deities don't normally do that.

It is unsurprising that General Okamura found solace in Chiang Kaishek's promise of a benevolent approach to the vanquished. Soviet forces in Manchuria were doing their best to make good on Stalin's pronouncement that they would wreak revenge for Russia's defeat by Japan in the 1905 Russo–Japanese War.[10] Two atomic bombs, Big Boy and Fat Man, had destroyed the cities of Hiroshima and Nagasaki, completing the strategic bombardment of Japan by 21st Bomber Command of 20th Air Force, which had already laid waste to many Japanese cities. The two cities had been left off target lists until then so that accurate assessments of the impact of the new bombs could be made. With a million troops and about as many Japanese citizens to look after, General Okamura had to worry about the retribution that the Chinese populace might exact once they learned that their former masters, under whose rule they had suffered so much, had fallen. Finally, he was faced with the task of convincing Japan's armies in China to accept the indignity of handing in their weapons to an enemy they had defeated time and time again. The general faced an extremely difficult situation, one for which no army manual provided guidance.

Chiang Kaishek's choice of General He Yingqing as his representative at the Nanjing surrender ceremony was intended to make General Okamura's task of surrendering Japanese forces in China easier to bear. Generals Okamura and He Yingqin had entered Japan's Military Academy in the same year, making them classmates – a bond of a much more meaningful, and hence useful, nature in Japan and China than in the West. The two had met across negotiating tables in the 1930s when the Nationalists were still pursuing their 'first unity then resistance' policy. General He Yingqing had acted for Chiang Kaishek at these occasions, so that if things went wrong any blame for signing these (for the Nationalists) embarrassing treaties would fall on his shoulders. As he had served Chiang loyally with little regard for his own reputation, the choice of General He to preside over China's acceptance of the Japanese surrender not only made life easier for General Okamura, it was also a way of telling the entire Chinese nation that it should have no doubt about the ultimate loyalty of General He.

General Okamura accepted Chiang Kaishek's invitation to participate in the surrender ceremony not because he had no choice. The Japanese were down, but not out. In China they still controlled a very large army perfectly capable of continuing the war. On the evening of Emperor Hirohito's broadcast, General Okamura and his most senior colleagues toyed with the idea of concentrating all Japanese forces near the port of Qingdao in Shandong province, in a 'semi-independent deployment'. On 16 August, General Okumara came to the conclusion that 'the revival of East Asia now depends on the prosperity, wealth, and strength of China. Japan must give it all possible help.' That evening, he met with his vice chief of staff and the commander of Japanese forces in Shanghai; both had come to the same conclusion. On 18 August, General Okamura submitted 'Guidelines for Our China Policy after the Restoration of Peace' to Tokyo. He argued that Japan's aim should be to 'remove all ancient causes for enmity and we must concentrate all efforts on assisting and strengthening China in order to aid the resurgence of Japan and the revival of East Asia'. That meant, according to him, supporting the 'Central Government in Chongqing'. While 'the differences between Chongqing and Yan'an must be settled by the Chinese themselves, nonetheless, if Yan'an undertakes actions to resist and harm Japan, then we must resolutely punish them'.[11] This policy received the endorsement of army and navy leaders in Tokyo as well as Japanese military and civil authorities in China. Their considerations probably included the thought that China under the Nationalists would be a bulwark against the Soviet Union as well as the USA. It would also be helpful to Japan's economic recovery.

Nothing brings into better relief Japan's miscalculation in 1937. Had they supported the Nationalists then – or at least not stood in their way as they consolidated their rule – China and Japan would not have gone to war, none of this would ever have happened and this book would not have been written. In 1945 the Japanese ended up defending a government which in 1937 they had believed to be such a grave threat to their security that they had gone to war with it with the aim of vanquishing it or rendering it irrelevant. This was all avoidable.

On the same day as Emperor Hirohito's broadcast, General Okamura had received a radio message from Chiang Kaishek instructing him to order his forces to cease all military operations and to send a delegate to an air field in Yushan county, Jiangxi province to receive instructions from General He Yingqin. Having decided to support the Nationalists, General Okamura replied to Chiang Kaishek saying that he would sent Major General Takeo Imai, the vice chief of the General Staff of the China Expeditionary Army, in an unmarked twin-engine aeroplane. Because heavy rain made that air field inoperable, on 19 August Chiang told General Okamura to send General Takeo to the Zhijiang air base in western Hunan instead. He issued very clear instructions: the aeroplane should fly at 5,000 feet, take off at 10 a.m. Chongqing time, have the Japanese flag painted on the undersides and tops of its wings, and trail 4-metre-long strips of red cloth from its wing tips. Three Allied planes would accompany the plane from Wuhan and, once it was near Zhijiang, the pilot was to make himself known to ground control with the message 'King Able air control, repeat, King Able air control' sent on the 5860KC radio frequency.[12]

On 21 August, General Takeo received General He's instructions on the Zhijiang air base with the order to take them to General Okamura. They required General Okamura to ensure that all Japanese units stayed in their present positions; safeguarded all materiel, supplies and archives; maintained social order; and accepted orders only from Chiang Kaishek or General He Yingqing.[13] Nationalist liaison officers flew back with General Takeo. An advance party of 175 personnel were transported in twelve US aeroplanes to Nanjing on 27 August to prepare for the arrival of General He and the re-establishment of the Nationalist supreme headquarters in the capital of the Republic of China.[14] The liaison officers kept stressing that Japanese forces should remain where they were and take responsibility for preserving order, both in large cities such as Shanghai, Nanjing, Beijing and Tianjin and along the main transport links.[15]

There were, of course, problems. Many Japanese troops at the front, where Emperor Hirohito's radio broadcast had not come through clearly, had assumed that the Emperor had taken to the airwaves to spur them on to even greater effort. Although many senior officers had seen the writing on the wall, the majority were convinced that one or two major campaigns on the Japanese homeland or in China would convince the Allies to accept more favourable surrender terms. Most members of the rank and file remained convinced that Japan's final triumph lay not far into the future. As the truth began to dawn, there was widespread consternation, a good deal of anger and a considerable outpouring of grief. Some troops threatened to kill their commanding officers unless they agreed to carry on the war. There were an unknown number of suicides. General Okamura was aware of around twenty in the lower Yangzi region alone. For himself, as he wrote in his diary, he had decided that 'I shall neither seek life nor death'.[16]

The officers of the Imperial Japanese Army regained control over their subordinates after a number of days had gone by. They kept their men busy with martial arts, sports, exercise, singing, music, painting and Japanese chess. Some Nanjing citizens went on the rampage, looting and burning buildings and extorting money and valuables from the Japanese (in a scenario no doubt repeated across the country). A battle broke out in the streets of Nanjing between forces of the Wang Jingwei government and a group which presented itself as a Chongqing commando force. However, according to General Okamura, 'in general the attitude of Chinese officials and citizens towards us, Japanese, was surprisingly good' – something he attributed to Chiang Kaishek's broadcast, whose message was repeated in the Nationalist newspapers, which resumed publishing in Shanghai and Beijing as early as 17 August.[17]

On 8 September General He Yingqin, escorted by nine fighter planes, flew in the twin-engined 'Meiling', named after Madame Chiang Kaishek, to the Gugong air field near Nanjing. Here he was welcomed by the senior staff of his advance party. After he had descended the steps of the plane, specially selected Nanjing residents handed him bouquets of flowers and banners of propitious phrases.[18] When General He entered the city, 'excited, flag-waving crowds cheered the procession of cars', reported the *Manchester Guardian*.[19] 'A holiday spirit swept the newly liberated capital', according to *The New York Times*, 'as throngs braved the hot Sunday sun to celebrate the official surrender of the Japanese forces.'[20] Thousands of Nationalist flags were flying, the words 'peace' and 'victory' adorned memorial arches at street entrances, and 'curious onlookers joyfully mobbed American soldiers', who had also just arrived. After the surrender ceremony, in order to reinforce the image of Nationalist benevolence, General He Yingqin issued orders rescinding all taxes and levies to alleviate 'the hardship of the people'.

The date 9–9–9 never became 11–11–11. Although 9 September was an excellent date on which to stage Japan's surrender ceremony, in order for it to be imbued with a wider significance – in this case as a display of Nationalist supremacy – it needed to be taken up, or at least quietly accepted, by all parties. While the Japanese were willing to perform their roles as drafted in the Nationalists' script, the Communists were not. They were not willing to participate in a performance in which Chiang was crowned as a great victor, let alone accept him as China's ruler, sage or otherwise.

Civil War

The Communists had been preparing for Japan's surrender since the spring. Now they sprang into action. On 9 August, the day the USA exploded the second of its atomic bombs over Japan, Mao Zedong ordered his forces to 'destroy enemy forces, seize their weapons and materiel, and aggressively expand liberated areas' – with the word 'enemy' referring here to the Japanese.[21] The next day, the CCP Central Committee activated plans to seize Shanghai, Nanjing, Beijing, Tianjin, Tangshan and Baoding.[22] General Zhu, the Communist commander-in-chief, ordered his commanders 'to send ultimatums to all enemy units and command posts in nearby towns and along important communication lines to hand over all their weapons to our combat forces'.[23] On 11 August, Zhu De instructed Communist forces in Shandong province and north China to move units into Manchuria and join up with Soviet forces there. Mao Zedong stated in Yan'an the next day that 'it is obvious that the fruits of victory belong to us'.[24]

On 14 August, a Yan'an radio broadcast called Chiang Kaishek 'the Fascist chieftain'. It denounced him as leading a 'Kuomintang [Nationalist] reactionary clique' and accused him of trying to use Japanese forces 'to kill Chinese Communists and destroy the peace of China and the world'. The broadcast compared Chiang Kaishek to Wang Jingwei, suggesting that Chiang too was trying to take control of the country by relying on Japanese troops.[25] It also claimed the victory over Japan for the Communists. 'Unrecognized and not receiving one iota of supply from the Kuomintang Government, anti-Japanese armies of liberated China independently liberated vast territories and over 100,000,000 people, held back 56 per cent of the total Japanese troops invading China and 95 per cent of the total puppet troops by relying solely on their own efforts and the support of the people. Without these armies it is probable that Chiang would have had to choose between exile and surrender.'[26] The broadcast's use of numbers and statistics, suggesting scientific precision and exactness, contrasted with Chiang's resort to a moral register. It ended by making clear that the Communists did not recognise the legitimacy of the Nationalist government. 'We want to announce to our three great Allies, the people of China and the world that the Chungking High Command cannot represent the Chinese people.'

On the day of Emperor Hirohito's broadcast, General Zhu De despatched a memorandum to the USA, Britain and the Soviet Union to announce that he would not obey Chiang Kaishek's instruction for his forces to 'defend the areas in which they are stationed and await further orders', that is, accept Chiang's military authority.[27] The Communists had refused that from the beginning of the War of Resistance; they would not begin to do so now. General Zhu De also announced that 'the Nationalist government and its supreme command cannot represent the liberated areas of China or the people's true resistance forces in the occupied areas.' He added that 'in accordance with the Potsdam Declaration', the Chinese Communists had the right to 'accept the surrender of Japanese and puppet forces surrounded by our forces' and to be represented at all Allied surrender ceremonies. As Chiang Kaishek had done, General Zhu sent an instruction to General Okamura to surrender to him, 'except for those areas where your forces are surrounded by Nationalist army units'.[28] The next day, Mao Zedong accused Chiang Kaishek of having fired the starting gun for all-out civil war by insisting that the Japanese surrender to him alone.[29]

If Nationalist intelligence is to be believed, in the spring of 1945 the Communists had established contact with the Japanese well before their surrender in order to induce them to hand over to the Communists rather than the Nationalists when they did surrender.[30] An April 1945 report stated that Chen Yi, the future Communist mayor of Shanghai, had secretly visited the city and suggested that if the Japanese surrendered to the Communists, they would be given safe passage to a northern port through Communist-held territory. A purported meeting in June attended by Chen Yi as well as Pan Hannian, a top Communist secret service agent, and Liu Shaoqi, in charge of Communist operations in urban areas, supposedly led to a signed agreement that the Japanese would notify the Communists one week in advance of their withdrawal from Shanghai. The Communists would not attack them during that time and the Soviet Union would send a naval force to take control of the city, at which point the Japanese would make their way home. Without access to Communist archives, it is impossible to confirm whether this meeting took place. But that there was some sort of Japanese–Communist *modus vivendi* makes sense and such a meeting would have been logical.

The US diplomat John Paton Davies was born in China and served in the US Embassy in Chongqing. During the War of Resistance he served as political attaché to General Stilwell. He was also one of the instrumental figures behind the American Observers Group that went to Yan'an in July 1944. Following General Stilwell's dismissal, he was assigned to the US Embassy in Moscow. In a conversation with the Chinese Ambassador to the Soviet Union, Fu Bingchang, Davies stated that, while there was unlikely to be a formal deal, 'neither side really wants to fight', the Communists because they did not have the weapons and the Japanese because the Communist-held areas had no military value.[31]

Whatever the reality of Communist–Japanese contact, Communist forces went on the move immediately after Japan's surrender. On 15 August, *The New York Times* reported that Yan'an announced in a radio broadcast, picked up by the US, that their units were 'rapidly pushing northward into Suiyuen [Suiyuan], Chahar, Jehol [Rehe], and Liaoning and toward Kirin [Jilin]'.[32] Two days later it reported that 'unofficial but reliable reports said the Communist forces were persisting in military operations north of the Yellow River aimed at establishing control of Tsingtao [Qingdao], Tientsin [Tianjin], and other vital points and that Communist underground fighters had infiltrated into Shanghai. The Communists announced themselves that they were nearing the ancient Chinese capital of Peiping [Beijing].'[33] On 18 August, the paper again reported that '20,000 to 30,000 Communist guerrillas were converging on the Yangtze [Yangzi] River port of Wuhu in possible preparation for a sixty mile drive to Nanking [Nanjing]'.[34] Similar reports continued to be broadcast, and reported in the US press, for the next week.

But the Communists had to abort this campaign in order to seize large cities. This was in part because, as previously explained, the Japanese had decided to disregard General Zhu De's orders and instead obey those of the Nationalists. No fewer than 7,000 Japanese troops died resisting the Communist attacks on Japanese positions that followed this refusal.[35] But even more decisive in forestalling this démarche of the Chinese Communists was that the United States and the Soviet Union both opposed it.

The USA, as mentioned, was determined to repatriate its overseas forces as soon as possible. On 11 August, just days before Japan's surrender, the US Joint Chiefs of Staff ordered their senior military leaders in east Asia – General Douglas MacArthur, Admiral Chester Nimitz and General Alfred Wedemeyer – to occupy as many Chinese 'key ports and communication points as is practicable without any major land campaign'.[36] US forces were there 'to preserve law and order and to initiate a program of disarmament and demobilization of Japanese forces'. But if vast amounts of Japanese arms and ammunition fell into the hands of the Communists, this project would become difficult. 'If the US and the United Nations allowed an opposition party in China which has a military force to accept the Japanese surrender and to take over Japanese armaments, a civil war will be unavoidable,'[37] advised Ambassador Patrick Hurley.

The Russians also declined to support the CCP. They resisted Communist penetration of Manchuria and even evicted Communist units from cities there.[38] On 14 August, only a day before Japan's acceptance of the Potsdam Declaration, the Soviet Union signed a Treaty of Friendship and Alliance with the Nationalists, concluded in a few weeks of rushed negotiations in Moscow. In return for a promise to withdraw their forces from Manchuria within three months of the defeat of Japan, the treaty gave the Soviets acceptance by the Nationalists of Soviet domination of Outer Mongolia, recognition of the Soviet occupation of the southern Kurile and Sakhalin Islands, the internationalisation of the warm water port of Dalian (often called Dairen in Anglophone reporting at the time) and joint management of the China Eastern and Southern Manchurian railways. Together with the occupation of the northern part of the Korean peninsula, these concessions secured for the Soviets a buffer zone around their north-east Asian frontier in the same way that their occupation of east European countries had done on their western frontier.

Having made these gains, the Soviets had every reason to swing their support behind the Nationalists and to warn the Communists off their land grab. On 14 August, Chiang Kaishek wired Mao Zedong in Yan'an: 'Japan's surrender means that a new era of enduring peace will become a reality. I invite you to come as soon as possible to Chongqing so that we can discuss all important international and domestic affairs.'[39] Mao declined Chiang's offer, insisting that he first provide an answer to General Zhu De's demand that 'you acknowledge your errors and retract your instruction of the 11th', that is, the one in which Chiang had ordered Communist units to stay in position and obey his orders. Chiang declined to reply, but instead issued a second invitation on 20 August.

Mao's answer to this second invitation was that 'for the sake of unity' he had instructed Zhou Enlai to proceed to Chongqing. 'The reply was considered discourteous', The New York Times reported, doubtless correctly, because 'behind the politeness was a rejection of the invitation'.[40] Chiang Kaishek sent a third invitation on 24 August, in which he assured Mao that he would have been delighted to welcome Zhou Enlai to Chongqing, but 'in view of the urgency of the problems at hand he hoped Mr Mao himself would come "so these problems may be speedily resolved in the interest of the nation"'.[41] At this point, Stalin intervened, wiring Mao: 'China must not have another civil war. If it does take place, the risk is the disintegration of the country ... Chiang Kaishek has issued you an invitation three times. No one inside or outside of China will understand if you continue to refuse. If civil war breaks out, you will be held responsible.'[42]

Faced not only with the opposition of the USA and Japan but also of the Soviet Union, the Communists called off their attempts to seize large coastal cities.[43] Mao Zedong now declared that 'the present situation is that the war with Japan is over and we have entered the stage of peaceful reconstruction',[44] a wording that made the best of a climb-down that had become inevitable. He arrived in Chongqing on 28 August together with Zhou Enlai. To guarantee Mao Zedong's safety, Ambassador Hurley had flown to Yan'an and then flown back to Chongqing with the two Communist leaders. To indicate the Party's new stance, the Communist newspaper *New China Daily* began referring to Chiang Kaishek as President Chiang rather than as a 'fascist reactionary dictator' and to the 'National Government' as opposed to the 'Chungking regime'.[45]

Although no longer aiming to take over large cities, the Communist armies continued operations. They seized no fewer than 150 towns at county level and above in north China, pushed forces into Inner Mongolia, sent units and Party workers into Manchuria and lifted railway tracks across north and east China to prevent the Nationalists from using them to transport troops and government personnel.[46] Although they failed in their prime objective, the Communists nonetheless did well out of Japan's defeat. According to Communist statistics, they seized from the Japanese in north China alone as many as 73,000 rifles, 900 light and heavy machine guns and 160 pieces of artillery.[47] They would gain much more later in Manchuria.

In Chongqing, Communist negotiators submitted eleven 'main points for negotiation' to their Nationalist opposite numbers. Among their demands were: recognition of 'liberated areas'; 'the punishment of traitors'; 're-designation of surrender areas and participation in surrender work'; 'the implementation of democracy'; the appointment of Communists to the chairmanship of the five provinces of north China and to the vice-chairmanship of six provinces in eastern China; and approval for an army of forty-eight divisions – far more than the Nationalists had accepted before.[48] Chiang instructed his negotiating team to make clear that all these issues could be discussed except for two: the size of the Communists' army, which could be no larger than twelve divisions and which had to be incorporated in a single national command system, and the chairmanships and vice-chairmanships of specific provinces. Chiang did not rule out appointing Communists for these posts, but he insisted that all appointments would have to be made on the basis of merit rather than Party affiliation. Finally, Chiang refused to have any area of China called a 'liberated area', but made clear that he would accept a less confrontational term such as 'special area'.[49]

The negotiations culminated in a text, published on 10 October, called 'Main Points of the Discussions between the Government and the Chinese Communist Party' – a document more snappily, and optimistically, referred to as the 'Double Ten Agreement', in reference to the 1911 Revolution. The agreement paid lip service to 'peaceful national reconstruction', 'avoidance of civil war' and the 'implementation of constitutional rule', but it could not disguise the fact that the interlocutors had failed to agree on fundamental issues.

Both sides made some concessions. The Communists were prepared to recognise Chiang Kaishek as the country's leader, while Chiang Kaishek agreed to the creation of a coalition government and Communist inclusion in surrender ceremonies.[50] But both sides stuck to the same red lines that had barred a settlement of their differences throughout the War of Resistance. Chiang Kaishek insisted on a single command for all forces in China as well as a single government, although he was prepared to condone virtually independent autonomous areas. As to the Communists, they would not give up control over their own forces.[51]

On 27 September Chiang Kaishek left Chongqing for a short break in Xichang, a city in the hills of south-west Sichuan province with a beautiful lake and a comfortable climate. During the flight, he read a Reuter's report on an interview with Mao, who once again boasted about having an army of 1.2 million soldiers and claimed that the Communists should control China north of the Huai river, which flows east–west in between the Yangzi and Yellow rivers. The anger that had been seething within Chiang exploded into rage: 'this most heinous and evil criminal not only shows no remorse but even demands an army of 1.2 million soldiers and a separatist region north of the Huai and Yellow Rivers … If I do not bring him to justice, how can I possibly face in Heaven the spirits of the soldiers and people who have sacrificed their lives in the War of Resistance?'[52] Chiang Kaishek even seriously contemplated arresting Mao Zedong, although once he calmed down he decided not to. This was partly because it might cause the Soviets to renege on their promise to leave Manchuria after three months, partly because he feared a media backlash, and also partly because it was not the appropriate thing to do for a benevolent ruler who bends people to his will through his virtue. Rather than arresting Mao and putting him before a court martial, he did the opposite. On 10 October he bestowed victory medals on both Mao Zedong and Zhu De.[53]

Chiang Kaishek and Mao Zedong met for personal discussions on the afternoon of 10 October and again the next morning. But these failed to break the deadlock. Mao left Chongqing on 11 October 'looking thinner than when he arrived'.[54] Back in Yan'an, he reported to a CCP Party congress that '"the ruling cliques of the Kuomintang" were preparing for civil war after the evacuation of the Japanese'.[55] Churchill's personal representative in China, the one-eyed, one-armed General Carton de Wiart, who had met Mao during the negotiations, reported back to the British Cabinet that 'Mao is quite a good type of man, but a fanatic, and I cannot believe he really means business.'[56] Mao had told him that he had tried to cooperate with Chiang, to which Carton de Wiart had responded that 'it was quite true that both Mao's and the Generalissimo's forces had fought the Jap, but the whole time they were looking over their shoulders at each other and hoping they might have a chance to deal each other a crippling blow. I pointed out that in my opinion cooperation was only effective if both parties trusted each other.' That trust did not exist.

Japan's surrender did, however, solve some of the problems the 1911 Revolution had thrown up. Where China was geographically located was now clear, by and large, with the Allies accepting that it included Taiwan and Manchuria, and the Nationalists abandoning claims over Outer Mongolia. But the deeper questions, such as how China should be governed, what it should stand for and how it should be positioned in international relations remained unresolved.

Surviving Momentous Times

Chi Pang-yuan's memoir is an important reminder that for most ordinary people the question was less about who would win the War of Resistance, the Japanese or the Chinese, or who on the Chinese side would emerge as the most powerful party, the Nationalists or the Communists. For them the aim was to survive an ordeal over which they had no control while hanging on as best they could to the loves, friendships and values they treasured most. Some of the most poignant passages in Pang-yuan's memoir record her response to Japan's surrender.

'In my whole life I never saw such ecstasy as in Chongqing when Japan formally surrendered,' she wrote. 'People abandoned their normal reserve and embraced on the streets. They danced and laughed. They sang patriotic songs such as "Our mountains and rivers are beautiful, our flags flutter in the wind" … all streets were lit up by people marching with big torches and cries of "Long Live the Republic of China" resounded through the heavens.'[57] Chi Pang-yuan joined the throngs with her brother and cousins. But soon she was overcome with grief and ran home, tears streaming down her face. 'To my startled mother I said, "I can't stand this wild partying." I spent the night of our victory in inconsolable grief.'[58]

Chi Pang-yuan was grieving for Zhang Dafei. After he had joined the Chinese air force, when Pang-yuan was young, she had written him a weekly letter out of a sense of semi-sisterly obligation. Dafei spent his leaves with the Chi family; his stoic acceptance of his likely fate and Pang-yuan's pride in his service in the one branch of the Chinese armed forces that could claim to be successful ensured that during their walks along the Jialing river their friendship deepened into love. Dafei confessed his feelings only once. He embraced Pang-yuan briefly, but withdrew immediately, realising that 'I can only cause her grief, both while I am alive and while I am dead.'[59]

While Zhang Dafei was away fighting, Chi Pang-yuan was studying well out of danger at Happy Mountain (Leshan) in western Sichuan. There she read a great deal and studied with Zhu Guangqian, a famous professor of literature, who had studied at Edinburgh University, University College London and the University of Strasbourg. He had run literary salons in the 1930s attended by some of the great literary lights of the period, including Zhu Ziqing, Zheng Zhenduo, and Shen Congwen. Under Professor Zhu, Pang-yuan developed a special fondness for Wordsworth, Shelley and Keats – as many romantic teenagers do.

The Wuhan University officials who decided that Happy Mountain should be its wartime locale made an inspired choice. Happy Mountain was where one of China's greatest poets, Du Fu, had found respite during an equally unhappy time in Chinese history, the eighth-century Tang Dynasty, when the Dynasty's fate was hanging in the balance because of rebellion, famine, floods and wars with the Tibetan Empire, which then occupied a vast swath of what we now think of as China. Du Fu aspired to a civil service career but failed the examinations and, from the mid 750s, lived a life turned upside down by war, moving from one place to the next, witnessing close-up all the suffering that came with the upheavals of his time, to which he bore witness in his sensitive, sombre and wise poetry. It was also at Happy Mountain that Du Fu found quiet and rest; his poetry of the time focuses on his peaceful time there. When they chose Happy Mountain, the Wuhan University officials were reminding their charges that they lived in a place where someone of no less a stature than Du Fu, one of whose poems provides an epigraph to this chapter, had found escape from the horrors of his own time, thus providing them with a meaningful and evocative link with China's past, and telling them that even in war studying and writing had a place.

'When you read this letter, I will be dead', Zhang Dafei's last letter to Pang-yuan began. He was right. He died in the skies above southern Henan on 18 May 1944, during the Ichigo offensive. He had prepared the letter beforehand and made arrangements for it to be sent to Pang-yuan's brother together with, in an act of gentlemanly decency, all the letters she had sent to him in two bundles. In the letter he reiterated his love for Pang-yuan, but also noted that the two had set off on such different paths, he serving in the army, prepared to die for China, while she enveloped herself in literature at Happy Mountain.

In retelling this history, Chi Pang-yuan shows us how war drove two intelligent, sensitive, serious and well-meaning young people, who had much in common and were deeply in love, in two completely different directions, one to defend their country in the here and now against the aggressor, and the other into a life of study of the great literature of China and the West, to make sure that those who survived could pass on the deeper values of human civilisation, including, of course, an appreciation of learning, art and beauty but also of mutual respect, dignity and affection.

On 15 August Pang-yuan grieved not only for the death of Dafei but also because she, too, sensed from her father that peace was unlikely and the future might well bring more suffering: 'While the whole country celebrated, my father was in a sombre mood, not saying anything while in deep thought.'[60] He was thinking about Manchuria, the place of his birth, where the Soviets had now replaced the Japanese. 'Disregarding our sovereignty, Stalin on August 23 declared "Manchuria has been liberated".' At university, she had personal experience of the spread of Communism, which was tearing the student body apart. One day a fellow student gave Pang-yuan a political dressing-down: 'Someone's father is a big shot in Chongqing but still collects a monthly stipend. Very brazen, this. Always reciting "Ode to a Skylark", but ignoring the suffering of the people. Shameless.' The next day the same student said: 'Someone doesn't want others to know she is establishment scum … a daughter of a corrupt official. Get lost. You're nothing special.'[61] 'For the next sixty years,' writes Pang-yuan, 'I never involved myself in politics, not even campus politics when I was teaching.'[62]

Guo Moruo, the author of '1644', now offered the services of his learning and his pen, or brush, to the Communists. But '1644' was not a simple endorsement of the Communists; it also contained a warning to Mao, one that Mao could not fail to have grasped. Guo Moruo, who, incidentally, hailed from Happy Mountain, described Li Zicheng as a great peasant movement leader. He had started out with a small force but in the space of ten years had built up a vast following. He was personally brave but had resisted the temptations that came with his growing power and fame, eating unpolished rice and refusing to indulge himself. He had suffered severe defeats but had re-emerged undaunted every time. But, Guo pointed out, Li Zicheng's fortunes had truly taken off only after he had accepted on his staff a highly educated, morally upright and principled son of a high Ming official. That man had warned Li Zicheng: 'in gaining all under Heaven, the foundation is winning the hearts of the people. Do not kill.' Whereupon Li Zicheng had scaled down his use of violence. The good words spoken about him by this educated young man had helped him gain a wide following.

Once victorious, Li Zicheng had cast the young man aside. Li Zicheng's inner circle had become drunk with victory. They had spent lavishly on celebrations, but had also extorted money from all and sundry, imposed harsh punishments on the vanquished and divided into factions, fighting among themselves for appointments after their victory. They had been blind to the danger emerging at the frontier, with the result that within a few weeks they had lost the empire for which they had struggled so hard. Guo was warning the Communist leadership, including Mao, not to give in to their worst instincts, not to cast aside the educated elites who were now speaking up for them, to be generous to others in victory and, especially, to behave less violently. This was a complex message, self-serving to a degree, but also expressing fears for the future which would prove all too prescient. Men like Guo knew their history.

PART IV

THE NEW CHINA

TWELVE

CRASH AND BURN

When one is losing, the first thing that strikes one's imagination, and indeed one's intellect, is the melting away of numbers … Next comes the break-up of the original line of battle, the confusion of units, and the dangers inherent in the retreat … Once that begins, you have to leave stragglers and a mass of exhausted men behind; among them generally the brave … The feeling of having been defeated, which on the field of battle has struck only the senior officers, now runs through the ranks down to the very privates. Worse still is the growing loss of confidence in the high command, which is held more or less responsible by every subordinate for his own wasted efforts. What is worse, the sense of being beaten is not a mere nightmare that may pass; it has become a palpable fact that the enemy is stronger.

Carl von Clausewitz, *On War* (1832)[1]

Just after Japan's formal surrender in Tokyo, Chiang Kaishek once more addressed his countrymen through a radio broadcast. He made two pledges and issued one appeal.[2] His first pledge was a tax holiday for rural China. Areas previously occupied by Japan would be exempt from taxes for the first year after the war and the rest of the country the year after. His second promise was what he called 'the return of political power to the people'. 'Our goal in carrying out a revolution and fighting the War of Resistance was not simply to vanquish the enemy, but to establish a new China based on the Three Principles of the People.'[3] One-party rule would be brought to an end after the adoption of a new constitution by a national convention. He had promised this before; now was the time to make it a reality. The appeal was for unity: 'for the future of the country and the prosperity of our people … I call on my fellow country-men to commit to the nationalization of all armed forces and the creation of a single national administration.'[4] This admonition was addressed to all those whose military strength had grown during the War of Resistance, not just the Communists.

Before making his speech, Chiang Kaishek led senior officials in a cere-mony 'to pay homage from afar to the spirit of Sun Yatsen'.[5] In the speech, Chiang stated: 'we offer our thanks to Sun Yatsen, our teacher in heaven who established our Republic of China; to the martyrs who died for our national revolution; and to all heroes, civil and military, who sacrificed their lives in the War of Resistance'. Just as he had done in 1928 after the Northern Expedition, at his moment of triumph Chiang attempted to lift people's gaze away from the harsh realities in which most Chinese struggled towards the uplands of a China rebuilt on the basis of nationalism, democracy and the people's livelihood, that is, Sun Yatsen's Three People's Principles. Having made his speech, Chiang Kaishek stepped into an open car. A jubilant Chongqing hailed him as he drove through the city's streets, leaving Chiang 'moved beyond description'.[6]

Not one ever to let down his guard, Chiang Kaishek was unable to surrender totally to the moment. 'My mind was not fully free from old and new worries.'[7] A few days earlier he had learned that some civil and military personnel dispatched to Nanjing to prepare Japan's surrender ceremony had behaved atrociously. At Nanjing's air field, Nationalist soldiers had 'sacked warehouses'. Officers of advance units of the General Headquarters had acted 'arrogantly and immorally'.[8] A furious Chiang had scolded them, warning, '[D]o not forfeit our victory.'[9] These incidents, minor as they were, proved to be straws in the wind. By the spring of 1947, less than two years after Japan's surrender, demoralisation, economic disaster, the USA's withdrawal of support and the burgeoning Communist revolution led many to predict that the days of the Nationalists were numbered.

Demoralisation

With the help of the US 10th and 14th Air Forces, as well as US naval vessels, Nationalist officials and troops made their way to Shanghai, Nanjing, Beijing, Tianjin, Wuhan, Canton, Fuzhou, Xiamen, Taiyuan, Ji'nan, Zhengzhou and Hefei, that is, strategic cities along the Yangzi river and on China's coast as well as key cities in central and northern China. The Nationalists also incorporated a large number of forces recruited and armed by the Japanese, while Japanese troops were ordered to stay and maintain control over the main transport links. In this way, the Nationalists hoped to recover control over the areas they had given up to the Japanese before the Communists could seize them.[10]

For civilians, the journey home was an education in disappointment. A few made the trip by aeroplane, more did so by train, boat and bus, but many made large parts of the journey on foot. Only 10 per cent of China's rail network was operational, much shipping had been destroyed and many rivers had been mined.[11] Troop movements always had priority over civilians. Various routes ran from the Great Rear, as it was called, back to coastal China. One expensive route led south, to Canton and Hong Kong, and then by ship back to the nearest port to home. Another went north, through the mountains ringing Sichuan province, to Xi'an, and then back home by train if there was space available, or else by bus or on foot.[12] Agnes Norman had been the head statistician of the Shanghai Municipal Council before the war and afterwards worked in China for the Far East Division of the United Nations Relief and Rehabilitation Agency. She wrote that 'one of the major human problems resulting from wartime dislocation is the creation of armies of homeless, wandering people ... the migration of 50 million people is the greatest trek in history.'[13]

If people found the journey home arduous, arriving there was often shocking and disorienting. Feng Zikai, the Buddhist artist whose wartime propaganda posters had made him a household name, was able to complete his return to Shimenwan, a small town in the Yangzi delta, only in the spring of 1947. His essay 'Returning Home in Victory' records his experience: 'When our small boat moored at the dock near the bridge of the southern bank of Shimenwan, I looked up. I thought that we had ended up in the wrong place.'[14] Little remained of the prosperous town he had left behind. Along once bustling streets, 'there was nothing but grass huts, ruins, and unfamiliar faces ... I felt like Rip van Winkle in Irving's *Sketchbook*. I was overcome and said to no one in particular: "Here was the rice shop of the Yangs", "Here abouts was Yin Family Alley", and "Wow, look, the stone pier is still there".' He left the next day. The village China of before the war, which many had thought about with affection and longing, was no more.

In the first year after the war Chi Pang-yuan remained at Wuhan University's wartime campus on Happy Mountain. Because of the lack of transport, the Nationalists had ordered universities which had moved away from Japanese-occupied areas to stay put for a year. In the summer of 1946, Pang-yuan was fortunate. She hitched a ride on the aeroplane of a US pilot who was courting her then-boyfriend's sister. Her first stop was Shanghai, where she stayed in the home of her boyfriend's family. They had suffered little during the war. In modish Shanghai, Pang-yuan felt 'vulgar' in her 'Chongqing outfit', which consisted of a baggy cotton dress and 'round leather shoes with soles made of tyre'.[15] Unwilling to be seen with Pang-yuan in her wartime dress, her boyfriend's sister took her clothes shopping. When Pang-yuan looked into a shop mirror, 'I saw someone I did not recognize.'

Pang-yuan did not stay long in Shanghai, but travelled on to Nanjing. Her father, in Nanjing as an official of the Manchurian Affairs Bureau, came to collect her. When she returned to the city where she had spent her happy youth, she found that 'following eight years of occupation by a foreign people, the capital ... had become dilapidated', with rubble and bricks from bombed-out buildings everywhere. 'Even young persons like me had to walk with caution.' Only the Drum Tower was still clearly recognisable. Pang-yuan attended a church service to commemorate the life of Zhang Dafei. Her grief re-awakened, she turned against what she regarded as self-indulgent Shanghai and let her relationship with her Shanghai boyfriend peter out.[16]

After the summer, Pang-yuan travelled to Wuhan, where her university was now relocated, to finish her education. In a quiet act of defiance, she took a course on Dante's *Divine Comedy*. University officials had wanted to cancel the course because her fellow students all preferred Soviet literature. But Pang-yuan was persistent, the teacher of the course made no objection, and so for a year she and her teacher studied the *Divine Comedy*, meeting at her teacher's home, which inevitably gave rise to rumours.

After she graduated in 1947, Pang-yuan travelled to Beijing to stay with her mother, who had set up the new family home there. Accompanying Pang-yuan on the ship taking her down the Yangzi river on the first leg of the journey were 'nearly a hundred young boys – fresh army recruits – tied together to the railing'. They appeared to be extremely thirsty, but when Pang-yuan sneaked them some water 'an officer ... asked us not to give them water to maintain military discipline'.[17]

At the end of the summer, Chi Pang-yuan moved to Taiwan. She had applied for a position at the Foreign Languages and Literatures Department of Central University in Nanjing, but, like most universities, it hired only its own graduates. A friend of the family who was an academic suggested that she should try applying to the Foreign Languages and Literature Department of Taiwan University. 'They have nothing, just two Japanese professors awaiting repatriation.' Others counselled against the move because of the February 28 Incident of 1947 – an uprising against the Nationalists resulting from the deep anger felt by the Taiwanese towards the Nationalist occupation of the island.

Most Taiwanese did not share the Nationalists' hostility towards the Japanese, as Taiwan had prospered under the Japanese occupation. Inevitably they were angered when the Nationalists not only took the most important government posts for themselves, but also requisitioned many buildings and residences, ousted Taiwanese from their positions in government sugar, tobacco and tea monopolies, and seized their businesses. Inflation skyrocketed when the Nationalists drained commodities from Taiwan in order to support the war effort on the mainland. Living standards for the Taiwanese plummeted while Nationalist officials lived it up and Nationalist businessmen made huge profits. When a tobacco monopoly enforcement team mistreated a pedlar of contraband cigarettes, Taiwan erupted, with protesters – some of whom wore Japanese uniforms – attacking police buildings, occupying radio stations and trying to seize military installations. The crackdown, conducted by troops shipped in for the purpose, left thousands dead, including many members of Taiwanese elite families. Despite these events, Chi Pang-yuan decided to try her luck in Taiwan. 'All of China is in a political maelstrom. Either you are left or right, with not even a small hole for an ostrich in which to stick its head.'[18]

By 1947 Chen Kewen, too, was looking to the future with foreboding. His career went from triumph to triumph, but many Nationalist officials were losing heart. 'When senior officials meet,' he wrote in his diary on 21 February 1947, 'the first thing they say is "What do we do?" The value of gold and dollars is rising so fast, the markets are in such disarray. How are millions of soldiers and teachers, plus hundreds of thousands of students, to survive?'[19] Chen was put in charge of implementing a rationing system for civil servants, but it failed. 'Prices have gone through the roof, rice riots are taking place everywhere, and people are panicking,' he reflected. For wont of a better idea, the decision was made to double the salaries of civil servants in the full knowledge that this would only worsen inflation: 'this is like drinking poison to quench a thirst.'[20] Chen Kewen had enjoyed being in Nanjing before the war. Now 'every day all that I hear and see, both about public and private affairs, causes me to despair. Nothing gives me a sense of satisfaction. I groan in my sleep.'[21]

Chen Kewen did, however, derive a quiet sense of dignity from visiting Chen Bijun, the widow of Wang Jingwei and the torch-bearer of the doomed peace movement. The Superior Court of Jiangsu province had found her guilty of collaboration in April 1946. At her trial she had been defiant, arguing that she and her husband had helped many people in occupied areas and calling those who had fled the real cowards. In a statement that elicited applause from the audience, she charged those who were now back in power in Nanjing with selling out the country to the Americans and running a regime of astounding corruption and incompetence.[22] In jail, however, bravado gave way to despair. Chen Bijun became addicted to daily injections of an expensive tranquilising drug. After her death in 1959, the Communists allowed a relative from Hong Kong to collect her ashes. They were scattered over the waves of the Pacific Ocean from the southern edge of Hong Kong Island, the thought being that, Wang Jingwei's remains having floated down the Yangzi into the Pacific, this famously devoted couple might be reunited in death.[23]

One movie released in 1947 caught the public mood perfectly. *A Spring River Flows East* told the story of a poor young couple driven apart by the war against Japan, with the husband rising from poverty to wealth in Chongqing while his wife slaves away in a Shanghai refugee camp to earn enough money to feed their one child. After the war, the husband returns to Shanghai with a new wife plus a mistress. His first wife drowns herself after she discovers the truth at a party at which she is a servant and he a guest. The title of the film references a famous tenth-century lament by Emperor Li Yu, the third and last ruler of the Southern Tang Dynasty, a leftover of one of the most glorious eras of Chinese history. The two most famous lines of Li Yu's poem read 'You ask how large my sorrow is/Like a river in spring flowing east'.[24] *Spring River* was a hit, watched by millions of people, many of whom will readily have associated their own times with those of the Southern Tang.

Relief and Rehabilitation

The Nationalists' demise was partly the result of circumstance, of decisions by others over which they had no control, and of developments that took everyone by surprise. Things might have turned out differently had the Soviets not seized Manchuria in the last week of the War of Resistance, had Japan surrendered earlier, had the Americans and the Soviets found a way to collaborate, or had the world economy revived more quickly. In history, nothing is ever really inevitable; chance and contingency play critical parts.

Even so, deep-seated structural problems existed. One was the lack of a sound fiscal basis. Before 1937, the Nationalists depended on revenue derived from international commerce, excises on alcohol and tobacco, and taxes levied on industry and on the salt trade. The war destroyed that financial foundation. It also destroyed the monetary system, in part because the Japanese military and the Wang Jingwei government had issued their own currencies, but also because the Nationalists had relied on printing money to fund the very large armies they believed they needed. Nothing is quite as effective in bringing out the worst in people as the debilitation of the monetary system.

Another serious issue was that the Nationalists were made up of a small elite with no deep tradition of government and without extensive social networks, especially in the countryside but also among elites outside their core region of the lower Yangzi provinces. Even so, they were internally divided, as the frequent rebellions against Chiang Kaishek's rule in the 1930s demonstrated. The War of Resistance had added new enmities to old grievances, including a deep resentment between those who had gone with the Nationalists to Chongqing and those who had stayed behind. This riven elite not only faced the task of re-establishing Nationalist rule in its core region and reviving its economy, but also of incorporating Manchuria, which had been part of their world for just a few years and then only nominally, as well as Taiwan and Tibet, which had never even been that. Nor were the Nationalists only intent on recovering their pre-war position. They were determined to push ahead with the project of building their version of a New China.

As the history of the United Nations Relief and Rehabilitation Agency (UNRRA) in China shows, just restoring China to a minimal level of functionality was a gargantuan task, let alone achieving the Nationalists' more ambitious aims. In 1943, the Allies, well aware that the destruction caused by the war was already so deep that many countries would need help getting back on their feet, established the UNRRA. Its purpose was to 'plan, coordinate, administer, or arrange … the relief of victims of war in any area under the

control of any of the United Nations through the provision of food, fuel, clothing, and other basic necessities'.[25] The United Nations in this case referred not
to the UN as we now know it, which did not yet exist, but to the forty-four
countries that made up the Allies.

Organisationally the UNRRA reflected President Roosevelt's vision of a new
world order. Its main business was carried out by a central council made up of
representatives of the USA, the Soviet Union, the UK and China. The Allies met
twice a year for a general meeting to frame policy. To respect national sovereignty, the UNRRA would deliver supplies to the country of destination, where
that country's partner agency – in the case of China, the Chinese National
Relief and Rehabilitation Agency – would take over. With 70 per cent of its
funding provided by the USA and many Americans serving in its programmes,
the UNRRA was both an expression of American generosity and an exemplar
of a new 'can do' form of humanitarianism. But it was only given a year and
a half to complete its mission. This timescale was put in place to reassure the
US Congress that a cap existed on the financial commitment it was making
but also reflected a determination not to have any country become dependent
on foreign aid, a state of affairs that could easily slide into colonialism, which
President Roosevelt was determined to avoid.

In the first half of 1944, a UNRRA mission visited China to draw up an estimate of the country's relief and rehabilitation needs in 'health, social welfare,
displaced persons, transport, Yellow River flood control, food, clothing, agriculture, industry, and shelter'.[26] The mission's September 1944 report held that
China required 'ten million tons of relief and rehabilitation supplies at an estimated cost of US$ 2.5 billion'. The priority was feeding 'seven million people
on the point of starvation and another 33 million on a diet barely above starvation'.[27] The commission proposed that the UNRRA pay for slightly under US$
1 billion of this amount, with China to supply the remainder. The final agreed
allocation for relief and rehabilitation in China was US$ 518 million, making
China the largest recipient of UNRRA assistance in absolute terms, if rather
less in relative ones. Poland received US$ 477 million and Italy received US$
418 million.[28]

The China Office files of the UNRRA make for grim reading. They are
important because they give insight into conditions in urban and rural China
at the conclusion of the War of Resistance from a politically neutral source. The
UNRRA's Tianjin office reported in early 1946 that in Hebei province 'large
scale starvation' could be prevented only if hundreds of thousands of tons of
grains were imported.[29] Japan's collapse had brought with it the disintegration
of the grain supply network on which the province, a chronic food deficit area,
depended. 'Before the war this deficiency was made up by large scale flour
imports from the US and Australia.' The Japanese had switched to sourcing

grain from Manchuria, north Jiangsu and Shandong, but 'the Japanese food control and collection system broke down completely during late summer and early fall'. The continuing violence in the province made the situation worse: 'livestock [is] being taken by warlord armies' and 'passing troops' helped themselves.

Guangxi province in south China had a population of around 15 million people. A UNRRA report estimated that 5,000 of the 24,000 or so villages in the province had been 'almost completely destroyed', agricultural production had fallen by 50 per cent and '4 large cement plants, several sugar refineries, an established tung-oil industry, and various tanneries and other industrial developments' were in ruins. The province's transport network was unusable: 'over 1,000 kilometres of main highway are practically impassable' and 'the lack of normal dredging and maintenance during the war years' was making 'transportation by river extremely limited, difficult, uncertain, and slow'.[30]

So it went on. In Jiangsu province, one of the wealthiest in China, the grain shortage from the beginning of April to the end of July 1946 was estimated at 404,700 tons of rice.[31] The problem was made worse by refugees from Communist areas. 'The total number is variously estimated at one to three million, with up to one fourth of them crowded in makeshift camps.'[32] The annual surplus production of rice in neighbouring Jiangxi province normally reached 1.3 million tons. The UNRRA Jiangxi regional office estimated that the 1946 crop would not be sufficient to feed the province's population of 13.5 million people, let alone to export grain to other regions. Land was lying idle because of a severe shortage of oxen, used in rice paddy fields for ploughing.[33] The UNRRA estimated that China had lost 24 per cent of its oxen, 30 per cent of its donkeys, 22 per cent of its sheep and 33 per cent of its pigs.[34]

The UNRRA did much good. In China, the food, clothing and shelter it provided to refugees as they made their long and arduous journey back home along a chain of 50 principal, 100 secondary and 350 support stations were very welcome. The seed, fertiliser, drought animals, pesticides and tractors distributed to rural China helped many areas restart agricultural production. Without the food the UNRRA distributed to large cities such as Shanghai, Beijing, Tianjin, Wuhan and Canton, their populations would have starved very quickly. Its most eye-catching achievement was the re-diversion of the Yellow river back to its pre-1938 course. Just closing the breach at Huayuankou involved the mobilisation of 50,000 workers and consumed '1,000 pine pilings and 800,000 board-feet of lumber from Oregon, 2,300 rolls (300 tons) of iron wire mesh, and 43 tons of steel cable'.[35] According to the US engineer who oversaw the project, the re-diversion would 'increase the world's food supply by an estimated two million tons annually through the rehabilitation of nearly two million acres of good farmland'.[36]

Nonetheless, the UNRRA's impact in China was limited. Transport was the key problem. By December 1945, 200,000 tons of supplies were stacked high on the Shanghai docks with nowhere to go. The 'the take-away capacity of vessels still plying the Yangtze River was limited to 10,000 tons a month', as one analysis commented.[37] The railways could not take up the slack because 'Chinese dismantled or destroyed railroads in many areas as they retreated [at the beginning of the war] ... [at the end] bridges, shops, locomotives and rolling stock were chief targets for US air forces'.[38] Dorothy Borg, later a leading historian of American–Asian relations but then a *Far Eastern Survey* correspondent, reached the depressing conclusion that 'China could not absorb a large amount of economic aid'.[39]

Money was another issue – not just the total amount that was available, but the politics of its allocation. The Nationalists promised the CNRRA the equivalent of US$ 105 million per year. But Song Ziwen, who was premier at the time, feared that the CNRRA was 'building up to become the biggest single economic force in post-war China' and would undermine his domination of China's economic affairs.[40] The CNRRA was a subordinate organisation of the Executive Yuan, of which Song as premier was in charge. He starved it of funding until he had established full control of it.

The UNRRA's record in China shows just how difficult the clean-up after the War of Resistance was. The same was true in Europe. After a few days of carnivalesque celebrations following the end of the Second World War, Europe's people had to come to terms with a reality that was grim, and would remain so for years. In France average daily rations after the war were just 1,000 calories.[41] The situation was similar or worse in most other places. Diseases associated with malnutrition ripped through the weakened populations. Waves of ethnic cleansing crashed through Poland, Hungary, the Ukraine, Romania and elsewhere.[42] Political violence in France and Italy and outright civil war in Greece and Yugoslavia meant that the savagery did not stop once the politicians declared that peace had returned. Recovery in Europe began in earnest only after 1948, in no small measure due to the US$ 5 billion pumped into the European economies by the Marshall Plan.

The lesson to draw from the devestated condition of post-war China is not that the Nationalists were irredeemably venal and corrupt, even if that was often true, but that industrialised war leaves behind it a wreckage from which recovery is difficult, takes time and is costly. For Clausewitz, the transition to peace was not much of an issue. That is unsurprising, given that in most wars before the twentieth century, normality returned after negotiations that followed a battlefield clash led to the payment of an indemnity, the adjustment of a border or the realignment of a succession. The destruction of total war is too deep and too widespread for that; in the same way that military histories should look at the transition to peace, so should military planning. If Clause-witz needs updating, it is not just by including naval and economic warfare (a point that is often made), but also by including transitions to peace, which is as much a military as a political issue.

A Cold War Kiss of Death

Japan's surrender was celebrated around the world, of course. Japan's collapse, however, left a booby-trapped peace in its wake. In east, south-east and south Asia – descriptors that only then gained some meaning – a return to the status quo ante was impossible. Where France, Britain and the Netherlands attempted to re-assert their pre-war positions in the region, the outcome was violent processes of decolonisation. In China, having signed new treaties with the USA and the UK on the basis of equality, a return to a situation in which foreign powers had a large say in Chinese affairs was impossible. Popular national independence movements, based in the countryside and armed during the war, strove to overthrow old elites with close connections to Western powers, not just in China but also in French Indochina and across south-east Asia. Adding yet deeper complexities to these new instabilities was the drift towards competition between the USA and the USSR. In China, these developments came together in a toxic mix in Manchuria, the Balkans of east Asia. Developments there would shape the post-war order fundamentally.

The historian Melvyn Leffler characterises the US policy in east Asia at the end of the war against Japan as driven by the concern that the Soviets 'would ensconce themselves in Manchuria, northern China, and Korea, integrate the resources of this region with the Soviet Far East, and establish a power complex in East Asia that resembled in its force and threat the one that the Japanese had created'.[43] Increasingly concerned about Soviet behaviour in eastern Europe, even before the end of the war with Japan the Americans had tried to keep them out of east Asia. President Truman approved the dropping of atomic bombs on two Japanese cities to shorten the war and so save American lives, but also in the hope that Japan's surrender would take place before Soviet armed forces entered Korea and Manchuria. However, the Soviets had their own fears, including a revival of Japanese militarism and concern about the Americans' ultimate objectives. The Soviet Red Army entered Korea and Manchuria in the last week of the war, drew Outer Mongolia into its orbit and sought to build up its influence in Xinjiang.

This was a new situation, in which the policies of both the Soviet Union and the USA changed frequently and at times dramatically. When the USA put forces into southern Korea shortly after Japan's surrender, the USA and the Soviet Union improvised a deal that made the 38th parallel the dividing line between their two areas of occupation. That level of cooperation proved short-lived. When in November 1945 the Soviet Union failed to comply with its undertaking in its Treaty of Friendship with China to withdraw its forces from Manchuria three months after Japan's surrender, President Truman dispatched General George Marshall to China. The mission's aim was to effect 'a cessation of hostilities' between Nationalist and Communist forces, assist the Nationalists in disarming, and repatriating Japanese forces and bringing about 'peace, unity, and democratic reform'.[44] These goals were considered essential to nurture China into being 'amenable to American influence, capable of establishing stability, and intent on circumscribing Russian power', as Leffler puts it.[45]

General Marshall spent a most miserable year in China. The initial omens were good. Shortly after his arrival, on 10 January 1946, he secured acceptance of a ceasefire agreement from both the Communists and the Nationalists. Over the next two weeks, meetings of the Political Consultative Committee resulted in a raft of further agreements, whose main points were that a constitution would be prepared and submitted to a National Assembly, that the State Council would be changed so that half of its members were non-KMT members, and that an army demobilisation programme would be put in place to reduce China's armed forces to sixty divisions, fifty Nationalist and ten Communist.[46] These paper achievements proved the high watermark of the Marshall Mission.

Having the Nationalists and Communists make promises was easy; having them put into practice proved impossible. Marshall succeeded in arranging the repatriation of 2,986,438 Japanese, thus fulfilling the part of his mission that ensured that there was no risk of a revival of Japanese militarism in China.[47] In order to enable him to stand any chance of achieving the other parts of his assignment, Truman handed Marshall a powerful weapon. He made it clear that if China did not respond positively to Marshall's suggestions, 'American assistance in post-war reconstruction, including credits and loans, and the development of China's national army might not be forthcoming.'[48] The similarities of that arrangement with the one that had led to the Stilwell debacle would not have escaped the Nationalists' notice.

Dependent on US assistance, the Nationalists behaved as if they were heeding Marshall's advice; in practice Chiang Kaishek declined to serve 'as an instrument of US policy'.[49] Manchuria became the rock on which the Marshall Mission foundered. The area was important to the Nationalists, primarily economically. A report by the Nationalist Minister of Economic Affairs made much of Japan's development of Manchuria's heavy industry. After they seized Manchuria, the Japanese established twenty state enterprises, including for fuels, coal, rail, iron and steel, textiles, wheat flour, fertiliser, concrete and timber. By 1944 Manchuria was producing 5 million tons of pig iron and 2 million tons of steel, generating 2.6 million watts of electricity and producing 1 million tons of crude oil per year.[50] The Manchuria plains were highly productive, its railway network was intact, and the Japanese had left behind a vast amount of arms, ammunition and food. This made control over Manchuria imperative for the Nationalists, who regarded its recovery as a war aim. This had been accepted by the USA and the UK at the Cairo Conference in November 1943, where Chiang Kaishek secured recognition of China's territorial demands. Manchuria was also important for China's security; it had, after all, been the jumping-off point for Japan's invasion of China south of the Great Wall.

The USA fully supported Chiang Kaishek's ambitions in Manchuria because that would prevent the Soviet Union from building up a new power base in north-east Asia. 'China without Manchuria,' US officials judged, 'would be no effective counterpoise to maintain the balance of power in the Far East.'[51] Marshall's truce agreement therefore excluded 'movements of the National Army for the purpose of restoring Chinese sovereignty', that is, moving troops into Manchuria.[52] US transport planes were put at the disposal of the Nationalists to ferry 200,000 troops to Manchuria and US$ 500 million-worth of surplus military supplies were transferred to the Nationalists.[53] When the Soviets stayed in Manchuria beyond November 1945, the USA put pressure on them to leave.[54]

As to the Soviets, they initially kept the Chinese Communists at arms' length; the Treaty of Friendship had given them much of what they wanted. But in October, before the first deadline for their withdrawal from Manchuria, the Soviets switched tack. They suggested to the Chinese Communists that they deploy 300,000 troops into southern Manchuria.[55] Soviet policy changed again in late 1945 and early 1946. Besides agreeing to the Nationalist proposal to delay their departure, because the Nationalists were not ready to move in, they suggested to the Communists that 'the French way' had much to recommend it. This was a reference to the agreement made by the French Communists after the end of the war in Europe to incorporate resistance forces into France's national army.[56] Leading Chinese Communists, including Zhou Enlai, spoke in favour of this option. Marshall secured his truce agreement during this period.

In April and early May, unwilling to risk a direct confrontation with the Americans, the Soviets completed their troop withdrawal.[57] But to hedge their bets, they also armed the Chinese Communists. We do not know the precise numbers or types of weapons the Soviets handed over to their Chinese comrades, something that will remain unclear as long as Communist archives remain closed. Peking University historian Yang Kuisong asserts that a first transfer of arms and ammunition took place in November 1945. This involved 120,000 rifles, 4,000 machine guns, 150,000 grenades, 20,000 overcoats, 30,000 boots, 8 million rounds of ammunition, an unspecified amount of communications equipment, 6 small transport planes and several railway carriages.[58] In the spring of 1946, when the Soviets made their main withdrawal, in the city of Harbin alone they handed over 100,000 rifles, 10,000 heavy machine guns and 1,000 artillery pieces.[59] In May, June, July and August 1946, the Soviets made further deliveries, one of which contained 83 heavy machine guns, 32 light machine guns and 10,000 chests of medicine, another consisted of 12,145 rifles, 182 heavy machine guns, 506 light machine guns, 167 grenade throwers and 10 million rounds of ammunition, and yet another consisted of 100 freight cars with arms from Korea.[60] The Soviets continued to supply the Communists with arms in subsequent years. In 1947, the value of these shipments reached 151 million roubles, followed over the next two years with transfers worth 335 million and 420 million roubles.[61] As British military intelligence put it, 'the Russians have seen to it that all Chinese Communist troops in Manchuria are suitably equipped and ready for any eventuality.'[62]

Chiang Kaishek did not oppose the outcome that Marshall wanted, which was a coalition government with the Nationalists in a dominant position, but he did believe that the Communists should be given a good hiding before any negotiations. In dealing with rebellions before 1937, he had either threatened or used military force and then negotiated an agreement. After Japan's surrender he took the same approach. General Long Yun in Yunnan province remained virtually independent during the War of Resistance. After Japan's surrender, Chiang transferred some of Long Yun's forces to north Vietnam on the pretext that they were to accept Japan's surrender there, and then ordered forces loyal to him to surround General Long Yun's residence. Chiang gave General Long Yun a choice: come to Chongqing to accept an appointment as Minister of Forestry or face Chiang's armies. General Long Yun did not take long to make up his mind. Chiang wanted to negotiate from a position of strength.

Exploiting the provision in the truce agreement that Nationalist forces could assert Chinese sovereignty in Manchuria, in the spring of 1946 the Nationalists not only took over Soviet positions, they swept from north China into Manchuria to clear out the Communists, moving from Jinzhou in south Manchuria to Shenyang, and then on towards Changchun. The Communists fought back with the result that the fighting spread quickly and Marshall's truce became unstruck. The Battle of Siping ended on 12 May, but only 'after twenty-three days of bitter house-to-house fighting'.[63] Siping was strategically important. Sitting astride the two railway lines that connect Manchuria to northern China, anyone wishing to control Manchuria needed to capture the city. The battle for Changchun was equally bitter.[64] But by the end of May, the Nationalists had succeeded in driving the Communists across the Songhua, or Sungari, river into northern Manchuria.[65]

The truce agreement also included the words 'destruction of and interference with all lines of communication will cease'.[66] The Nationalists used this clause to justify operations to clear parts of the east–west-running Longhai railway in north China, as well as parts of the Beijing–Wuhan and Qingdao–Ji'nan rail lines. Furious at having been taken for a mug by Chiang, Marshall threatened to resign his mission unless Chiang ordered an immediate cease-fire, including in Manchuria. Chiang only agreed to a fifteen-day truce 'to give the Communist Party an opportunity to demonstrate in good faith their intention to carry out the agreements they had previously signed', including 'the demobilization, reorganization, and integration of the armed forces of China'.[67] The truce agreement was enough to convince Marshall to stay, but the fighting soon resumed. This sequence of events has led some to lay the blame for the eventual defeat of the Nationalists on Marshall. That, though, ignores a raft of other factors and the fact that the fighting resumed after just two weeks.

While Chiang Kaishek was prepared to make many concessions, his bottom line was a single army and unified government under his leadership. He had battled for this his whole adult life, and now, after the defeat of Japan, he was trying to make it a reality. The Communists for their part were unwilling to give up their own armed forces. Marshall might have had a greater chance of success if he had proposed a deal by which the Nationalists were recognised as China's official government but the Communists were allowed to govern their own area and maintain forces in it. Throughout the War of Resistance, negotiations between the Communists and the Nationalists accepted the principle of such a solution, which had precedents in China's political tradition. Today, with the Communists in control of mainland China but the Nationalists firmly established in Taiwan, such a situation has in fact come about, although with the Nationalists and the Communists in reverse positions. For Marshall, coming from a country that had nearly destroyed itself in a ferocious civil war that was partly about that same issue, this solution might not have seemed obvious.

Besides resisting Nationalist offensives, the Communists intensified a propaganda campaign that depicted the Americans as imperialists and the Nationalists as their lackeys. It was not a difficult case to make. American armed forces occupied Shanghai, the Beijing–Tianjin region and Qingdao, the port city and naval base on the southern coast of Shandong province. The fact that the UNRRA's 1,000 mostly American staff members were attached to Nationalist government ministries, including Health, Communications, Agriculture, Water Conservancy and Domestic Affairs, suggests that they were indeed under US supervision. Seven hundred and fifty US army and 165 navy officers of the American Military Advisory Group in China, inevitably known as MAGIC, strove to strengthen Nationalist military efficiency.[68] US enterprises, including some set up by Claire Chennault, had carved out prominent positions in trade and commerce. As the British Ambassador Ralph Stevenson reported back to London in January 1947, a fear for 'American enslavement' was widespread even in Nationalist areas.[69]

In August 1946, after the fighting resumed, Chiang Kaishek announced unilaterally that he would press ahead with the convening of a National Assembly in November to adopt a 'draft constitution' and 'institute constitutional government'. He insisted that his 'only demand' to the Chinese Communist Party was that it 'change its policy of seizing power by military force and transform into a peaceful party'.[70] The Communists declined to comply, for the obvious reason that doing so amounted to submission to Chiang Kaishek. Instead, they made steps towards forming a 'United Association of Liberated Areas' as an alternative government.[71] Chiang announced a unilateral ceasefire just before the opening of the Nationalist Assembly on 15 November, so that constitutional rule formally began at a time of peace, but after Zhou Enlai declared that 'the assembly would perpetuate the personal dictatorship of Chiang Kaishek',[72] he flew back to Yan'an. Chiang's attempt to beat the Communists to the negotiating table had failed.

In January 1947, Truman decided to bring Marshall's mediation in China to an end. Chiang's failure to do as they wished was one reason, but there were others. The hope was that distancing the USA from the Nationalists would reduce the chances of a Soviet intervention in east Asia and might convince the Chinese Communists to follow Tito's example in Yugoslavia and retain a degree of autonomy from Moscow.[73] To put pressure on Chiang Kaishek to become more compliant with US wishes, an arms embargo imposed in August 1946 remained in place and a US financial loan was put on ice.[74] Truman's policy, a US State Department official told UK diplomats in Washington, was to wait 'until conditions in China improve', at which point 'we are prepared to consider aiding in the carrying out of policies, unrelated to civil strife, which would encourage economic reconstruction and reform'.[75] Unless he changed his ways, Chiang Kaishek would have to face a future without US military assistance.

The consequences were predictable. Brigadier F. Field, the UK military attaché, believed that 'we have now reached the stage where – assuming the Government's ammunition supplies can last them for offensive purposes to July or August – they must, after that, go on the defensive'.[76] British naval intelligence concurred. Its assessment was that the Communists were 'very well armed, mostly with Japanese arms taken over after the Japanese surrender … in all sectors the Nationalists are nervous and uneasy about their position'.[77] In April 1947, US Ambassador Leighton Stuart, who had frequent meetings with Chiang Kaishek, told UK Ambassador Ralph Stevenson that he did not believe the Nationalists had the military wherewithal to score telling victories over the Communists over the next few months and that a Nationalist collapse was likely to follow soon.[78] UK Ambassador to Washington Archibald Clark Kerr was succinct in his views: 'all this amounts to letting the Chinese stew in their own juices.'[79]

In the spring of 1947, the Nationalists undertook two more offensives, one of which saw them take Yan'an, while the other was a thrust into Communist areas in Shandong province. They also threw back a Communist attempt to retake the city of Siping in June 1947. But from then on a lack of munitions forced the Nationalists to go on the defensive, as predicted. In September, Ambassador Stuart made an urgent appeal to Washington to replenish Nationalist ammunition stocks. General Albert Wedemeyer, who had just completed a fact-finding mission to China, also believed that the situation was critical. He 'went so far as to secure conditional agreement from [General Douglas] MacArthur' to make a shipment of arms from US stores in Japan. Ambassador Stuart was 'anxious about delay in view of the apparent imminence of Communist offensives in Manchuria'.[80] But Marshall, who had become Secretary of State and was now concentrating on salvaging the peace in Europe, declined to give his approval.[81] He held firm to his conviction that China's problems could not be solved by military means alone, and certainly not by the Nationalist military. 'Chiang Kaishek is faced with a problem. He is losing 40% of supplies to the enemy,' he told one Chinese interlocutor.[82] Aiding the Nationalists effectively meant aiding the Communists. President Truman agreed. 'Pouring sand in a rat hole' was how he typified further aid to the Nationalists.[83]

By the spring of 1947, the Nationalists were in a terrible situation. Demoralisation had the country in a vice-like grip, the economy showed no signs of recovery, rural conditions were deplorable, Nationalist armies were running out of ammunition, and the USA had decided to support them no further. Panics about Communist infiltration in cities triggered crackdowns which corroded what little remained of the Nationalists' standing among the educated urban youth. In February 1947, a 'black terror' descended over Beijing when 3,000 students were arrested after a demonstration.[84] 'It is said,' wrote the British diplomat Lionel Lamb, that 'one third have been shot, one third released, and one third jailed.'[85] Chiang Kaishek's authority hung by a thread. Ambassador Stevenson reported to London that 'there is talk of Chiang Kaishek stepping aside'.[86] General Li Zongren, the leader of the Guangxi Clique, told Ambassador Stuart that he 'would continue to support Chiang Kaishek as long as he conscientiously could',[87] thereby indicating that his commitment was conditional. Meanwhile, a group of lesser southern military leaders were sounding out foreign diplomats about what response they might expect if they seized power.[88] China was ripe for revolution.

— THIRTEEN —

NATIONAL LIBERATION WAR

It is wrong to think of guerrilla warfare as primitive, unorganized, and small scale for there is no other warfare that entails so much complicated strategy and tactics, and relies so heavily on political and economic factors.
Kusano Fumio, 'Chinese Communist Guerrilla Warfare' (1948)[1]

The overthrow of the enemy is the aim in war; the destruction of hostile armed forces, the means both in attack and defence.
Carl von Clausewitz, On War (1832)[2]

Preserving their forces rather than wasting them on territorial operations that were unlikely to succeed was an important part of the Communists' strategy. When in November 1945 Nationalist armies entered the Liaoxi Corridor, the strategically important slice of land that connects Manchuria to north China, the Communist commander-in-chief in Manchuria, General Lin Biao, wrote to Mao Zedong:

Our forces which have engaged in battle are completely exhausted and have lost their cohesion. Their combat strength is weak and we have many new recruits who have not been trained … we lack arms and ammunition and are not receiving resupplies. We do not have enough uniforms and shoes, we are not accustomed to eating sorghum, and we have no money. From our general headquarters down, we have no maps, we do not know the terrain, our communication systems are in chaos, the local people are not yet supportive, and there are many bandit groups.[3]

Mao approved Lin's request to move his troops 200 kilometres north.[4]

When Chiang Kaishek went on the offensive in 1946, the Communist forces again fell back, allowing the Nationalists to take territory. An anonymous British intelligence officer travelled for six months through north Jiangsu while the Nationalist forces were clearing the Tianjin–Nanjing and Longhai railways. At first it seemed to him that the Nationalists 'would destroy the Communist forces in the area'. However, he soon learned that, while 'that was the aim, it was never achieved. The Communist New Fourth Army withdrew practically intact.'[5] These offensives gained the Nationalists little except broken railways and endless harassment from guerrilla units on their flanks and in their rear.

Waiting – 'waiting for failure to ripen before plucking it', as Lionel Lamb put it in October 1948 – was also part of the Communists' operational strategy.[6] They could not fail to notice that the Nationalists were feeling increasingly overwhelmed by their problems, that growing sections of both urban and village Chinese were turning against them, and that the Americans' impatience with Nationalist strategies was intensifying day by day. Waiting for these processes to deepen made eminent sense.

Wrecking was another element of the Communists' strategy, one that speeded up Nationalist disintegration. They pulled up large sections of railway line, not only to hamper Nationalist troop movements but also to damage local economies. In north Jiangsu, the Communists 'stripped everything in a most thorough matter. Most of the industrial plants are stripped of vital parts ... the dykes of the Grand Canal and various rivers have been broken.'[7] A UNRRA report from the capital of Shandong province, Ji'nan, stated that the Communists prevented coal, wheat and cotton from reaching the city by blocking rail traffic and occupying coal mines.[8] In southern Hebei, 'all bridges have been completely destroyed', the UK Consul General in Tianjin reported.[9] In their destruction of railway tracks, the Communists were nothing if not thorough; in Hebei they had the rails sawn into pieces and carried off into the mountains. The UK Foreign Office's China Department concluded from information from a range of sources that the Communists were following a policy of 'systematically wrecking any communications and plants essential to the economic life of the country'.[10]

But victory did not simply fall into the laps of the Communists. Prevailing by default as the last man standing would not deliver what they wanted; in order to have the authority to impose their vision of the New China, they needed an overwhelming victory. For that they would have to mobilise the population, recruit large armies and equip and train them to fight serious battles. These were not easy or painless processes. They needed a helping hand.

Village China in Revolution

Kusano Fumio, whose remark provides one of the epigraphs for this chapter, was a Japanese civil servant who worked for his country's Foreign Ministry in Beijing throughout the War of Resistance and went on to become a China specialist writing extensively on Chinese communism after the war. In a document translated by the CIA in 1948, he wrote that a 'guerrilla army is generally placed in such a circumstance that it must choose between wholehearted support and bitter conflict with the masses. If an army is to be successful in guerrilla warfare, it must first win wide popularity with the masses ... and it must strive not to be confused with bandit groups.'[11]

When General Lin Biao's troops arrived in Manchuria, they were entering an area in which there were a variety of hostile forces, including local militia, criminal gangs, groups of bandits and the puppet Manzhouguo Army which the Japanese had used to help them control the region. Lin Biao's men were driven by these various forces to north Manchuria, where they set about building a new base area. Imposing order was their first task. They began by conducting a bandit extermination campaign, clearing the area one county at a time.

Dealing with minor bandit groups was easy: they were surrounded and disarmed, or driven into the hills, where the harshness of the winter ensured their rapid diminution. Larger forces posed a tougher challenge. Xie Wendong, a local commander of the Manzhouguo Army, initially agreed to incorporate his troops into General Lin Biao's but then went over to the Nationalists. It took many months before General Lin was able to destroy them. First he picked off Xie's weakest units and destroyed all the food and arms stockpiles he could locate. Then he cut off Xie's support in the villages, no doubt by punishing those found to be supplying Xie's troops, and chased as many of them as possible into the mountains. When the Communists finally captured Xie Wendong himself, they did not kill him immediately but paraded him through several villages in the area. Having got their message over loud and clear, they executed him at a mass rally.[12]

For the Communists, securing popular support was far from straightforward because, like the Nationalists, they were facing a desperate economic situation. A combination of the pressures of war, recruitment drives which now exceeded the limits they had set for themselves during the War of Resistance, and bad weather meant that in Yan'an in late 1946, out of a total population of several million people, 40,000 were short of food. In February 1947, that figure rose to 200,000, and 400,000 two months later. The result was starvation and fleeing refugees.[13] In Manchuria, grain requisitions in 1947 reached 23 per cent of the harvest on average, and exceeded 30 per cent in its most northerly province, Jilin. Communist work assignments took up a third of the villagers' time, reducing the amount they had available for agricultural work. In 1947 in Shaan-Gan-Ning, another north China base area, the rural population paid more than 6 million litres of grain as tax and worked half of their time for the Communists. In one county, a local Communist official pleaded for a reduction in taxes and work quotas. The villagers for whom he was responsible paid 60 per cent of their earnings in taxes and, out of a population of 20,000, 4,500 were serving in the Communist forces. Of the remaining 15,500, nearly all of whom were subsistence farmers, 10,760 could not till their own land because of the work they were performing for the Communists.[14] Much land was left uncultivated. By 1947, these exactions reached levels considered unsustainable in the long run even by the Communists themselves.[15] Without any countervailing programme, the Communists would have ended up 'in bitter conflict' with the population, as Kusano Fumio argued.

To avoid this, they opted for land revolution. 'China's irrational landholding system is the greatest obstacle to our country's democratization, industrialization, independence, unification, and wealth and power,' declared the Central Committee of the CCP on 10 October 1947, at that year's anniversary of the 1911 Revolution.[16] An outline land law published the same day declared: 'China's rural system is unjust in the extreme … landlords and rich peasants, who make up less than 10 per cent of the rural population, hold approximately 70 to 80 per cent of the land, cruelly exploiting the peasantry.'[17] The law ordered the confiscation of all land owned by landlords and rich peasants, ancestral shrines, temples and schools, and for it to be distributed to 'all the village people' equally.[18] Collectivisation was not yet on the agenda; that would come in the 1950s.

The historian Ch'en Yung-fa has demonstrated that a large amount of land had in fact already been redistributed before the publication of the land law.[19] The Communists had halted land seizures at the beginning of the War of Resistance, but after Japan's surrender they confiscated land from people they designated as collaborators, evil gentry (wealthy and powerful local families) and local tyrants (people exploiting their positions of power in the government or other local institutions). Not yet willing to declare their intent publicly, the Communists disguised land revolution as the implementation of Sun Yatsen's call to return 'land to the tiller'. But land revolution it was.

Land was hugely important to China's peasants, far more so than money – especially at this time of high inflation and general food shortages. But the aim behind land revolution was not just to give China's peasants pieces of land and so make them beneficiaries of the revolution; by and large that had already been accomplished. 'The land revolution that Mao Zedong had always wanted … in truth was closely connected with war mobilization,' concluded Ch'en Yung-fa.[20] This was not only because in land revolution the peasants received the land but also because the Communists retained the money confiscated from large landowners and rich peasants. Land revolution was also a way of inspiring and mobilising village China for the fight to come.

Clausewitz wrote *On War* after the French Revolution. While *ancien régime* Europe feared its populations, the *levée en masse* conscripted the French masses into the army. It was their energy and passion that enabled revolutionary France to trounce the professional standing armies of its opponents. Clausewitz stressed the importance of what he called 'moral forces', the commitment to the fight made by the armed forces and the broader population.[21] The land revolution was a way for the Communists to gain the support of village China by exemplifying in practice that it would stand up for the poor, that it was opposed to the abuse of their positions by the locally wealthy and powerful (including Communist officials) and that it had the power to enforce its will.

William Hinton's famous 1966 book *Fanshen: A Documentary of Revolution in a Chinese Village* illustrated the process. Educated at Harvard and Cornell Universities, Hinton was a UNRRA tractor technician who stayed in China after the organisation brought its activities to a halt in 1947, when he took up the post of English teacher at Northern University in Shanxi province.[22] When he learned of land revolution, he was thrilled: 'I want to see and take part in it more than I have ever wanted to do anything in my life.'[23] *Fanshen* became a classic. Based on numerous interviews, eight months of observation and attendance at countless village meetings in the village of Long Bow in Lucheng County, Shanxi province, the book provided a vivid account of land revolution. It succeeded in giving voice and face to those Long Bow villagers who had benefitted from the land revolution, something missing not just from the accounts of those who opposed it, but also from Communist reports, in which statistics and generalisations, rather than individual human stories, dominated. Hinton followed the Communists' preferred narrative – naturally so, given his sympathies – but also laid bare the innards of land revolution.

Hinton began by sketching out economic relations in Long Bow, as was only appropriate for a supporter of the Communist cause. The Catholic Church, a local mutual aid society and 'a handful of families' owned most of the land in the village. One landlord, Sheng Jinghe, owned twenty-three acres. He lived on the rents paid to him for his land as well as 'usurious interest rates, profits from commercial and industrial offices, the spoils of public office, and graft or commissions from the management of temple, church, and clan affairs'.[24] Another landlord, 'the Catholic Fan Buzi', owned fourteen acres, plus 'a flock of sheep, a distillery, and a liquor store'.[25] But most Long Bow villagers were poor. One told Hinton that during a recent famine 'the whole family went out to beg ... Many mothers threw new born children in the river ... We had to sell our eldest daughter.'[26]

Communism made its appearance in Long Bow during the War of Resistance, a linkage stressed in Hinton's narrative in order to underscore the Communists' patriotic credentials. The Japanese requisitioned labour, built fortifications, imposed a new village leadership and recruited a militia in the village. One resident, Shi Fuyuan, had joined the Communists and regularly slipped back into Long Bow, using his connections to build up a small network of sympathisers. Among the early recruits were 'the poor nephew of the village head' of a neighbouring village and 'the hired labourer Shen Suozi'. Their first assignments were simple. They collected food, clothing and shoes for the Communists and passed on information about Japanese troop move-ments.[27] They also helped Communist guerrillas enter the village and kill a local collaborator.[28]

Following Japan's defeat, Long Bow Communists used the Chinese New Year, a time of celebration and excitement but also often used for settling debts, to attack landlord Sheng Jinghe. The Long Bow Peasant Association decided that Sheng Jinghe owed '400 bags of milled grain' to pay for past exploitation. As they entered his home:

> It was very cold so we built bonfires [in the courtyard] and the flames shot up toward the stars. It was very beautiful. We went in to register his grain and altogether found but 200 bags of unmilled millet – only a quarter of what he owed us. Right then and there we decided to call another meeting. People all said he must have a lot of silver dollars – they thought of the wine plant, and the pigs he raised on the distillers' grains, and the North Temple Society and the Confucius Association. We called him out of his house and asked him what he intended to do since the grain was not nearly enough. He said, 'I have land and a house.' 'But all this is not enough,' shouted the people. So then we began to beat him. Finally he said, 'I have 40 silver dollars under the kang [his bed].' We went in and dug it out. The money stirred up everyone. We beat him again. He told us how to find another hundred after that.[29]

Land revolution was violent, and meant to be so: it was a display of power.

Sheng Jinghe, by now 500 Chinese dollars lighter, fled the village the very next day for a nearby city, as many landlords in Communist areas did. One purpose of land revolution was to polarise the population between urban and rural, between rich and poor, and between the defenders of an abusive status quo and the standard bearers of a better future.

In 1947, when the land revolution had gone public, Zhang Chunxu, the Com-munist village head, was made to confess his sins in front of a village gathering. 'A hush settled over the room and soon spread even to the rowdy crowd outside' as he began to speak, declaring: 'I chose the best piece of land for myself' when land was confiscated from landlords in 1946. In allocating tax quotas, he admit-ted, he had demanded too much from poor peasants. After long discussion, the meeting agreed to impose a fine, which Zhang Chunxi could pay after the harvest, and to suspend his Party membership for five months.[30] An important part of land revolution was the punishment of local officials, including Com-munist ones. In a culture where local officials are habitually held responsible for all the ills that befall the people for whom they are supposed to care, that formed an astute way of demonstrating that the Communist Party was on the side of the good and, just as importantly, that it had the power to enforce its will.

In the spring of 1948, the land revolution was declared to have been completed. In Long Bow, a final meeting was convened. Members of the audience 'rose to their feet and bowed their heads three times before a large poster-style portrait of Chairman Mao' before singing the Internationale. A new Communist culture was being embedded into village life to replace that of the Nationalists. Party members who had survived the intense vetting process took to the stage.[31] Among them was Zhang Chunxi; his sins had been forgiven. This was the first time Long Bow Communist Party members acknowledged their Party membership in public. While the Party membership of a number of them had been widely surmised, that of others, especially those who were normally looked down upon, occasioned some startled remarks.

The public unveiling of the local Communist Party branch also took Hinton by surprise. 'With Kuomintang [Guomindang] assassins still roaming the countryside, with the Civil War battlefront only a hundred miles away, with a massive counter-attack still under preparation by Nationalist generals, who could guarantee the life of a Communist? If Governor Yen [General Yan Xishan]'s troops ever returned, every active revolutionary in the village would most certainly be hunted down and killed.'[32] That, of course, was the point. The Long Bow Communists had made a step from which there could be no return.

For those on the wrong side of land revolution, the process was terrifying and regularly fatal. Even though he was enthusiastic about it in general, Hinton acknowledged that 'at least a dozen people were beaten to death by angry crowds; some hardworking small holders were wrongly dispossessed; revolutionary leaders at times rode roughshod over their followers.'[33] One Pastor Wang, in charge of a locally influential church, ended up in front of a 'people's court' after he refused to hand over to the Communists the contributions his flock had made to the church. 'A meeting of the various societies was convened. Pastor Wang was accused before the group of being unproductive and depending on the offerings of the church members.' When Pastor Wang defended himself, the Communist official in charge of the meeting asked the audience: '"Do you all approve of what Mr Wang has said?" The reply was given in a prompted chorus. "We disapprove." They were asked, "If you are not satisfied, how will you act?" They answered, "Drag him". Therefore several men took a rope and tied Pastor Wang's feet together. The village people pulled on the rope and dragged him around the village.' This process was repeated several times. The property of the church was confiscated and Pastor Wang was accused of being a Nationalist spy.[34] Pastor Wang's sister tried but failed to secure his release. We do not know what happened to him, but it is unlikely that he survived.

General Lin Biao in Manchuria

It was the Communist forces under General Lin Biao in Manchuria that inflicted the first major blow against the Nationalists. General Lin had a reputation as an expert in battlefield tactics. Edgar Snow describes him in *Red Star over China* as 'rather slight, oval-faced, handsome' and 'shy and reserved'.[35] Unlike many Second World War commanders, Lin made no effort to become popular with his troops; the development of a personal cult was not for him. But, Snow reports, he was known as a genius at 'feints, masked strategy, surprises, ambushes, flank attacks, pounces from the rear'. In the Jiangxi Soviet in the 1930s, Lin's First Red Army Corps of 20,000 men 'became the most dreaded' of all the Communist forces because of 'Lin's extraordinary talent as a tactician'. In the autumn of 1948, the general led 700,000 Communist troops to victory over a Nationalist force of 550,000 men in the Battle of Liaoning and Shenyang, often known as the Liaoshen Campaign.[36] That blow was decisive, starting a Communist sweep south that gained momentum like an avalanche rolling down a mountain, eventually pushing the Nationalists out of mainland China.

The Communists prevailed in the Civil War not just because they were better at mobilising popular support in the countryside, but because the Communist Party was a far more disciplined organisation than the Nationalists, and they were also able to secure the support of urban youths and many intellectuals. The Japanese arms the Soviets delivered and the supplies they provided to the Communists ensured that, during the Liaoshen Campaign, General Lin Biao enjoyed not just superiority of numbers but in terms of arms and ammunition too. 'Between the years 1947–48, during all major engagements the Communist artillery was at least four times that of the Nationalists', Professor Li Chen of People's University in Beijing has concluded from his research.[37]

The Soviets did more than furnish arms and ammunition. Several thousand Soviet military personnel provided 'technical guidance and medical aid'.[38] They did so in the Lüshun–Dalian area, on the southern tip of the Manchurian peninsula, where they maintained a large number of troops,[39] as was permitted under the 1945 Treaty of Friendship between China and the Soviet Union.[40] By 1948 the annual production of Communist arsenals there and in north Manchuria had reached 2,000 60mm artillery shells, 500,000 mortar rounds, 1.5 million grenades and 17 million rounds of rifle ammunition.[41] The Chinese Communists also 'conscripted 8,000 Japanese doctors and nurses to set up hospitals for wounded soldiers', and an unknown number of Japanese experts were made to work in Communist military industries, air force academies and artillery schools.[42] While the Americans ensured that most Japanese were repatriated speedily from Nationalist held areas, the Soviets and the Chinese Communists did not move with such speed. About half a million of the 2.7 million Japanese soldiers in Soviet hands were put to work in 700 labour camps all over the Soviet Union, building railway lines, restoring factories and working on the land, [43] while a substantial number were conscripted into Communist armies. Repatriation was eventually completed in 1956, but a number remained missing.

The Communists had to learn to use all the equipment they now had in their hands. Many of the leading Communists in Manchuria had received training in the Soviet Union. After General Lin Biao went there to receive medical care in 1938, he stayed until 1942, probably studying Soviet battle planning at the Frunze Military Academy. General Zhu Rui spent five years in the Soviet Union in the 1920s, three of them at the Mikhail Kalinin Artillery School. General Zhu Rui was despatched to Manchuria in November 1946 together with 1,000 teachers and students of the Yan'an Artillery School, almost its entire staff and student body. General Liu Yalou also studied at the Frunze Military Academy, from 1939 to 1941. He then received a commission in the Soviet Red Army and fought the Germans on the Soviets' western front. A serious student of both European and Chinese warfare, he wrote an article about the Battle of Stalingrad and translated the 'Regulations on Field Staff Work' of the Soviet Red Army into Chinese. [44]

While General Zhu Rui ensured that General Lin Biao's forces were trained in the effective use of artillery, General Liu Yalou trained up staff officers to organise and coordinate the combined artillery and infantry operations. General Zhu Rui instructed artillery units in indirect fire techniques. Until then, Communist commanders deployed cannons at the front in a haphazard way, having them fire at targets in sight, using them like high-tech battering rams. In indirect fire, the artillery is moved to the rear, and usually hidden in camouflaged positions. Forward observers communicate target coordinates to widely dispersed artillery units, enabling them to deliver concentrated barrages on the most critical points in the enemy position or lay down screening fire in front of advancing infantry. [45]

Indirect fire requires rapid coordination and close cooperation between the artillery and the infantry. This is where General Liu Yalou came in. [46] He trained thousands of staff officers at a military academy established in Manchuria in 1946. In guerrilla warfare, staff officers did little more than prepare battle orders. General Liu's staff officers were a different breed. They collected and interpreted intelligence, supervised the implementation of battle plans and ensured that commanders were supplied with up-to-date information. [47] They constructed and supervised flows of information from troops in the field to higher unit headquarters. 'Once camped,' General Liu insisted, staff officers 'should immediately produce a report with a map and then submit it to regimental and divisional headquarters within 20 minutes. A division should send a report to the general headquarters within one hour after its troops have reached a given location.[48] Large-scale operations were possible only if such a flow of information was in place.

General Lin Biao developed battle tactics designed to reduce losses resulting from primitive tactics. Until then, when launching offensive operations, the Communists had usually simply thrown men at enemy fronts. That did not matter much during the War of Resistance when the Communists restricted their operations to mobile guerrilla warfare or in attacks on poorly trained and armed puppet or bandit forces. But against Nationalist forces equipped with machine guns and powerful artillery, and supported by a substantial air force of about 1,000 aeroplanes, such human wave tactics were not just costly but ineffective.

In Manchuria, General Lin Biao drilled his units in implementing his tactics and in a system of troop organisation that became known as 'One point, two flanks' and 'the 3–3 system'. 'One point, two flanks' entailed the concentration of superior numbers of men on two or more points in the flank or rear of the enemy, while a small force tied down its front line. He also insisted on wedge formations. The sharp point of the wedge was to open up a breech in the enemy position. The troops behind the point then flooded through the opening and attacked the defenders in their rear and on their flanks. 'According to Soviet battle experience,' Lin wrote, 'whether in the case of the German Army attacking the Soviet Union or the Red Army counter-attacking Germany, their approach to the offensive was to deploy in the shape of a wedge.'[49] National revolutionary war did not emerge in China without any outside influence.

In the '3–3 system' of troop organisation, a squad was made up of three or four teams of three soldiers. The squad leader and his deputy (usually an experienced and politically reliable soldier) took charge of a team each, while the other team or teams selected their own leader. Operating in triangular formations, teams provided covering fire for each other as the squad advanced.[50] The '3–3' system allowed formations to spread out according to the terrain and enemy fire patterns and so reduce casualty figures. Six to eight paces separated each soldier but cohesion was maintained as team leaders stayed within earshot of their squad leader. The system facilitated night fighting, which nullified Nationalist air superiority, and helped the Communists incorporate large numbers of new recruits.

General Lin Biao's first efforts in large-scale warfare were disasters. In February 1947, four Communist divisions equipped with ninety pieces of artillery and a number of tanks attacked an isolated Nationalist unit with just 5,000 troops. The Communists were quickly put to flight.[51] In June, General Lin Biao concentrated 100,000 troops in an attempt to retake the city of Siping and so offset the loss of Yan'an. He once again suffered a beating. According to the

British air attaché's report, the defeat had come about as a result of factors such as rain turning the roads to mud, malfunctioning logistics and a lack of coordination, but also the Nationalists' 'effective use of airpower'.[52] Lin Biao lost half his troops.[53]

Burnt by the disaster, General Lin Biao put his forces through a major retraining programme that lasted six months. He had his units rehearse basic skills such as cleaning weapons, firing accurately in coordinated patterns, setting up camp and entrenching. Small unit exercises inculcated Lin Biao's tactics of 'one point, two flanks' and 'four fasts and one slow'. The latter was a post-Siping addition to Lin Biao's tactical prescriptions. It insisted that speed and aggression were important in everything except in deciding when to launch an offensive. Commanders should take their time to make careful preparations so that they knew the terrain and were accurately informed about enemy positions, and could make sure that their own units were in the right place and understood their assignments fully.[54] Platoon commanders and squad leaders received training in the exercise of command, the organisation of fields of fire, the use of explosives and the construction of fortifications. At division level and above, the focus was on staff work, liaison, communication and the coordination of troop movements.[55] Under General Liu Yalou's overall guidance, each squad developed a special skill. There were fire squads, assault squads and demolition squads. Others developed night-fighting techniques or became adept at scaling walls.[56]

The training programme also aimed at strengthening morale and heightening aggression. At 'speak bitterness' meetings, soldiers talked about how they and their friends and families had suffered in the past. They attended performances of revolutionary operas such as *The White Haired Girl*, the story of a poor peasant daughter whose father was killed by a landowner to whom he was indebted. Following a series of unhappy events, including being taken as a concubine by her father's killer, the story ends happily when the daughter is re-united with her fiancé, a Communist soldier. Slogans such as 'Defeat Chiang Kaishek, Liberate China' and 'All Poor People under Heaven are One Family' were drummed into the soldiers.[57]

By autumn 1948, Lin Biao's forces were as ready as they would ever be. Short of ammunition, the Nationalists had withdrawn into Manchuria's largest cities – Changchun, Shenyang and Jinzhou – to hunker down behind high city walls. Land revolution had altered power relations in the countryside, giving a large number of people a stake in a Communist victory. Strong emotions had been let loose and a simple but effective narrative about the Communists freeing China from a bad past and taking it to a bright future had been spread widely. Nationalist demoralisation deepened further. In July 1948, Ralph Stevenson wrote that 'war weariness and economic distress resulting from continual civil war are approaching point of desperation'.[58] At the same time, the Communists knew that they could not sustain their current level of mobilisation for much longer. The waiting, the wrecking and the avoidance of battle had done their work. It was time to strike.

The Liaoshen Campaign

Changchun, 'eternal spring' in Chinese, is a city in north Manchuria. Its name defies the severe cold the city experiences every winter, when average temperatures fall to below freezing for four months and strong winds add a severe chill factor to the cold. The Japanese made Changchun the capital of Manzhouguo, renaming it Xinjing or New Capital. Seeking to turn the city into a monument to the benefits of the Japanese empire, they fitted it with wide boulevards lined with trees, grand ministries, spacious parks and elegant villas.[59]

In May 1947, just as spring was finally beginning to break through, General Lin Biao ordered his forces to put Changchun's 500,000 residents and 100,000-strong garrison under siege, an idea that originated more with him than with Mao Zedong. The two had been debating which city in Manchuria to attack: Jinzhou in the Liaoxi Corridor; Shenyang, 250 kilometres north of Jinzhou and Manchuria's largest city, main transportation hub and most important industrial centre; or Changchun, another 300 kilometres north from Shenyang. Lin pushed for Changchun on the grounds that Nationalist forces were weaker there, that an attack on Jinzhou would allow Nationalist forces in Changchun to withdraw south to Shenyang, and that supplying his troops in south Manchuria would impose serious transport difficulties. Mao accepted Lin's arguments, but only grudgingly, believing that Lin Biao was being too cautious.[60]

General Lin Biao was not wrong to worry about the ability of his troops, then still in the middle of their training programme, to take large cities by assault. At the beginning of the siege of Changchun, he ordered seven divisions to destroy two Nationalist divisions at the city's two air fields They failed and the Nationalist divisions were able to escape back into the city, leading Mao to wonder, 'Are the troops still using the old tactics of charging *en masse*?'[61] The logistical difficulties Lin Biao faced were also all too real. The Communists restored the railways in the areas they occupied, but their carrying capacity was limited. During the Liaoshen Campaign, they pressed 1.6 million men into service and requisitioned 6,000 ox carts to haul supplies. Even so, front-line troops survived by living off the land.[62]

General Lin Biao's men isolated Changchun, shutting down both its air fields blocking its roads and severing its railway connection to Shenyang. In August General Lin Biao ordered the encirclement to be tightened in order to prevent the Nationalists from getting hold of the crops then ripening in the fields around the city. Its residents soon began to starve. Thousands of people crammed into a no-man's land between Nationalist and Communist lines. When refugees left Changchun, the Nationalists soldiers stripped them of all their valuables, 'pots and pans as well as gold and silver and even salt'.[63] Then they became stuck. Communist sentries ignored 'the pleas of mothers holding aloft starving children on the other side of the barbed-wire barricades'.[64] An August 1947 report to Mao from Manchuria, signed by Lin Biao among others, describes the impact of this cruel policy on the Communist soldiers:

> Not allowing the starving people to leave the city and pushing back those who have left is extremely difficult to explain to both the starving people and the soldiers. The starving people ... kneel in front of our soldiers begging to be let through; some of them leave their babies and children and then run away; some bring rope and hang themselves in front of our sentries.[65]

The siege was not lifted.

Instead the Communists requisitioned all grain within a 20–30-kilometre radius.[66] Changchun's commander-in-chief, General Zheng Dongguo, told a Presbyterian missionary that 'the majority of the people are living on grass and bark, social order has completely broken down, and cases of cannibalism are frequent.'[67] On 7 October, *The New York Times* reported that 'refugees who recently arrived in Mukden [Shenyang] drew a picture of dead bodies littering the streets, with one pound of kaoliang (millet) selling for more than $50 (US) while hungry civilians were surviving on soy bean cake and tree bark and leaves. They estimated that the population had dwindled to half.'[68] Today, the death toll of the siege of Changchun is reckoned to lie between 120,000 and 330,000.[69] Zhang Zhenglong, author of the widely read but banned 1989 history of Communist forces in Manchuria, *White Snow, Red Blood*, recently drew a parallel between Hiroshima and Changchun. 'The casualties were about the same. Hiroshima took nine seconds; Changchun took five months.'[70] He could have added Nanjing to the list if he had wanted to be truly provocative.

The Communists also isolated the city of Shenyang.[71] There, too, the situation became grim, although the encirclement was less tight than at Changchun. Supplies reached the city by air and the Nationalists controlled the surrounding countryside. Even so, Henry Lieberman reported for *The New York Times* on 2 July that 'an estimated 300,000 persons, one fourth of Mukden [Shenyang]'s population, are slowly starving to death ...With Mukden cut off by land from China proper and living off a restricted hinterland, the poorest quarter of the population is existing mainly on cattle fodder. Some are eating tree leaves and bark.'[72] While 1,500 Shenyang residents fled the city every day, Lieberman went on to say that 'at least an equal number of refugees are pouring into the city from Communist-controlled areas. Mayor Tung Wen-chi said today that the

Reds were forcing refugees into Mukden as part of the campaign to starve the city.'

On 7 September, Mao Zedong instructed Lin Biao to take Jinzhou. The harvest was now in and therefore supplies were at their most plentiful. To wait longer, possibly until the next winter had passed, risked foregoing the opportunity altogether. In attacking Jinzhou rather than Shenyang or Changchun, the aim was 'to close the door and beat the dog', that is, to seal off Manchuria by taking this key city. With Jinzhou in Communist hands, no relief force from north China could come to the aid of the Nationalist armies in Manchuria, who would also be prevented from withdrawing through the Liaoxi Corridor.[73] The Communists could then set to work to destroy the Nationalist armies in Changchun and Shenyang.

Once the decision to assault Jinzhou was made, General Lin Biao took two weeks to move his forces into position. Seventh and Fourth Columns blocked the railway line south of Jinzhou. Eleventh Column surrounded port towns along the coast south of the city in order to prevent Nationalist withdrawals through these. Other forces surrounded Jinzhou itself. From high ground near the city, Communist artillery pounded Jinzhou's one usable air field, thus preventing an attempt by the Nationalists to airlift divisions from Shenyang to Jinzhou.[74]

To complete the encirclement of Jinzhou, General Lin Biao had to take the town of Yixian, located along the railway line from Jinzhou to Shenyang. Yixian was surrounded by thick strong walls and counted an elite division armed with US equipment among its defenders. When Yixian had still not been captured after three weeks, Mao pressed Lin Biao to make haste: 'our forces moved out on the ninth, twenty days ago, and you have not yet begun to attack Yixian.'[75] But General Lin Biao stuck to his 'four fasts and one slow' principle. He worked methodically, initially severing Yixian's railway connection with Shenyang and encircling the city. He then ordered a pause to allow his commanders to complete their preparations while General Zhu Rui's artillery bombarded the town. On 1 October, after the artillery had blasted a hole in the town wall, Lin's forces advanced on a narrow front through this breech, and then spread out. Four hours later the city was in Communist hands.[76] This was a stunning success, marred only by the death of General Zhu Rui, who stepped on a land mine.[77]

Chiang Kaishek tried to turn the tables on Lin Biao. His plan for snatching victory from the jaws of defeat was to use Jinzhou to tie down General Lin Biao's forces and then smash them by sending relief forces from north China and Shenyang. Chiang Kaishek's American advisor, General David Barr, wrote later that 'the plans made and the orders given were sound and, had they been obeyed, the results would probably have been favorable'.[78] On being informed of the plan, General Lin Biao took fright, remarking that 'we prepared a feast for one table, but now we have two tables of guests – what are we to do?'[79] He was so concerned that he even proposed to Mao to abort the battle. Mao Zedong, too, was worried, but he ordered General Lin to attack immediately, before the Nationalists could complete their deployments, which Mao believed would take three weeks.[80]

We will never know whether Chiang Kaishek's plan could have worked. Opposition by his most senior military leaders in north China and Manchuria meant that it was not given a chance. General Wei Lihuang, commander-in-chief at Shenyang, believed that his best option was to sit tight in Shenyang rather than send his forces out into the Manchurian countryside where they would be exposed to Communist attacks. General Fu Zuoyi in north China, already engaged by the Communists, also doubted the wisdom of diluting his force strength there. Only after Chiang Kaishek shuttled back and forth between Shenyang and Beijing for nine days was he able to convince them, a fact that underscored the fragility of his authority by this time. While the relief force from north China arrived just before the commencement of the Battle of Jinzhou, the force from Shenyang never came close. Valuable time was lost in dithering and bickering.

Before beginning the assault on Jinzhou on 14 October, Lin Biao's 250,000 Communist forces dug many kilometres of trenches, some to within earshot of Nationalist front lines. They shut down the water supply to the city, closed all roads leading in and out of it and cut its telephone lines. The attack began with an artillery barrage delivered by 900 cannons. A planned second barrage was called off when Communist tank units began their advance prematurely due to a communications mix-up. It did not matter. Through a breech in the city wall, their infantry poured into the city. By nightfall all meaningful resistance had ended and the city was in Communist hands.[81] They could not believe their good luck. Jinzhou was chock-full of supplies destined for Shenyang and Changchun. Besides vast piles of grain, they took possession of arms and ammunition for 60,000 troops, 'a large amount of industrial equipment', 1,000 bolts of cotton cloths, 200,000 kilos of cotton yarn and 400 trucks.[82]

The Siege of Changchun ended a few days later, on 20 October, when commander-in-chief Zheng Dongguo ordered his headquarter's units to lay down their arms after a symbolic last stand at the city's Central Bank building. From the middle of September, desertion, either individually or by small units of troops, had become common. On 13 October, the whole 60th Army defected, its commanders having been in discussion with the Communists about such a move for weeks.[83] It is unlikely to be a coincidence that the defection happened the day before General Lin Biao ordered the attack on Jinzhou. Following the fall of Jinzhou, holding out in Changchun became pointless. The Communists treated the surrendered Nationalist commanders well, as an inducement to

Nationalist commanders elsewhere to follow suit. The siege also showed that the Communists were prepared to inflict terrible pain on cities that defied them. After Changchun, no city would be defended to the death.

Following the fall of Jinzhou, General Wei Lihuang favoured recalling to Shenyang the relief force that he had sent south. Its commander, General Liao Yaoxiang, had consistently favoured withdrawal of all forces from Manchuria. He continued to argue that the attempt should be made, not through Jinzhou, of course, but through Yingkou, which was in Communist hands but where their troop numbers were low. On 19 October, a compromise was worked out in Shenyang whereby General Liao Yaoxiang's forces would attack General Lin Biao's northerly positions. If these attacks were victorious, the relief force would continue on to Jinzhou; if not, it would head for Yingkou. General Lin Biao first drew Shengyang's relief force south by pulling back his advance units; he then encircled and annihilated it methodically and thoroughly.[84]

With only some 100,000 troops left to defend it, Shenyang was doomed. General Lin Biao's units raced to the city, reaching it on 29 October, and prepared his assault. The lesson of Changchun was fresh in the minds of the defenders. The one division that refused to surrender was crushed on 2 November.[85] *The New York Times* reported that day: 'the Communists entered this thriving industrial center this morning, started disarming scattered government troops, and were in full control by 3 p.m.'[86]

The Communists had pulled off one of the greatest military feats in Chinese, or even world history. They had outmanoeuvred and out-thought a huge Nationalist force. They had first drawn the Nationalists out over much of Manchuria and then isolated their armies there. They had identified where precisely the critical point was in the Nationalist deployment and, having rapidly transferred a vast number of troops, had attacked it with overwhelming force. Lionel Lamb, whose acting position as Britain's ambassador to China had now been converted into a permanent one, visited Beijing and Tianjin after the fall of Jinzhou. He concluded that 'the morale among the civilian population no less than in Central Government armies is at an extremely low ebb ... the military, economic, and political collapse of the Central Government is a foregone conclusion.'[87]

He was right. Hot on the heels of the Liaoshen disaster came the Huai-Hai Campaign, which lasted from 6 November 1948 until 10 January the following year. This caused the Nationalists even greater losses. By this time, the Nationalists were no longer capable of fighting as a cohesive force or following a cohesive strategy. The enormous resilience that had sustained them during the War of Resistance was dissolving in a sea of economic, political and social problems.

During the Civil War, the Nationalists relied on the printing press to finance their military effort, as they had during the War of Resistance, with hyper-inflation the result. Twice they attempted to bring the inflationary spiral under control. In February 1947, price caps were imposed on essential commodities such as rice, cotton and fuel, and wages were frozen. The reforms failed because they were only enforced in the Shanghai–Nanjing area, but also because the price cap disincentivised rural producers and prompted, for instance, grain merchants to hoard their stocks. A black market grew up as the food supply situation inevitably worsened, resulting in rice riots. The second anti-inflation-ary attempt by the Nationalists, in August 1948, involved forcing the public to sell gold, silver and foreign currencies to the government in return for a new paper currency, the Gold Yuan. Prices and wages were again frozen, but once again the reform had to be abandoned after only a few weeks. The introduction of the Gold Yuan became seen as the daylight robbery of urban China of US$ 170 million-worth of gold, silver and hard currency.[88]

One consequence of the Nationalists' fiscal policy and the subsequent deteri-oration of living standards in the cities was industrial unrest. Before the War of Resistance, strikes were not uncommon in Shanghai, China's industrial centre, but they were counted in the hundreds. In 1946, 1,716 strikes took place in Shanghai. That figure rose to 2,538 the following year.[89] The freezing of salaries, the collapse of the rice market and the advent of hyperinflation hit teachers, college professors, writers, journalists, government employees and students. The value of their salaries and stipends had already been reduced to a frac-tion of what they had been in 1937; afterwards the situation worsened further. Most people's salaries were insufficient to pay for even their families' basic needs. Unsurprisingly, an anti-war movement took hold, which the National-ists attributed to Communist agents and which led, as we have seen, to harsh suppression measures which only made the Nationalists more unpopular.[90]

The Liaoshen and Huai-Hai defeats also caused the Nationalists to disin-tegrate politically. The re-election of Harry S. Truman to the US presidency in November 1948, which came as a surprise to many people, including in the USA, scotched any hope that a new administration might change course and resume US aid to the Nationalists. In December, pressure on Chiang Kaishek to resign reached a crescendo. In his 1949 New Year's message, he attempted to take the moral high ground by declaring that he was prepared to restart discus-sions with the Communists, laying down as his conditions that the constitution would remain in effect, that the government would not be changed, and that the Communists would agree to reject violent means to pursue their goals. This attempt to shift the blame for the Civil War on to the Communists failed. They declared that their conditions for the resumptions of negotiations were '(1) The punishment of war criminals; (2) The abolition of the bogus constitution; ... (4) The reorganization of all reactionary military forces on the basis of democratic principles; (5) The confiscation of bureaucratic capital [assets held by the government and its officials]; and (6) reform of the land system.'[91]

On 8 January, Chiang Kaishek gave in and communicated his decision to resign to Li Zongren, the head of the Guangxi Clique, who formally took over on 21 January, but only as acting president – an arrangement that guaranteed instability as Chiang could resume the presidency at any moment. In addition, Sun Ke, Sun Yatsen's son and China's premier at the time, moved the Executive Branch to Canton. Li Zongren may now be acting president, but he had no government.

Li Zongren declared an end to martial law, released political prisoners, allowed journals and newspapers that had been closed to publish again and reined in the secret police. He also initiated negotiations with the Communists. He declared that he was willing to accept a number of the demands the Communists had made earlier, including the confiscation of bureaucratic capital and the abolition of the constitution, which he suggested should be replaced after negotiations involving both parties. He proposed that both Nationalist and Communist forces would maintain their current positions and begin voluntary troop reductions. The Communist response was to demand the punishment of war criminals, the incorporation of Nationalist forces into the Communist order of command, the cancellation of all treaties and international agreements made by the Nationalists, the replacement of Nationalist government organisations with democratically elected ones, and the nationalisation of all banks, mines, industrial factories, shipping lines and companies. Essentially, they insisted that the Nationalists surrender and that their leadership sign its own death warrant. They set 20 April as the last date for acceptance of their demands.[92]

Unsurprisingly, that day came and went, after which the Communists crossed the Yangzi river in force, thus shattering any hope the Nationalists might have had of hanging on to south China. Acting President Li Zongren fled to his home province of Guangxi. A delegation from Canton convinced him to resume his acting presidency in Canton, but the diary of Chen Kewen, who worked closely with Li Zongren during this time, makes clear that Li was thoroughly demoralised and could see no way to restore Nationalist fortunes. In the middle of October 1949, when the Communist forces reached Canton, the Nationalists moved their capital to Chongqing, hoping that Sichuan province might save them again. Not this time. In the middle of November, they had to relinquish Chongqing, and shortly afterwards, on 8 December, they moved their government to Taipei.

Individual commanders such as General Bai Chongxi and Hu Zongnan still continued to fight, but they were unable to stem the Communist advance. Forces other than those of Lin Biao were involved in rounding them up, including the East China Field Army of Generals Su Yu and Chen Yi, the Central Plains Army of General Liu Bocheng and Political Commissar Deng Xiaoping, General Nie Rongzhen's army in the Shanxi–Hebei–Chahar Border Region, and the forces of General He Long in Shanxi and Suiyuan provinces.[93] But General Lin Biao's army was the best armed and trained and did most of the work. They marched all the way south, defeating Nationalist forces in the provinces of Hubei, Hunan, Jiangxi and Guangdong, including at Canton. The Lin Biao juggernaut only came to a halt after it rolled through Hainan, the large island off the south China coast in the South China Sea. It could go no further.

In *On War*, Clausewitz wrote that 'a swift and vigorous assumption of the offensive – the flashing sword of vengeance – is the most brilliant point in the defensive.' The Nationalists' Winter Offensive of 1939–40 had been an attempt to achieve that feat, but it proved a damp squid. Had the War of Resistance lasted longer, General Albert Wedemeyer's plan to train up and equip a thirty-plus division army might have been completed. The Nationalists might well then have been able to wage a powerful offensive against Japanese positions in China. But that was not to be, with the result that the Communists succeeded where the Nationalists had failed. They wielded the flashing sword of vengeance, crushingly and decisively.

FOURTEEN

EXHAUSTION

There is no instance of a nation benefitting from prolonged warfare.

Sun Tzu, *The Art of War* (Fifth century BC)

A s so often in China's history, events along its borders would have a major impact on the outcome of the Civil War. Chiang Kaishek did not surrender, he just moved to Taiwan, together with the country's gold and between 1 and 2 million soldiers, officials and citizens, hoping to launch a comeback from this difficult-to-invade island. General Hu Zongnan had retreated with his troops to still-independent Tibet. In Gansu province in north-west China, Muslim forces allied with the Nationalists to resist the Communists. Several thousand Nationalist soldiers withdrew to Burma and Thailand; they, too, did not accept that the Civil War was over. Xinjiang, China's far west province with a large Muslim population, was far from secure, not just because of Muslim resistance to Communist rule but also because of Soviet penetration. To the south of China, Ho Chi Minh's Viet Minh had begun fighting the French in Vietnam. In Korea, the 38th parallel divided two governments each claiming to rule the whole country. Events in any of these border regions could have triggered a chain reaction leading to a different outcome for China. But it was in Korea that the final act took place, an act that ended with the Communists firmly taking control of mainland China and the Nationalists ensconced on Taiwan.

As we have seen, at the end of the war against Japan, Soviet and US forces entered Korea and made the 38th parallel the line demarcating their zones of occupation. Instead of granting the country immediate independence, the Allies decided at a conference in Moscow in December 1945 to place Korea under joint Soviet and US trusteeship for a period of five years.[1] An attempt in 1946 to establish a single government failed because of Korean opposition and because of the distrust between the USA and the USSR. The Soviets instituted a government in North Korea, with their man in Korea, the 38-year-old Kim Il-sung, as president. Seventy-one-year-old Syngman Rhee, the USA's counterpart to Kim, was put in charge of the US-sponsored South Korean government.

Initially Stalin rebuffed Kim Il-sung every time he mooted his desire to launch an offensive to unify Korea by force, but at a meeting held in April 1950, he gave his approval.[2] Three developments led to Stalin's change of heart. The

USA had announced that it regarded neither Korea nor Taiwan as critical to its security, making a US intervention unlikely. The completion of its troop withdrawal programme by July 1949 provided concrete evidence that the USA was serious.[3] Secondly, the USA was turning Japan into an anti-Communist bastion in the western Pacific. That stoked the Soviets' fears about the security of their eastern frontier zone. Finally, South Korea seemed ripe for invasion. In 1946, the Soviet Union had imposed order efficiently in North Korea; by contrast, the US administration in the south was beset by problems ranging from food shortages, strikes and corruption to a serious uprising, the suppression of which came at a cost of 30,000 dead.[4] Syngman Rhee's government lacked a strong popular base because many of its officials came from an elite which had close connections with the Japanese. Finally, the Chinese Civil War was over. Thus, in the spring of 1950, a conjuncture of developments came together to suggest that an invasion of South Korea stood every chance of success.

When Stalin gave his blessing to Kim Il-sung, he told him that the Soviet Union would not become directly involved in the offensive and that Kim must secure Mao Zedong's concurrence.[5] Before Kim arrived in Beijing for his discussions with Mao Zedong, Stalin informed the latter that, while he personally approved of 'the proposal of the Koreans to move toward reunification', the final decision rested with 'the Chinese and Korean comrades together, and in case of disagreement by the Chinese comrades, the decisions should be postponed'.[6] In Beijing, Kim did not ask for any assistance other than the transfer back to Korea of three Korean divisions which had fought with General Lin Biao during the Liaoshen Campaign. Also, Mao Zedong judged that 'the Americans would not become engaged in a Third World War for such a small territory'.[7] With the invasion of South Korea promising the definitive removal of US influence from the Korean peninsula, and the ousting of a hostile South Korean government with links to Chiang Kaishek on Taiwan, and little being asked of the Chinese in the way of support, Mao Zedong readily gave his approval.

On 25 June, Kim Il-sung hurled his forces across the entire length of the 38th parallel. Using heavy artillery and tanks, including the Soviets' mighty T-34s, the North Koreans made mincemeat of Syngman Rhee's forces. They took Seoul three days after their offensive had begun. By then, the collapse of the South Korean forces was so complete that only 22,000 out of 100,000 troops could be accounted for and they had lost most of their heavy weapons and ammunition.[8] US forces flown in from Japan were unable to halt the North Korean juggernaut, to both their surprise and mortification. By early August, American and South Korean forces had been pushed back all the way to the southern edge of South Korea, where they defended a precarious perimeter along the Naktong river west of Pusan.[9]

The Korean War

But Stalin, Kim and Mao had misjudged US intentions. In April 1950, at the same time that they were dismissing the probability of an American intervention, the US National Security Council adopted Paper 68, which became a cornerstone of US Cold War policy. Its premise was that the Soviet Union 'seeks to impose its authority everywhere' and so threatened 'the destruction not only of this Republic but of civilization itself'.[10] The paper also rejected as possible responses to the danger both isolation and war. With the Soviets now also having atomic bombs, the consequences of the latter were too awful to contemplate. NSC-68, as it became known, recommended 'a more rapid building up of the political, economic, and military strength of the free world' to contain the Soviet Union and prepare the West to defend itself in case of a Soviet attack.[11]

NSC-68 both fleshed out and reflected the policy of containment that had been articulated by the diplomat George Kennan in 1946 and 1947. In what came to be known as 'The Long Telegram', which he sent from his posting in Moscow to the State Department, Kennan argued that the USSR was an instinctively expansionist but ultimately weak state which could be contained through a series of flexible economic, political, ideological and, if need be, military countermeasures. In essence, he saw the world as in the midst of a struggle between a Communist bloc and the free world. This policy of containment, out of which grew the Truman Doctrine, led to the Marshall Plan of aid to Europe, support for Greece in its struggle with Communist rebels, and NATO. Kim Il-sung's attack on South Korea was not considered a strategic threat in its own right, but it was interpreted from this Cold War point of view. Not confronting Kim in South Korea might, it was felt, embolden Moscow to step up its efforts to bring more of Europe under its sway, and that was considered a threat to the security of the USA.

Korea, then, was the first test of US resolve in the new Cold War. On 27 June, two days after the invasion of South Korea began, President Truman authorised the deployment of US forces to Korea, a decision he later characterised as more difficult than ordering the detonation of the two atomic bombs above Japan.[12] From 7 July, the US forces were allowed to operate as UN Forces, after the UN Security Council condemned North Korea's attack as a 'breach of the peace' at a meeting which the Soviets had declined to attend because it was boycotting the Security Council at the time in protest at its continued recognition of the Nationalists as China's official government.[13] Units from Britain, Canada, New Zealand, Australia, France, the Philippines, the Netherlands and a few other countries assisted the Americans in Korea. General Douglas MacArthur, Supreme Commander of the Allied Powers in Japan, was the first UN Commander of the Korean War.

At Pusan, the North Korean forces were at the end of very long supply lines and, after more than a month of fighting, their combat strength had weakened. UN forces gradually firmed up the Pusan defensive perimeter and by the end of August it was clear that Kim Il-sung's forces would go no further. General MacArthur then masterminded a daring amphibious landing to the rear of the North Koreans, at Incheon, Seoul's sea port just south of the 38th parallel. Ten-metre high tides (among the highest in the world), strong currents of as much as eight knots in Incheon's two narrow approach channels, high sea-walls and long mudflats at low tide made any landing a gamble, but would also give it the element of surprise. Begun on 15 September, the landing by the US army's X Corps succeeded beyond anyone's wildest imaginings, except those of General MacArthur himself, who never lacked faith in his own ideas, and for whom the operation was to be the grand finale to an illustrious career. The North Koreans, assuming that a landing at Incheon was unlikely, had not even bothered to mine the approach channels.

Now it was the turn of the North Koreans to fall apart. UN Forces went on the offensive the day after the Incheon landings. The US army's 1st and 11th Corps had reinforced its 8th Army, which was facing the Koreans at Pusan, while USA's X Corps had landed at Incheon. Together with the X Corps, they threatened to encircle the by now tired and outgunned North Koreans. By 9 October, UN Forces had driven them back across the 38th parallel. On 26 October, the first South Korean units reached the Yalu river which marks the border between China and Korea.[14] Rather than North Korea uniting the country, it was Syngman Rhee's South Korea which stood on the brink of achieving that feat.

Mao Zedong now faced a difficult decision, one that could have cost him his revolution: intervene in Korea or stay out. Kim Il-sung would have preferred that the Soviets came to his assistance, but Stalin told him brusquely on 1 October that, if he needed help, he had better appeal to Beijing.[15] Stalin also put pressure on Mao to assist Kim: 'I think that if in the current situation you consider it possible to send troops to assist the Koreans, then you should move at least five or six divisions toward the 38th Parallel.'[16] The Chinese had already concentrated 120,000 troops at Shenyang; they could go into action in short order.

Some very good arguments counselled against the deployment of this force into Korea. The Chinese Communists faced many urgent and difficult problems within China. Disarming the bandit gangs that were operating throughout the country, ensuring sufficient food supplies for its hungry population, and bringing order to a society in turmoil were only the most pressing of these. Rather than sending troops to Korea, the Communists would have preferred to invade Taiwan. Apart from anything, taking on the Americans was a far greater undertaking. General Lin Biao opposed intervention because he did not believe that the Communist forces were capable of succeeding and because he feared that it might trigger US attacks by air on China's railway lines, ports and cities, possibly with atomic weapons. He declined to be appointed as commander-in-chief of any expeditionary force that might be despatched to Korea.[17]

On 3 October, Mao informed Stalin that 'having thought this over', he had concluded that now was not the time to invade: 'in the first place, it is very difficult to resolve the Korean question with a few divisions (our troops are extremely poorly equipped); ... in the second place, it is most likely that this will provoke an open conflict between the USA and China.'[18] Pessimism reigned at a Communist Party Politburo meeting of 4 October, which rehearsed all the arguments against Chinese intervention: the inferiority of their troops; their unfamiliarity with the mountainous terrain of North Korea; the bitter cold of the now fast approaching winter; the problems of supplying troops outside China; and the possibility that the war might have a destabilising effect domestically.[19]

Stalin did not take no for an answer. He counselled Mao that a Fabian policy of waiting for events to develop carried great risks. 'If a war is inevitable,' Stalin told him, 'then let it be waged now, and not in a few years' time when Japanese militarism will be restored as an ally of the USA and Japan will have a ready-made bridgehead on the continent in a form of the entire Korea run by Syngman Rhee.'[20] A US victory in Korea would mean, Stalin argued, that 'China would fail to get back even Taiwan, which at present the United States clings to as a springboard, not for Chiang Kaishek who has no chance to succeed, but for themselves or for a militaristic Japan.'[21] Reversing the USA's earlier stance that it would not stand in the way of a Communist invasion of Taiwan, on 27 June President Truman had ordered the Seventh Fleet into the Taiwan Straits. Even if the ultimate aim of the Chinese Communists was to control Taiwan, helping Kim Il-sung to beat back the Americans made sense.

Stalin's arguments and a promise of Soviet air cover for their ground forces swayed Mao and his Politburo colleagues. On 5 October they agreed that China would intervene. The night before, Mao Zedong had persuaded the seasoned Communist General Peng Dehuai, who had fought with Mao since the early 1930s, to accept the position of commander-in-chief. At the meeting on 5 October, General Peng Dehuai spoke out strongly in favour of intervention, arguing that if the Americans were not stopped, they would be able to attack China from Korea and Taiwan.[22] Mao Zedong told Stalin that China would 'send to Korea nine, not six divisions'.[23]

Following the meeting, Zhou Enlai, recently installed as China's premier, travelled with General Lin Biao to the Black Sea resort of Sochi for talks with Stalin. To their consternation, Stalin told them that no Soviet air cover would be provided for at least the first couple of months.[24] Informed of this unwelcome surprise, Mao Zedong ordered a halt to all preparations for the invasion. Stalin, in turn, told Kim Il-sung that 'you must prepare to evacuate completely into China and/or the USSR'.[25] More meetings followed in Sochi and Beijing. Mao Zedong was overcome by doubt, not knowing whether to go ahead with an intervention or stay out of the conflict in Korea. He suffered many nights of insomnia, and 'remained undecided even when our forces reached the Yalu river', as one Chinese Communist general remembered.[26] But on 19 October, Chinese Communist forces began to enter Korea as China's People's Volunteers, a disguise that fooled nobody but which indicated that the Chinese Communists did not want the fighting to be understood as being between China and the USA directly.

We do not know what, precisely, motivated Mao to approve China's entry into the Korean War. Perhaps, at some dark moment in the middle of the night, as his mind was churning, he recalled Guo Moruo's '1644', the article in which Guo recounts how the peasant leader Li Zicheng, too busy indulging in victory celebrations in Beijing, failed to pay attention to threats mounting on his frontier and so lost his new dynasty to the Manchus in weeks. Stalin's warning about the dangers of allowing the Americans to build up strong positions in Korea and Taiwan may have hit home, even haunted Mao, precisely because it echoed Guo's. When Premier Zhou Enlai spoke on 24 October at a gathering of members of the People's Political Consultative Conference, he made the same point: 'If the DPRK [North Korea] is subjugated by the US imperialists, there will be no security for the Northeast [Manchuria].'[27]

It all worked out for Mao Zedong and his colleagues. The Korean War greatly enhanced the young People's Republic's international position, stabilised Communist rule in China and strengthened Mao Zedong's own position in the Communist Party yet further. Over a period of two weeks, the Chinese Communists smuggled four armies and three artillery divisions across the Yalu river into North Korea. US intelligence failed to spot them, partly as a result of plain incompetence but also because of an unwarranted sense of superiority, disdain for Chinese Communist military capabilities and victory fever. With the North Koreans on the run and the USA's 10th Corps and 8th Army thrusting towards the Yalu, General MacArthur and his staff, many of whom were under the spell of his charisma, bragged about being home before Christmas.

As in Manchuria, the Chinese Communists faced an enemy with modern weapons, this time with ample supplies and a powerful air force to boot. Neither a frontal assault nor establishing a defensive line and trying to hold it were promising options. Instead, the Chinese People's Volunteers exploited the weak intelligence capabilities of the UN forces and the fact that their sumptuous equipment tied them to low-lying roads. Following a first probing attack, they withdrew and allowed UN units moving north to pass them by. They concentrated superior numbers on the UN forces' flanks and rear, prepared battlefields and ambushes in the way of retreating forces, took up positions on high ground and gathered intelligence to identify the weaker units among the UN forces.[28]

On 25 November, the Chinese People's Volunteers first hit Korean forces incorporated into the US 8th Army. Two days later they took on the 10th Corps, whose units were far too dispersed to be able to assist each other. Taken by complete surprise, the stunned UN commanders ordered the retreat.[29] Even several days into the offensive, some senior commanders failed to realise what was happening. One told a subordinate commander that 'the enemy who is delaying you for the moment is nothing more than remnants of Chinese divisions fleeing north'.[30] On 3 December, UN forces evacuated Pyongyang in disarray, alongside 300,000 refugees. The Chinese People's Volunteers had Seoul in their hands a month later.

The collapse was one of the worst in US military history. The shock was so severe that a successful retreat, such as that of the First Marine Division and the 7th US Army Division at Changjin reservoir, became celebrated in the US press as an act of outstanding heroism, in the same way that the evacuation of the defeated British Expeditionary Force from Dunkirk in 1940 was turned into an inspiring tale of British defiance and pluck. 'Surrounded and vastly outnumbered by savage enemies, fighting in temperatures as low as 25 below zero [Fahrenheit], not certain that there was any possible escape', the US forces at Changjin reservoir 'moved down in perfect order', according to one *New York Times* article.[31]

Had the US journalists or UN commanders known that the Chinese People's Volunteers had suffered tens of thousands of casualties and had to all intents and purposes been put out of action, the story of the battle for Changjin reservoir would have been told differently. And had they been aware of the assessment of Soviet advisors in Korea, it would have been told differently again. One Soviet advisor wrote that the Volunteers 'deployed strength and equipment evenly along the front, and thus failed to concentrate for an offensive. Every army conducted its own isolated attacks. No powerful offensive was launched against the enemy's vulnerable point.'[32] Some of Lin Biao's tactical principles had apparently been forgotten. The Chinese general in charge of logistics reported that the offensive went in two divisions short of its planned number and those troops that were involved 'did not have enough to eat, [and] their winter uniforms were too thin … as a result, there occurred a large number of non-combat casualties', that is, soldiers died from lack of food and exhaustion as well as being literally frozen to death.[33] The UN disaster resulted from a collapse of nerve on its part as much as from superior Chinese intelligence, movement and aggression.

A new US commander, General Matthew Ridgway, who replaced General Walker after he was killed in a traffic accident, was able to revive the morale of the UN forces. Exploiting the UN's superior air power, he brought the retreat to a halt 100 kilometres south of Seoul and succeeded in firming up a defensive line.[34] In January 1950, the Chinese commander-in-chief, General Peng Dehuai, reached the conclusion that no further offensive operations should be conducted until his forces had been resupplied and had a chance to rest. But Mao, his confidence restored following the early victories of the People's Volunteers, judged that the UN forces would withdraw after a symbolic defence and ordered Peng to keep the pressure on. Peng did as he was told and in February began another offensive. Although he managed to put the 8th Division of the South Korean army out of action, he made no further headway. With many Chinese divisions severely weakened, UN forces prepared to counter-attack. What was left of Seoul was back in their hands by 15 March.[35]

With UN forces back at the 38th parallel, President Truman had to decide whether to dig in or once again move on to the Yalu river. MacArthur favoured the latter option, and even called for expanding the war to China and bringing in the Nationalists. Truman definitely did not want that. He had ordered the US Seventh Fleet into the Taiwan Straits not only to prevent a Communist invasion of Taiwan, but also to prevent the Nationalists from moving the other way. Despite presidential orders to the contrary, MacArthur vented his ideas in public and blamed Washington for making him fight with one hand tied behind his back. When President Truman received intelligence that the Soviets were considering joining the war in Korea if the Chinese People's Volunteers were defeated, he secretly sent atomic bombs to east Asia in readiness for any eventuality. But he also judged that General MacArthur was too unpredictable, too independent and too cavalier about instructions from Washington to be relied upon at this critical time. He therefore recalled him, a difficult decision that could not but damage Truman's domestic popularity, given the general's enormous personal popularity. But Truman was determined to contain the fighting to Korea and therefore did not want to take any risks. UN forces did not cross the 38th parallel.[36]

Still convinced that the Chinese People's Volunteers could defeat the UN forces, in May Mao Zedong ordered General Peng Dehuai to go on the offensive once more. General Peng attacked with 1 million men. The fighting was heavy and the Chinese and North Korean forces were able to punch a bulge in UN lines. However, when UN forces threatened to encircle these, General Peng ordered his forces to retreat. Some UN commanders wanted to pursue them. 'We had him beaten and could have destroyed his armies', General James van Fleet claimed later.[37] But that was not Washington's aim and UN forces stayed at the 38th parallel, leaving the Chinese People's Volunteers free to lick their wounds.

After this last Chinese offensive, the Korean War entered a stalemate. From then until an armistice was agreed in 1953, the front lines did not change very much, even though the fighting still resulted in a large number of casualties. President Truman was ready to agree to a truce in the spring of 1951. He suggested a ceasefire plan to the UN Security Council which, had Mao accepted it, would have left the North Koreans with a larger territory, including Seoul, than they eventually did. But Mao rejected it.[38] Only after the failure of a further offensive and the incurrence of yet more losses did he and Kim Il-sung accept that they were not going to prevail over the UN forces. Truce negotiations began in July 1951 but were concluded only after Stalin's death on 5 March 1953. Having US forces embroiled in fighting the Chinese in Korea had suited him just fine.

The armistice was finally signed on 27 July 1953, at the village of Panmunjom, following long-drawn-out negotiations in which the repatriation of prisoners of war was the most contentious issue. It brought to an end a conflict in which 2–3 million Korean citizens from both the North and the South lost their lives, with air power and the climate responsible for a large proportion of this terrible death toll. The USA dropped more bombs on Korea in three years than in the Pacific during the whole of the Second World War. Most of North Korea's largest towns were at least partly destroyed, many dams – important for irrigation and hence for food production – were broken, railway lines and bridges were smashed, and napalm rains first drenched and then burned enemy troop formations as well as the villages and forests suspected of harbouring them.[39] The South Korean armed forces suffered 163,000 dead (including 25,000 classed as missing presumed dead) and 429,000 wounded. The figures for US armed forces are 36,574 dead (of whom 7,926 were missing presumed dead) and 103,284 wounded.[40] No reliable casualty figures exist for Chinese and North Korean combatants, but it is unlikely that they will have been any less than those for South Korea, that is, around half a million casualties each.[41]

A Cold War Peace

At the time of the Korean War, different futures for Asia remained in play. A new order based on Communist comradeship was one possibility. This inspired not just the Chinese and Korean Communists, but had large followings elsewhere, in French Indochina, for instance, but also in Japan. Japanese Pan-Asianism was dead, of course, but yearnings for Asian solidarity were not. When the Chinese Nationalists learned that the Americans might try to abolish the use of characters in Japan, they were greatly concerned until the Japanese premier Yoshida Shigeru told them that he would not allow this to happen and that Confucianism was the shared foundation for both Chinese and Japanese modernity.[42] The Indian prime minister Jawaharlal Nehru, who had discussed with Chiang Kaishek the glories of Asian civilisations in Chong-qing during the War of Resistance, now talked about a 'Third Way' based on common Asian values and independence from both Moscow and Washington. Britain promoted the British Commonwealth as the post-war successor to the British Empire, not just to sustain its pre-war global network of trade connec-tions but also as an alternative to a US-dominated Cold War order.

After the outbreak of the Korean War, the Truman administration decided that the goal of containing the Soviet Union could be best achieved by tying Japan as well as Taiwan, the Philippines, Australia and New Zealand to the USA through a series of defence treaties, trade agreements and economic aid accords. John Foster Dulles led the diplomatic negotiations that culminated in a series of treaties that achieved this aim, inventing shuttle diplomacy as he went about it. He was a Republican but, as Secretary of State in the Eisenhower administration after 1952, he continued the policy of containing communism that his Democrat predecessor Dean Acheson had pioneered in Korea, doing so in south-east Asia. In the Truman administration he had served as a 'special consultant' to Acheson, when US policy was to contain communism rather than to fight back against it.[43]

The US decided that peace needed to be restored between Japan and its former enemies, both to return sovereignty to Japan and so bring it into the new order as an independent nation and to lay the basis for collaboration among states in east and south-east Asia in the defence against the spread of communism. In early January 1951, Dulles formulated the principles for what would become the San Francisco Peace Treaty: the end of the state of war between Japan and its enemies; Japan's renouncement of sovereignty over Korea, Taiwan and the small nearby island of Penghu; and the requirement that Japan should apply for UN membership. The peace treaty would also commit Japan to adhere to Article 2 of the UN Charter, that is, to use only peaceful means in resolving dis-putes with other countries. It was thought necessary to include this stipulation in the treaty because of the possibility that the Soviet Union might use its veto in the Security Council to block Japanese membership of the United Nations.

Dulles's diplomacy hit a roadblock when Britain and the USA fell out over which China should attend the peace conference: the People's Republic of Mao Zedong or the Nationalist government of Chiang Kaishek? Britain had recog-nised the People's Republic, in part because it had substantial interests in the country, but also simply in recognition of the fact that the Communists were in control of China. As well, significant sympathy for the Communists existed in south and south-east Asian nations, whose support the British needed if the British Commonwealth was to be a success.

The UK suggested as a solution the inclusion of an accession clause to the peace treaty and to hand to the Far East Commission the decision as to which

China should be allowed to avail itself of this facility. That commission, of which the Soviet Union was a member, formally oversaw the Allied occupation of Japan. The proposal was unacceptable to the USA as it was likely that it would be outvoted on the commission. Another issue that divided the USA and the UK was that the UK argued that 'a formula should be worked out about what should be done with Formosa [Taiwan] and the Pescadores [Penghu] rather than leaving the matter up in the air'.[44] Dulles rejected that, arguing that 'at present we were only providing that Japan should relinquish its claim to Formosa and that we were not attempting to indicate what the final settlement of the Formosa problem should be'.[45] When it became clear that the USA and the UK were unable to arrive at a common position, they decided that neither Beijing nor Taipei would be invited to the peace conference. Given that China had been both their ally and one of Japan's main enemies, this was awkward, but only on that basis could the two co-convenors of the San Francisco Peace Conference move forwards.

Nehru wanted a peace conference involving only Asian countries. India declined an invitation to attend the San Francisco Peace Conference and protested at the United States' 'continued occupation of the Ryukyu (Okinawa) and Bonin islands, the failure to restore Formosa to China, and the provision that US troops stay as part of a US–Japan defensive agreement'.[46] Krishna Menon, the head of the Indian delegation at the UN, declared that India would develop good will with Beijing by not attending the conference and that then 'the whole of South Asia and the Far East would acclaim India'.[47]

Other important issues proved controversial, including whether Japan should pay war reparations, but the peace conference went ahead anyway and a treaty was signed on 8 December 1951, on the tenth anniversary of Japan's Nanshin operation, its attack on south-east Asia and Pearl Harbor. Its provisions were in line with the American design for the treaty. Japan abandoned any claims to Taiwan and Penghu as well as to the Kurile and southern Sakhalin islands. No war reparations were imposed on it but Japan also committed to the use of peaceful means in settling international disputes.[48]

The Soviet ambassador to the United Nations, Andrei Gromyko, attended the conference, not to sign the treaty but to denounce it. He called Dulles a warmonger, accused the USA of turning Japan into a military base and argued that the treaty was an injustice against China.[49] In Beijing on 15 August – yet again a date chosen for its historical resonance (the surrender of Japan) – Premier Zhou Enlai echoed Gromyko's criticism, adding that the failure of the treaty to restore Chinese sovereignty over Taiwan amounted to the US occupation of China's 'sovereign territory'.[50]

Even though the San Francisco Peace Treaty restored independence to Japan, Japan was less than thrilled. The treaty bound Japan to sign a treaty with any of its former enemies who wished to do so, an oblique but clear reference to China.[51] At San Francisco, Yoshida Shigeru told Dean Rusk, the US Under Secretary of State for Far Eastern Affairs, that 'he had been trying to think of some "contribution" Japan might make to the common cause of bringing peace and stability to East Asia ... as a repayment for the enormous generosity and forbearance the Americans had shown during the occupation'.[52] Rusk concluded that Premier Yoshida was preparing him for a Japanese decision not to sign with Taipei but with Beijing. Yoshida faced pressure from pro-Communist parliamentarians in the Diet as well as from business interests to develop good relations with Beijing.[53] As *The New York Times* explained, 'many merchants and politicians [in Japan] look to Red China as an eventual and inevitable market for Japan's resurgent industry'.[54]

Dulles made sure that Japan opted for the Nationalists. Five days after the US occupation of Japan ended and the country became an independent nation again, Dulles handed Premier Yoshida a memorandum stating: 'the US Senate, Congress, and American people generally will insistently want to know whether Japanese Government intends to pursue foreign policies in Asia generally compatible with those of the United States.'[55] The memorandum went on to say that the Nationalist government 'is recognized as the lawful government of China by the United States; ... it has a seat, voice, and vote in the UN, including the Security Council ... It is suggested that Japanese interests might best be served if the Japanese Government were to negotiate with the National Government.'[56] After the USA promised to guarantee Japan's security and access to new markets including in south-east Asia, Yoshida bowed to US pressure,[57] and ordered a negotiator to Taipei. The Asia Bureau of Japan's Foreign Office issued a public statement stating that 'Japan has no relation whatsoever with the Peiping [Beijing] regime, and it is inconceivable that she will sign any treaty with that government.'[58] This was clear as a bell.

The negotiations in Taipei were short but fractious. Japan aimed not at a full-blown peace treaty but one that treated the Nationalists as a local government in control of a piece of territory with which Japan arranged a number of practical issues such as trade, postal communications, air transport, the citizenship of Taiwan's residents and the delineation of fishing grounds. Japan, then, implicitly tried to treat the Nationalist government as they had attempted to do during the War of Resistance, as a minor local administration, no doubt to their astonishment and anger. The Nationalists, in their turn, hoped to secure Japan's recognition that they were the sovereign government of all of China, including the mainland.

The issue came to a head in discussions about the geographical area to which the treaty should apply. After long debate, Japan's plenipotentiary negotiator, Isao Kawada, and the Nationalists' Foreign Minister, Yeh Kung-ch'ao, settled on the following wording: 'the present treaty ... shall, in respect of the Republic of China, be applicable to all territories which are now, or which may hereafter be, under the control of its government.' While the English text of the treaty was authoritative, Yeh and Isao agreed that the Chinese translation would use the word *lingtu*, which connotes 'sovereign territory' and that the Japanese translation would speak of *ryoiki,* a vaguer term. The head of the Asia Desk of Japan's Foreign Minister explained to the Diet that 'in common international practice some cases are found where the term "territory" is not so strictly interpreted as to mean "state territory"'.[59] The wording allowed Japan to argue that the treaty applied only to areas actually under the control of the Nationalists and that it did not necessarily even regard these as sovereign territory of the Nationalists. In 1978, the Japanese also signed a treaty of peace and friendship with the People's Republic of China.

In contrast to his diplomats and lawyers, Chiang Kaishek did not believe the issue to be all that important. His greatest concern was that the treaty recognised the Nationalists as one of the victors of the Second World War, as it indeed did by being termed a peace treaty. On 27 April, the day before the treaty was signed, Chiang wrote in his diary: 'we are able to sign a Treaty of Peace with Japan as one of the victors. Doubtless this is a major blow to the bogus Communist organization, although of course this cannot erase my responsibility for the defeat of the revolution.'[60] 'Bogus Communist organization' was Chiang's choice of words for the People's Republic of China. He had lost the Civil War and was a much-diminished figure, of course, but recognition as one of the victorious allies of the Second World War brought enormous advantages. This way he kept hold of the diplomatic gains he had secured during the War of Resistance, including a seat for Taiwan on the UN Security Council. Last but not least, the peace treaty denied Mao Zedong the total victory he had been after. The Nationalists were safe in Taiwan. They lived to fight another day, or so they hoped.

Naturally, America's drive to shore up its Cold War front line in the western Pacific triggered a reaction in Beijing. A China Peace Committee was established, of which Guo Moruo, the author of '1644', was chair. He and Sun Yatsen's widow, Song Qingling, issued invitations for an Asian and Pacific Peace Conference in Beijing to discuss 'the validity of the Japanese Peace Treaty', the 'revival of Japanese militarism' and 'the menace of atomic, chemical, and bacteriological warfare', which Beijing was accusing the USA of waging at the time.[61] The conference went ahead in October 1952 and was attended by representatives from thirty-seven countries, mostly from non-governmental organizations. When the conference opened, the *People's Daily* accused the USA of conducting biochemical and bacterial warfare, suppressing independence movements and stalling on truce talks in Korea, while China's Minister of Foreign Affairs called on the American people to campaign for the removal of the trade embargo imposed on China in 1949.[62] The conference had a long-term impact by promoting the idea of peaceful coexistence which, for instance, shaped the non-aligned movement, that group of states that wished to keep both Moscow and Washington at a distance. It also gained Beijing sympathisers the world over. But it did not succeed in changing the basic outlines of the new US-dominated Cold War order that had now come about in east Asia; the hard truth was that the People's Republic of China lacked the military power to achieve that aim.

The Cold War peace was a strange sort of peace, a jerry-rigged armed peace, if it can be called a peace at all. The 38th parallel remains a potent symbol of the dislocations that came with the new order: divisions within and between states; fears about ideological others triggering panics, purges and suppression; and families split apart for decades. This was a peace shorn of any grand principles about equality among nations, rights to self-determination, democracy and human rights. It did not give hope, nor did it foster reconciliations, but instead it fuelled fears of nuclear war and Armageddon.

For south-east Asia, the consequences of the new order were abysmal. When the US Cold War strategy turned aggressive, Vietnam paid a heavy price, as first French and then US forces brought their mechanical superiority to bear on a national liberation war whose architects and leaders learned from and were helped by their Chinese neighbours. In 1954, at the Battle of Dien Bien Phu, artillery was important, as it had been during the Liaoshen Campaign. The North Vietnamese strategy of spreading the war out over vast areas and surrounding cities from the countryside followed that of the Communists in China. In Vietnam napalm rained down on forests and villages with devastating consequences which were captured in photographs and newsreels, whose distribution undermined support for the war in the USA. Other areas in south-east Asia were affected, including Malaysia, where a Communist insurgency lasted from 1948 until 1960. Not the least significant victims of the new Cold War order were the cross-Asian trade networks, flows of people and solidarities that had long linked east and south-east Asia. It is only in the last decade or two that they have begun to re-emerge.

The USA, and other Western countries, were impacted by the new order, and not only because of the blood and money they spilled in fighting national liberation wars in south-east Asia and elsewhere. The McCarthyite paranoia about Communist infiltration of the US government was a symbol of the kind of nightmares that kept Americans in their grip and which shaped the USA's international policies and interventions, not just until détente began in 1969, but well after; until the fires that had been set alight during the Second World War began to die down; the fears of a Third World War fought with nuclear arms began to lose their grip; and the habit of seeing the world as engaged in a fight to the end between two radically different alternatives – capitalism and communism – began to lose their persuasiveness.

But east Asia did reap real benefits from the new order, not least because, after the signing of the two treaties, the armies in the region have stayed largely in their barracks, despite occasional border wars. These include: China's 1955 testing of the USA's resolve when it attacked Nationalist-controlled offshore islands, a test which the USA met with ease; China's clash with India in 1962; and its invasion of Vietnam in 1978. The internal violence in China took much longer to die down. In the early 1950s, the Campaign to Suppress Counter Revolutionaries and the implementation of land revolution in areas where it had not yet taken place were important in consolidating Communist control; estimates of death tolls range from a low (and officially acknowledged) 800,000 to 2 or even 5 million.[63] The Anti-Rightist Campaign in the late 1950s and the Cultural Revolution of the 1960s were still to come. Violent class struggle – effectively, another form of civil war – ended only when Deng Xiaoping outlawed it in 1978. Even so, the new order made an economic miracle possible first in Japan, then in South Korea and Taiwan, and finally, after Deng Xiaoping came to power in 1978, in China, whose economic miracle transformed the lives of hundreds of millions of people. The case for peace has rarely been better made.

TRANSITIONS

Peace is at once the mother and the nurse of all that is good for man; war, on a sudden and at one stroke, overwhelms, extinguishes, abolishes, whatever is cheerful, whatever is happy and beautiful, and pours a foul torrent of disasters on the life of mortals. Peace shines upon human affairs like the vernal sun. The fields are cultivated, the gardens bloom, the cattle are fed upon a thousand hills, new buildings arise, riches flow, pleasures smile, humanity and charity increase, arts and manufactures feel the genial warmth of encouragement, and the gains of the poor are more plentiful.

Erasmus, 'Antipolemus, or, the Plea of Reason, Religion, and Humanity against War' (1515)

In the People's Republic, the new order meant not a return to ordinary times but a society hellbent on revolution, as Mao Zedong abandoned his pre-1949 caution and began to rush history. Many joined this world with enthusiasm. The Communists were the embodiment of hope, not just in China, but in the rest of Asia, in the Middle East and Africa, and even in the West, although more so in Europe than in the USA. Communist China represented an alternative to militarised Cold War American capitalism and appeared to offer cures for the ills of atomised, urban-centred, industrialised modernity. Thousands of overseas Chinese returned to China to offer their talents as engineers, scientists, economists, doctors, nurses and teachers to assist the Communists in giving birth to their New China. The vast majority of those who had the means and the money to make their way to Taiwan, Hong Kong, Australia, the USA, or Europe – including writers, journalists, bankers, film-makers, businessmen, teachers and students – decided not to do so. The Nationalists were the past; the Communists were the future.

Few knew then that the suppression of counter-revolutionaries in China's cities and land revolution in its villages in the 1950s had cost hundreds of thousands, probably millions of lives; many of those who did know probably thought that this was a price worth paying for a new future. None could know in the 1950s, as we do now, that the 1958–61 famine resulting from the Great Leap Forward, when the Communists reorganised China into communes, would result in 18 to 45 million deaths.[1] Real successes in the 1950s bolstered hopes that a new dawn had broken. The Communists brought inflation under control, cleansed China's cities of prostitution and opium-smoking, restarted rural production and pushed ahead with industrialisation. If what we now know takes the shine off these achievements, it is important to remember the early optimism, the new mood of hope, which the Communists brought to China.

Qian Liqun, today one of China's most eminent scholars of Chinese literature, was among the stay-behinders. His father, who had been educated at Cornell University and was the vice head of the Nationalist Ministry of Agriculture, did opt to go to Taiwan, but his mother, his maternal grandfather and 'uncles who worked in banks' all rejected that choice. Qian Liqun witnessed the arrival of the Communist troops in Shanghai on 23 June 1949, as a ten-year-old boy. 'So as not to be a burden to the people, they slept on the streets ... in contrast to wounded Nationalist soldiers who molested everybody.'[2] That impressed him. Qian became an enthusiastic Maoist and joined the Cultural Revolution as a Red Guard when it began in 1966. In a series of lectures given in Taiwan in 2009, he explained why intellectuals like him became Maoists, drawing his audience into the moments, such as the arrival of the Communist troops in Shanghai, that attracted him to Maoism. He remained a believer until the Cultural Revolution sowed disenchantment in his mind and the dangers of falling foul of the authorities were brought home to him and his family, with his mother doing everything possible to shield her children from what was unfolding.[3]

We lack the kinds of diaries and memoirs of people like Chen Kewen and Chi Pang-yuan to help us understand how ordinary people in mainland China experienced the beginning of this new phase in China's history. During the Cultural Revolution, many consigned their writings to the fire for fear of repercussions if they fell into the wrong hands. Important archives remain firmly closed as well. But an emphasis on the human toll of the Communist consolidation of power risks missing the point that while the Communists were undoubtedly tough enforcers of a new order, they were not mindless. For one thing, if Mao Zedong was convinced that power came out of the barrel of a gun, he also insisted that 'the Party commands the gun, and the gun must never be allowed to command the Party'.[4]

To begin with, the People's Republic was divided into military regions, with the army in total control, but in the meantime Party organisation and government offices were built up, banditry was suppressed and weapons were taken out of civil society. Then, after three years, the generals who had headed up the military regions were recalled to Beijing and civilian authorities took over. The armed forces returned to barracks and were kept separate from civil society, to the extent that they did not even share the same telephone network. In 1955, twelve People's Liberation Army generals, including General Lin Biao, were given the grand title of Marshal, but none was allowed to hold a major political office and the title was never granted again. The fate of demobilised soldiers was often an unhappy one. Whole units were despatched to China's frontier regions to bring new areas under cultivation, lay railway lines or develop oil fields. The majority were sent back to their original home regions, where many received little assistance in finding a job or in reintegrating into civilian life.[5] The Communists were deadly serious about demilitarising Chinese society.

A second major policy was the introduction of a household registration system. Public security organs began registering urban households and all their members in 1950. In 1953, when the first population census was conducted, rural households were also registered. The system allowed the authorities to stop people moving around the country, and especially to prevent rural household-ers from moving to urban areas, which became virtually impossible after 1958. A raft of official approvals would become necessary for anyone, even in cities, to move from one place to another. Soon sharp differences emerged between rural and non-rural citizens as the People's Republic used rural production to finance rapid urbanisation in the cities. Urban work units provided their staff with apartments, health care and educational facilities, as well as food and textile rations. The countryside was deprived of such beneficence. During the Great Leap Forward of 1958–62, the aim of which was the rapid industri-alisation of China, food was scarce in the cities but famine raged through the countryside. Village China had made revolution possible, but it profited little from that revolution. In recent decades, village residents have moved to cities in their tens or even hundreds of millions in search of a better life. They have usually ended up in low-end jobs in retail and hospitality, on construction sites or in factories.

For Chi Pang-yuan, the transition to a new life in Taiwan was difficult and eventful but in many ways fortunate. Twenty-five years old in 1947, she was now Assistant Professor in the Department of Foreign Literature at Taiwan University in Taipei. The conditions were primitive and she felt desperately lonely in a city in which she knew nobody and where everything was strange, from the food to the floor coverings (which were Japanese tatami mats). But small comforts such as a Thermos and a washbasin, small kindnesses such as being invited by family friends to share a meal, and signs of human normality such as the crying of a baby in a neighbouring room helped her bear up.

At a meeting of Wuhan University graduates in Taiwan, Pang-yuan met a young man called Luo Zhenyu, who had studied electronics and telecommu-nications but had decided to apply for a posting with the railways rather than for a more lucrative job with the electricity company. 'When in Sichuan he had been ridiculed by students from elsewhere because he had never seen a train.'[6] Zhenyu gave Pang-yuan a radio he had made himself, and in the evenings 'I listened to classical music recordings left by the Japanese as well as Japanese songs.' This made her realise that the Japanese were human, too. 'The several million of Japanese who died invading China, although they are hated enemies, they too have families waiting for their return in the cold night.' In Taipei, Japanese soldiers awaiting repatriation sold their belongings on street stalls. 'I felt no real sympathy for them, but I also became aware that they should not be the object of our vengeance.'[7]

However, Chi Pang-yuan was reluctant to develop her relationship with Luo Zhenyu further because her family faced rough times in mainland China. One day he wrote to her saying that he had broken down in tears after watching the 1943 film *Madame Curie*, which tells the story of how Marie Curie, while in exile in Paris from her native Poland, toiled together with her husband for years in the discovery of radium. The film convinced him, he said, that he needed to dedicate his energies to achieve his life's goals, even if times were difficult and it meant 'reducing meaningless social interactions to a minimum'.[8] Impressed by his determination and reassured by friends that Luo Zhenyu was a good man, she married him. Together they would work for a better future.

Chi Pang-yuan's mother, father, sisters and brother all came to Taipei, her father catching the last plane out of Chongqing on 28 November 1949. Pang-yuan soon became pregnant, and so the couple decided to move to Taizhong, a city in the middle of Taiwan, where Luo Zhenyu became chief of the Taizhong railway bureau. Although the job was a move sidewards, a demotion even, Taizhong was a better place to raise a family than Taipei: their house was larger and came with a tree-shaded courtyard. More importantly, 'we were worried about the political complexities Taiwan faced', which would affect life in Taipei more than in Taizhong.[9] For the next seventeen years the couple lived in Taizhong, raising their children as Luo Zhenyu put the rail network in the Taizhong region in order, an achievement from which they both derived enormous pride. Chi Pang-yuan taught at the local school and later built a career as a scholar of Chinese and English literature, writer and translator – eventually doing that for which she had been prepared during the War of Resistance: promoting human values and upholding civilisation.

Chi Pang-yuan and Luo Zhenyu were right. After the Korean War broke out, in order to firm up the Chiang family's control of Taiwan, Chiang Kaishek and his son, Ching-kuo, began a crackdown on suspected Communists and spies. Chi Pang-yuan's father, Chi Shiying, had continued to publish *Time and Tide*, the journal he had been editing; had spoken up for human rights and freedom; and had denounced increases in the military budget in the Legislative Branch. He was expelled from the KMT, put under surveillance and was not allowed to work. High-level protection spared him from jail. 'Nothing shows better the muddle-headedness of their dictatorship than that the KMT could not accommodate a Central Committee member who had been so loyal for twenty years,'

Chi Pang-yuan commented in an uncharacteristically angry passage of her memoir.[10]

Guilt about the fate of Manchurian resistance workers left behind on mainland China haunted Chi Pang-yuan's father for the rest of his life. Before all postal communications with mainland China were cut, he received a letter stating: 'We braved untold dangers. You encouraged us. Now you have abandoned us. Can you be at peace with yourself?' After surgery to remove a lung tumour shortly after his arrival in Taiwan, he had a nightmare in which 'a head dripping blood hung from a city wall opened its mouth and asked "Who is looking after our women and children?"'[11] The Cold War peace came with many costs.

Chen Kewen had a ringside seat at the disintegration of the Nationalists in mainland China. He remained loyal almost to the end. In April 1947, he decided to compete for a seat in the Legislative Branch.[12] Given the context of civil war, hyperinflation, rice riots, student demonstrations, collapsing morale, labour strikes, secret service round-ups and unrest in the military, the conditions for a successful transition to democracy could hardly have been less favourable. The attempt to do so now smacked of desperation. One of Chen's friends commented that 'the situation our country faces is not dissimilar to that in France and Russia before their revolutions'.[13] But Chen Kewen believed it his duty to do his best to make democracy work.[14] He was elected and became one of the legislators. He and Chi Pang-yuan's father therefore may have met; if they did, they would have found that they shared much in common.

Disappointments piled up quickly. Chen Kewen's diary entry for 27 May 1948 records that 'Chiang Kaishek made a very impolite speech' to legislators he had invited to a banquet. In the speech Chiang made clear that he would quit as president if the legislators demanded, as was their right, that his nominees for certain posts were summoned to the Legislative Branch to set out their views.[15] The Legislative Branch defied Chiang, with the result that a tug of war between the two paralysed the Nationalist government at the worst possible moment.[16] 'We are really immature when it comes to parliamentary government. We all lack experience. We must study harder,' was Chen Kewen's conclusion.[17]

The political infighting did not improve. Legislators squabbled about their entitlements, vied for the best appointments and turned deliberations into increasingly badly attended 'speech contests'.[18] Chiang Kaishek found it difficult to live with the rowdy realities of democracy, stating at one meeting that 'everybody has become drunk with democracy, believing that it does not need the guidance of the party. This is a serious mistake.'[19] He soon began simply bypassing the Legislative Branch altogether.[20]

When the Nationalists moved to Canton in April 1949, after the Communists seized Nanjing, Chen went with them. There he supported an attempt to organise a new party. 'These days many people have lost faith in the Nationalists and oppose the Communists,'[21] he said at a preparatory meeting. 'They hope for a party committed to democracy and freedom to take charge.' However, with no money and no senior figure in the country willing to assume its leadership, the idea proved stillborn. When the Nationalists next moved, to Chongqing on 15 April, Chen Kewen resigned his post of Chief Secretary of the Legislative Branch and moved to Hong Kong.

Hong Kong was the destination of choice for many wealthy Nationalists, especially southerners who had been connected with the Wang Jingwei faction. Chen Kewen first bought a small property at Shek O, on the southern shore of Hong Kong island, and then a larger one in the nearby town of Stanley. In both he enjoyed the ocean views, the beaches – and the calm. For the first few years after he arrived in Hong Kong, Chen Kewen sought to make a living as an investor and businessman, putting money into real estate projects, managing office and apartment buildings and trading with mainland China in kerosene and cotton. But he was not a natural businessman and, after his funds dwindled, he became a schoolteacher. He remained so for the next twenty-six years, ending his career as he had begun it while editing *Free Men* in his spare time.[22] He had given up any hope that the Nationalists might realise his May Fourth idealism, but not the idealism itself.

Guo Moruo, the author of '1644', was among those intellectuals who decided to stay on in China – unsurprisingly, given his close association with the Communist Party. He became President of the Academy of Sciences, was awarded the Stalin Peace Prize in 1951 and lived in a splendid traditional home in the heart of Beijing – although he was among the first to be criticised during the Cultural Revolution, during which two sons of his died. Today he is generally regarded as having gone a little too far in toadying up to Mao. Deng Tuo, the man who wrote about famine in Chinese history, also stayed. He became the editor of the *People's Daily,* the Communist Party's main mouthpiece. In the early 1960s, together with some colleagues, he wrote a series of satirical pieces with titles such as 'Big Empty Words', which criticised the agricultural collectivisation of the Great Leap Forward that led to mass starvation. Thus he remained true to his concern for China's peasantry. Attacked as a member of an anti-Party clique in May 1966 at the beginning of the Cultural Revolution, Deng took his own life with an overdose of sleeping pills.[23]

A year before Guo Moruo published '1644' about the collapse of the Ming Dynasty, historian Wu Han published a biography of its founder, Zhu Yuanzhang. Zhu had been born into a poor farming household and lived as a beggar and a monk before leading his armies to victory over the Mongols and seizing the emperorship. Central to Wu Han's biography was the conflict between the imperative to truthfulness of the historian and the compromises that might have to be made by those who wished to serve their society in an autocratic age. Wu Han became a leading figure in the China Democratic League, a political party founded in 1941 committed to steering China towards a democratic future. After 1949, he stayed in China to serve the new government and even went so far as to criticise other scholars when the Communists demanded that.

But in 1961 he published *Hai Rui Dismissed from Office,* a play about an honest local official who works for the good of his local community but is dismissed by the Emperor after he remonstrates against the dishonesty and abuse of power by other local officials. The play was a success. Coming in the wake of the Great Leap Forward, however, Mao understood its message only too well. The Cultural Revolution began when Mao ordered the play and its author to be criticised. Wu Han had been a deputy mayor of Beijing, but was purged and in 1969 he died in prison. Any hope that the moral voice of intellectuals, so important in Chinese history, might continue to have a role in the New China proved largely illusory.[24]

But not totally. The historian Chen Yinke's response to the dilemmas of his time was unique.[25] Chen was from an esteemed scholarly establishment family. Born in 1890 in the same province as Mao Zedong, Hunan, and roughly the same age as him, he did not seek his future in the Chinese countryside but travelled the world, studying at its great universities, including Tokyo Gakuin, Harvard, Berlin, Zurich and the Institute d'Etudes Politiques in Paris. He amassed an astonishing range of languages – Mongolian, Japanese, Manchu, Tangut, French, Sanskrit, Pali, and others – and acquired wide knowledge of fields such as philology, history, art history and literature. Before the War of Resistance, he wrote stunning pieces of scholarship that reconstructed the social and political history of the Tang Dynasty. He showed that the greatness of the Tang Dynasty did not result from the recovery of a quintessential Chinese-ness from the corruption of Buddhism, a foreign religion, but from the cosmopolitan mingling of Central Asian and Chinese elites in which women played a prominent role.

At the outbreak of the War of Resistance, Chen Yinke left Beijing when his university, Qinghua, relocated to Yunnan province. He taught at Southwest Associated University, made up of Qinghua University and two others, including Peking University, and where Wu Han was one of his colleagues. In 1939 he was offered the professorship of Chinese at Oxford, but the outbreak of war in Europe prevented him from taking up the post. After Japan's surrender, he returned to Beijing, teaching again at Qinghua. In 1948, before the Communists seized Beijing, he moved to Canton, where he taught at Zhongshan, or Sun Yatsen, University. The Nationalists and the Communists vied for his loyalty. He stayed in Canton, in the People's Republic but far away from Beijing. He replied to an invitation to become head of the Institute of History at

Guo Moruo's Academy of Sciences with the demand that it be exempted from complying with Marxist doctrines and holding political study meetings, and insisting that he receive a letter to this effect signed by Mao Zedong personally. That letter was not forthcoming.

Chen Yinke was well aware of Guo Moruo's '1644'. His response, a retort really, was a decade in the making and was not published until over ten years after his death. This was *The Unofficial History of Liu Rushi*, published in 1980, which gave an account of the life of a Ming courtesan from a lowly background who became famous for her poetry, erudition, good taste and enjoyment of life. It 'lay before the mind's eye a late Ming elite world of poetry, pleasure, elegance, and opulence amidst the ponds, streams, gardens, and pavilions of central China'.[26] Some ten years into the new Qing Dynasty, Liu Rushi was pressured to take her own life after the death of her husband, also a Ming loyalist. Chen Yinke's version of the fall of the Ming was the celebration of a world of friendship, literature and play, as well as a record of the pain that comes when that world is inevitably lost when a new dynasty takes over.

In the early years of the People's Republic, Chen Yinke was treated well, given a large apartment, books, films, extra allocations of food and Western medicines. The highest officials, including the provincial secretary, visited him to show their veneration for the master. But Chen's eyesight was failing, making *Liu Rushi* even more of an achievement. Three assistants were allocated to help him with his research and note down the narrative as he told it to them. But he fell out of favour during the Cultural Revolution and died on 7 October 1969 after being attacked by Red Guards. His books became famous in the 1980s after Deng Xiaoping began the reform period. *Liu Rushi* was even made into a film.

Until the 1980s, the Communists dismissed anything that went before the Communist revolution as feudal and tolerated history only if it repeated Communist models and phrasings. But then different pasts were allowed to rise to the surface,[27] partly to give the country a new source of national pride as the longest continuous civilisation on Earth and partly as a source of inspiration for films, televisions series, novels, advertisements – and restaurant decors. But the past also came back as a new source of ideas with which to contemplate what it means to be Chinese today, what the country should stand for, and what its position in the world should really be, thus illustrating that much of the Sun Yatsen question – that is, who is to have what say and on what grounds in China's public affairs, what does it mean to be Chinese, and what is the country's place in the world – has yet to be answered. Where that will lead is impossible to say: no one owns the past; no government controls its interpretation for very long; history can come back to bite, as even Mao Zedong found out; and no historian ever has the last word.

NOTES

CHOC – *The Cambridge History of China*, see Selected Bibliography, under John K. Fairbank.
ZHMGZYSLCB – Zhonghua Minguo Zhongyao Shiliao Chubian, see Selected Bibliography, under Qin Xiaoyi.
FRUS – Foreign Relations on the USA. See https://uwdc.library.wisc.edu/collections/frus.
SLGB – See Academia Historica, *Jiang Zhongzheng Zongtong Dang'an: Shilue Gaoben (The Archives of President Chiang Kaishek: Basic Biographical Documents)*.

Introduction

1. Leon Trotsky, foreword, Harold Isaacs, *The Tragedy of the Chinese Revolution* (London: Secker & Warburg, 1938), xii.
2. Rana Mitter, *China's War with Japan, 1937–1945: The Struggle for Survival* (London: Penguin Books, 2014), 8–14, and 'China's Good War', in Sheila Miyoshi Jager and Rana Mitter, *Ruptured Histories: War, Memory, and the Post-Cold War in Asia* (Cambridge, MA: Harvard University Press, 2007), 173–4.
3. Contribution by Pamela Crossley, 'What is China's Big Parade All About?: A ChinaFile Conversation', 2 September 2015. http://www.chinafile.com/conversation/what-chinas-big-parade-all-about
4. Mitter, *China's War with Japan*, 384.
5. For an analysis of these issues, see Philip A. Kuhn, *Origins of the Modern Chinese State* (Stanford, CA: Stanford University Press, 2002).
6. Dennis Showalter, 'Introduction to Part III', in Roger Chickering, Dennis Showalter and Hans van de Ven, eds., *The Cambridge History of War: Volume 4: War and the Modern World* (Cambridge: Cambridge University Press, 2012), 413.
7. Michael W. S. Ryan, *Decoding Al-Qaeda's Strategy: The Deep Battle against America* (New York: Columbia University Press, 2013), 84–96.
8. Adam Tooze, 'The War of the Villages: The Interwar Agrarian Crisis and the Second World War', in Michael Geyer and Adam Tooze, eds., *The Cambridge History of the Second World War, Volume 3: Total War: Economy, Society and Culture* (Cambridge: Cambridge University Press, 2015), 385–411.
9. David Reynolds, 'The Origins of the Two "World Wars": Historical Discourse and International Politics', *Journal of Contemporary History*, vol. 38: 1 (January 2003), 29.
10. 'The Naming of World War II', 11 September 1945, http://www.ibiblio.org/pha/policy/post-war/1945-09-11a.html
11. Alessio Patalano, 'Feigning Grand Strategy: Japan', in John Ferris and Edward Mawdsley, eds., *The Cambridge History of the Second World War: Volume I: Fighting the War* (Cambridge: Cambridge University Press, 2015), 164–5.
12. Reynolds, 'The Origins of the Two "World Wars"', 34.
13. Ibid., 39–41.

14. Lizzie Collingham, *The Taste of War: World War Two and the Battle for Food* (London: Allen Lane, 2011), 96–101, 339–43.

15. 'Facing up to Germany's Past', *The New York Times Magazine*, 23 June 1985.

16. J. L. van der Pauw, 'Door Eendracht Victorie: De Geschiedenis van geen Verzetsorganizatie' ('Victory through Unity: The History of a Pseudo Resistance Organisation'), in *Scyedam*, vol. 22: 2 (1996), 67–9.

17. Rita Steblin, *A History of Key Characteristics in the Eighteenth and Early Nineteenth Centuries* (Rochester, NY: University of Rochester Press, 2002), 124.

Chapter 1: Chiang Kaishek. Saving China

1. http://www.loebclassics.com/view/thucydides-history_peloponnesian_war/1919/pb_LCL108.143.xml

2. Yang Tianshi, 'Jiang Jieshi Wei He Cesha Tao Chengzhang?' ('Why Did Chiang Kaishek Murder Tao Chengzhang?'), in *Zhaoxun Zhenshi de Jiang Jieshi: Jiang Jieshi Riji Jiedu (In Search of the Real Chiang Kaishek: Reading the Chiang Kaishek Diaries)* (Taiyuan: Shanxi Renmin Chubanshe, 2008), 1–10.

3. Yang Tianshi, 'Cong Jiang Jieshi Riji Kan Tade Zaonian Sixiang' ('An Examination of Chiang Kaishek's Early Thought on the Basis of his Diary'), in *Jiang Jieshi Midang yu Jiang Jieshi Zhenxiang (The Secret Archive of Chiang Kaishek and Chiang Kaishek's True Identity)* (Beijing: Social Sciences and Documents Press, 2002), 11–37.

4. Chiang Kaishek, *Kunmianji (Diary Entries on Striving in Adversity)*, Huang Zijin and Pan Guangzhe, eds., (Taipei: Guoshiguan, 2011), 47.

5. Yang Tianshi, 'Cong Jian Jieshi Riji Kan Tade Zaonian Sixiang', 11–13, provides a list culled from Chiang's diary.

6. Ibid., 21.

7. Ibid., 21.

8. Ibid., 21.

9. Ibid., 16.

10. For a detailed discussion of Chiang Kaishek's use of Confucianism to curb what he saw as his character flaws, see Yang Tianshi, 'Song Ming Daoxue yu Jiang Jieshi de Zaonian Xiushen', ('Song and Mind Dynasty Studies of the Way and Chiang Kaishek's Self-cultivation in His Early Years'), in *Jiang Jieshi Midang yu Jiang Jieshi Zhenxiang (The Secret Archive of Chiang Kaishek and Chiang Kaishek's True Identity)* (Beijing: Social Sciences and Documents Press, 2002), 38–57.

11. Ibid., 38–9.

12. Paul S. Reinsch, *An American Diplomat in China* (New York: Doubleday, Page & Co., 1922), 241–6.

13. Yang Tianshi, 'Cong Jiang Jieshi Riji Kan Tade Zaonian Sixiang', 17.

14. Ibid., 18.

15. Ibid.

16. Hans van de Ven, *War and Nationalism in China, 1925–1945* (London: Routledge, 2003), 70.

17. Yang Tianshi, 'Jiang Weiguo "Shenshi" zhi Mi yu Jiang Jieshi, Song Meiling de Ganqing Weiji' ('The Mystery of Chiang Wei-kuo's "Life Experiences" and the Crisis in Relations between Chiang Kaishek and Song Meiling') in Yang Tianshi, *Xunzhao*

Zhenshi de Jiang Jieshi (*In Search of the Real Chiang Kaishek*) (Taiyuan: Shanxi Renmin Chubanshe, 2008), no page numbers.

18. Yang Tianshi, '1923 Nian Jiang Jieshi de Sulian Zhi Xing Ji Qi Junshi Jihua' ('Chiang Kaishek's Journey to the Soviet Union in 1923 and His Military Plan'), in *Jiang Jieshi Midang yu Jiang Jieshi Zhenxiang* (*The Secret Archive of Chiang Kaishek and Chiang Kaishek's True Identity*) (Beijing: Social Sciences and Documents Press, 2002), 87–106.

19. Ibid., 90.

20. Ibid., 104.

21. Ibid., 105.

22. Van de Ven, *War and Nationalism in China*, 83–4.

23. Ibid., 79–93.

24. Wu Hung, *Remaking Beijing: Tiananmen Square and the Creation of a Political Space* (Chicago: University of Chicago Press, 2005), 69.

25. 'Hong Kong Mourns Dr Sun', *The New York Times*, 17 March 1925.

26. 'Many Races Honor Dr Sun's Memory', *The New York Times*, 23 March 1925.

27. Yang Zhiyi, 'The Road to Lyric Martyrdom: Reading the Poetry of Wang Zhaoming', *Chinese Literature: Essays, Articles, Reviews (CLEAR)*, vol. 37 (2015), 139.

28. Van de Ven, *War and Nationalism in China*, 83.

29. Ibid.

30. Ibid., 46.

31. Ibid., 97–9.

32. Ibid., 99.

33. Ibid., 100.

34. Chiang Kaishek, *Kunmianji*, 51.

35. Ibid.

36. Ibid., 162.

37. 'Chinese War: Solemn Ceremony at Peking: Victory Announced to Sun Yat-sen', *The Times*, 7 July 1928.

38. Van de Ven, *War and Nationalism in China*, 134.

Chapter 2: Nation Building

1. Chiang Wei-kuo, *Kangzhan Yuwu* (*The War of Resistance and Fighting Humiliation*) (Taipei: Liming Wenhua Shiye Gongsi, 1978), vol. 1, 40.

2. Hans van de Ven, *War and Nationalism in China, 1925–1945* (London: Routledge, 2003), 136.

3. Zhang Xianwen, *Zhonghua Minguo Shi* (*History of the Republic of China*) (Nanjing: Nanjing University Press, 2005), vol. 2, 71.

4. Quoted in Zhang Xianwen, *Zhonghua Minguo Shi*, vol. 2, 358.

5. I am grateful to my Ph.D. student Wu Rong for pointing out the popularity in China of Friedrich von Bernardi in China at this time.

6. Zhang Xianwen, *Zhonghua Minguo Shi*, vol. 2, 53.

7. For Max Bauer, see Adam Tooze, *The Deluge: The Great War and the Remaking of the Global Order, 1916–1931* (London: Viking, 2014), 112.

8. Chiang Jui-te, 'The Nationalist Army on the Eve of the War', in Mark Peattie, Edward J. Drea and Hans van de Ven, eds., *The Battle for China: Essays on the Military History of the Sino-Japanese War* (Stanford, CA: Stanford University Press, 2011), 94.

9.   Ibid., 92–3.
10.   Van de Ven, *War and Nationalism in China*, 166.
11.   Ibid., 164–6.
12.   'Queding Jiaoyu Zongzhi Ji Qi Shishi Fangzhen An' ('Proposal for Determining the General Aim of Education and Guidelines for Its Implementation', 25 March 1929, in ZHMGZYSLCB, series 2, vol. 3, 409.
13.   Liu Cuirong and Zhong Jideng, *Zhonghua Minguo Fazhanshi: Jingji Fazhan (The Historical Development of the Republic of China: Economic Development)* (Taipei: Cheng-chi University Press, 2011), vol. 2, 356–7.
14.   Lloyd E. Eastman, 'Nationalist China during the Nanjing Decade, 1927–1937', CHOC, vol. 13, 155.
15.   Zhang Xianwen, *Zhonghua Minguo Shi*, vol. 2, 464–80; Etu Zen Sun, 'The Growth of the Academic Community', CHOC, vol. 13, 361–420; Ramon Myers, 'The Agrarian System', CHOC, vol. 13, 256–7.
16.   Prasenjit Duara, *Culture, Power, and the State: Rural North China, 1900–1942* (Stanford, CA: Stanford University Press, 1988). For the *baojia*, see van de Ven, *War and Nationalism in China*, 142–6.
17.   Van de Ven, *War and Nationalism in China*, 142–6.
18.   Zhang Xianwen, *Zhonghua Minguo Shi*, vol. 2, 490–91.
19.   Frank Dikötter, *The Age of Openness: China before Mao* (Berkeley, CA: University of California Press, 2008).
20.   Peter Mauch, 'Asia-Pacific: The Failure of Diplomacy, 1931–1941', in Richard J. B. Bosworth and Joseph A. Maiolo, eds., *The Cambridge History of the Second World War: Volume 2: Politics and Ideology* (Cambridge: Cambridge University Press, 2015), 259.
21.   Chiang Kaishek, 'Di Hu? You Hu?' ('Friend or Enemy?'), in Qin Xiaoyi, ZHMGZYSLCB: series 3, supplementary materials, vol. 3, 614.
22.   Ibid., 616–17.
23.   'Soong, Here, Denies China is in Chaos', *The New York Times*, 23 May 1933.
24.   'Conference Speeches', *The Times*, 16 June 1933.
25.   For Jiang Tingfu's experiences in the Soviet Union, see his *Jiang Tingfu Huiyilu (Memoirs of Jiang Tingfu)* (Changsha: Yuelu Press, 2003), 156–78 and, especially, 199–216.
26.   Hans van de Ven, *Breaking with the Past: The Maritime Customs Service and the Global Origins of Modernity in China* (New York: Columbia University Press, 2014), 223.
27.   'China War Lord Era Near End, Says Mme Chiang in Broadcast', *Washington Post*, 22 February 1937.
28.   Myers, 'The Agrarian Crisis', CHOC, vol. 13, 265.
29.   For details, see http://www.disasterhistory.org.
30.   Dr John H. Finley, foreword, Walter H. Mallory, *China: Land of Famine* (New York: American Geographical Society, 1926).
31.   Guy S. Alitto, *The Last Confucian: Liang Shu-ming and the Dilemma of Chinese Modernity* (Berkeley, CA.: University of California Press, 1979) and Charles W. Hayford, *To the People: James Yen and Village China* (New York: University of Columbia Press, 1990).
32.   Zhang Xianwen, *Zhonghua Minguo Shi*, vol. 2, 180–87.
33.   'Szechwan Famine Taking Heavy Toll', *The New York Times*, 22 March 1937.

34. 'Famine in China is Wide', *The New York Times*, 12 March 1937
35. 'Making Smuggling Easier', *Manchester Guardian*, 25 June 1937.

Chapter 3: Nanjing, Nanjing

1. Ye Zhaoyan, *Nanjing 1937: A Love Story*, Michael Berry, trans. (London: Faber & Faber, 2004), 112.
2. Charles D. Musgrove, *China's Contested Capital: Architecture, Ritual, and Response in Nanjing* (Honolulu, HI: University of Hawaii Press, 2013), 56.
3. Ibid., 55–88.
4. 'China's "Washington"', *The New York Times*, 3 June 1929.
5. Musgrove, *China's Contested Capital*, 128.
6. Ibid.
7. Lai Delin, 'Searching for a Modern Chinese Monument: The Design of the Sun Yat-sen Mausoleum in Nanjing', *Journal of the Society for Architectural Historians*, 64 (March 2005), 25. The following paragraphs are based on Lai's article as well as on Charles D. Musgrove, 'Monumentality in Nanjing's Sun Yat-sen Memorial Park', *Southeast Review of Asian Studies*, 29 (2007), 1–19.
8. Lai Delin, 'Searching for a Modern Chinese Monument', 47–9.
9. This point is elaborated fully in John Fitzgerald, *Awakening China: Politics, Culture, and Class in the Nationalist Revolution* (Stanford, CA: Stanford University Press, 1996).
10. Sun Yatsen, 'The Three Stages of Revolution' (1918), in Wm Theodore de Bary and Richard Lufrano, *Sources of Chinese Tradition, Volume 2: From 1600 through the Twentieth Century* (Second edition, New York: Columbia University Press, 2000), 328–30.
11. Musgrove, *China's Contested Capital*, 144.
12. Henrietta Harrison, *The Making of the Republican Citizen: Political Ceremonies and Symbols in China, 1911–1929* (Oxford: Oxford University Press, 2000), 49–60; and https://www.powerhousemuseum.com/hsc/evrev/mao_suit.htm
13. Reba Soffer, 'Conservatism as a Crusade: F. J. C. Hearnshaw' in *History, Historians and Conservatism in Britain and America: From the Great War to Thatcher and Reagan* (Oxford: Oxford University Press, 2008), 51–78.
14. On Liang Shuming, see Guy S. Alitto, *The Last Confucian: Liang Shu-ming and the Chinese Dilemma of Modernity* (Berkeley, CA.: University of California Press, 1979).
15. Chi Pang-yuan, *Juliuhe (The Great Flowing River)* (Taipei: Yuanjian Tianxia, 2014), 27–8.
16. Ibid., 37.
17. Ibid., 22.
18. Ibid., 53.
19. Ibid., 76.
20. Ibid., 63.
21. Ibid., 54.
22. Ibid., 71.

Chapter 4: To War

1. 'Happy Ending in China: Chiang Kaishek Released', *The Times*, 28 December 1936.

2.   Hallett Abend, 'Leniency is Asked by Nanking Leader for Rebel's Chiefs', *The New York Times*, 27 December 1936.

3.   'Happy Ending in China', *The Times*.

4.   Zang Yunhu, 'Qiqi Shibian Yiqian de Riben Duihua Zhengci Ji Qi Yanbian' ('Japan's China Policy before the 7 July 1937 Incident'), in *Kang Ri Zhanzheng Yanjiu* (*Research on the War of Resistance*), vol. 64 (2007), 1–29.

5.   'Japan's Mongolian Policy', *The Times*, 30 April 1936.

6.   'Japan Sees Hope for China Amity', *The New York Times*, 3 February 1935.

7.   Chiang Kaishek, *Kunmianji* (*Diary Entries on Striving in Adversity*), Huang Zijin and Pan Guangzhe, eds., (Taipei: Guoshiguan, 2011), 523.

8.   Hans van de Ven, *War and Nationalism in China 1922–1945* (London: Routledge, 2003), 185.

9.   Ibid.

10. Jiang Yongjing, 'Xi'an Shibian Qian Zhang Xueliang "Yi Er Yue Nei Ding You Biandon" He Zhi' ('Zhang Xueliang's Suggestion before the Xi'an Incident That Changes Will Take Place in One to Two Months'), in *Jindaishi Yanjiu* (*Research on Modern History*), 1997, vol. 2, 266–72.

11. Chiang Kaishek, *Kunmianji*, 517.

12. Jiang Yongjing, 'Zhang Xueliang's Suggestion before the Xi'an Incident', 271.

13. Zhang Xianwen, *Zhonghua Minguo Shi* (*History of the Republic of China*) (Nanjing: Nanjing Daxue Chubanshe, 2005), vol. 2, 527–9.

14. Van de Ven, *War and Nationalism in China*, 185.

15. Ibid., 184.

16. Chiang Kaishek, *Kunmianji*, 527–8.

17. Hallett Abend, *My Life in China 1926–1941* (New York: Harcourt, Brace & Co., 1943), 233–5.

18. Chiang Kaishek, *Kunmianji*, 531.

19. 'Soviet Sure Chang is Japan's Agent', *The New York Times*, 20 December 1936.

20. Riben Fangweiting Fangwei Yanjiusuo Zhanshishi (Office of War History, Defence Research Institute, Department of Defence, Japan), *Zhongguo Shibian Lujun Zuozhan Zhanshi* (*History of the Army's Campaigns during the China Incident*), Tian Qizhi, trans. (Beijing: Zhonghua Shuju, 1979), vol. 1:1, 26–8, 58–9.

21. 'Soviet Sure Chang is Japan's Agent', *The New York Times*, 20 December 1936.

22. Ibid.

23. Van de Ven, *War and Nationalism in China*, 187.

24. 'New Difficulties are Seen', *The New York Times*, 20 December 1936.

25. Yang Kuisong, *Geming* (*Revolution*) (Nanning: Guangxi Renmin Chubanshe, 2012), vol. 3, 395–402; 'Anti Chiang Plot is Laid to Nanjing', *The New York Times*, 12 January 1937.

26. 'General Han Becomes Ally of Nanking', *The New York Times*, 14 December 1936.

27. SLGB, vol. 42 (July–December 1938), 689.

28. Song Ziwen diary in TV Soong Papers, Hoover Institution Archives, box 591, folder 21.

29. Quoted in Jonathan Fenby, *Generalissimo: Chiang Kai-shek and the China He Lost* (London: Free Press, 2003), 9.

30. Abend, *My Life*, 234.

31. Ibid., 234–45.

32. 'Great Welcome for Chiang Kaishek', *The Times of India*, 28 December 1936.

33. Yang Kuisong, *Geming*, vol. 3, 395–428.
34. Chiang Kaishek, *Kunmianji*, 535.
35. Zhou Enlai, 'Our Strategy in Negotiations with the Nationalists', 24 February 1937, in *Zhou Enlai Shuxin Xuanji (Selected Correspondence of Zhou Enlai)* (Beijing: Zhongyang Wenxian Chubanshe, 1988), 129.
36. Chiang Kaishek, *Kunmianji*, 551.
37. Shao Minghuang, 'A Temporary Farewell to Nanjing: Chiang Kaishek's Comings and Goings after the Xi'an Incident' in *Jindai Zhongguo (Modern China)*, vol. 160 (2005), 166–7.
38. Chiang Kaishek, *Kunmianji*, vol. 2, 544; Shao Minhuang, 'A Temporary Farewell to Nanjing', 173.
39. 'The Consul General at Shanghai (Gauss) to the Ambassador in China (Johnson), 25 June 1937' in *Foreign Relations of the United States Diplomatic Papers, 1937: The Far East, Undeclared War between China and Japan*, 122.
40. Shao Minghuang, 'A Temporary Farewell to Nanjing', 174.
41. Chiang Kaishek, *Kunmianji*, 559.
42. Ibid., 543.
43. Ibid., 551.
44. Ibid., 549.
45. Ibid., 550.
46. Edward J. Drea, 'The Japanese Army on the Eve of the War', in Mark Peattie, Edward J. Drea and Hans van de Ven, eds., *The Battle for China: Essays on the Military History of the Sino-Japanese War* (Stanford, CA: Stanford University Press, 2011), 130–31.
47. 'Fighting near Peking', *The Times*, 9 July 1937.
48. Zhang Xianwen, *Zhonghua Minguo Shi*, vol. 3, 1–5; Hallett Abend, 'Japanese Battle Chinese at Peiping', *The New York Times*, 8 July 1937.
49. 'The Issues in China', *The Times*, 29 July 1937.
50. Rana Mitter, *China's War with Japan, 1937–1945: The Struggle for Survival* (London: Penguin Books, 2014), 79.
51. Zhang Xianwen, *Zhonghua Minguo Shi*, vol. 2, 299–307.
52. 'Chinese Demonstrate in Protest', *The New York Times*, 16 September 1932.
53. 'Chinese Mourn Seizure of Mukden 2 Years Ago', *The New York Times*, 18 September 1933.
54. 'Peiping Students Beaten by Police', *The New York Times*, 17 December 1937.
55. 'Anti Japan Parade Routed in Tientsin', *The New York Times*, 17 June 1936.
56. 'Japanese Protest Attack in Chengtu', *The New York Times*, 27 August 1936.
57. Mark Peattie, 'The Dragon's Seed: Origins of the War', in Peattie et al., *The Battle for China*, 75–6.
58. 'Sato Would Solve Minor China Issues', *The New York* Times, 7 May 1937.
59. George E. Taylor, 'Popular Front in China', *Manchester Guardian*, 12 February 1937.
60. Chiang Kaishek, diary entry for 2 November 1937, *Kunmianji (Exertions under Pressure)* (Taipei: Guoshiguan, 2011), 583.
61. Kazuo Yagami, *Konoe Fumimaro and the Failure of Peace in Japan, 1937–1941: A Critical Appraisal of the Three-time Prime Minister* (Jefferson, NC: McFarland & Co., 2006), 47–9.
62. Ibid.

63. Ibid., 560–63.
64. Chiang Kaishek, *Kunmianji*, 560.
65. Ibid.
66. 'Forebodings in Peking', *The Times*, 14 July 1937.
67. 'The Limit of Our Endurance', *Collected Wartime Messages of Generalissimo Chiang Kai-shek, 1937–1945* (New York: John Day Company, 1946), vol. 1, 23–4; 'Forebodings in Peking', *The Times*, 14 July 1937.
68. 'The Limit of Our Endurance', *Collected Wartime Messages of Generalissimo Chiang Kai-shek, 1937–1945*, vol. 1, 23–4; Zhang Xianwen, *Zhongguo Kang Ri Zhanzheng Shi (History of China's War of Resistance)* (Nanjing: Nanjing Daxue Chubanshe, 2001), 250.
69. 'More Fighting in China', *The Times*, 27 July 1937.
70. Zhang Xianwen, *Zhongguo Kang Ri Zhanzheng Shi*, 246.
71. 'Nanking and the Settlement', *The Times*, 24 July 1937.
72. Van de Ven, *War and Nationalism in China*, 194.
73. Zhang Xianwen, *Zhongguo Kang Ri Zhanzheng Shi*, 247.
74. 'Peace or War in China', *The Times*, 2 August 1937.
75. 'Anxious Time in China', *The Times*, 6 August 1937.
76. Van de Ven, *War and Nationalism in China*, 194–5.
77. Ibid.
78. Ibid., 197.
79. 'Chinese Government Defiant', *Manchester Guardian*, 30 July 1937.
80. Qi Houjie, 'Kangzhan Baofa Hou Nanjing Guomin Zhengfu Guofang Lianxi Huiyi Jilu' ('Minutes of the Joint National Defence Meeting of Nanjing's Nationalist Government after the Outbreak of the War of Resistance'), *Minguo Dang'an* (Republican Archives), vol. 1 (1996), 27–33.

Chapter 5: The Battle of Shanghai
1. Chiang Kaishek, *Kunmianji (Diary Entries on Striving in Adversity)*, Huang Zijin and Pan Guangzhe, eds., (Taipei: Guoshiguan), 582.
2. Frank Dorn, *The Sino-Japanese War, 1937–41: From Marco Polo Bridge to Pearl Harbor* (New York: Macmillan, 1974); Hsi-sheng Ch'i, *Nationalist China at War: Military Defeats and Political Collapse, 1937–45* (Ann Arbor, MI: University of Michigan Press, 1982); US Department of State, *The China White Paper, August 1949* (Stanford, CA: Stanford University Press, 1967); Peter Harmsen, *Shanghai, 1937: Stalingrad on the Yangtze* (Oxford: Casemate Books, 2013) is a recent and thorough corrective.
3. Edward J. Drea, 'The Japanese Army on the Eve of the War', in Mark Peattie, Edward J. Drea, and Hans van de Ven, eds., *The Battle for China: Essays on the Military History of the Sino-Japanese War* (Stanford, Calif.: Stanford University Press, 2011), 107–14.
4. Riben Fangweiting Fangwei Yanjiusuo Zhanshishi (Office of War History, Defence Research Institute, Department of Defence, Japan), *Zhongguo Shibian Lujun Zuozhan Zhanshi (History of the Army's Campaigns during the China Incident)*, Tian Qizhi, trans. (Beijing: Zhonghua Shuju, 1979). vol. 1: 1, 86–90.
5. Drea, 'The Japanese Army on the Eve of the War', 109–11.
6. Chang Jui-te, 'The Nationalist Army on the Eve of the War', in Peattie et al., eds., *The Battle for China*, 88–9.

7.   'Air Attaché', 19 July 1937, in 'Sino-Japanese Situation in North China', UK National Archives, FO 676/327.

8.   Quoted in Chang Jui-te, 'The Nationalist Army on the Eve of the War', 91.

9.   Quoted in Peter Harmsen, *Shanghai, 1937*, 51.

10. Ibid., 158–9.

11. Chang Jui-te, 'The Nationalist Army on the Eve of the War', 86–7.

12. Ibid., 92–3.

13. 'Telegram to FO', 2 February 1938, in 'Shanghai Siege', UK National Archives, FO 676/397; Riben Fangweiting Fangwei Yanjiusuo Zhanshishi, *Zhongguo Shibian Lujun Zuozhan Zhanshi*, vol. 1: 1, 233–9; vol. 1: 2, 55–84.

14. Harmsen, *Shanghai, 1937*, 38.

15. 'Knatchbull-Hugessen to Halifax', 17 August 1937, in Ann Trotter, Kenneth Bourne, D. Cameron Watt, eds., *British Documents on Foreign Affairs: Reports and Papers from the Foreign Office Confidential Print: Part 2, From the First to the Second World War, Series E, Asia, 1914–1939* (Frederick, MD: University Publications of America, 1991–7), 45 (July 1937–March 1938), 68.

16. Ibid.

17. Quoted in Rana Mitter, *China's War with Japan, 1937–1945: The Struggle for Survival* (London: Penguin Books, 2014), 93.

18. Harmsen, *Shanghai, 1937*, 38–41.

19. '1,000 Dead in Shanghai', *The Times*, 16 August 1937.

20. Claire Lee Chennault, *Way of a Fighter: The Memoirs of Claire Lee Chennault* (New York: G. P. Putnam's Sons, 1946), 45–6.

21. *North China Herald*, 18 August 1937.

22. Harmsen, *Shanghai, 1937*, 62.

23. '1,000 Dead in Shanghai', *The Times*, 16 August 1937.

24. Harmsen, *Shanghai, 1937*, 50.

25. Ibid., 51.

26. Chen Cheng, *Chen Cheng Huiyilu: Kang Ri Zhanzheng* (*Chen Cheng Memoirs: The War of Resistance*) (Taipei: Guoshiguan, 2005), 19.

27. Harmsen, *Shanghai, 1937*, 69–75, 81–4.

28. Harmsen, *Shanghai, 1937*, 93–7.

29. Riben Fangweiting Fangwei Yanjiusuo Zhanshishi, *Zhongguo Shibian Lujun Zuozhan Zhanshi*, vol. 1: 2, 79–81.

30. Kazuo Horiba, *Riben Dui Hua Zhanzheng Zhidao Shi* (*History of Strategic Planning in Japan's War against China*), Wang Peilan, trans. (Beijing: Junshi Kexue Chubanshe, 1988), 75–6.

31. Chen Cheng, *Chen Cheng Huiyilu*, 19.

32. Guangxi Army sources quoted in Harmsen, *Shanghai, 1937*, 184.

33. Harmsen, *Shanghai, 1937*, 119–22, 129–33, 151–5, 161–5, 187–95; Zhang Xianwen, *Zhongguo Kang Ri Zhanzheng Shi* (*History of China's War of Resistance*) (Nanjing: Nanjing Daxue Chubanshe, 2001), 278–87.

34. Harmsen, *Shanghai, 1937*, 212.

35. Ibid., 223.

36. Chen Cheng, *Chen Cheng Huiyilu*, 19.

37. Yang Tianshi, 'Chiang Kaishek and the Battles of Shanghai and Nanjing', in Peattie, et al, eds., *The Battle for* China, 154.

38. Zhang Xianwen, *Zhongguo Kang Ri Zhanzheng Shi*, 297–339.

39. Chiang Kaishek, *Kunmianji*, 582.

40. Hallett Abend, *My Life in China 1926–1941* (New York: Harcourt, Brace & Co., 1943), 258.

41. Ibid.

42. 'Shanghai Consul to British Ambassador Knatchbull-Hugessen', 11.30 a.m., 14 August 1937, in 'Sino-Japanese Dispute', UK National Archives, FO 676/328.

43. Harmsen, *Shanghai, 1937,* 63–4.

44. *Oriental Affairs*, November 1937.

45. H. J. Timperley, *What War Means: The Japanese Terror in China; a Documentary Record* (London: Victor Gollancz, 1938), 119–43.

46. Frank Oliver, *Special Undeclared War* (London: Jonathan Cape, 1934), 145.

47. Chi Pang-yuan, *Juliuhe* (*The Great Flowing River*) (Taipei: Yuanjian Tianxia, 2014), 79.

48. Ibid., 78.

49. Chen Kewen, *Chen Kewen Riji* (*Chen Kewen's Diary*), Chen Fangzheng, ed. (Taipei: Zhongyang Yanjiuyuan Jindaishi Yanjiusuo, 2012), 94.

50. Ibid., 104.

51. Ibid.

52. Ibid., 114.

53. *Oriental Affairs*, November 1937, 254.

54. Ibid., 161.

55. John Rabe, *The Good Man of Nanking: The Diaries of John Rabe* (New York: Alfred A. Knopf, 1998), 10.

56. 'Kalkutta, 26 July 1937', in 'Political Relations Germany–China, July 1936–December 1937', UK National Archives, GFM 33/2951.

57. Ibid.

58. 'Ernst von Weizsäcker, Berlin, to Tokyo', 7 July 1937, in UK National Archives, GFM 33/115.

59. 'Soviet Warning to Japan', *The Times of India*, 28 September 1937.

60. Chen Kewen, *Chen Kewen Riji*, 104.

61. Trotter et al., eds., *British Documents on Foreign Affairs: Reports and Papers from the Foreign Office Confidential Print: Part 2, From the First to the Second World War, Series E, Asia, 1914–1939*, 45 (July 1937–March 1938), 'Japanese note', 110.

62. Abend, *My Life in China*, 270.

63. Ibid.

64. Ibid., 274–83.

65. Roads Farmer, *Shanghai Harvest: A Diary of Three Years in the China War* (London: Museum Press, 1945), 86.

66. Chen Kewen, *Chen Kewen Riji*, 128.

67. 'Despatch by Major General A. P. D. Telfer-Smollett, C.B., D.S.O., M.C. on the Shanghai Emergency', UK National Archives, WO 32/4347.

68. Quoted in David Sutton, *Simon: A Political Biography of Sir John Simon* (London: Aurum Press, 1992), 125.

69. Robert Bickers, *Britain in China: Community, Culture, and Colonialism, 1900–49* (Manchester: Manchester University Press, 1999).

70. For instance, Robin Hyde, *Dragon Rampant*; C. R. Shepherd, *The Case against Japan*; H. J. Timperley, *What War Means*; O. M. Green, *China's Struggles with the Dictators*; and J. Gunnar Andersson, *China Fights for the World*.

71. J. Gunnar Andersson, *China Fights for the World*, Arthur G. Chater, trans. (London: Kegan Paul, Trench, Trubner & Co., 1938), 261.

72. Chiang Kaishek, *Kunmianji*, 571.

73. Van de ven, *War and Nationalism in China, 1925–1945* (London: Routledge, 2003), 200.

74. Bai Chongxi, *Bai Chongxi Huiyilu* (*Bai Chongxi Memoirs*), Shu Zhirong et al., eds. (Beijing: Jiefangjun Chubanshe, 1987), 139.

75. Ibid., 139–48.

76. Bai Chongxi, *Bai Chongxi Xiansheng Fangwen Jilu* (*Interviews with Bai Chongxi*), Zhongyang Yanjiuyuan Jindaishi Yanjiusuo, ed. (Taipei: Academia Sinica, 1984), 147; Harmsen, *Shanghai, 1937*.

77. Harmsen, *Shanghai, 1937*, 185.

78. Van de Ven, *War and Nationalism in China*, 199–200.

79. Ibid., 195–6, 201.

80. Quoted in Zhang Xianwen, *Zhongguo Kang Ri Zhanzheng Shi*, 287.

81. Ibid., 287.

82. Yang Kuisong, *Shiqu de Jihui: Kangzhan Qianhou Guo Gong Tanpan Shilu* (*Lost Chance: A Record of Communist–Nationalist Negotiations around the Time of the War of Resistance*) (Beijing: Xinxing Chubanshe, 2010), 41, 57, 59; Zhang Xianwen, *Zhongguo Kang Ri Zhanzheng Shi*, 290–92.

83. Yang Kuisong, 'Nationalist and Communist Guerrilla Warfare in North China', in Peattie et al., eds., *The Battle for China*, 309.

84. Ibid.

85. 'Costs of Shanghai Campaign', *Washington Post*, 21 December 1937.

86. Parks M. Coble, *China's War Reporters: The Legacy of Resistance against Japan* (Cambridge, MA: Harvard University Press, 2015), 23.

87. Ibid., 24.

88. Ibid., 35.

89. Ibid., 25.

90. Ibid., 28.

91. Ibid., 35, 38.

92. Coble, *China's War Reporters*, 32–3.

93. Wang Qisheng, 'Kangzhan Chuqi de "He" Sheng' ('Voices for "Peace" at the Beginning of the War of Resistance'), in Lü Fangshan, ed., *Zhanzheng de Lishi yu Jiyi* (*The History and Memory of the War*) (Taipei, Guoshiguan, 2015), 27.

94. Ibid., 32.

95. Ibid., 37–55.

96. Hung Chang-tai, *War and Popular Culture: Resistance in Modern China, 1937–1945* (Berkeley, CA: University of California Press, 1994), 136–50.

97. Chen Kewen, *Chen Kewen Riji* (*Chen Kewen's Diary*), Chen Fangzheng, ed. (Taipei: Zhongyang Yanjiuyuan Jindaishi Yanjiusuo, 2012), 97.

98. Chen Kewen, *Chen Kewen Riji*, 120.

99. Coble, *China's War Reporters*, 35–7.

Chapter 6: Trading Space for Time

1.   Carl von Clausewitz, *On War*, J. J. Graham, trans., revised by F. N. Mause, abridged by Louise Wilmot (London: Wordsworth, 1997), 287.
2.   Carl von Clausewitz, *On War*, Michael Howard and Peter Paret, trans. (Princeton: Princeton University Press, 1989), 89.
3.   Zhang Xianwen, *Zhongguo Kang Ri Zhan Zheng Shi* (*History of China's War of Resistance*) (Nanjing: Nanjing Daxue Chubanshe, 2001), 531–2.
4.   Parks M. Coble, *China's War Reporters: The Legacy of Resistance against Japan* (Cambridge, MA: Harvard University Press, 2015), 169–71.
5.   Chen Kewen, *Chen Kewen Riji*, 141.
6.   Ibid., 137.
7.   Ibid., 140.
8.   Yang Tianshi, 'Jiang Jieshi yu 1937 Nian de Songhu Nanjing zhi Zhan' ('Chiang Kaishek and the Battles of Shanghai and Nanjing'), in *Xunzhao Zhenshi de Jiang Jieshi*, (*Searching for the Real Chiang Kaishek*), no page numbers.
9.   'All Captives Slain', *The New York Times*, 18 December 1937.
10.   Bai Chongxi, *Bai Chongxi Huiyilu* (*Bai Chongxi Memoirs*), Shu Zhirong et al., eds. (Beijing: Jiefangjun Chubanshe, 1987),149.
11.   Zhang Xianwen, *Zhongguo Kang Ri Zhanzheng Shi*, 367.
12.   Yang Tianshi, 'Chiang Kaishek and the Battles of Shanghai and Nanjing', in Mark Peattie, Edward J. Drea and Hans van de Ven, eds., *The Battle for China: Essays on the Military History of the Sino-Japanese War* (Stanford, Calif.: Stanford University Press, 2011), 157.
13.   Ibid.
14.   Ibid. See also Li Yuzhen, 'Chiang Kaishek and Joseph Stalin during World War II', in Hans van de Ven, Diana Lary, Stephen MacKinnon, eds., *Negotiating China's Destiny in World War II* (Stanford, CA.: Stanford University Press, 2015), 148–9.
15.   Chen Kewen, *Chen Kewen Riji*, 139.
16.   Zhang Xianwen, *Zhongguo Kang Ri Zhanzheng Shi*, 370.
17.   Ibid., 375.
18.   Report, 1937, quoted in Zhang Xianwen, *Zhongguo Kang Ri Zhanzheng Shi*, 376.
19.   Tillman Durdin, 'Japanese Atrocities Marked Fall of Nanking', *The New York Times*, 9 January 1938.
20.   Zhang Xianwen, *Zhongguo Kang Ri Zhanzheng Shi*, 164.
21.   Hattori Satoshi with Edward J. Drea, 'Japanese Operations from July to December 1937', in Peattie et al., eds., *The Battle for China*, 177.
22.   Ibid.
23.   Tillman Durdin, 'Japanese Atrocities Marked Fall of Nanking', *The New York Times*, 9 January 1938.
24.   Ibid.
25.   Ibid.
26.   Hattori Satoshi with Drea, 'Japanese Operations from July to December 1937', 179. On the Nanjing Massacre, see Zhang Xianwen, ed., *Nanjing Datusha Shiliao Ji* (*Historical Materials for the Nanjing Massacre*); Masahiro Yamamoto, *Nanking: Anatomy of an Atrocity*; Yang Daqing, 'Challenges of Trans-national History', 'Convergence

or Divergence' and 'Revisionism and the Nanjing Atrocity'; Timothy Brook, ed., *Documents on the Rape of Nanking*.

27. Tillman Durdin, 'Japanese Atrocities Marked Fall of Nanking', *The New York Times*, 9 January 1938.
28. Ibid.
29. Masahiro Yamamoto, *Nanking: Anatomy of an Atrocity: Separating Fact from Fiction* (Westport, CT: Praeger, 2000), 93.
30. Ibid., 95.
31. Ibid., 97.
32. Zhang Xianwen, *Zhongguo Kang Ri Zhanzheng Shi*, 379.
33. Masahiro Yamamoto, *Nanking*, 102–4.
34. Ibid., 99.
35. Tillman Durdin, 'All Captives Slain', *The New York Times*, 18 December 1937.
36. Tillman Durdin, 'Japanese Atrocities Marked Fall of Nanking', *The New York Times*, 9 January 1938.
37. Masahiro Yamamoto, *Nanking*, 106–7.
38. Hallett Abend, 'Reign of Disorder Goes on in Nanking', *The New York Times*, 25 January 1938.
39. Tillman Durdin, 'All Captives Slain', *The New York Times*, 18 December 1937.
40. Masahiro Yamamoto, *Nanking*, 137.
41. Masahiro Yamamoto, *Nanking*, 1–8, 81–127.
42. Yang Daqing, 'Challenges of Trans-national History: Historians and the Nanjing Atrocity', in *SAIS Review* 19:2 (1999), 143; Mashiro Yamamoto, *Nanking*, 109–17.
43. Mashiro Yamamoto, *Nanking*, 115.
44. Chen Kewen, *Chen Kewen Riji*, 141.
45. Ibid., 155.
46. Ibid., 147.
47. Ibid., 147.
48. Ibid., 145–6.
49. Ibid., 152–3.
50. Ibid., 153.
51. Ibid., 163.
52. Ibid., 186.
53. Xie Bingying, *A Woman Soldier's Own Story: The Autobiography of Xie Bingying*, Lily Chia Brissman and Barry Brissman, trans. (New York: Columbia University Press, 2001), 270.
54. Chen Kewen, *Chen Kewen Riji*, 154.
55. Ibid., 220.
56. Hans van de ven, *War and Nationalism in China, 1925–1945* (London: Routledge, 2003), 218–19.
57. Ibid., 201.
58. Chen Kewen, *Chen Kewen Riji*, 174.
59. SLGB, vol. 41 (January–June 1938), 87–8; James C. Hsiung and Steven I. Levine, eds., *China's Bitter Victory: War with Japan, 1937–45* (London: Routledge, 1992), 53.
60. Chen Kewen, *Chen Kewen Riji*, 234.

61. Stephen R. MacKinnon, *Wuhan, 1938: War, Refugees, and the Making of Modern China* (Berkeley, CA: University of California Press, 2008), 93.

62. Ibid., 75–80.

63. Quoted in MacKinnon, *Wuhan, 1938*, 98.

64. Zhang Xianwen, ed., *Kang Ri Zhanzheng de Zhengmian Zhanchang (Battles at the Front during the War of Resistance)* (Zhengzhou: Henan Renmin Chubanshe, 1996), vol. 1, 18–19; Zhang Xianwen, *Zhongguo Kang Ri Zhanzheng Shi*, 410–11.

65. Stephen MacKinnon, 'The Defence of the Central Yangtze', in Peattie et al., eds., *The Battle for China*, 191.

66. Zhang Xianwen, *Zhongguo Kang Ri Zhanzheng Shi*, 425.

67. Ibid., 437–45; Tobe Ryoichi, 'The Japanese Eleventh Army in Central China', in Peattie et al., eds., *The Battle for China*, 209.

68. 'Million Chinese Hail 1st Victory', *Washington Post*, 8 April 1938.

69. 'Japanese Force in Flight', *The Times*, 8 April 1938.

70. 'Chinese Increase Shantung Victory', *The New York Times*, 9 April 1938.

71. Chen Cheng, *Chen Cheng Huiyilu: Kang Ri Zhanzheng (Chen Cheng Memoirs: The War of Resistance)* (Taipei: Guoshiguan, 2005), 21–2.

72. 'Wartime Organic Law', ZHMGZYSLCB, series 4, vol. 1, 48–51.

73. Wang Chaoguang, 'Kangzhan yu Jianguo: Guomindang Linshi Daibiao Dahui Yanjiu' ('The War of Resistance and National Reconstruction: An Investigation of the Emergency National Conference of the Nationalists'), paper presented at History and Memory of the War: A Conference to Mark the Seventieth Anniversary of the Victory in the War of Resistance, Taipei, 7 July 2015, 8.

74. Ibid.

75. Ibid., 9.

76. Ibid., 10.

77. Van de Ven, *War and Nationalism in China*, 265–6.

78. Ibid., 266.

79. Chen Kewen, *Chen Kewen Riji*, 254.

80. Ibid.

81. 'Chinese Hurl Army across Yellow River', *Washington Post*, 16 April 1938.

82. MacKinnon, 'The Defence of the Central Yangtze', 194.

83. De Fremery, report no. 11, in Gerke Teitler and Kurt Werner Radtke, eds., *A Dutch Spy in China: Reports on the First Phase of the Sino-Japanese War (1937–1939)* (Leiden: Brill, 1999), 193, 200.

84. 'Secret Telegram from Li Zongren', 13 April 1937, in Zhang Xianwen, ed., *Kang Ri Zhanzheng Zhengmian Zhanchang*, vol. 1, 619.

85. MacKinnon, *Wuhan, 1938*, 112.

86. Riben Fangweiting Fangwei Yanjiusuo Zhanshishi (Office of War History, Defence Research Institute, Department of Defence, Japan), *Zhongguo Shibian Lujun Zuozhan Zhanshi (History of the Army's Campaigns during the China Incident)*, Tian Qizhi, trans. (Beijing: Zhonghua Shuju, 1979), vol. 2: 2, 87–112.

87. Chen Kewen, *Chen Kewen Riji*, 235.

88. Ibid., 154.

89. Ibid., 303.

90. SLGB, vol. 42 (July–December 1938), 204.

91. Yang Weizhen, '1938 Nian Changsha Dahuo Shijian de Diaocha yu Jiantao' ('An Investigation and Evaluation of the Great Fire of Changsha of 1938'), in Wu Sufeng, ed., *Buke Hulue de Zhanchang* (*A Battlefield That Must Not be Ignored*) (Taipei: Guoshiguan, 2013), 66–7.

92. Ibid., 66–70.

93. 'Japanese Rush On', *The New York Times*, 9 November 1937.

94. '12,000 stay to fight', *The New York Times*, 10 November 1937.

95. 'Japan Lays Gains to Massing of Foe', *The New York Times*, 9 December 1937.

96. 'Chinese Wreck Vast Japanese Mill Interests', *Washington Post*, 20 December 1937.

97. 'Military Affairs Council Battle Plan for the Third Period', Zhang Xianwen, ed., *Kang Ri Zhanzheng de Zhengmian Zhanchang*, vol. 1, 18–19.

98. 'Suchow is Occupied by the Japanese', *The New York Times*, 20 May 1938.

99. 'Chengchow Being Razed', *The New York Times*, 11 June 1938.

100. Quoted in Micah S. Muscolino, *The Ecology of War in China: Henan Province, the Yellow River, and Beyond, 1938–1950* (New York: Cambridge University Press, 2015), 26.

101. CKS material.

102. Ma Zhonglian, 'Huayuankou Jueti de Junshi Yiyi' ('The Military Significance of the Breaking of the Yellow River Dike at Huayuankou'), in *Kang Ri Zhanzheng Yanjiu* (*Studies on the War of Resistance*), vol. 4 (1999), 207.

103. Muscolino, *The Ecology of War in China*, 29.

104. Ibid., 30–31.

105. Ibid., 87.

106. 'Panic Rules Capital', *Washington Post*, 25 October 1938.

107. 'Japanese Battle Way into Blazing Cities', *Washington Post*, 26 October 1938.

108. Yang Weizhen, 'An Investigation and Evaluation of the Great Fire of Changsha of 1938', 71.

109. Ibid., 73.

110. Ibid., 73–7; Li Zhiyu, *Jingxuan: Wang Jingwei de Zhengzhi Shengya* (*The Startled Bow: The Political Life of Wang Jingwei*) (Hong Kong: Oxford University Press, 2014), 195.

111. Hallett Abend, *Chaos in Asia* (London: The Bodley Head, 1940), 120–25; *Canton Current Events and Rumours*, 16–31 October 1938, in Archives of the Inspectorate General of Customs, Second Historical Archives of China, 679(1)/32417.

112. Quoted in Chi Pang-yuan, *Juliuhe* (*The Great Flowing River*) (Taipei: Yuanjian Tianxia, 2014), 102.

113. Wang Qisheng, 'Kangzhan Chuqi de "He" Sheng' ('Voices for "Peace" at the Beginning of the War of Resistance'), in Lü Fangshan, ed., *Zhanzheng de Lishi yu Jiyi* (*The History and Memory of the War*) (Taipei: Guoshiguan, 2015), 24.

114. Lei Haizong, 'Jianshe – Zai Wang de Di San Zhou Wenhua' 'Reconstruction – Anticipating a Third Cycle', in Lei Haizong, *Zhongguo Wenhua yu Zhongguo de Bing* (*Chinese Culture and China's Armed Forces*) (Hong Kong: Longmen Shudian, 1968), 214.

115. Ibid., 212–13.

116. Ibid., 222.

117. Ibid., 214.

118. MacKinnon, *Wuhan, 1938*, 47.

119. Chen Kewen, *Chen Kewen Riji*, 143.

120. Chi Pang-yuan, *Juliuhe*, 82.

121. Ibid., 82.
122. Ibid., 87.
123. Ibid., 85–6.
124. Ibid., 92.
125. https://en.wikipedia.org/wiki/Along_the_Sungari_River
126. Chi Pang-yuan, *Juliuhe*, 89–96.
127. Ibid., 98.
128. Ibid., 100.
129. Ibid., 99.
130. Ibid., 103.
131. Ibid.
132. Zhang Xiangwen, *Zhongguo Kang Ri Zhanzheng Shi*, 531.
133. For a summary, see ibid., 586.
134. Chiang Kaishek, 'First Speech at the Nanyue Military Conference', ZHMGZYSLCB, I, 132.

Chapter 7: Regime Change

1. James Baldwin, *No Name in the Street* (New York: Dial Press, 1972), 88–9.
2. Quoted in Zhang Xianwen, *Zhonghua Minguo Shi* (*History of the Republic of China*) (Nanjing: Nanjing University Press, 2005), vol. 3, 89.
3. Kazuo Horiba, *Riben Dui Hua Zhanzheng Zhidao Shi* (*History of Strategic Planning in Japan's War against China*), Wang Peilan, trans. (Beijing: Junshi Kexue Chubanshe, 1988), 195–205.
4. Zhang Xianwen, *Zhonghua Minguo Shi*, vol. 3, 89.
5. Ibid., 500.
6. Quoted in ibid., 500–501.
7. James W. Morley, ed., *The China Quagmire: Japan's Expansion on the Asian Continent, 1933–1941* (New York: Columbia University Press, 1983), 290–91.
8. Kazuo Horiba, *Riben Dui Hua Zhanzheng Zhidao Shi*, 110.
9. John Thompson, *A Sense of Power: The Roots of America's Global Role* (Ithaca, NY: Cornell University Press, 2015), 147–8.
10. John W. Garver, *Chinese–Soviet Relations, 1937–1945: The Diplomacy of Chinese Nationalism* (Oxford: Oxford University Press, 1988), 38–41. See Jonathan Haslam, *The Soviet Union and the Threat from the East, 1933–41, Volume 3: Moscow, Tokyo and the Prelude to the Pacific War* (Basingstoke: Palgrave Macmillan, 1992), 93–4, for slightly different figures.
11. Chiang Kaishek, *Kunmianji* (*Diary Entries on Striving in Adversity*), Huang Zijin and Pan Guangzhe, eds., (Taipei: Guoshiguan, 2011), 645.
12. SLGB, vol. 42 (July–December 1938), 689.
13. Chiang Kaishek, *Kunmianji*, 646.
14. Ibid.
15. Quoted in Yang Zhiyi, 'The Road to Lyric Martyrdom: Reading the Poetry of Wang Zhaoming', *Chinese Literature: Essays, Articles, Reviews (CLEAR)*, vol. 37 (2015), 142.
16. John Hunter Boyle, *China and Japan at War, 1937–1945: The Politics of Collaboration* (Stanford, CA: Stanford University Press, 1972), 194–205. The agreement did not mention dates, on the grounds that the schedule of implementation might have to be

changed, depending on the circumstances; Rana Mitter, *China's War with Japan, 1937–1945: The Struggle for Survival* (London: Penguin Books, 2014), 205–6.

17. Boyle, *China and Japan at War*, 203–5.
18. Ibid., 13.
19. Kazuo Horiba, *Riben Dui Hua Zhanzheng Zhidao Shi*, 215–16.
20. Boyle, *China and Japan at War*, 215.
21. Ibid., 220.
22. Cai Dejin, *Lishi de Guaitai: Wang Jingwei Guomin Zhengfu (A Historical Monster: The Wang Jingwei Government)* (Guilin: Guangxi Shifan Daxue Chubanshe, 1993), 35–50.
23. Ibid., 35–40.
24. Mitter, *China's War with Japan*, 203.
25. Ibid., 80.
26. Quoted in Li Zhiyu, *Jingxuan: Wang Jingwei de Zhengzhi Shengya (The Startled Bow: The Political Life of Wang Jingwei)* (Hong Kong: Oxford University Press, 2014), 176–7.
27. Ibid., 187.
28. Ibid., 188 and SLGB, vol. 42 (July–December 1938), 497.
29. Boyle, *China and Japan at War*, 200–201.
30. Li Zhiyu, *Wang Jingwei de Zhengzhi Shengya*, 192.
31. Ibid., 212–22.
32. 'Guo Taiqi to Wang Jingwei', 27 December 1938, in Zhou Gu, ed., *Hu Shi Ye Gongchao Shi Mei Waijiao Wenjian Shougao (The Diplomatic Messages of Hu Shi and Yeh Kung-ch'ao as Ambassadors to the USA)* (Taipei: Lianjing Chuban Gonsi, 2001), 6.
33. Ibid., 217.
34. Ibid., 216.
35. Boyle, *China and Japan at War*, 227.
36. Ibid., 227–8.
37. Ibid., 223.
38. Shao Minghuang, 'Xiao Zhenying Gongzuo' ('The Xiao Zhenying Project'), 15–16. http://jds.cass.cn/UploadFiles/zyqk/2010/12/201012091549026982.pdf; SLGB, vol. 42 (July–December 1938), 341.
39. SLGB, vol. 42 (July–December 1938), 341–3, 407.
40. 'Chen Kewen to Wang Jingwei', 4 January 1939, in Chen Kewen, *Chen Kewen Riji*, 349.
41. Ibid., 408.
42. Li Zhiyu, *Wang Jingwei de Zhengzhi Shengya*, 232.
43. Ibid., 240–41; Boyle, *China and Japan at War*, 226.
44. Li Zhiyu, *Wang Jingwei de Zhengzhi Shengya*, 243–4.
45. Boyle, *China and Japan at War*, 230–31; Zhang Xianwen, *Zhonghua Minguo Shi*, vol. 3, 58–62.
46. Li Zhiyu, *Wang Jingwei de Zhengzhi Shengya*, 240–52.
47. Ibid., 249.
48. Kazuo Horiba, *Riben Dui Hua Zhanzheng Zhidao Shi*, 321–42.
49. 'Tokyo is Launching Monopolies in China', *The New York Times*, 30 December 1939.
50. Boyle, *China and Japan at War*, 271–6.
51. 'Wang Puppet Rule in China in Danger', *The New York Times*, 23 January 1940.
52. SLGB, vol. 43 (January–July 1940), 70–71.
53. Boyle, *China and Japan at War*, 294.

54. Ibid., 293–4.
55. Ibid., 294.
56. Ibid., 304.
57. Edna Tow, 'The Great Bombing of Chongqing and the Anti-Japanese War, 1937–1945', in Mark Peattie, Edward J. Drea and Hans van de Ven, eds., *The Battle for China: Essays on the Military History of the Sino-Japanese War of 1937–45* (Stanford, CA: Stanford University Press, 2011), 259–60.
58. '101 Japanese Planes Raid Chinese Airfield', *The New York Times*, 28 December 1939.
59. 'Bomb Kills Chiang's First Wife', *The New York Times*, 25 December 1939.
60. Xu Yong, *Zhengfu Zhi Meng: Riben Qinhua Zhanlue (The Dream of Conquest: Japan's Strategy in Invading China)* (Nanning: Guangxi Shifan Daxue Chubanshe, 1993), 224.
61. Riben Fangweiting Fangwei Yanjiusuo Zhanshishi (Office of War History, Defence Research Institute, Department of Defence, Japan), *Zhongguo Shibian Lujun Zuozhan Zhanshi (History of the Army's Campaigns during the China Incident)*, Tian Qizhi, trans. (Beijing: Zhonghua Shuju, 1979), vol. 2: 2, 187–8.
62. Mitter, *China's War with Japan*, 2.
63. 'Air Raid Kills 200 in China's Capital', *The New York Times*, 16 January 1939.
64. 'Thousands Leave Chungking in Raids', *The New York Times*, 16 January 1939.
65. Riben Fangweiting Fangwei Yanjiusuo Zhanshishi, *Zhongguo Shibian Lujun Zuozhan Zhanshi*, vol. 2: 2, 190–93.
66. Tow, 'The Great Bombing of Chongqing and the Anti-Japanese War', 249.
67. I am grateful to Richard Frank for providing me with this nice detail.
68. Riben Fangweiting Fangwei Yanjiusuo Zhanshishi, *Zhongguo Shibian Lujun Zuozhan Zhanshi*, vol. 3: 2, 35–40.
69. Tow, 'The Great Bombing of Chongqing and the Anti-Japanese War', 264–5.
70. Ibid., 271.
71. Ibid.
72. Ibid., 268–71.
73. Riben Fangweiting Fangwei Yanjiusuo Zhanshishi, *Zhongguo Shibian Lujun Zuozhan Zhanshi*, vol. 3: 2, 44.
74. Chi Pang-yuan, *Juliuhe (The Great Flowing River)* (Taipei: Yuanjian Tianxia, 2014), 123.
75. Ibid., 124.
76. Ibid., 123.
77. Ibid.
78. Ibid., 144.
79. Ibid.
80. Chen Kewen, *Chen Kewen Riji*, 420.
81. Ibid., 639.
82. Tow, 'The Great Bombing of Chongqing and the Anti-Japanese War', 273.
83. Ibid., 275.
84. 'Japanese Bombing is Called Stupid', *The New York Times*, 12 December 1939.
85. 'Jiang Weiyuanzhang Dui Diyici Nanyue Junshi Huiyi Xunci' ('Generalissimo Chiang's Address to the First Nanyue Military Conference'), 25 November 1938, in ZHMGZYSLCB, series 2, vol. 1, 128.
86. Ibid., 129.

87. Zhang Xianwen, *Zhongguo Kang Ri Zhanzheng Shi* (*History of China's War of Resistance*) (Nanjing: Nanjing Daxue Chubanshe, 2001), 645.

88. Ibid.

89. Xu Yong, *Zhengfu Zhi Meng*, 273.

90. Quoted in Tobe Ryoichi, 'The Japanese Eleventh Army in Central China', in Peattie, et al., eds., *The Battle for China*, 220.

91. 'President Obtains Data on China War', *The New York* Times, 21 December 1939.

92. Zhang Xianwen, *Zhongguo Kang Ri Zhanzheng Shi*, 651.

93. Ibid., 647–8.

94. 'State that 13,000 Chinese Have Been Killed in South, 15,000 near Hankow', *The New York Times,* 17 December 1939.

95. Tobe Ryoichi, 'The Japanese Eleventh Army in Central China', 220.

96. Xu Yong, *Zhengfu Zhi Meng*, 273.

97. Barak Kushner, *The Thought War: Japanese Imperial Propaganda* (Honolulu, HI: University of Hawaii Press, 2006), 1–49.

98. Riben Fangweiting Fangwei Yanjiusuo Zhanshishi, *Zhongguo Shibian Lujun Zuozhan Zhanshi*, vol. 3: 2, 1–28.

99. Lyman Van Slyke, 'The Battle of the Hundred Regiments: Problems of Coordination and Control during the Sino-Japanese War', in *Modern Asian Studies*, vol. 30:4 (1996), 979–1005.

100. SLGB, vol. 43 (January–June 1940), 523.

101. Arthur Waldron, 'China's New Remembering of WWII: The Case of Zhang Zizhong', *Modern Asian Studies* 30:4 (1996), 953–4.

102. Quoted in ibid., 954.

103. Ibid., 965–9.

104. Chen Kewen, 'Recollecting Chen Bijun and Chen Chunpu', in Chen Kewen, *Chen Kewen Riji*, 1435–6.

105. Yang Zhiyi, 'The Road to Lyric Martyrdom', 162.

106. Boyle, *China and Japan at War*, 6–11.

Chapter 8: War Communism

1. https://www.csee.umbc.edu/~stephens/POEMS/brecht1.

2. Lyman Van Slyke, 'The Chinese Communist Movement during the Sino-Japanese War 1937–1945', in CHOC, vol. 13, 632.

3. Edgar Snow, *Red Star over China* (originally published London: Victor Gollancz, 1937; New York: Grove Press, 1961), 63–4; Mark Selden, *The Yenan Way in Revolutionary China* (Cambridge, MA: Harvard University Press, 1971), 3.

4. J. C. Keyte, *The Passing of the Dragon*, 227, quoted in Selden, *The Yenan Way*, 4.

5. Alexander Pantsov and Steven I. Levine, *Mao: The Real Story* (New York: Simon & Schuster, 2012), 289.

6. Ibid., 287–8.

7. Li Zhisui, *The Private Life of Chairman Mao: The Inside Story of the Man Who Made China* (London: Chatto & Windus, 1994), 568.

8. Xinhua, 'Zhengque Chuli Mao Zedong "Ganxie Ribin Qinlue" Yiyu' ('Correctly Handling Mao Zedong's Statement "With Thanks to Japanese Aggression"', 17 December 2008 http://news.163.com/08/1217/08/4TBQLDI200011247.html

9. Karl Marx, *The Class Struggles in France*, in Lewis S. Feuer, ed., *Marx and Engels: Basic Writings on Politics and Philosophy* (Garden City, NY: Doubleday, 1959), 319.

10. Karl Marx, *The Eighteenth Brumaire of Louis Bonaparte,* chapter 7, https://www.marxists.org/archive/marx/works/1852/18th-brumaire/ch07.htm

11. On Tawney as a moral economist, see Tim Rogan, *The Moral Economists: R. H. Tawney, Karl Polanyi, E. P. Thompson and the Critique of Capitalism* (Princeton, NJ: Princeton University Press, 2017). R. H. Tawney, *Land and Labor in China* (Boston, MA: Beacon Press, 1966), 74.

12. Timothy Cheek, *Propaganda and Culture in Mao's China: Deng Tuo and the Intelligentsia* (Oxford: Clarendon Press, 1997), 49–51.

13. For an excellent introduction to literary and scholarly writings about the countryside, see Zhang Yu, *To the Soil: The Rural and the Modern in Chinese Cultural Imagination, 1915–1935* (Stanford University Ph.D. dissertation, 2014), chapter 1.

14. Pantsov and Levine, *Mao*, 11–21.

15. Quoted in Hans van de Ven, *From Friend to Comrade: The Founding of the Chinese Communist Party, 1920–1927* (Berkeley: University of Califonria Press, 1991), 23.

16. Ibid., 157–60.

17. Cheek, *Propaganda and Culture in Mao's China,* 43.

18. Ibid., 47.

19. Hans van de Ven, *From Friend to Comrade: The Founding of the Chinese Communist Party, 1920–1927* (Berkeley, CA: University of California Press, 1992), 52.

20. Quoted in Su Yu, *Su Yu Zhanzheng Huiyilu* (*War Memoirs of Su Yu*) (Beijing: Jiefangjun Chubanshe, 1988), 72.

21. Stephen Averill, 'The Origins of the Futian Incident', in Tony Saich and Hans van de Ven, *New Perspectives on the Chinese Communist Revolution* (Armonk, NY: M E. Sharpe, 1995), 100–110.

22. Mao Zedong, *On Protracted War*, in *Selected Works of Mao Tse-tung* (Beijing: Foreign Languages Press, 1969), vol. 2, 131.

23. Pantsov and Levine, *Mao*, 255.

24. Quoted in Pantsov and Levine, *Mao*, 268.

25. Mao Zedong, 'A Single Spark Can Start a Prairie Fire', in *Selected Works of Mao Tse-tung*, vol. 1, 124.

26. Pantsov and Levine, *Mao*, 280.

27. Snow, *Red Star over China*, part 3, chapter 1.

28. James M. Bertram, *North China Front* (London: Macmillan & Co., 1939), 151.

29. Panstov and Levine, *Mao*, 309.

30. Ibid., 279.

31. Raymond F. Wylie, *The Emergence of Maoism: Mao Tse-tung, Chen Po-ta, and the Search for Chinese Theory 1935–1945* (Stanford, CA: Stanford University Press, 1980).

32. Jin Chongji, *Mao Zedong Zhuan, 1883–1949* (*Biography of Mao Zedong, 1893–1949*) (Bejing: Zhongyang Wenxian Chubanshe, 1996), 498.

33. Jin Chongji, *Mao Zedong Zhuan*, 497–8; Wu Xiuquan, 'Zai Yan'an Junwei Zongbu' ('At the Yan'an HQ of the Military Affairs Committee'), in Zhongguo Renmin Jiefangjun Lishi Ziliao Congshu Bianshen Weiyuanhui, eds., *Zhongguo Renmin Jiefangjun Lishi Ziliao: Zong Canmou Bu Huiyi Shiliao* (*Historical Materials for the People's Liberation*

Army: Recollections from the General Staff Office) (Beijing: Jiefangjun Chubanshe, 1995), 125.

34. Mao Zedong, *On Protracted War*, in Stuart R. Schram, ed., *Mao's Road to Power, 1912–1949: Volume 6: The New Stage, August 1937–1938* (Armonk, NY: M. E. Sharpe, 2004), 356–9.
35. Ibid., 329.
36. https://www.marxists.org/reference/archive/mao/selected-works/volume-2/mswv2_08.htm. May 1938. This is a draft of a piece that Mao abandoned.
37. Mao Zedong, *On Protracted War*, in Schram, ed., *Mao's Road to Power*, vol. 6, 374.
38. Ibid.
39. Ibid.
40. Ibid.
41. Ibid.
42. Carl von Clausewitz, *On War*, J. J. Graham, trans., revised by F. N. Mause, abridged by Louise Wilmot (London: Wordsworth, 1997), 150–51.
43. Van Slyke, 'The Chinese Communist Movement during the Sino-Japanese War', in CHOC, vol. 13, 646–58.
44. Peng Zhen, quoted in ibid., 654.
45. Quoted in Yang Kuisong, 'Nationalist and Communist Guerrilla Warfare in North China', in Mark Peattie, Edward J. Drea and Hans van de Ven, eds., *The Battle for China: Essays on the Military History of the Sino-Japanese War of 1937–45* (Stanford, CA: Stanford University Press, 2011), 321.
46. Ch'en Yung-fa, 'The Blooming Poppy under the Red Sun', in Tony Saich and Hans van de Ven, eds., *New Perspectives on the Chinese Communist Revolution* (Armonk, NY: M.E. Sharpe, 1995), 263–98.
47. Peter Vladimirov, *The Vladimirov Diaries: Yenan, China, 1942–1945* (London: Robert Hale, 1976), 43.
48. Zhang Xianwen, *Zhonghua Minguo Shi* (*History of the Republic of China*) (Nanjing: Nanjing University Press, 2005), vol. 2, 343–57.
49. Ibid., vol. 3, 24–5.
50. Ibid., vol. 3, 22.
51. Yang Kuisong, *Geming* (*Revolution*) (Nanning: Guangxi Renmin Chubanshe, 2012), vol. 3, 446.
52. Ibid., vol. 3, 448.
53. Quoted in Lloyd E. Eastman, *The Nationalist Era in China, 1927–1949* (Cambridge: Cambridge University Press, 1991), 207.
54. Mao Zedong, 'The Luochuan Meeting Will Discuss Major Military Issues', 18 August 1937, in Schram, ed., *Mao's Road to Power*, vol. 6, 22; 'Three Telegrams from Mao Zedong on the Issue of Guerrilla Warfare', September 1937 and April 1938, in Tony Saich and Bingzhang Yang, eds., *The Rise to Power of the Chinese Communist Party: Documents and Analysis* (Armonk, NY: M. E. Sharpe, 1996), 793–5.
55. Mao Zedong, 'Resolutely Maintain the Principle of Independent and Self-Reliant Warfare', in Schram, ed., *Mao's Road to Power*, vol. 6, 51.
56. Mao Zedong, 'Opinion Concerning the 115th Division Advancing to Hebei, Shandong, and Other Places in Three Steps', in Schram, ed., *Mao's Road to Power*, vol. 6, 218–19.

57. Mao Zedong, 'We Must Deploy Sufficient Forces on Exterior Lines', in Schram, ed., *Mao's Road to Power*, vol. 6, 222–5.

58. Mao Zedong, 'Opinion Concerning the 115th Division Advancing to Hebei, Shandong, and Other Places in Three Steps', in Schram, ed., *Mao's Road to Power*, vol. 6, 218–19.

59. Van Slyke, 'The Chinese Communist Movement during the Sino-Japanese War', CHOC, vol. 13, 640.

60. Ibid., 641.

61. Sherman Lai, *A Springboard to Victory: Shandong Province and Chinese Communist Military and Financial Strength, 1937–1945* (Leiden: Brill, 2011), 15–17.

62. Van Slyke. 'The Chinese Communist Movement during the Sino-Japanese War', CHOC, vol. 13, 620–21.

63. Zhang Guotao, 'Earnest Letter to the Chinese People', 6 May 1938, in Saich and Yang, eds., *The Rise to Power of the Chinese Communist Party*, 762, 764.

64. Quoted in Yang Kuisong, 'Kangzhan Shiqi Zhonggong Junshi Fazhan Biandong de Shishi Kaoxi' ('An Examination of the Facts about Changes in the Military Development of the Chinese Communist Party during the War of Resistance'), in *Jindaishi Yanjiu (Research on Modern Chinese History)*, vol. 210 (2015: 11), 5.

65. See Yang Kuisong, 'Kangzhan Shiqi Zhonggong Junshi Fazhan Biandong de Shishi Kaoxi', http://jds.cass.cn/ztyj/gms/201605/t20160506_3324941.shtml.

66. Chiang Kaishek, *Kunmianji (Diary Entries on Striving in Adversity)*, Huang Zijin and Pan Guangzhe, eds., (Taipei: Guoshiguan, 2011), 648.

67. Yang Kuisong, *Geming*, vol. 3, 468.

68. Ibid., 462.

69. Ibid., 476–7.

70. Ibid., 477.

71. Van Slyke, 'The Chinese Communist Movement during the Sino-Japanese War', in CHOC, vol. 13, 659.

72. Ibid., 620–21.

73. Lai, *A Springboard to Victory*, 44.

74. Ibid., 46–7.

75. Ibid., 47– 9.

76. Quoted in Yang Kuisong, *Geming*, vol. 3, 479.

77. Yang Kuisong, *Geming*, vol. 3, 483–5.

78. Ibid., 485–512.

79. Jin Chongji, *Mao Zedong Zhuan*, 624–5.

80. Ibid., 639, quoting 'Mao Zedong Zai Zhongyang Xuexizu Fayan Jilu' ('Record of Mao Zedong's Speeches at the Central Study Group'), 28 May 1942.

81. 'To 10 from 12', 12 October 1944, in Government Code and Cypher School: Decrypts of Communist International Messages, in UK National Archives, HW 17/42.

82. Quoted in Jin Chongji, *Mao Zedong Zhuan*, 653.

83. Quoted in Van Slyke, 'The Chinese Communist Movement during the Sino-Japanese War', in CHOC, vol. 13, 690.

84. The definitive work is Gao Hua, *Hong Taiyang Shi Zen Yang Shengqide: Yan'an Zhengfeng Yundong De Lailong Qumai (How Did the Red Flag Rise Above Yan'an: The History of the Yan'an Rectification Movement)* (Hong Kong: Chinese University of Hong Kong Press, 2002).

85. Jin Chongji, *Mao Zedong Zhuan*, 651.
86. Quoted in Van Slyke, 'The Chinese Communist Movement during the Sino-Japanese War', in CHOC, vol. 13, 692.
87. David E. Apter and Tony Saich, *Revolutionary Discourse in Mao's Republic* (Cambridge, MA: Harvard University Press, 1994), 285.
88. Ibid., 285.
89. This collection would become *Liuda Yilai* (*Since the Sixth Congress*), published internally in 1950 and 1980 by the Office of the Central Committee of the CCP. The collection *Zhonggong Zhongyang Wenjian Xuanji* (*Selection Documents of the CCP Central Committee*) (Beijing: Central Party School, 1989–1992) is based on these.
90. Vladimirov, *The Vladimirov Diaries*, 105–10.
91. Apter and Saich, *Revolutionary Discourse in Mao's Republic*, 287.
92. Dai Qing, *Wang Shiwei and 'Wild Lilies': Rectification and Purges in the Chinese Communist Party, 1942–1944* (Arnak, NY: M. E. Sharpe, 1994), 5.
93. Jin Chongji, *Mao Zedong Zhuan*, 652.
94. Apter and Saich, *Revolutionary Discourse in Mao's Republic*, 289.
95. Jin Chongji, *Mao Zedong Zhuan*, 653.
96. Quoted in ibid., 655.
97. See Saich and Yang, eds., *The Rise to Power of the Chinese Communist Party*, 912–29.
98. Ibid., 915.
99. Ibid., 928.
100. Ibid., 927.

Chapter 9: The Allies at War

1 Sir Adrian Carton de Wiart, *Happy Odyssey: The Memoirs of Lieutenant-General Sir Adrian Carton de Wiart* (London: Jonathan Cape, 1950; Barnsley: Pen & Sword Military, 2007), 271.
2 Winston S. Churchill, *History of the Second World War, Volume 3: The Grand Alliance* (London: Cassell & Co. Ltd, 1950), 538–40.
3 https://www.loc.gov/exhibits/churchill/wc-sword.html
4 SLGB, vol. 47 (September–December 1941), 593.
5 Ibid., 487–92.
6 Ibid., 492–530.
7 'Omita to Currie', 27 November 1941, in Hoover Institution Archives, Laughlin Currie Papers, Owen Lattimore Correspondence.
8 'Sharp Statement Indicates Talks with Kurusu Near Collapse', *Washington Post*, 4 December 1941.
9 Jay Taylor, 'China's Long War with Japan', in John Ferris and Evan Mawdsley, eds., *The Cambridge History of the Second World War, Volume 1: Fighting the War* (Cambridge: Cambridge University Press, 2015), 65.
10 SLGB, vol. 47 (September–December 1941), 607–8.
11 Chiang Kaishek, *Kunmianji* (*Diary Entries on Striving in Adversity*), Huang Zijin and Pan Guangzhe, eds. (Taipei: Guoshiguan, 2011), 813.
12 Ibid.
13 John Thompson, *A Sense of Power: The Roots of America's Global Role* (Ithaca, NY: Cornell University Press, 2015), 194, 201–2.

14 Barbara W. Tuchman, *Stilwell and the American Experience in China, 1911–1945* (London: Macmillan, 1971), 320.

15 Quoted in Thomas G. Mahnken, 'US Grand Strategy', in Ferris and Mawdsley, eds., *The Cambridge History of the Second World War, Volume 1: Fighting the War,* 193.

16 Mark A. Stoler, *Allies and Adversaries: The Joint Chiefs of Staff, the Grand Alliance, and the US Strategy in WWII* (Chapel Hill, NC: University of North Carolina Press, 2000), 31.

17 Mark Watson http://www.history.army.mil/books/wwii/csppp/ch12.htm

18 'Notes of Meeting at the White House', Larry Bland, ed, *The Papers of George Catlett Marshall* (6 volumes) (Baltimore, MD: Johns Hopkins University Press, 1981), vol. 3, 30–34.

19 Chiang Kaishek, *Kunmianji*, 813–15.

20 SLGB, vol. 47 (September–December 1941), 713.

21 Zhang Xianwen, *Zhonghua Minguo Shi* (*History of the Republic of China*) (Nanjing: Nanjing University Press, 2005), vol. 3, 135.

22 Mahnken, 'US Grand Strategy', in Ferris and Mawdsley, eds., *The Cambridge History of the Second World War: Volume 1: Fighting the War,* 189.

23 'The Military Mission in China to the War Department', 10 February 1942, in FRUS, 1942, China, 13–16.

24 'Airmen Decorated', *The New York Times,* 20 May 1942.

25 'The Chinese Campaign', *The New York Times,* 7 June 1942.

26 R. Keith Schoppa, *In a Sea of Bitterness: Refugees during the Sino-Japanese War* (Cambridge, MA: Harvard University Press, 2011), 249.

27 Schoppa, 'Self-inflicted Wounds: Scorched Earth Strategies in Zhejiang, 1937–1945', paper presented at the Conference on the Scars of War at the University of British Columbia, April 1998, 15.

28 Tuchman, *Stilwell and the American Experience in China,* 359.

29 *The New York Times,* 21 April 1942.

30 'We Mean Business, Stilwell Asserts', *The New York Times,* 21 March 1942.

31 Thompson, *A Sense of Power,* 199.

32 Hans van de Ven, *War and Nationalism in China, 1925–1945* (London: Routledge, 2003), 22–3.

33 Ibid., 22–4.

34 For relevant documents, see ZHMGZYSLCB, series 2, vol. 3, 221–60, consisting of minutes of discussions between Chiang Kaishek and General Joseph Stilwell, as well as Chiang Kaishek's instructions to his commanders.

35 Tuchman, *Stilwell and the American Experience in China,* 330.

36 Hsi-sheng Ch'i, *The Much Troubled Alliance: US–China Military Cooperation during the Pacific War, 1941–1945* (Singapore: World Scientific Publishing, 2015), 65.

37 Ibid., 85.

38 Peter Paret, ed., *Makers of Modern Strategy from Machiavelli to the Nuclear Age* (Princeton, NJ: Princeton University Press, 1986), 681.

39 Theodore H. White, ed., *The Stilwell Papers* (New York: William Sloane Assoc., 1948), 214, 315, 340.

40 Ibid., 53.

41 Ibid., 80.

42   'Stilwell, After "a Beating" in Burma Would Hit Back', *The New York Times*, 26 May 1942.

43   Hsi-sheng Ch'i, *The Much Troubled Alliance*, 140.

44   Ibid.

45   'What Caused It', *The New York Times*, 26 May 1942.

46   Chiang Kaishek, *Kunmianji*, 845; Hsi-sheng Ch'i, *The Much Troubled Alliance*, 137.

47   I am grateful to Richard Frank for bringing this detail to my attention.

48   I am grateful to Richard Frank for spelling out in this way the implications of the logistical problems the Allies faced in supplying China.

49   'Record of Conversation following Chiang Kaishek's Welcoming Banquet for General Stilwell, Chief of Staff of Allied Forces in the China Theatre', 9 March 1942, ZHMGZYSLCB, series 2, vol. 3, 221–3.

50   Tuchman, *Stilwell and the American Experience in China*, 404–5.

51   Ibid., 418–19.

52   Charles F. Romanus and Riley Sunderland, *China–Burma–India Theater: Stilwell's Mission to China* (Washington, DC:, Office of the Chief of Military History, 1956), 152–8; Louis Allen, *Burma: The Longest War 1941–45* (London: J. M. Dent, 1984), 156; Tuchman, *Stilwell and the American Experience in China, 1911–1945*, 386–7.

53   'Subject: Retaking of Burma', in Bland, ed., *The Papers of George Catlett Marshall*, vol. 3, 319–20.

54   Tuchman, *Stilwell and the American Experience in China*, 389.

55   'Subject: Operation in Burma, March 1943', in Bland, ed., *The Papers of George Catlett Marshall*, vol. 3, 476–7.

56   Claire Lee Chennault, *Way of a Fighter: The Memoirs of Claire Lee Chennault* (New York: G. P. Putnam's Sons, 1946), 4.

57   Ibid., 21.

58   Herbert O. Yardley, *The Chinese Black Chamber: An Adventure in Espionage* (Boston, MA: Houghton Mifflin Company, 1983).

59   Carton de Wiart, *Happy Odyssey*, 124–5.

60   Ibid., 89.

61   Chennault, *Way of a Fighter*, 73.

62   Ibid., 114–15.

63   'Labels Americans "Flying Tigers"', *The New York Times*, 27 January 1942.

64   Chennault, *Way of a Fighter*, 144.

65   https://www.youtube.com/watch?v=TqoivpKAvn4.

66   *Washington Post*, 17 April 1942.

67   Romanus and Sunderland, *China–Burma–India Theater: Stilwell's Mission to China*, 253–4; Wesley Marvin Bagby, *The Eagle–Dragon Alliance: America's Relations with China in World War II* (Newark, NJ: University of Delaware Press, 1992), 75.

68   Ibid., 74.

69   'To Lieutenant General Joseph Stilwell', in Bland, ed., *The Papers of George Catlett Marshall*, vol. 3, 503–4.

70   Letter to Stilwell, 9 April 1943, Marshall Papers, vol. 3, 637.

71   'Plan of Operation in China', 30 April 1943, Hoover Institution Archives, Chennault Papers, box 9.

72   Bagby, *The Eagle–Dragon Alliance*, 76.

304 CHINA AT WAR

73   Commentary, in Bland, ed., *The Papers of George Catlett Marshall*, vol. 3, 584–6 and 674–75; 'Memorandum for General Stilwell', 3 May 1943, in ibid., 675.

74   Bagby, *The Eagle–Dragon Alliance*, 76.

75   Chi Pang-yuan, *Juliuhe* (*The Great Flowing River*) (Taipei: Yuanjian Tianxia, 2014), 210, 216–17.

76   'Oh Captain! My Captain!' in *Leaves of Grass* (Philadelphia, PA: David McKay, 1891) https://www.poetryfoundation.org/poems-and-poets/poems/detail/45474.

77   Chi Pang-yuan, *Juliuhe*, 216.

78   Winston S. Churchill, *The Second World War, Volume 5: Closing the Ring* (London: Cassell & Co., 1954), 82.

79   Tuchman, *Stilwell and the American Experience in China*, 437.

80   'Minutes of Conference Held at Generalissimo's Residence, 18 October 1943', ZHMGZYSLCB, series 2, vol. 3, 395–411.

81   Tuchman, *Stilwell and the American Experience in China*, 400–401.

82   Van de Ven, *War and Nationalism in China*, 43.

83   'Views Regarding the Burma Offensive of Lin Wei', ZHMGZYSLCB, series 2, vol. 3, 427.

84   Mary Barbier, 'The War in the West, 1943–1945', in Ferris and Mawdsley, eds., *The Cambridge History of the Second World War: Volume 1: Fighting the War*, 400.

85   Churchill, *The Second World War, Volume 5: Closing the Ring*, 495.

86   'Chiang Kaishek to Roosevelt', 1 January 1944, in 'Use of the Yunnan Force', in UK National Archives, PREM 3/148/6.

87   Yang Tianshi, 'Chiang Kaishek and Jawaharlal Nehru', in Mark Peattie, Edward Drea and Hans van de Ven, eds., *The Battle for China: Essays on the Military History of the Sino-Japanese War of 1937–45* (Stanford, CA: Stanford University Press, 2011), 129.

88   Ibid., 127–8. See also Yang Tianshi, 'Jiang Jieshi yu Nihelu' ('Chiang Kaishek and Nehru'), in *Zhongguo Wenhua*, vol. 30 (2009), 132–3.

89   Yang Tianshi, 'Chiang Kaishek and Jawaharlal Nehru', 128, and Yang Tianshi, 'Jiang Jieshi yu Nihelu', 133.

90   12 February 1942, Churchill Archives, CHAR 20/70/18.

91   Yang Tianshi, 'Chiang Kaishek and Jawaharlal Nehru', 131–4.

92   'Telegram from General Chiang Kaishek', 24 February 1942, FRUS, 1942, General, 605.

93   'Exchange of Views between Generalissimo Chiang Kaishek and President Roosevelt Regarding Situation in India', FRUS, 1942, China, 761.

94   Elliott Roosevelt, *As He Saw It* (New York: Duell, Sloan, and Pearce, 1946), 37.

95   Auriol Weigold, *Churchill, Roosevelt, and India: Propaganda During World War II* (London: Routledge, 2008), 48–50.

96   'Memorandum by the Chief of the Division of Far Eastern Affairs', 27 March 1942, FRUS, 1942, China, 273.

97   'The British Embassy to the Department of State', 12 May 1942, FRUS, 1942, China, 276.

98   ZHMGZYSLCB, series 3, vol. 3, 696.

99   Ibid., 696–7.

100   '"V" Tapped on Liberty Bell', *Time* magazine, October 1942.

101   'Chiang Kaishek to Roosevelt', 11 October 1942, in Qin Xiaoyi, ed., *Zhonghua Minguo Zhongyao Shiliao Chubian: Disan Bian: Zhanshi Waijiao* (*A Preliminary Collection of Important Historial Documents for the Republic of China: Part 3: Wartime Foreign Relations*) (Taipei: Zhongyang Wenwu Gongying Chubanshe, 1981), 7.

102 'Text of the Two Addresses before Congress by Mme Chiang Kaishek', *The New York Times*, 19 February 1943.

103 'A Camera Report of Mme Chiang's First Official Visit', *The New York Times*, 3 March 1942.

104 Jane Park, '"The China Film": Madame Chiang Kaishek in Hollywood', *Screening the Past*, vol. 4, 2011 http://www.screeningthepast.com/2011/04/the-china-film

105 Gordon H. Chang, 'Chinese Painting Comes to America: Zhang Shuqi and the Diplomacy of Art', in Cynthia Mills, Lee Glazer and Amelia Goerlitz, eds., *East–West Interchanges in American Art: A Long and Tumultuous Relationship* (Washington, DC: Smithsonian Contributions to Knowledge, 2012), 131–2.

106 Christopher Thorne, *The United States, Britain, and the War against Japan, 1941–1945* (Oxford: Oxford University Press, 1978), 420–21.

107 Keith Sainsbury, *The Turning Point: Roosevelt, Stalin, Churchill and Chiang Kai-shek, 1943: The Moscow, Cairo and Teheran Conferences* (Oxford: Oxford University Press, 1985), 146.

108 Chiang Kaishek, *Kunmianji*, 935.

109 Ibid., 934–5.

110 Ibid., 941.

111 Ibid., 937–8.

112 Ibid., 937–8.

113 Ibid., 937.

114 Churchill, *The Second World War, Volume 5: Closing the Ring*, 289–90.

115 Lord Moran, *Winston Churchill: The Struggle for Survival, 1940–65* (London: Constable & Co. Ltd, 1966), 135–7.

116 G. F. Hudson, minute, 4 February 1944, in 'Foreign Office: Political Departments: Chinese Post-War Territorial Aims', UK National Archives, FO 371/41627.

Chapter 10: The Turning Point

1 See *Johann Gottfried Herder on World History: An Anthology*, Hans Adler and Ernest A Menze, eds. (London: Routledge, 1996).

2 Ch'en Yung-fa, 'Guanjian de Yinian: Jiang Zhongzheng yu Yu Xiang Gui Da Kuibai' '('The Crucial Year: Chiang Kaishek and the Major Defeat at Ichigo'), in Liu Cuirong, ed., *Zhongguo Lishi de Zai Sikao (Reconsiderations of Chinese History)* (Taipei: Liangjing, 2015), 349.

3 Chiang Kaishek, *China's Destiny: Chinese Economic Theory*, Philip Jaffe, trans. (London: Dennis Dobson, 1947), 44.

4 Ibid., 201–2.

5 Ibid., 201.

6 Chen Kewen, *Chen Kewen Riji (Chen Kewen's Diary)*, Chen Fangzheng, ed. (Taipei: Zhongyang Yanjiuyuan Jindaishi Yanjiusuo, 2012), 925.

7 Barbara W. Tuchman, *Stilwell and the American Experience in China, 1911–1945* (London: Macmillan, 1971), 607.

8 Chen Kewen, *Chen Kewen Riji*, 901; Ch'en Yung-fa, 'Guanjian de Yinian', 350.

9 Ibid., 854–5.

10 Ch'en Yung-fa, 'Guanjian de Yinian', 410.

11   Wu Sufeng, 'The Nationalist Government's Attitude toward Post-war Japan', in Hans van de Ven, Diana Lary and Stephen R. MacKinnon, eds., *Negotiating China's Destiny in WWII* (Stanford, CA: Stanford University Press, 2014), 201.

12   Hara Takeshi, 'The Ichigo Offensive', in Mark Peattie, Edward J. Drea and Hans van de Ven, eds., *The Battle for China: Essays on the Military History of the Sino-Japanese War of 1937–45* (Stanford, CA: Stanford University Press, 2011), 395–6.

13   Ibid., 397–8.

14   Edward J. Drea, *In the Service of the Emperor: Essays on the Imperial Japanese Army* (Lincoln, NE: University of Nebraska Press, 1998), 188.

15   Hans van de Ven, *War and Nationalism in China, 1925–1945* (London: Routledge, 2003), 272.

16   Lloyd E. Eastman, 'Facets of an Ambivalent Relationship: Smuggling, Puppets, and Atrocities during the War, 1937–45', in Akira Iriye, ed., *The Chinese and the Japanese: Essays in Political and Cultural Interactions* (Princeton, NJ: Princeton University Press, 1980), 275–303.

17   Ch'en Yung-fa, 'Guanjian de Yinian', 353–4.

18   Ibid., 351–6.

19   Ibid., 354.

20   Ibid., 368.

21   'Millions Starving in Vast Chinese Area', *The New York Times*, 20 October 1942.

22   Rana Mitter, *China's War with Japan, 1937–1945: The Struggle for Survival* (London: Penguin, 2014), 271.

23   Claire Lee Chennault, *Way of a Fighter: The Memoirs of Claire Lee Chennault* (New York: G. P. Putnam's Sons, 1946), 286.

24   Van de Ven, *War and Nationalism in China*, 252–93; see also Arthur N. Young, *China's Wartime Finance and Inflation, 1937–1945* (Cambridge, MA: Harvard University Press, 1965); Chang Kia-Ngau, *The Inflationary Spiral, The Experience in China, 1939–1950* (Cambridge, MA: The MIT Press, 1958).

25   Wang Qisheng, 'The Battle of Hunan and the Chinese Military's Response to Operation Ichigo', in Peattie et al., eds., *The Battle for China*, 405.

26   Ch'en Yung-fa, 'Guanjian de Yinian', 363–4.

27   Zhang Xianwen, *Zhongguo Kang Ri Zhanzheng Shi* (*History of China's War of Resistance*) (Nanjing: Nanjing Daxue Chubanshe, 2001), 1059.

28   Ibid., 1061–5.

29   Chen Kewen, *Chen Kewen Riji*, 863.

30   Zhang Xianwen, *Zhongguo Kang Ri Zhanzheng Shi*, 1054–9.

31   Ibid., 1064–7.

32   Ch'en Yung-fa, 'Guanjian de Yinian', 361.

33   Ibid., 371.

34   Ibid., 362.

35   Ibid., 349.

36   Stephen R. Platt, *Autumn in the Heavenly Kingdom: China, the West, and the Epic Story of the Taiping Civil War* (New York: Alfred A. Knopf, 2012), 358–9.

37   Wang Qisheng, 'The Battle of Hunan and the Chinese Military's Response to Operation Ichigo', in Peattie et al., eds., *The Battle for China*, 407–8; Van de Ven, *War and Nationalism in China*, 19–63.

38   Ch'en Yung-fa, 'Guanjian de Yinian', 376.

39   Zhang Xianwen, ed., *Kang Ri Zhanzheng de Zhengmian Zhanchang* (*Battles at the Front during the War of Resistance*) (Zhengzhou: Henan Renmin Chubanshe, 1996), 1069–74.

40   Ibid., 1076–8; Ch'en Yung-fa, 'Guanjian de Yinian', 378–81.

41   Zhang Xianwen, *Zhongguo Kang Ri Zhanzheng Shi*, 1082–4; Hara Takeshi, 'The Ichigo Offensive', 394; Ch'en Yung-fa, 'Guanjian de Yinian', 382–3.

42   Ch'en Yung-fa, 'Guanjian de Yinian', 384.

43   Ibid., 385–6.

44   Zhang Xianwen, *Zhongguo Kang Ri Zhanzheng Shi*, 1084–7.

45   Quoted in ibid., 1087.

46   Ibid., 1088.

47   Ibid.

48   Ibid.

49   Chen Yung-fa, 'Guanjian de Yinian', 390–91.

50   Deng Ye, 'Chiang Jieshi Dui Fang Xianjue Tou Di de Caijue' ('Chiang Kaishek's Ruling on Fang Xianjue's Surrender'), in *Lishi Yanjiu* (*Historical Research*), vol. 5 (2006), 136–48; Ch'en Yung-fa, 'Guanjian de Yinian', 391–3.

51   'Major General Claire Chennault to President Roosevelt', 19 April 1944, FRUS, 1944, vol. 6, China, 83.

52   Van de Ven, *War and Nationalism in China*, 52–3.

53   Chennault, *Way of a Fighter*, 258.

54   Chen Kewen, *Chen Kewen Riji*, 898.

55   Ibid., 906.

56   Ibid.

57   Ibid., 717.

58   'The Chinese Famine', *The Times*, 5 February 1944.

59   Chen Kewen, *Chen Kewen Riji*, 885.

60   Chi Pang-yuan, *Juliuhe* (*The Great Flowing River*) (Taipei: Yuanjian Tianxia, 2014), 196.

61   Ibid., 197.

62   Ibid., 198.

63   Chen Yung-fa, 'Guanjian de Yinian', 394.

64   'Behind the Removal of General Stilwell', *The New York Times*, 30 October 1944.

65   Tuchman, *Stilwell and the American Experience in China*, 624. 'US Air Base Peril', *The New York Times*, 26 October 1944.

66   'Consul at Kweilin (Ringwalt) to Ambassador (Gauss)', 25 May 1944, FRUS, 1944, vol. 6, China, 83.

67   Chen Yung-fa, 'Guanjian de Yinian', 399.

68   Ibid., 403–4.

69   'Albert Wedemeyer to Dwight Eisenhower', February 1946, Hoover Institution Archives, Wedemeyer Papers, box 86, folder 3.

70   'Albert Wedemeyer to George Marshall', 10 December 1944, Hoover Institution Archives, Wedemeyer Papers, box 82, folder 23.

71   'Albert Wedemeyer to Stanley Embick', 7 December 1945, Hoover Institution Archives, Wedemeyer Papers, box 81, folder 4.

72   Chen Yung-fa, 'Guanjian de Yinian', 406.

73   Wesley Frank Craven and James Lea Cate, eds., *The Army Air Forces in World War II: Volume 5: The Pacific – Matterhorn to Nagasaki, June 1944 to August 1945* (Washington DC: Office of Air Force History, 1983), 142–4; http://www.afhso.af.mil/shared/media/document/AFD-101105-012.pdf.

74   Okamura Yasuji, *Gangcun Ningci Huiyilu* (*Memoirs of Okamura Yasuji*), Tianjin Shi Zhengxie Weiyuanhui, trans. (Beijing: Xinhua Shudian, 1981), 248–9.

75   Mitter, *China's War with Japan*, 377–80.

76   Theodore H. White, ed., *The Stilwell Papers* (New York: William Sloane Assoc., 1948), 45.

77   Tuchman, *Stilwell and the American Experience in China*, 329.

78   Ibid., 347.

79   Ibid., 547.

80   White, ed., *The Stilwell Papers*, 305.

81   Tuchman, *Stilwell and the American Experience in China*, 531.

82   'Carton de Wiart to PM', 18 December 1943, in 'Use of Yunnan Force', UK National Archives, PREM 3/148/6.

83   Larry Bland, ed., *The Papers of George Catlett Marshall* (6 volumes) (Baltimore, MD: John Hopkins University Press, 1981), vol. 4, 568, nn. 1 and 2. See also 'Prime Minister to General Carton de Wiart' and 'Prime Minister to Chiang Kaishek', in ZHMGZYSLCB, series 2, vol. 3, 468–71.

84   Tuchman, *Stilwell and the American Experience in China*, 567, 579.

85   Ibid., 596–7.

86   Mitter, *China's War with Japan*, 331.

87   Ibid., 332; Tuchman, *Stilwell and the American Experience in China*, 596–7.

88   'Political Obstacles to Military Unity', *The New York Times*, 18 December 1944.

89   Ibid.

90   Tuchman, *Stilwell and the American Experience in China*, 600–601.

91   Ibid., 302.

92   Van de Ven, *War and Nationalism in China*, 56.

93   Tuchman, *Stilwell and the American Experience in China*, 631.

94   Ibid.

95   Message from Chiang Kaishek, passed on by Ambassador Patrick J. Hurley, see 'Major General Patrick Hurley to President Roosevelt', FRUS, 1944, vol. 6, China, 167–9.

96   Daniel Katz, 'The Polls and the 1944 Election', in *Public Opinion Quarterly*, vol. 8 (1944–5), 468, 481.

97   'President Roosevelt to Generalissimo Chiang Kaishek', 5 October 1944, FRUS, 1944, vol. 6, China, 165.

98   'Ambassador Hurley to President Truman', 20 May 1945, FRUS, 1945, vol. 8, China, 107.

99   'Draft of Message from the President to the Generalissimo', 16 October 1944, in Bland, ed., *The Papers of George Catlett Marshall*, vol. 4, 627.

100 Tuchman, *Stilwell and the American Experience in China*, 646; 'Long Schism Seen', *The New York Times*, 31 October 1944.

101 'Long Schism Seen', *The New York Times*, 31 October 1944.

102 Van de Ven, *War and Nationalism in China*, 60.

103 'Albert Wedemeyer to Dwight Eisenhower', February 1946, Hoover Institution Archives, Wedemeyer Collection, box 86, folder 3.

104 'Marshall to Stilwell', 26 May 1944, in Bland, ed., *The Papers of George Catlett Marshall*, vol. 4, 466.

105 'George Marshall to Joseph Stilwell', 7 June 1944, in Bland, ed., *The Papers of George Catlett Marshall*, vol. 4, 472–3.

106 'Superforts Make Records in Orient', *The New York Times*, 17 December 1944.

107 Ibid.

108 Jeremy Harwood, *World War II: From Above: An Aerial View of the Global Conflict* (Brighton: Qu:id Publishing, 2014), 150–52, 192.

109 Craven and Cate, eds., *The Army Air Forces in World War II: Volume 5: The Pacific – Matterhorn to Nagasaki June 1944 to August 1945*, 142–4; Chennault, *Way of a Fighter*, 295; Wuhan Shizhi Biancuan Wiyuanhui (Editorial Committee for the Wuhan Local Gazetteer), eds., *Wuhan Shizhi: Junshi Zhi (Gazetteer of Wuhan: Military Gazetteer)*, 412.

110 'Hankow Blow to be Type', *The New York Times*, 22 December 1944.

111 Quoted in Richard Overy, *The Bombing War: Europe 1939–1945* (London: Allen Lane, 2013), 637.

112 'Albert Wedemeyer to George Marshall', 1 August 1945, in Keith E. Eiler, ed., *Wedemeyer on War and Peace* (Stanford, CA: Hoover Institution Press, 1987), 127.

113 'Albert Wedemeyer to Dwight Eisenhower', February 1946, Hoover Institution Archives, Wedemeyer Papers, box 86, folder 3.

114 Ibid.

115 'Albert Wedemeyer to George Marshall', 25 April 1945, Hoover Institution Archives, Wedemeyer Papers, box 82, folder 23.

116 'Albert Wedemeyer to Stanley Embick', 7 December 1944, Hoover Institution Archives, Wedemeyer Papers, box 81, folder 4.

117 'Efficiency Report', 25 January 1945, Hoover Institution Archives, Wedemeyer Papers, box 87, folder 9.

118 'Smuggling in China', Claire Chennault Papers, Hoover Institution Archives, box 9, folder 8.

119 Ibid.

120 'Albert Wedemeyer to Dwight Eisenhower', February 1946, Hoover Institution Archives, Wedemeyer Papers, box 86, folder 3.

121 Albert Wedemeyer, 'Memorandum for Chiang Kaishek', 10 November 1945, Hoover Institution Archives, Wedemeyer Papers, box 81, folder 2.

122 'Albert Wedemeyer to George Marshall', 16 August 1945, Hoover Institution Archives, Wedemeyer Papers, box 87, folder 1.

123 'George Marshall to Arthur Wedemeyer', 12 and 14 August 1945, Hoover Institution Archives, Wedemeyer Papers, box 87, folder 1.

124 Lyman Van Slyke, 'The Chinese Communist Movement during the Sino-Japanese War 1937–1945', in CHOC, vol. 13, 708–9.

125 Yang Zhesheng, *Qingbao Yingxiong Xiong Xianghui: Zai Hu Zongnan Shenbian de Shiernian (Intelligence Hero Xiong Xianghui: Twelve Years by the Side of Hu Zongnan)* (Shanghai: Shanghai Renmin Chubanshe, 2007), 191–208.

126 Van Slyke, 'The Chinese Communist Movement during the Sino-Japanese War', in CHOC, vol. 13, 709.

127   Deng Ye, *Lianhe Zhengfu yu Yidang Xunzheng: 1944–1946 Nian jian Guo Gong Zhengzhen* (*Joint Government and One Party Political Tutelage: The Political Struggle between the Communists and the Nationalists, 1944–1946*) (Beijing: Shehui Wenxue Wenxian Chubanshe, 2011), 17.
128   Ibid., 49.
129   Ibid., 47–8.
130   Ibid.
131   Ibid., 6.
132   Ibid., 7–10.
133   Ibid., 14.
134   Ibid., 31.
135   Ibid., 35.
136   Ibid., 35–6.
137   Guo Moruo, 'Jiashen Sanbainian Ji' ('In Commemoration of the 300th Anniversary of 1644'), in Guo Moruo, *Guo Moruo Wen Ji* (1937; reprinted Ann Arbor: University of Michigan Press, 2009).
138   *Zhongyang Ribao* (*Central Daily News*), 24 March 1944.
139   Mao Zedong, 'Our Study and the Current Situation', in *Selected Works of Mao Tse-tung* (Beijing: Foreign Languages Press, 1969), vol. 3, 174.
140   Chen Yung-fa, 'Guanjian de Yinian', 410.

Chapter 11: Japan's Surrender in China

1   Carl von Clausewitz, *On War*, Michael Howard and Peter Paret, trans. (Princeton, NJ: Princeton University Press, 1989), 227.
2   http://www.chinese-poems.com/due.html
3   Guo Dajun, *Yuxue Banian Shu Fengbei: Shouxiang yu Shenpan* (*A Monument Erected in Eight Blood-drenched Years: The Acceptance of Surrender and the Judgment after Trial*) (Guilin: Guangxi Shifan Daxue Chubanshe, 1994), 96.
4   'Nanking Acclaims Japan's Surrender', *The New York Times,* 10 September 1945.
5   Okamura Yasuji, *Gangcun Ningci Huiyilu* (*Memoirs of Okamura Yasuji*), Tianjin Shi Zhengxie Weiyuanhui, trans. (Beijing: Xinhua Shudian, 1981), 50–55; Guo, *Yuxue Banian Shu Fengbei*, 100–114; Wan Jinyu, 'Riben Touxiang he Zhongguo Lujun Zongbu Shouxiang Neimu' ('Japan's Surrender and the Background to the Reception of the Surrender by the Supreme Headquarters of the Chinese Army'), in *Zhonghua Wenshi Ziliao Quanji* (*Compilation of Materials for the Culture and History of China*), vol. 5, 2, 911–27.
6   Guo Dajun, *Yuxue Banian Shu Fengbei*, 65.
7   Okamura Yasuji, *Gangcun Ningci Huiyilu*, 28–32.
8   Ibid., 26.
9   Ibid., 23–8.
10   Ibid., 33.
11   The text is replicated in ibid., 45–6.
12   Guo Dajun, *Yuxue Banian Shu Fengbei*, 78–9.
13   Ibid., 85–6.
14   Ibid., 92–4.
15   Ibid., 95.

16   Okamura Yasuji, *Gangcun Ningci Huiyilu*, 30–31.

17   Guo Dajun, *Yuxue Banian Shu Fengbei*, 78; Okamura Yasuji, *Gangcun Ningci Huiyilu*, 33.

18   Guo Dajun, *Yuxue Banian Shu Fengbei*, 97–8.

19   'Nanking Welcomes the Chinese C-in-C', *Manchester Guardian*, 10 September 1945.

20   'Nanking Acclaims Japan's Surrender', *The New York Times*, 10 September 1945.

21   Mao Zedong, 'Dui Ri Kou de Zui Hou Yi Zhan' ('One Final Battle with the Japanese Invader'), in Mao Zedong, *Mao Zedong Junshi Wenji* (*Collected Military Writings of Mao Zedong*) (Beijing: Military Sciences Press, 1993), vol. 2, 817.

22   Yang Tianshi, *Zhaoxun Zhenshi de Jiang Jieshi: Jiang Jieshi Riji Jiedu* (*In Search of the Real Chiang Kaishek: Reading the Chiang Kaishek Diaries*) (Taiyuan: Shanxi Renmin Chubanshe, 2008), vol. 2, 422.

23   Guo Dajun, *Yuxue Banian Shu Fengbei*, 67.

24   Quoted in Guo Dajun, *Yuxue Banian Shu Fengbei*, 69–70.

25   'Text of Yenan Charges against Chiang', *The New York Times*, 14 August 1945.

26   Ibid.

27   Guo Dajun, *Yuxue Banian Shu Fengbei*, 71.

28   Ibid., 73–4.

29   Ibid., 74.

30   See Hans van de Ven, *War and Nationalism in China, 1925–1945* (London: Routledge, 2003), 58–9.

31   Ibid., 59.

32   'Red Offensive Announced', *The New York Times*, 15 August 1945.

33   'China Communists Ask Part in Peace', *The New York Times*, 17 August 1945.

34   'Reds Warn Chiang to Avert Civil War', *The New York Times*, 20 August 1945.

35   Okamura Yasuji, *Gangcun Ningci Huiyilu*, 36.

36   'Joint Chiefs of Staff to MacArthur, Nimitz, and Wedemeyer', 11 August 1945, in Hoover Institution Archives, Wedemeyer Papers, box 87, folder 1.

37   'From COMGENCHINA to WARCOS', 1 August 1945, in Hoover Institution Archives, Wedemeyer Papers, box 83, folder 40.

38   Brian Murray, 'Stalin, the Cold War, and the Division of China: A Multi-Archival Mystery', Working Paper 12, Cold War International Project, June 1995, 2–6; Shen Zhihua, *Mao, Stalin, and the Korean War: Trilateral Communist Relations in the 1950s* (Abingdon: Routledge, 2012), 2–4.

39   'Telegram from Chiang Kaishek to Mao Zedong Inviting Mao Zedong to Chongqing', ZHMGZYSLCB, series 7, vol. 2, 23.

40   'Chungking and Reds Claim New Gains in Wide Areas', *The New York Times*, 25 August 1945.

41   Ibid.

42   Quoted in Yang Tianshi, *Zhaoxun Zhenshi de Jiang Jieshi*, vol. 2, 423; Murray, 'Stalin, the Cold War, and the Division of China', 2.

43   'Zhongyang Guanyu Duoqu Da Chengshi yu Jiaotung Yaodao Gei Huazhongju de Zhishi' ('Instruction from the Centre to the Central China Bureau about Seizing Large Cities and Main Transport Routes'), available at http://cpc.people.com.cn/ GB/64184/64186/66647/4490962.html. 'Zhonggong Zhongyang Zhongyang Junwei Guanyu Gaibian Zhanlue de Zhishi' ('Instruction from the CCP Central Committee

and the Central Military Affairs Committee about Changing Our Strategic Guideline'),
available at http://cpc.people.cn/GB/64184/64186/66647/4490941.html.

44   Shen Zhihua, *Mao, Stalin, and the Korean War*, 49.
45   'Mao in Chungking for Talk on Unity', *The New York Times*, 29 August 1945.
46   Guo Dajun, *Yuxue Banian Shu Fengbei*, 76.
47   Ibid.
48   'Key Issues for Negotiation Raised by Communist Representatives Zhou Enlai and
     Wang Ruofei', ZHMGZYSLCB, series 7, vol. 2, 39–41.
49   Ibid., 41–5.
50   Ibid., 41–2.
51   Ibid., 41–2.
52   Quoted in Yang Tianshi, *Zhaoxun Zhenshi de Jiang Jieshi*, vol. 2, 430.
53   Ibid., 434–8.
54   'Chungking, Reds in Limited Accord', *The New York Times*, 12 October 1945.
55   'Mao Tse-tung Charges Plot', *The New York Times*, 14 October 1945.
56   'Extract of a letter by Carton de Wiart to General Ismay', in 'Personal Correspondence
     with General Sir Carton de Wiart', National Archives UK, CAB 127/28.
57   Chi Pang-yuan, *Juliuhe* (*The Great Flowing River*) (Taipei: Yuanjian Tianxia, 2014),
     218–19.
58   Ibid., 219.
59   Ibid., 212.
60   Chi Pang-yuan, *Juliuhe*, 224.
61   Ibid., 203–4.
62   Ibid., 204.

Chapter 12: Crash and Burn
1   Carl von Clausewitz, *On War*, Michael Howard and Peter Paret, trans. (Princeton, NJ:
     Princeton University Press, 1989), 254.
2   SLGB, vol. 62 (August– September 1945), 439–54.
3   Ibid., 442.
4   Ibid., 449–50.
5   Ibid., 439.
6   Ibid., 453–4.
7   Ibid., 454.
8   Ibid., 414.
9   Ibid., 417.
10   Zhang Xianwen, *Zhonghua Minguo Shi* (*History of the Republic of China*) (Nanjing:
     Nanjing Daxue Chubanshe, 2005), vol. 4, 1–10.
11   Morrison-Knudsen Construction Group, 'Report on Requirements of Railroads of
     China South of the Great Wall of China' (Shanghai, 1946), 11.
12   Diana Lary, 'Flowing East in Victory', paper presented at the conference 'The Sino-
     Japanese War and Its Impact on Asia', Taipei, December 2015, 6–8.
13   Agnes Norman, 'Immediate Needs', *China Newsweek*, 20 Decemberr 1945, in 'Chinese
     National Relief and Rehabilitation Administration and the United Nations', UK
     National Archives, WO 208/484.

14　Feng Zikai, 'Shengli Huanxiang Ji' ('Returning Home in Victory'), in *Feng Zikai Sanwen Xuanji (Selected Prose Essays by Feng Zikai)* (Tianjin: Baihua Wenyi Chubanshe, 1991), 194.

15　Chi Pang-yuan, *Juliuhe (The Great Flowing River)* (Taipei: Yuanjian Tianxia, 2014), 254–5.

16　Ibid., 278–8.

17　Ibid., 281–2.

18　Ibid., 287.

19　Chen Kewen, *Chen Kewen Riji (Chen Kewen's Diary)*, Chen Fangzheng, ed. (Taipei: Zhongyang Yanjiuyuan Jindaishi Yanjiusuo, 2012), 1034.

20　Ibid., 1059.

21　Ibid., 1027.

22　Charles D. Musgrove, 'Cheering the Traitor: The Post-war Trial of Chen Bijun, April 1946', in *Twentieth-century China*, 30:5 (2005), 3.

23　Chen Kewen, 'Yi Chen Bijun yu Chen Chunpu' ('Recollecting Chen Bijun and Chen Chunpu'), in Chen Kewen, *Chen Kewen Riji*, 1435–6.

24　Diana Lary, *China's Civil War: A Social History, 1945–1949* (Cambridge: Cambridge University Press, 2015), 67.

25　'Agreement for UNRRA', November 1943, http://www.ibiblio.org/pha/ policy/1943/431109a.html

26　Ruth E. Pardee, 'First Aid for China', *Pacific Affairs*, vol. 19:1 (March 1946), 75.

27　'CNRRA: Its Purpose, Functions, and Organization', in 'Chinese National Relief and Rehabilitation Administration and United Nations', UK National Archives, WO 208/484.

28　Katherine Green, 'UNRRA's Record in China', in *Far Eastern Survey*, vol. 20:10 (1951), 100–102.

29　'Food Supply Survey Peiping – Tientsin', Hoover Institution Archives, UNRRA China Office Files, box 8.

30　'Kwangsi Regional Office Summary Report', Hoover Institution Archives, UNRRA China Office Files, box 6.

31　'Answers to Questions on the Amount of Food Production, Consumption, and Shortage of Food in Kiangsu', Hoover Institution Archives, UNRRA China Office Files, box 6.

32　Carl Hopkins, 'Report No. 7', 21 June 1946, Hoover Institution Archives, UNRAA China Office Files, box 6.

33　T. Harman, 'Agricultural Conditions and CNRRA Operations in Kiangsi (as of March 1946)', Hoover Institution Archives, UNRRA China Office Files, box 6.

34　'Agicultural Rehabilitation in China during the UNRRA Period', 31 July 1947, Hoover Institution Archives, UNRRA China Office Files, box 7.

35　Micah S. Muscolino, *The Ecology of War in China: Henan Province, the Yellow River, and Beyond, 1938–1950* (New York: Cambridge University Press, 2015), 201–2.

36　Muscolino, *The Ecology of War in China*, 173.

37　Pardee, 'First Aid for China', 75.

38　Morrison-Knudsen Construction Group, 'Report on Requirements of Railroads of China South of the Great Wall of China' (Shanghai, 1946)'.

39　Dorothy Borg, 'ECA and US Policy in China', *Far Eastern Survey*, vol. 18:17 (1949), 198.

40　'China Must Supply Relief Work Fund', *The New York Times*, 10 June 1946.

41   Keith Lowe, *Savage Continent: Europe in the Aftermath of World War II* (London: Viking, 2012), 36–40.

42   Ibid., 212–48.

43   Melvyn P. Leffler, *A Preponderance of Power: National Security, the Truman Administration, and the Cold War* (Stanford, CA: Stanford University Press, 1992), 127.

44   'Statement by President Truman on United States Policy toward China', 15 December 1945, in US Department of State, *The China White Paper, August 1949* (Stanford, CA: Stanford University Press, 1967), vol. 2, 607–9.

45   Leffler, *A Preponderance of Power*, 128.

46   US Department of State, *The China White Paper*, vol. 1, 138–43.

47   'Statement by President Truman on the United States Policy toward China', 18 December 1946, in US Department of State, *The China White Paper*, vol. 2, 693.

48   'Truman Says Aid to China Hinges on Ending of Strife and Unification of Nation', *The New York Times*, 16 December 1945.

49   Leffler, *A Preponderance of Power*, 128.

50   Ministry of Economic Affairs, 'An Overview of the Economy in the Northeast', 26 January 1944, Taipei, Academia Historica (Guoshiguan), 055/1336.

51   Leffler, *A Preponderance of Power*, 128.

52   'Press Release on Order for Cessation of Hostilities', in US Department of State, *The China White Paper*, vol. 2, 610.

53   Leffler, *A Preponderance of Power*, 128.

54   Ibid., 127.

55   Niu Jun, *From Yan'an to the World: The Origin and Development of Chinese Communist Foreign Policy* (Norwalk, CT: EastBridge, 2005), 210–12.

56   Yang Kuisong, *Zhongjian Didai de Geming: Guoji Da Beijing Xia Kan Zhonggong Chenggong Zhi Dao* (*A Middle Zone Revolution: Looking at the Chinese Communist Party's Road to Success from an International Context*) (Taiyuan: Shanxi Renmin Chubanshe, 2010), 496.

57   Niu Jun, *From Yan'an to the World*, 210–12; Odd Arne Westad, *Decisive Encounters: The Chinese Civil War, 1946–1950* (Stanford, CA: Stanford University Press, 2003), 141.

58   Yang Kuisong, *Zhongjian Didai de Geming*, 479.

59   Ibid., 504.

60   Ibid., 507.

61   Ibid., 508.

62   'BAS Washington to War Office', 9 April 1946, in 'China: Reports on Russian Military Activities', UK National Archives, WO 208/4736.

63   'Szepingkai's Fall Reported', *The New York Times*, 13 May 1946.

64   'Manchuria: Communist Activities', April 1946, and 'Report from Peiping', 17 April 1946, in WO 208/4736.

65   'The Communist Armies in Manchuria' (nd) in WO 208/4725.

66   'Press Release on Order for Cessation of Hostilities', 10 January 1946, US Department of State, *The China White Paper*, vol. 2, 609.

67   'Statement by Generalissimo Chiang Kaishek', 6 June 1946, US Department of State, *The China White Paper*, vol. 2, 641.

68   US Department of State, *The China White Paper*, vol. 1, 338–51; Leffler, *A Preponderance of Power*, 128.

69 'Ralph Stevenson to Foreign Office', 25 January 1947, in 'Situation in China: Visit of General Marshall: Abandonment of US Mediation in Communist–Kuomintang Negotiations', UK National Archives, FO 371/63318.

70 'Statement by Generalissimo Chiang Kaishek', 13 August 1946, US Department of State, *The China White Paper,* vol. 2, 651; 'Chiang Gives Reds 8-point Peace Bid', *The New York Times,* 17 October 1946.

71 'Telegram, Zhou Enlai to the Central Committee and Mao Zedong, August 10, 1946' and 'Telegram, CCP Central Committee to Zhou Enlai, September 2, 1946', in Shuguang Zhang and Jian Chen, eds., *Chinese Communist Foreign Policy and the Cold War in Asia: New Documentary Evidence, 1944–1950* (Chicago, IL: Imprint Publications, 1996), 73–4, 77–8.

72 'China Reds Defied', *The New York Times,* 15 November 1946.

73 Leffler, *A Preponderance of Power,* 170–71.

74 Westad, *Decisive Encounters,* 49; 'Year's Work Halts', *The New York Times,* 30 January 1947.

75 Minute to 'Lord Inverchapel to Foreign Office', 15 February 1947, in 'Situation in China: Visit of General Marshall', UK National Archives, FO 371/63318.

76 Brigadier Field, 'Conversation with Pai Chung-hsi', 11 March 1947, in 'Situation in China: Visit of General Marshall', UK National Archives, FO 371/63322.

77 'Naval Intelligence to China Department', 25 January 1947, in 'Situation in China: Visit of General Marshall', UK National Archives, FO 371/63321.

78 'Ralph Stevenson to FO', 30 April 1947, in 'Situation in China: Visit of General Marshall', UK National Archives, FO 371/63322.

79 'Lord Inverchapel from Washington to FO', 15 February 1947, in 'Situation in China: Visit of General Marshall', FO 371/63318.

80 'Ralph Stevenson to FO', 29 September 1947, in 'Situation in China: Visit of General Marshall', UK National Archives, FO 371/63327.

81 Westad, *Decisive Encounters,* 159–62.

82 Ibid., 160–61.

83 Arnold A. Offner, *Another Such Victory: President Truman and the Cold War, 1945–1953* (Stanford, CA: Stanford University Press, 2002), 307.

84 'British Consul General M. C. G. Gillett to Wallinger', 27 February 1947, in 'Situation in China: Visit of General Marshall', FO 371/63321.

85 Report by Lionel Lamb, attached to 'British Embassy, Nanjing, to Foreign Office', 26 April 1947, in 'Situation in China: Visit of General Marshall', UK National Archives, FO 371/63317.

86 'R. Stevenson to Bevin', 22 June 1947, in 'Situation in China: Visit of General Marshall', UK National Archives, FO 371/63317.

87 Ralph Stevenson, 'Situation in China: Visit of General Marshall', 17 July 1947, Kitson minute, in 'Situation in China: Visit of General Marshall', UK National Archives, FO 371/63321.

88 'Ralph Stevenson to Foreign Office', 7 July 1947, 'Situation in China: Visit of General Marshall', UK National Archives, FO 371/63321.

Chapter 13: National Liberation War

1   Kusano Fumio, 'Chinese Communist Guerrilla Warfare', Translated Foreign Documents Branch, CIA, 9 September 1948, in 'Communist Army: General', UK National Archives, WO 208/4731.

2   Carl von Clausewitz, *On War*, Michael Howard and Peter Paret, trans. (Princeton, NJ: Princeton University Press, 1989), 322.

3   Lin Biao, 'Proposal that at Present Our Forces Avoid Rush to Fight Back' in Lin Doudao, ed., *Lin Biao Junshi Wenxuan (Selected Military Texts of Lin Biao)* (Hong Kong: Zhongguo Wenge Lishi Chubanshe, 2012), 184.

4   'Telegram, CCP Central Committee to CCP Northeast Bureau', 28 November 1945, Shuguang Zhang and Jian Chen, eds., *Chinese Communist Foreign Policy and the Cold War in Asia: New Documentary Evidence, 1944–1950* (Chicago, IL: Imprint Publications, 1996), 51.

5   'China: Northern Kiangsu – Conditions in', undated, no author, forwarded by Naval Intelligence, in 'Situation in China: Visit of General Marshall', UK National Archives, FO 371/63321.

6   'Lionel Lamb to FO', 28 October 1948, in 'Situation in China: Situation Reports from Nanking', in UK National Archives, FO 371/69541.

7   'China: Northern Kiangsu – Conditions in', undated, no author, forwarded by Naval Intelligence, in 'Situation in China: Visit of General Marshall', UK National Archives, FO 371/63321.

8   'Economic Life of Tsinan District', 17 April 1946, Hoover Institution Archives, UNRRA China Office Files, box 7.

9   'H. M. Consul Tianjin, Whitamore, to Ambassador R. Stevenson', 26 March 1947, in 'Situation in China: Visit of General Marshall', UK National Archives, FO 371/ 63317.

10   China Department, UK Foreign Office, 'The Chinese Communists', 1 April 1947, in 'Situation in China: Situation Reports from Nanking', UK National Archives, FO 371/69537.

11   Kusano Fumio, 'Chinese Communist Guerrilla Warfare', Translated Foreign Documents Branch, CIA, 9 September 1948, in 'Communist Army: General', UK National Archives, WO 208/4731.

12   Harold M. Tanner, *Where Chiang Kai-shek Lost China: The Liao-shen Campaign, 1948* (Bloomington, IN: Indiana University Press, 2015), 129–30; Odd Arne Westad, *Decisive Encounters: The Chinese Civil War, 1946–1950* (Stanford, CA: Stanford University Press, 2003), 126–8.

13   Ch'en Yung-fa, 'Neizhan, Mao Zedong, He Tudi Gemfing: Cuowu Panduan Haishi Zhengzhi Genmou' ('Civil War, Mao Zedong, and Land Revolution: Mistaken Assessment or Political Intrigue?'), in *Dalu Zazhi (Mainland Magazine)* 1996, vol. 92:1, 14.

14   Ibid., 13.

15   Ibid., 12.

16   'Zhongguo Gongchandang Zhongyang Weiyuanhui Guanyu Gongbu Zhongguo Tudifa Dagang de Jueyi' ('Resolution of the Central Committee of the Chinese Communist Party about the Outline Land Law for China') in 'Zhonggong Zhongyang Wenjian Xuanji' ('Selected Documents of the CCP Central Committee') (Beijing: Zhonggong Zhongyang Dangxiao Chubanshe, 1992), 546.

17   'Outline of China's Land Law' in Tony Saich and Bingzhang Yang, eds., *The Rise to Power of the Chinese Communist Party: Documents and Analysis* (Armonk, NY: M. E. Sharpe, 1996), 1295.

18   Ibid., 1296.

19   Ch'en Yung-fa, 'Neizhan, Mao Zedong, He Tudi Gemfing', 1–2; Liu Shaoqi, 'Directive of the CCP CC on Settling Accounts, Rent Reduction, and the Land Question', 2 May 1946, in Saich, ed., *The Rise to Power of the Chinese Communist Party,* 1281.

20   Ch'en Yung-fa, 'Neizhan, Mao Zedong, He Tudi Gemfing', 17.

21   Carl von Clausewitz, *On War,* J. J. Graham, trans., revision by F. N. Mause, abridged by Louise Wilmot (London: Wordsworth, 1997), 288.

22   William Hinton, *Fanshen: A Documentary of Revolution in a Chinese Village* (New York: Monthly Review Press, 1967), 12–13.

23   Ibid., 13.

24   Ibid., 29.

25   Ibid., 33.

26   Ibid., 42–3.

27   Ibid., 89–91.

28   Ibid., 92.

29   Ibid., 137.

30   Ibid., 332–40.

31   Ibid., 319–20.

32   Ibid., 321.

33   Ibid., xi.

34   'Condition in North Honan, Kaifeng', 1 June 1947, unsigned letter, enclosed in 'T.C. Davis, Canadian Ambassador to China, to R. S. Stevenson', 25 June 1947, 'Situation in China: Visit of General Marshall', UK National Archives, FO 371/63325.

35   Quoted in Harrison E. Salisbury, *The Long March: The Untold Story* (London: Macmillan, 1985), 191–2; Edgar Snow, *Red Star over China* (originally published London: Victor Gollancz, 1937; New York: Grove Press, 1961), 135.

36   Tanner, *Where Chiang Kai-shek Lost China,* 4.

37   Li Chen, 'From Burma Road to the 38th Parallel: The Chinese Forces' Adaptation in War 1942–1953', (Cambridge University Ph.D. dissertation, 2013), 174.

38   'Chinese Communist–Soviet Secret Pact on Manchuria Revealed, as Reported 17 May 1946', in 'Military Attaché: Monthly Reports', in 'Manchuria', UK National Archives, WO 208/4736.

39   'China: Soviets on the Kuantung Peninsula', 27 April 1948, 'South Manchuria: Military: Kwantung Peninsular: Russian Occupied Territory', UK National Archives, WO 208/4722.

40   'Military Information: Soviets and Chinese Communists: Kuantung Peninsula', 12 September 1947, in 'Manchuria', UK National Archives, WO 208/4721; 'Russian Activities in the Far East', 22 March 1946, in 'Manchuria', UK National Archives WO 208/4736.

41   Tanner, *Where Chiang Kai-shek Lost China,* 146.

42   Yang Kuisong, *Zhongjian Didai de Geming: Guoji Da Beijing Xia Kan Zhonggong Chenggong Zhi Dao (A Middle Zone Revolution: Looking at the Chinese Communist*

Party's Road to Success from an International Context) (Taiyuan: Shanxi Renmin Chubanshe, 2010), 509.

43   William Nimmo, *Behind a Curtain of Silence: Japanese in Soviet Custody, 1945–1956* (Westport, CT: Praeger Publishers, 1988).

44   Liu Yalou, 'Jiaqiang Wo Jun Jianshe he Fazhan de Jidian Yijian' ('Suggestions for Strengthening and Developing Our Army'), in Liu Yalou, *Liu Yalou Junshi Wenji* (*Collected Military Writings of Liu Yalou*) (Beijing: Lantian Chubanshe, 2010), 90–93.

45   Liu Yalou, 'Guanyu Paobing de Shiyong Wenti' ('On the Use of Artillery'), in Liu Yalou, *Liu Yalou Junshi Wenji* (*Collected Military Writings of Liu Yalou*) (Beijing: Lantian Chubanshe, 2010), 136–40.

46   Liu Yalou,' 'Jiaqiang Wo Jun Jianshe he Fazhan de Jidian Yijian' ('Suggestions for Strengthening and Developing Our Army'), 90–104.

47   Liu Yalou, 'Silian "Hongjun Yezhan Canmou Yeweu Tiaoling" Yiban Xuyan' ('Foreword to the Translation of Field Staff Officers Manual of the Red Army'), in Liu Yalou, *Liu Yalou Junshi Wenji* (*Collected Military Writings of Liu Yalou*) (Beijing: Lantian Chubanshe), 112–15.

48   Quoted in Tanner, *Where Chiang Kai-shek Lost China*, 153.

49   Lin Biao, 'Yidian Liangmian Zhanshu' ('The Tactics of One Point and Two Flanks'), in Lin Doudou, ed., *Lin Biao Junshi Wenxuan* (*Selected Military Writings of Lin Biao*) (Hong Kong: Zhongguo Wenge Lishi Chubanshe, 2012), 188–92. See also Tanner, *Where Chiang Kai-shek Lost China*, 58–61.

50   Lin Biao, 'San San San Zhi Zhanshu' ('The Tactics of the Three–Three System'), in Lin Doudou, ed., *Lin Biao* (*Selected Military Writings of Lin Biao*) (Hong Kong: Zhongguo Wenge Lishi Chubanshe, 2012), 193–7.

51   Tanner, *Where Chiang Kai-shek Lost China*, 78.

52   'Air Attaché Annual Report 1947', in 'Air Attaché, Nanking: Annual Report for 1947', UK National Archive, FO 371/69637.

53   'Szepingkai Victors Find Many Dead Reds', *The New York Times*, 2 July 1947.

54   Lin Biao, 'Guanyu Sikuai Yimian' ('Concerning Four Fasts and One Slow'), in Lin Doudou, ed., *Lin Biao Junshi Wenxuan*, 266–72.

55   Tanner, *Where Chiang Kai-shek Lost China*, 155–7.

56   Liu Yalou, 'Formations Used in Combat In Depth', in Liu Yalou, *Liu Yalou Junshi Wenji*, 132–4; Liu Yalou, 'On the Use of Artillery', 136–40.

57   Tanner, *Where Chiang Kai-shek Lost China*, 151.

58   Quoted in 'Ralph Stevenson to FO', 9 July 1948, in 'Situation in China: Situation Reports from Nanking', UK National Archives, 371/69536.

59   Frank Dikötter, *The Tragedy of Liberation: A History of the Chinese Revolution, 1945–57* (London: Bloomsbury, 2013), 4.

60   Quoted in Tanner, *Where Chiang Kai-shek Lost China*, 173.

61   Quoted in ibid., 173.

62   Tanner, *Where Chiang Kai-shek Lost China*, 175–80.

63   Dikötter, *The Tragedy of Liberation*, 5.

64   'China is Wordless on Traumas Inflicted in Communists' Rise', *The New York Times*, 1 October 2009.

65   Tanner, *Where Chiang Kai-shek Lost China*, 240.

66   Ibid., 234.

67 W. G. Graham, 'The Plight of Refugees in the Chang-ch'un Area', 13 September 1948, in 'Military, Industrial, and Economic Situation in Manchuria', UK National Archives, FO 371/69591.

68 'Changchun Left to Reds by Chinese', *The New York Times*, 7 October 1948.

69 Tanner, *Where Chiang Kai-shek Lost China*, 326, n. 4.

70 'China is Wordless on Traumas Inflicted in Communists' Rise', *The New York Times*, 1 October 2009.

71 Tanner, *Where Chiang Kai-shek Lost China*, 262.

72 '300,000 Starving in Mukden's Siege', *The New York Times*, 2 July 1948; Dikötter, *The Tragedy of Liberation*, 1–8.

73 Tanner, *Where Chiang Kai-shek Lost China*, 184.

74 Ibid., 187–9.

75 Ibid., 189.

76 Ibid., 189–91.

77 Ibid., 191.

78 Quoted in ibid., 195.

79 Quoted in ibid., 197.

80 Quoted in ibid., 198.

81 Ibid., 210–16.

82 'Military Situation: Loss of Chinchow', in 'Military, Industrial, and Economic Situation in Manchuria', UK National Archives, FO 371/69591.

83 Tanner, *Where Chiang Kai-shek Lost China*, 243–9.

84 Ibid., 252–61.

85 Ibid., 261–7.

86 'Mukden is Bombed by Nanking as Reds Capture City', *The New York Times*, 2 November 1948.

87 Lionel Lamb to Foreign Office', 28 October 1948, in 'Situation in China: Situation Reports from Nanking', UK National Archives, FO 371/69541.

88 Suzanne Pepper, 'The KMT–CCP Conflict, 1945–1949', in CHOC, vol. 13, 743–6.

89 Ibid., 742.

90 Ibid., 745–7.

91 Zhang Xianwen, Zhang Xianwen, *Zhonghua Minguo Shi (History of the Republic of China)* (Nanjing: Nanjing Daxue Chubanshe, 2005), vol. 4, 245–7.

92 Ibid., vol. 4, 251–61.

93 'China, Military', 16 September 1948, in 'Manchuria: Area A: Communist Army', UK National Archives, WO 208/4725.

Chapter 14: Exhaustion

1 Sheila Miyoshi Jager, *Brothers at War: The Unending Conflict in Korea* (London: Profile, 2013), 13.

2 Alexander Pantsov and Steven I. Levine, *Mao: The Real Story* (New York: Simon & Schuster, 2012), 377.

3 Miyoshi Jager, *Brothers at War*, 59.

4 Ibid., 49, 53.

5 Ibid., 58–60; Pantsov and Levine, *Mao*, 375–9.

6 Pantsov and Levine, *Mao*, 378.

7   Ibid., 377–9.

8   Miyoshi Jager, *Brothers at War*, 69–71.

9   Ibid., 73–9.

10 'NSC 68: United States Objectives and Programs for National Security', https://fas.org/irp/offdocs/nsc-hst/nsc-68-1.htm.

11 Ibid.

12 Miyoshi Jager, *Brothers at War*, 72.

13 'Resolution 84 (1950)', http://www.refworld.org/docid/3b00f1e85c.html.

14 Miyoshi Jager, *Brothers at War*, 80–85, 113–16.

15 Pantsov and Levine, *Mao*, 380–81.

16 Ibid., 379.

17 Chen Jian, *China's Road to the Korean War: The Making of the Sino-American Confrontation* (New York: Columbia University Press, 1994), 173–5.

18 Pantsov and Levine, *Mao*, 381; Miyoshi Jager, *Brothers at War*, 121 and 511, n. 25.

19 Chen Jian, *China's Road to the Korean War*, 182.

20 Miyoshi Jager, *Brothers at War*, 111–21.

21 Ibid., 121; Pantsov and Levine, *Mao*, 383.

22 Pantsov and Levine, *Mao*, 383.

23 Ibid.

24 Miyoshi Jager, *Brothers at War*, 123; Pantsov and Levine, *Mao*, 384.

25 Pantsov and Levine, *Mao*, 384.

26 Mihoshi Jager, *Brothers at War*, 123.

27 'Speech, Zhou Enlai, at the 18th Meeting of the Standing Committee of the Chinese People's Political Consultative Conference', in Shuguang Zhang and Jian Chen, eds., *Chinese Communist Foreign Policy and the Cold War in Asia: New Documentary Evidence, 1944–1950* (Chicago, IL: Imprint Publishing, 1996), 186–7.

28 Li Chen, 'From Civil War Victor to Cold War Guard: Positional Warfare in Korea and the Transformation of the Chinese People's Liberation Army, 1951–1953', in *Journal of Strategic Studies*, vol. 38 (2015), 183–214.

29 Miyoshi Jager, *Brothers at War*, 136.

30 Ibid., 134.

31 'Retreat from Changjin', *The New York Times*, 11 December 1950.

32 Li Chen, 'From Civil War Victor to Cold War Guard', 189.

33 Miyoshi Jager, *Brothers at War*, 138.

34 Ibid., 130–63.

35 Ibid., 162–73.

36 Miyoshi Jager, *Brothers at War*, 173–7.

37 Ibid., 192.

38 Ibid., 165–6.

39 Bruce Cumings, *The Korean War: A History* (New York: Modern Library, 2010), 150–61.

40 Miyoshi Jager, *Brothers at War*, 481–3.

41 Roughly the numbers suggested in Pantsov and Levine, *Mao*, 387.

42 Shen Jinding, 'Canjia Zhu Ri Daibiaotuan de Huiyi' ('Recollections of My Participation in China's Delegation in Japan'), in ZHMGZYSLCB, series 7, vol. 4, 667.

43 For this and the following paragraphs, see Hans van de Ven, 'The 1952 Treaty of Peace between China and Japan', in Hans van de Ven, Diana Lary and Stephen MacKinnon,

eds., *Negotiating China's Destiny in World War II* (Stanford, CA: Stanford University Press, 2014), 222–3.

44 Ibid., 223.

45 Ibid.

46 Ibid., 224.

47 Ibid.

48 'Treaty of Peace with Japan', https://treaties.un.org/doc/Publication/UNTS/Volume%20 136/volume-136-I-1832-English.pdf.

49 Van de Ven, 'The 1952 Treaty of Peace between China and Japan', 225.

50 Quoted in ibid., 225.

51 'Treaty of Peace with Japan', https://treaties.un.org/doc/Publication/UNTS/Volume%20 136/volume-136-I-1832-English.pdf.

52 Van de Ven, 'The 1952 Treaty of Peace between China and Japan', 230.

53 Quoted in ibid., 230.

54 'Japan Recognizes Chiang Regime as Ruler of All China and Bars Pact with Peiping', *The New York Times*, 19 June 1952.

55 Van de Ven, 'The 1952 Treaty of Peace between China and Japan', 231.

56 Quoted in ibid., 231.

57 Melvyn P. Leffler, *A Preponderance of Power: National Security, the Truman Administration, and the Cold War* (Stanford, CA: Stanford University Press, 1992), 391–5, 413–29.

58 'Japan Recognizes Chiang Regime as Ruler of All China and Bars Pact with Peiping', *The New York Times*, 19 June 1952.

59 Van de Ven, 'The 1952 Treaty of Peace between China and Japan', 235.

60 Diary entry for 27 April 1952 in *Diary of Chiang Kaishek*, Hoover Institution Archives, box 49, folder 12. I am grateful for Lin Hsiao-ting for this reference.

61 'Red China Calls "Peace" Gathering', *The New York Times*, 15 May 1952.

62 'Red "Peace Parley" Sounds Amity Note', *The New York Times*, 3 October 1952.

63 Julia Strauss, 'Morality, Coercion, and State Building by Campaign in the Early PRC: Regime Consolidation and After, 1949–1956', *China Quarterly* 188 (2006), 901.

Epilogue: Transitions

1 Julia Strauss, 'Morality, Coercion, and State Building by Campaign in the Early PRC: Regime Consolidation and After, 1949–1956', *China Quarterly* 188 (2006), 892; Frank Dikötter, *Mao's Great Famine: The History of China's Most Devastating Catastrophe, 1958–62* (London: Bloomsbury, 2010), 324–34.

2 Qian Liqun, *Mao Zedong Shidai He Hou Mao Zedong Shidai* (*The Mao Era and the Post-Mao Era*) (Taipei: Lianjing Chuban Shiye Gufen Youxian Gongsi, 2012), 25.

3 Ibid., 7.

4 Mao Zedong, 'Zhanzheng He Zhanlue Wenti' ('Issues of War and Strategy'), November 1936, in Mao Zedong, *Mao Zedong Junshi Wenji* (*Collected Military Writings of Mao Zedong*) (Beijing: Military Sciences Press, 1993), vol. 2, 421.

5 Neil J. Diamant, *Embattled Glory: Veterans, Military Families, and the Politics of Patriotism in China, 1949–2007* (Lanham, MY: Rowman and Littlefield, 2008), chapters 2–5.

6 Chi Pang-yuan, *Juliuhe* (*The Great Flowing River*) (Taipei: Yuanjian Tianxia, 2014), 298.

7   Ibid., 298–9.
8   Ibid., 304.
9   Ibid., 316.
10   Ibid., 320.
11   Ibid., 319–26.
12   Chen Kewen, *Chen Kewen Riji* (*Chen Kewen's Diary*), Chen Fangzheng, ed. (Taipei: Zhongyang Yanjiuyuan Jindaishi Yanjiusuo, 2012), 1050.
13   Ibid., 1071–81.
14   Ibid., 1095.
15   Ibid., 1098–99.
16   Ibid., 1100.
17   Ibid., 1103–4.
18   Ibid., 1098.
19   Ibid., 1128–9.
20   Ibid., 1148.
21   Ibid., 1247.
22   Chen Fangzheng, 'Bianzhe Xu' ('Foreword by the Editor'), in Chen Kewen, *Chen Kewen Riji*, xiv–xv.
23   Timothy Cheek, *Propaganda and Culture in Mao's China: Deng Tuo and the Intelligentsia* (Oxford: Clarendon Press, 1997), 279–306.
24   Mary G. Mazur, *Wu Han, Historian: Son of China's Times* (Lanham, MY: Lexington Books, 2009).
25   The paragraphs below are based on Professor Yeh Wen-hsin's study of Chen Yinke and her reflections on his writings. I am deeply grateful for her agreement to borrow and repeat her trenchant ideas here.
26   Yeh Wen-hsin, 'Historian and Courtesan: Chen Yinke and the Writing of Liu Rushi Biezhuan', Morrison Lecture, Australia National University (July 2003) and *East Asian History* 27 (2004), 61.
27   Yeh Wen-hsin, 'Historian and Courtesan', 67–70.

SELECTED BIBLIOGRAPHY

Hallett Abend, *Chaos in Asia* (London: The Bodley Head, 1940).

Hallett Abend, *My Life in China, 1926–1941* (New York: Harcourt, Brace & Co., 1943).

Academia Historica, *Jiang Zhongzheng Zongtong Dang'an: Shilue Gaoben (The Archives of President Chiang Kaishek: Basic Biographical Documents)* (Taipei: Guoshiguan, 2011 ff).

Guy S. Alitto, *The Last Confucian: Liang Shu-ming and the Chinese Dilemma of Modernity* (Berkeley, CA: University of California Press, 1979).

Louis Allen, *Burma: The Longest War 1941–45* (London: J. M. Dent, 1984).

J. Gunnar Andersson, *China Fights for the World,* Arthur G. Chater, trans. (London: Kegan Paul, Trench, Trubner & Co., 1938).

David E. Apter and Tony Saich, *Revolutionary Discourse in Mao's Republic* (Cambridge, MA: Harvard University Press, 1994).

Wesley Marvin Bagby, *The Eagle–Dragon Alliance: America's Relations with China in World War II* (Newark, NJ: University of Delaware Press, 1992).

Bai Chongxi, *Bai Chongxi Xiansheng Fangwen Jilu (Interviews with Bai Chongxi)*, Zhongyang Yanjiuyuan Jindaishi Yanjiusuo, ed. (Taipei: Academia Sinica, 1984).

Bai Chongxi, *Bai Chongxi Huilyu (Bai Chongxi Memoirs)*, Shu Zhirong et al., eds. (Beijing: Jiefangjun Chubanshe, 1987).

James M. Bertram, *North China Front* (London: Macmillan & Co., 1939).

Robert A. Bickers, *Britain in China: Community, Culture, and Colonialism, 1900–49* (Manchester: Manchester University Press, 1999).

Larry Bland, ed., *The Papers of George Catlett Marshall* (6 volumes) (Baltimore, MD: Johns Hopkins University Press, 1981).

John Hunter Boyle, *China and Japan at War, 1937–1945: The Politics of Collaboration* (Stanford, CA: Stanford University Press, 1972).

Timothy Brook, ed., *Documents on the Rape of Nanking* (Ann Arbor, MI: University of Michigan Press, 1999).

Timothy Brook, 'The Tokyo Judgment and the Rape of Nanking', in *Journal of Asian Studies,* vol. 60:3 (2001), 673–700.

Cai Dejin, *Lishi de Guaitai: Wang Jingwei Guomin Zhengfu (A Historical Monster: The Wang Jingwei Government)* (Guilin: Guangxi Shifan Daxue Chubanshe, 1993).

Sir Adrian Carton de Wiart, *Happy Odyssey: The Memoirs of Lieutenant-General Sir Adrian Carton de Wiart* (London: Jonathan Cape, 1950; Barnsley: Pen & Sword Military, 2007).

Gordon H. Chang, 'Chinese Painting Comes to America: Zhang Shuqi and the Diplomacy of Art', in Cynthia Mills, Lee Glazer and Amelia Goerlitz, eds., *East–West Interchanges in American Art: A Long and Tumultuous Relationship* (Washington, DC: Smithsonian Contributions to Knowledge, 2012), 126–41.

Chang Jui-te, 'The Nationalist Army at the Eve of the War', in Mark Peattie, Edward J. Drea and Hans van de Ven, eds., *The Battle for China: Essays on the Military History of the Sino-Japanese War* (Stanford, CA: Stanford University Press, 2011), 83–104.

Timothy Cheek, *Propaganda and Culture in Mao's China: Deng Tuo and the Intelligentsia* (Oxford: Clarendon Press, 1997).

Chen Cheng, *Chen Cheng Huiyilu: Kang Ri Zhanzheng* (*Chen Cheng Memoirs: The War of Resistance*) (Taipei: Guoshiguan, 2005).

Chen Jian, *China's Road to the Korean War: The Making of the Sino-American Confrontation* (New York: Columbia University Press, 1994).

Chen Kewen, *Chen Kewen Riji* (*Chen Kewen's Diary*), Chen Fangzheng, ed. (Taipei: Zhongyang Yanjiuyuan Jindaishi Yanjiusuo, 2012).

Ch'en Yung-fa, 'The Blooming Poppy under the Red Sun', in Tony Saich and Hans van de Ven, eds., *New Perspectives on the Chinese Communist Revolution* (Armonk, NY: M.E. Sharpe, 1995), 263–98.

Ch'en Yung-fa, 'Neizhan, Mao Zedong, He Tudi Genfing: Cuowu Panduan Haishi Zhengzhi Genmou' ('Civil War, Mao Zedong, and Land Revolution: Mistaken Assessment or Political Intrigue?') in *Dalu Zazhi* (*Mainland Magazine*) (1996), vol. 92:1, 9–19; vol. 92:2, 41–8; and vol. 92:3, 11–29.

Ch'en Yung-fa, 'Guanjian de Yinian: Jiang Zhongzheng yu Yu Xiang Gui Da Kuibai' ('The Crucial Year: Chiang Kaishek and the Major Defeat at Ichigo'), in Liu Cuirong, ed., *Zhongguo Lishi de Zai Sikao* (*Reconsiderations of Chinese History*) (Taipei: Liangjing, 2015), chapter 16.

Claire Lee Chennault, *Way of a Fighter: The Memoirs of Claire Lee Chennault* ((New York: G. P. Putnam's Sons, 1946).

Hsi-sheng Ch'i, *Nationalist China at War: Military Defeats and Political Collapse, 1937–45* (Ann Arbor, MI: University of Michigan Press, 1982).

Hsi-sheng Ch'i, *The Much Troubled Alliance: US–China Military Cooperation during the Pacific War, 1941–1945* (Singapore: World Scientific Publishing, 2015).

Chiang Kaishek, *The Collected Wartime Messages of Generalissimo Chiang Kai-shek, 1937–1945*, Chinese Ministry of Information, ed. (New York: John Day Company, 1946).

Chiang Kaishek, *China's Destiny: Chinese Economic Theory*, Philip Jaffe, trans. (London: Dennis Dobson, 1947).

Chiang Kaishek, *Kunmianji* (*Diary Entries on Striving in Adversity*), Huang Zijin and Pan Guangzhe, eds. (Taipei: Guoshiguan, 2011).

Chiang Wei-kuo, *Kangzhan Yuwu* (*The War of Resistance and Fighting Humiliation*) (Taipei: Liming Wenhua Shiye Gongsi, 1978).

Roger Chickering, Dennis Showalter and Hans van de Ven, eds., *The Cambridge History of War: Volume 4: War and the Modern World* (Cambridge: Cambridge University Press, 2012).

Chi Pang-yuan, *Juliuhe* (*The Great Flowing River*) (Taipei: Yuanjian Tianxia, 2014).

CHOC, see John K. Fairbank.

Winston S. Churchill, *The Second World War, Volume 3: The Grand Alliance* (London: Cassell & Co., 1950).

Winston S. Churchill, *The Second World War, Volume 5: Closing the Ring* (London: Cassell & Co., 1954).

Carl von Clausewitz, *On War,* J. J. Graham, trans., revision by F. N. Mause, abridged by
Louise Wilmot (London: Wordsworth, 1997).

Carl von Clausewitz, *On War,* Michael Howard and Peter Paret, trans. (Princeton, NJ:
Princeton University Press, 1989).

Parks M. Coble, *China's War Reporters: The Legacy of Resistance against Japan* (Cambridge,
MA: Harvard University Press, 2015).

Lizzie Collingham, *The Taste of War: World War Two and the Battle for Food* (London: Allen
Lane, 2011).

Wesley Frank Craven and James Lea Cate, eds., *The Army Air Forces in World War II: Volume
5: The Pacific – Matterhorn to Nagasaki, June 1944 to August 1945* (Washington DC:
Office of Air Force History, 1983), http://www.afhso.af.mil/shared/media/document/
AFD-101105-012.pdf

Pamela Crossley, 'What is China's Big Parade All About?: A ChinaFile
Conversation', 2 September 2015. http://www.chinafile.com/conversation/
what-chinas-big-parade-all-about

Bruce Cumings, *The Korean War: A History* (New York: Modern Library, 2010).

Dai Qing, *Wang Shiwei and 'Wild Lilies': Rectification and Purges in the Chinese Communist
Party, 1942–1944* (Armonk, NY: M. E. Sharpe, 1994).

Deng Ye, 'Chiang Jieshi Dui Fang Xianjue Tou Di de Caijue' ('Chiang Kaishek's Ruling on
Fang Xianjue's Surrender'), in *Lishi Yanjiu (Historical Research),* vol. 5 (2006), 136–48.

Deng Ye, *Lianhe Zhengfu yu Yidang Xunzheng: 1944–1946 Nian jian Guo Gong Zhengzhen
(Joint Government and One Party Political Tutelage: The Political Struggle between
the Communists and the Nationalists, 1944–1946)* (Beijing: Shehui Wenxue Wenxian
Chubanshe, 2011).

Neil J. Diamant, *Embattled Glory: Veterans, Military Families, and the Politics of Patriotism in
China, 1949–2007* (Lanham, MY: Rowman and Littlefield, 2008).

Frank Dikötter, *The Age of Openness: China before Mao* (Berkeley, CA: University of
California Press, 2008).

Frank Dikötter, *Mao's Great Famine: The History of China's Most Devastating Catastrophe,
1958–62* (London: Bloomsbury, 2010).

Frank Dikötter, *The Tragedy of Liberation: A History of the Chinese Revolution, 1945–57*
(London: Bloomsbury, 2013).

Frank Dorn, *The Sino-Japanese War, 1937–41: From Marco Polo Bridge to Pearl Harbor* (New
York: Macmillan, 1974).

Edward J. Drea, *In the Service of the Emperor: Essays on the Imperial Japanese Army* (Lincoln,
NE: University of Nebraska Press, 1998).

Edward J. Drea, 'The Japanese Army on the Eve of the War', in Mark Peattie, Edward J. Drea
and Hans van de Ven, eds., *The Battle for China: Essays on the Military History of the
Sino-Japanese War* (Stanford, CA: Stanford University Press, 2011), 105–38.

Prasenjit Duara, *Culture, Power, and the State: Rural North China, 1900–1942* (Stanford:
Stanford University Press, 1988).

Lloyd E. Eastman, 'Facets of an Ambivalent Relationship: Smuggling, Puppets, and Atrocities
during the War, 1937–45', in Akira Iriye, ed., *The Chinese and the Japanese: Essays in
Political and Cultural Interactions* (Princeton, NJ: Princeton University Press, 1980),
275–303.

Lloyd E. Eastman, *The Nationalist Era in China, 1927–1949* (Cambridge: Cambridge University Press, 1991).

Lloyd E. Eastman, 'Nationalist China during the Nanjing Decade, 1927–1937', CHOC, vol. 13, 116–67.

Keith E. Eiler, ed., *Wedemeyer on War and Peace* (Stanford, CA: Hoover Institution Press, 1987).

John K. Fairbank and Albert Feuerwerker, eds., *The Cambridge History of China: Volume 13: Republican China, 1912–1949, Part 2* (Cambridge: Cambridge University Press, 1986).

Rhodes Farmer, *Shanghai Harvest: A Diary of Three Years in the China War* (London: Museum Press, 1945).

Jonathan Fenby, *Generalissimo: Chiang Kai-shek and the China He Lost* (London: Free Press, 2003).

Feng Zikai, *Feng Zikai Sanwen Xuanji* (*Selected Prose Essays by Feng Zikai*) (Tianjin: Baihua Wenyi Chubanshe, 1991).

John Ferris and Evan Mawdsley, eds., *The Cambridge History of the Second World War: Volume 1: Fighting the War* (Cambridge: Cambridge University Press, 2015).

Lewis S. Feuer, ed., *Marx and Engels: Basic Writings on Politics and Philosophy* (Garden City, NY: Doubleday, 1959).

John Fitzgerald, *Awakening China: Politics, Culture, and Class in the Nationalist Revolution* (Stanford, CA: Stanford University Press, 1996).

Gao Hua, *Hong Taiyang Shi Zen Yang Sheng Qi De: Yan'an Zhengfeng Yun Dong De Lai Long Qumai* (*How Did the Red Flag Rise Above Yan'an: The History of the Yan'an Rectification Movement*) (Hong Kong: Chinese University of Hong Kong Press, 2002).

John W. Garver, *Chinese–Soviet Relations, 1937–1945: The Diplomacy of Chinese Nationalism* (Oxford: Oxford University Press, 1988).

O. M. Green, *China's Struggles with the Dictators* (London: Hutchinson & Co. Ltd, 1941).

Guo Dajun, *Yuxue Banian Shu Fengbei: Shouxiang yu Shenpan* (*A Monument Erected in Eight Blood-Drenched Years: The Acceptance of Surrender and Judgment after Trial*) (Guilin: Guangxi Shifan Daxue Chubanshe, 1994).

Guo Moruo, 'Jiashen Sanbainian Ji' ('In Commemoration of the 300th Anniversary of 1644'), in Guo Moruo, *Guo Moruo Wen Ji* (1937; reprinted Ann Arbor, MI: University of Michigan Press, 2009).

Hara Takeshi, 'The Ichigo Offensive', in Mark Peattie, Edward J. Drea and Hans van de Ven, eds., *The Battle for China: Essays on the Military History of the Sino-Japanese War of 1937–45* (Stanford, CA: Stanford University Press, 2011), 392–402.

Peter Harmsen, *Shanghai, 1937: Stalingrad on the Yangtze* (Oxford: Casemate Books, 2013).

Henrietta Harrison, *The Making of the Republican Citizen: Political Ceremonies and Symbols in China, 1911–1929* (Oxford: Oxford University Press, 2000).

Jeremy Harwood, *World War II from Above: An Aerial View of the Global Conflict* (Brighton: Qu:id Publishing, 2014).

Jonathan Haslam, *The Soviet Union and the Threat from the East, 1933–41, Volume 3: Moscow, Tokyo and the Prelude to the Pacific War* (Basingstoke: Palgrave Macmillan, 1992).

Hattori Satoshi with Edward J. Drea, 'Japanese Operations from July to December 1937', in Mark Peattie, Edward J. Drea and Hans van de Ven, eds., *The Battle for China: Essays on the Military History of the Sino-Japanese War of 1937–45* (Stanford, CA: Stanford University Press, 2011), 159–180.

William Hinton, *Fanshen: A Documentary of Revolution in a Chinese Village* (New York: Monthly Review Press, 1967).

Kazuo Horiba, *Riben Dui Hua Zhanzheng Zhidao Shi* (*History of Strategic Planning in Japan's War against China*), Wang Peilan, trans. (Beijing: Junshi Kexue Chubanshe, 1988).

William Hung, *Tu Fu: China's Greatest Poet* (Cambridge, MA: Harvard University Press, 1952).

Robin Hyde, *Dragon Rampant: A Record of Things Seen and Heard during a Few Months of the Sino-Japanese War* (London, Hurst and Blackett, 1938).

Akira Iriye, ed., *The Chinese and the Japanese: Essays in Political and Cultural Interactions* (Princeton, NJ: Princeton University Press, 1980).

Sheila Miyoshi Jager, *Brothers at War: The Unending Conflict in Korea* (London: Profile, 2013).

Sheila Miyoshi Jager and Rana Mitter, eds., *Ruptured Histories: War, Memory, and the Post-Cold War in Asia* (Cambridge, MA: Harvard University Press, 2007).

Jiang Tingfu, *Jiang Tingfu Huiyilu* (*Memoirs of Jiang Tingfu*) (Changsha: Yuelu Press, 2003).

Jiang Yongjing, 'Xi'an Shibian Qian Zhang Xueliang Suowei "Yi Er Yue Nei Ding You Biandong" He Zhi' ('Zhang Xueliang's Suggestion before the Xi'an Incident that Changes Will Take Place in One to Two Months'), in *Jindaishi Yanjiu* (*Research on Modern History*), 1997, vol. 2, 266–72.

Jin Chongji, *Mao Zedong Zhuan, 1893–1949* (*Biography of Mao Zedong, 1893–1949*) (Bejing: Zhongyang Wenxian Chubanshe, 1996).

Philip A. Kuhn, *Origins of the Modern Chinese State* (Stanford, CA: Stanford University Press, 2002).

Barak Kushner, *The Thought War: Japanese Imperial Propaganda* (Honolulu, HI: University of Hawaii Press, 2006).

Lai Delin, 'Searching for a Modern Chinese Monument: The Design of the Sun Yat-sen Mausoleum in Nanjing', *Journal of the Society for Architectural Historians*, 64 (March 2005), 22–55.

Sherman Lai, *A Springboard to Victory: Shandong Province and Chinese Communist Military and Financial Strength, 1937–1945* (Leiden: Brill, 2011).

Diana Lary, *China's Civil War: A Social History, 1945–1949* (Cambridge: Cambridge University Press, 2015).

Diana Lary, 'Flowing East in Victory', paper presented at the conference The Sino-Japanese War and Its Impact on Asia, Taipei, December 2015, 6–8.

Melvyn P. Leffler, *A Preponderance of Power: National Security, the Truman Administration, and the Cold War* (Stanford, CA: Stanford University Press, 1992).

Lei Haizong, 'Jianshe – Zai Wang de Di San Zhou Wenhua' ('Reconstruction – Anticipating a Third Cycle'), in Lei Haizong, *Zhongguo Wenhua yu Zhongguo de Bing* (*Chinese Culture and China's Armed Forces*) (Hong Kong: Longmen Shudian, 1968).

Li Chen, 'From Civil War Victor to Cold War Guard: Positional Warfare in Korea and the Transformation of the Chinese People's Liberation Army, 1951–1953', in *Journal of Strategic Studies*, vol. 38 (2015), 183–214.

Li Zhisui, *The Private Life of Chairman Mao: The Inside Story of the Man Who Made China* (London: Chatto & Windus, 1994).

Li Zhiyu, *Jingxuan: Wang Jingwei de Zhengzhi Shengya* (*The Startled Bow: The Political Life of Wang Jingwei*) (Hong Kong: Oxford University Press, 2014).

Lin Doudou, ed., *Lin Biao Junshi Wenxuan* (*Selected Military Writings of Lin Biao*) (Hong Kong: Zhongguo Wenge Lishi Chubanshe, 2012).

Liu Cuirong and Zhong Jideng, *Zhonghua Minguo Fazhanshi: Jingji Fazhan* (*The Historical Development of the Republic of China: Economic Development*) (Taipei: Cheng-chi University Press, 2011).

Liu Yalou, *Liu Yalou Junshi Wenji* (*Collected Military Writings of Liu Yalou*) (Beijing: Lantian Chubanshe, 2010).

Keith Lowe, *Savage Continent: Europe in the Aftermath of World War II* (London: Viking, 2012).

Ma Zhonglian, 'Huayuankou Jueti de Junshi Yiyi' ('The Military Significance of the Breaking of the Yellow River Dike at Huayuankou'), in *Kang Ri Zhanzheng Yanjiu* (*Studies on the War of Resistance against Japan*), vol. 4 (1999), 203–14.

Roderick MacFarquhar, Eugene Wu and Timothy Cheek, eds., *The Secret Speeches of Chairman Mao: From the Hundred Flowers to the Great Leap Forward* (Cambridge, MA: Harvard University Press, 1989).

Stephen R. MacKinnon, *Wuhan, 1938: War, Refugees, and the Making of Modern China* (Berkeley, CA: University of California Press, 2008).

Walter H. Mallory, *China: Land of Famine* (New York: American Geographical Society, 1926).

Karl Marx, *The Eighteenth Brumaire of Louis Bonaparte*, https://www.marxists.org/archive/marx/works/1852/18th-brumaire/ch07.htm

Mao Zedong, *Selected Works of Mao Tse-tung* (Beijing: Foreign Languages Press, 1969).

Mao Zedong, *Mao Zedong Junshi Wenji* (*Collected Military Writings of Mao Zedong*) (Beijing: Military Sciences Press, 1993).

Peter Mauch, 'Asia-Pacific: The Failure of Diplomacy, 1931–1941', in Richard J. B. Bosworth and Joseph A. Maiolo, eds., *The Cambridge History of the Second World War: Volume 2: Politics and Ideology* (Cambridge: Cambridge University Press, 2015), 253–75.

Mary G. Mazur, *Wu Han, Historian: Son of China's Times* (Lanham, MY: Lexington Books, 2009).

Rana Mitter, *China's War with Japan, 1937–1945: The Struggle for Survival* (London: Penguin, 2014).

Lord Moran, *Winston Churchill: The Struggle for Survival 1940–1965* (London: Constable & Co. Ltd, 1966).

James W. Morley, ed., *The China Quagmire: Japan's Expansion on the Asian Continent, 1933–1941* (New York: Columbia University Press, 1983).

Brian Murray, 'Stalin, the Cold War, and the Division of China: A Multi-Archival Mystery', Working Paper 12, Cold War International Project, June 1995.

Micah S. Muscolino, *The Ecology of War in China: Henan Province, the Yellow River, and Beyond, 1938–1950* (New York: Cambridge University Press, 2015).

Charles D. Musgrove, 'Cheering the Traitor: The Post-war Trial of Chen Bijun, April 1946', in *Twentieth-Century China*, 30:5 (2005), 3–28.

Charles D. Musgrove, 'Monumentality in Nanjing's Sun Yat-sen Memorial Park', *Southeast Review of Asian Studies*, 29 (2007), 1–19.

Charles D. Musgrove, *China's Contested Capital: Architecture, Ritual, and Response in Nanjing* (Honolulu, HI: University of Hawaii Press, 2016).

Ramon Myers, 'The Agrarian System', CHOC, 230–69.

William Nimmo, *Behind a Curtain of Silence: Japanese in Soviet Custody, 1945–1956* (Westport, CT: Praeger Publishers, 1988).

Niu Jun, *From Yan'an to the World: The Origin and Development of Chinese Communist Foreign Policy* (Norwalk, CT: EastBridge, 2005).

Arnold A. Offner, *Another Such Victory: President Truman and the Cold War, 1945–1953* (Stanford, CA: Stanford University Press, 2002).

Okamura Yasuji, *Gangcun Ningci Huiyilu* (*Memoirs of Okamura Yasuji*), Tianjin Shi Zhengxie Weiyuanhui, trans. (Beijing: Xinhua Shudian, 1981).

Richard Overy, *The Bombing War: Europe 1939–1945* (London: Allen Lane, 2013).

Alessio Patalano, 'Feigning Grand Strategy: Japan', in John Ferris and Edward Mawdsley, eds., *The Cambridge History of the Second World War: Volume I: Fighting the War* (Cambridge: Cambridge University Press, 2015), 159–88.

Alexander Pantsov and Steven I. Levine, *Mao: The Real Story* (New York: Simon & Schuster, 2012).

Ruth E. Pardee, 'First Aid for China', *Pacific Affairs*, vol. 19:1 (March 1946), 75–89.

Peter Paret, ed., *Makers of Modern Strategy from Machiavelli to the Nuclear Age* (Princeton, NJ: Princeton University Press, 1986).

Jane Park, '"The China Film": Madame Chiang Kaishek in Hollywood', *Screening the Past*, vol. 4, 2011. http://www.screeningthepast.com/2011/04/the-china-film.

J. L. van der Pauw, 'Door Eendracht Victorie: De Geschiedenis van geen Verzetsorganizatie' ('Victory through Unity: The History of a Pseudo Resistance Organisation), in *Scyedam*, vol. 22: 2 (1996), 67–9.

Mark Peattie, Edward J. Drea and Hans van de Ven, eds., *The Battle for China: Essays on the Military History of the Sino-Japanese War of 1937–45* (Stanford, CA: Stanford University Press, 2011).

Suzanne Pepper, 'The KMT–CCP Conflict, 1945–1949', in CHOC, vol. 13, 723–88.

Riben Fangweiting Fangwei Yanjiusuo Zhanshishi (Office of War History, Defence Research Institute, Department of Defence, Japan), *Zhongguo Shibian Lujun Zuozhan Zhanshi* (*History of the Army's Campaigns during the China Incident*), Tian Qizhi, trans. (Beijing: Zhonghua Shuju, 1979).

Qi Houjie, 'Kangzhan Baofa Hou Nanjing Guomin Zhengfu Guofang Lianxi Huiyi Jilu' ('Minutes of the Joint National Defence Meeting of Nanjing's Nationalist Government after the Outbreak of the War of Resistance'), Minguo Dang'an (Republican Archives), vol. 1 (1996), 27–33.

Qian Liqun, *Mao Zedong Shidai He Hou Mao Zedong Shidai* (*The Mao Era and the Post-Mao Era*) (Taipei: Lianjing Chuban Shiye Gufen Youxian Gongsi, 2012).

Qin Xiaoyi, ed., *Zhonghua Minguo Zhongyao Shiliao Chubian: Duiri Kangzhan Shiqi* (*A Preliminary Collection of Important Materials for the History of the Republic of China: The War of Resistance against Japan*) (Taipei: Zhongyang Wenwu Gongying Chubanshe, 1981).

Qin Xiaoyi, ed., *Zhonghua Minguo Zhongyao Shiliao Chubian: Duiri Kangzhan Shiqi: Xubian* (*A Preliminary Collection of Important Materials for the History of the Republic of China: The War of Resistance against Japan: Supplementary Materials*) (Taipei: Zhongyang Wenwu Gongying Chubanshe, 1981).

Qin Xiaoyi, ed., *Zhonghua Minguo Zhongyao Shiliao Chubian: Disan Bian: Zhanshi Waijiao* (*A Preliminary Collection of Important Historical Documents for the Republic of China: Wartime Foreign Relations*) (Taipei: Zhongyang Wenwu Gongying Chubanshe, 1981).

David Reynolds, 'The Origins of the Two "World Wars": Historical Discourse and International Politics', *Journal of Contemporary History,* vol. 38:1 (January 2003), 29–44.

Tim Rogan, *The Moral Economists: R. H. Tawney, Karl Polanyi, E. P. Thompson and the Critique of Capitalism* (Princeton, NJ: Princeton University Press, 2017).

Charles F. Romanus and Riley Sunderland, *China–Burma–India Theater: Stilwell's Mission to China; Stilwell's Command Problems;* and *Time Runs out in CBI* (Washington, DC:, Office of the Chief of Military History, 1956, 1953 and 1959).

Elliott Roosevelt, *As He Saw It* (New York: Duell, Sloan, and Pearce, 1946).

Michael W. S. Ryan, *Decoding Al-Qaeda's Strategy: The Deep Battle against America* (New York: Columbia University Press, 2013).

Tony Saich and Bingzhang Yang, eds., *The Rise to Power of the Chinese Communist Party: Documents and Analysis* (Armonk, NY: M. E. Sharpe, 1996).

Tony Saich and Hans van de Ven, eds., *New Perspectives on the Chinese Communist Revolution* (Armonk, NY: M. E. Sharpe, 1995).

Keith Sainsbury, *The Turning Point: Roosevelt, Stalin, Churchill and Chiang Kai-shek, 1943: The Moscow, Cairo and Teheran Conferences* (Oxford: Oxford University Press, 1985).

Harrison E. Salisbury, *The Long March: The Untold Story* (London: Macmillan, 1985).

R. Keith Schoppa, 'Self-Inflicted Wounds: Scorched Earth Strategies in Zhejiang, 1937–1945', paper presented at the Conference on the Scars of War at the University of British Columbia, April 1998.

R. Keith Schoppa, *In a Sea of Bitterness: Refugees during the Sino-Japanese War* (Cambridge, MA: Harvard University Press, 2011).

Stuart R. Schram, ed., *Mao's Road to Power 1912–1949: Volume 6: The New Stage, August 1937–1938* (Armonk, NY: M. E. Sharpe, 2004).

Mark Selden, *The Yan'an Way in Revolutionary China* (Cambridge, MA Harvard University Press, 1971).

Shao Minghuang, 'Zhanbie Nanjing: Xi'an Shibian Hou Jiang Zhongzheng Xiansheng Zhi Jintui Chuchu' ('A Temporary Farewell to Nanjing: Chiang Kaishek's Comings and Goings after the Xi'an Incident'), in *Jindai Zhongguo* (*Modern China*), vol. 160 (2005), 165–84.

Shao Minghuang, 'Xiao Zhenying Gongzuo' ('The Xiao Zhenying Project'), http://jds.cass.cn/UploadFiles/zyqk/2010/12/201012091549026982.pdf

Shen Jinding, 'Canjia Zhu Ri Daibiaotuan de Huiyi' ('Recollections of My Participation in China's Delegation in Japan'), in ZHMGZYSLCB, series 7, vol. 4,

Shen Zhihua, *Mao, Stalin, and the Korean War: Trilateral Communist Relations in the 1950s* (Abingdon: Routledge, 2012).

C. R. Shepherd, *The Case against Japan: A Concise Survey of the Historical Antecedents of the Present Far Eastern Imbroglio* (London: Jarrolds, 1939).

E. B. Sledge, *China Marine: An Infantryman's Life after World War II* (New York: Oxford University Press, 2002).

SLGB, see Academia Historica.

Edgar Snow, *Red Star over China* (originally published London: Victor Gollancz, 1937; New York: Grove Press, 1961).

Reba Soffer, *History, Historians and Conservatism in Britain and America: From the Great War to Thatcher and Reagan* (Oxford: Oxford University Press, 2008).

Rita Steblin, *A History of Key Characteristics in the Eighteenth and Early Nineteenth Centuries* (Rochester, NY: University of Rochester Press, 1996).

Mark A. Stoler, *Allies and Adversaries: The Joint Chiefs of Staff, the Grand Alliance, and the US Strategy in WWII* (Chapel Hill, NC: University of North Carolina Press, 2000).

Julia Strauss, 'Morality, Coercion, and State Building by Campaign in the Early PRC: Regime Consolidation and After, 1949–1956', *China Quarterly* 188 (2006), 891–912.

Su Yu, *Su Yu Zhanzheng Huiyilu* (*War Memoirs of Su Yu*) (Beijing: Jiefangjun Chubanshe, 1988).

Sun Yatsen, 'The Three Stages of Revolution' (1918), in Wm Theodore de Bary and Richard Lufrano, *Sources of Chinese Tradition, Volume 2: From 1600 through the Twentieth Century* (Second edition, New York: Columbia University Press, 2000), 328–30.

David Sutton, *Simon: A Political Biography of Sir John Simon* (London, Aurum, 1992).

Harold M. Tanner, *Where Chiang Kai-shek Lost China: The Liao-shen Campaign, 1948* (Bloomington, IN: Indiana University Press, 2015).

R. H. Tawney, *Land and Labor in China* (Boston: Beacon Press, 1966).

Gerke Teitler and Kurt Werner Radtke, eds., *A Dutch Spy in China: Reports on the First Phase of the Sino-Japanese War (1937–1939)* (Leiden: Brill, 1999).

John Thompson, *A Sense of Power: The Roots of America's Global Role* (Ithaca, NY: Cornell University Press, 2015).

Christopher Thorne, *Allies of a Kind: The United States, Britain, and the War against Japan, 1941–1945* (Oxford: Oxford University Press, 1978).

H. J. Timperley, *What War Means: The Japanese Terror in China; a Documentary Record* (London: Victor Gollancz, 1938).

Tobe Ryoichi, 'The Japanese Eleventh Army in Central China', in Mark Peattie, Edward J. Drea and Hans van de Ven, eds., *The Battle for China: Essays on the Military History of the Sino-Japanese War of 1937–45* (Stanford, CA: Stanford University Press, 2011), 207–32.

Adam Tooze, *The Deluge: The Great War and the Remaking of the Global Order, 1916–1931* (London: Viking: 2014).

Adam Tooze, 'The War of the Villages: The Interwar Agrarian Crisis and the Second World War', in Michael Geyer and Adam Tooze, eds., *The Cambridge History of the Second World War, Volume 3: Total War: Economy, Society and Culture* (Cambridge: Cambridge University Press, 2015), 385–411.

Edna Tow, 'The Great Bombing of Chongqing and the Anti-Japanese War, 1937–1945', in Mark Peattie, Edward J. Drea and Hans van de Ven, eds., *The Battle for China: Essays on the Military History of the Sino-Japanese War* (Stanford, CA: Stanford University Press, 2011), 256–82.

Ann Trotter, Kenneth Bourne, D. Cameron Watt, eds., *British Documents on Foreign Affairs: Reports and Papers from the Foreign Office Confidential Print: Part 2, From the First to the Second World War, Series E, Asia, 1914–1939* (Frederick, MD: University Publications of America, 1991–7).

Barbara W. Tuchman, *Stilwell and the American Experience in China, 1911–1945* (London: Macmillan, 1971).

US Department of State, *The China White Paper, August 1949* (Stanford, CA: Stanford University Press, 1967).

Hans van de Ven, *From Friend to Comrade: The Founding of the Chinese Communist Party, 1920–1927* (Berkeley, CA: University of California Press, 1992).

Hans van de Ven, *War and Nationalism in China, 1925–1945* (London: Routledge, 2003).

Hans van de Ven, 'The 1952 Treaty of Peace between China and Japan', in Hans van de Ven, Diana Lary and Stephen MacKinnon, eds., *Negotiating China's Destiny in World War II* (Stanford, CA: Stanford University Press, 2014), 220–38.

Hans van de Ven, *Breaking with the Past: The Maritime Customs Service and the Global Origins of Modernity in China* (New York: Columbia University Press, 2014).

Hans van de Ven, Diana Lary and Stephen MacKinnon, eds., *Negotiating China's Destiny in World War II* (Stanford, CA: Stanford University Press, 2014).

Lyman Van Slyke, 'The Chinese Communist Movement during the Sino-Japanese War 1937–1945', in CHOC, vol. 13 (1986), 609–722.

Lyman Van Slyke, 'The Battle of the Hundred Regiments: Problems of Coordination and Control during the Sino-Japanese War', in *Modern Asian Studies*, vol. 30:4 (1996), 979–1005.

Peter Vladimirov, *The Vladimirov Diaries: Yenan, China, 1942–1945* (London: Robert Hale, 1976).

Arthur Waldron, 'China's New Remembering of WWII: The Case of Zhang Zizhong', *Modern Asian Studies* 30:4 (1996), 953–4.

Wang Chaoguang, 'Kangzhan yu Jianguo: Guomindang Linshi Daibiao Dahui Yanjiu' ('The War of Resistance and National Reconstruction: An Investigation of the Emergency National Conference of the Nationalists'), paper presented at History and Memory of the War: A Conference to Mark the Seventieth Anniversary of the Victory in the War of Resistance, Taipei, 7 July 2015.

Wang Jinyu, 'Riben Touxiang he Zhongguo Lujun Zongbu Shouxiang Neimu' ('Japan's Surrender and the Background to the Reception of the Surrender by the Supreme Headquarters of the Chinese Army'), in *Zhonghua Wenshi Ziliao Quanji (Compilation of Materials for the Culture and History of China)*, vol. 5: 2, 911–27.

Wang Qisheng, 'The Battle of Hunan and the Chinese Military Response to Operation Ichigo', in Mark Peattie, Edward J. Drea and Hans van de Ven, eds., *The Battle for China: Essays on the Military History of the Sino-Japanese War* (Stanford, CA: Stanford University Press, 2011), 403–20.

Wang Qisheng, 'Kangzhan Chuqi de "He" Sheng' ('Voices for "Peace" at the Beginning of the War of Resistance'), in Lü Fangshan, ed., *Zhanzheng de Lishi yu Jiyi (The History and Memory of the War)* (Taipei, Guoshiguan, 2015), 24–71.

Auriol Weigold, *Churchill, Roosevelt, and India: Propaganda During World War II* (London: Routledge, 2008).

Odd Arne Westad, *Decisive Encounters: The Chinese Civil War, 1946–1950* (Stanford, CA: Stanford University Press, 2003).

Theodore H. White, ed., *The Stilwell Papers* (New York: William Sloane Assoc., 1948).

Theodore H. White and Annalee Jacoby, *Thunder Out of China* (New York: William Sloane Assoc., 1946).

Wu Hung, *Remaking Beijing: Tiananmen Square and the Creation of a Political Space* (Chicago, IL: University of Chicago Press, 2005).

Wu Sufeng, ed., *Buke Hulue de Zhanchang* (*A Battlefield That Must Not be Ignored*) (Taipei: Guoshiguan, 2013).

Wu Sufeng, 'The Nationalist Government's Attitude toward Post-war Japan', in Hans van de Ven, Diana Lary and Stephen R. MacKinnon, eds., *Negotiating China's Destiny in WWII* (Stanford, CA: Stanford University Press, 2014), 193–204.

Wu Xiuquan, 'Zai Yan'an Junwei Zongbu' ('At the Yan'an HQ of the Military Affairs Committee') in Zhongguo Renmin Jiefangjun Lishi Ziliao Congshu Bianshen Weiyuanhui, eds., *Zhongguo Renmin Jiefangjun Lishi Ziliao: Zong Canmou Bu Huiyi Shiliao* (*Historical Materials for the People's Liberation Army: Recollections from the General Staff Office*) (Beijing: Jiefangjun Chubanshe, 1995).

Raymond F. Wylie, *The Emergence of Maoism: Mao Tse-tung, Chen Po-ta, and the Search for Chinese Theory 1935–1945* (Stanford, CA: Stanford University Press, 1980).

Xie Bingying, *A Woman Soldier's Own Story: The Autobiography of Xie Bingying*, Lily Chia Brissman and Barry Brissman, trans. (New York: Columbia University Press, 2001).

Xu Yong, *Zhengfu zhi Meng: Riben Qinhua Zhanlue* (*The Dream of Conquest: Japan's Strategy in Invading China*) (Nanning: Guangxi Shifan Daxue Chubanshe, 1993).

Kazuo Yagami, *Konoe Fumimaro and the Failure of Peace in Japan, 1937–1941: A Critical Appraisal of the Three-time Prime Minister* (Jefferson, NC and London: McFarland and Co., 2006).

Yamamoto Masahiro, *Nanking: Anatomy of an Atrocity: Separating Fact from Fiction* (Westport, CT: Praeger, 2000).

Yang Daqing, 'Challenges of Trans-national History: Historians and the Nanjing Atrocity', in *SAIS Review*, vol. 19: 2 (1999), 133–48.

Yang Daqing, 'Convergence or Divergence? Recent Historial Writings on the Rape of Nanjing', in *American Historical Review*, 104: 3 (1999), 842–65.

Yang Daqing, 'Revisionism and the Nanjing Atrocity', in *Critical Asian Studies*, vol. 43: 4 (2011), 625–48.

Yang Daqing, *Toward a History beyond Borders: Contentious Issues in Sino-Japanese Relations* (Cambridge, MA: Harvard University Press, 2012).

Yang Kuisong, *Shiqu de Jihui: Kangzhan Qianhou Guo Gong Tanpan Shilu* (*Lost Chances: A Record of Communist–Nationalist Negotiations around the Time of the War of Resistance*) (Beijing: Xinxing Chubanshe, 2010).

Yang Kuisong, *Zhongjian Didai de Geming: Guoji Da Beijing Xia Kan Zhonggong Chenggong Zhi Dao* (*A Middle Zone Revolution: Looking at the Chinese Communist Party's Road to Success from an International Context*) (Taiyuan: Shanxi Renmin Chubanshe, 2010).

Yang Kuisong, 'Nationalist and Communist Guerrilla Warfare in North China', in Mark Peattie, Edward J. Drea and Hans van de Ven, eds., *The Battle for China: Essays on the Military History of the Sino-Japanese War* (Stanford, CA: Stanford University Press, 2011), 308–27.

Yang Kuisong, *Geming* (*Revolution*) (Nanning: Guangxi Renmin Chubanshe, 2012).

Yang Kuisong, 'Kangzhan Shiqi Zhonggong Junshi Fazhan Biandong de Shishi Kaoxi' ('An Examination of the Facts about Changes in the Military Development of the Chinese Communist Party during the War of Resistance'), in *Jindaishi Yanjiu* (*Research on Modern Chinese History*), vol. 210 (2015: 11).

Yang Tianshi, *Jiang Jieshi Midang yu Jiang Jieshi Zhenxiang* (*The Secret Archive of Chiang Kaishek and Chiang Kaishek's True Identity*) (Beijing: Social Sciences and Documents Press, 2002).

Yang Tianshi, *Zhaoxun Zhenshi de Jiang Jieshi: Jiang Jieshi Riji Jiedu* (*In Search of the Real Chiang Kaishek: Reading the Chiang Kaishek Diaries*) (Taiyuan: Shanxi Renmin Chubanshe, 2008).

Yang Tianshi, 'Jiang Jieshi yu Nihelu' ('Chiang Kaishek and Nehru'), in *Zhongguo Wenhua*, vol. 30 (2009), 132–3.

Yang Tianshi, 'Chiang Kaishek and the Battles of Shanghai and Nanjing', in Mark Peattie, Edward J. Drea and Hans van de Ven, eds., *The Battle for China: Essays on the Military History of the Sino-Japanese War* (Stanford, CA: Stanford University Press, 2011), 143–58.

Yang Tianshi, 'Chiang Kaishek and Jawaharlal Nehru', in Mark Peattie, Edward J. Drea and Hans van de Ven, eds., *The Battle for China: Essays on the Military History of the Sino-Japanese War* (Stanford, CA: Stanford University Press, 2011), 127–40.

Yang Weizhen, '1938 Nian Changsha Dahuo Shijian de Diaocha yu Jiantao' ('An Investigation and Evaluation of the Great Fire of Changsha of 1938'), in Wu Sufeng, ed., *Buke Hulue de Zhanchang* (*A Battlefield That Must Not be Ignored*) (Taipei: Guoshiguan, 2013), 63–90.

Yang Zhesheng, *Qingbao Yingxiong Xiong Xianghui: Zai Hu Zongnan Shenbian de Shiernian* (*Intelligence Hero Xiong Xianghui: Twelve Years by the Side of Hu Zongnan*) (Shanghai: Shanghai Renmin Chubanshe, 2007).

Yang Zhiyi, 'The Road to Lyric Martyrdom: Reading the Poetry of Wang Zhaoming', *Chinese Literature: Essays, Articles, Reviews* (*CLEAR*), vol. 37 (2015), 135–64.

Herbert O. Yardley, *The Chinese Black Chamber: An Adventure in Espionage* (Boston, MA: Houghton Mifflin Company, 1983).

Yeh Wen-hsin, 'Historian and Courtesan: Chen Yinke and the Writing of Liu Rushi Biezhuan', Morrison Lecture, Australia National University (July 2003) and *East Asian History* 27 (2004), 57–70.

Ye Zhaoyan, *Nanjing 1937: A Love Story*, Michael Berry, trans. (London: Faber & Faber, 2004).

Shuguang Zhang and Jian Chen, eds., *Chinese Communist Foreign Policy and the Cold War in Asia: New Documentary Evidence, 1944–1950* (Chicago, IL: Imprint Publications, 1996).

Zang Yunhu, 'Qiqi Shibian Yiqian de Riben Duihua Zhengci Ji Qi Yanbian' ('Japan's China Policy before the 7 July 1937 Incident'), in *Kang Ri Zhanzheng Yanjiu* (*Research on the War of Resistance*), vol. 64 (2007), 1–29.

Zhang Xianwen, ed., *Kang Ri Zhanzheng de Zhengmian Zhanchang* (*Battles at the Front during the War of Resistance*) (Zhengzhou: Henan Renmin Chubanshe, 1996).

Zhang Xianwen, *Nanjing Datusha Shiliao Ji* (*Historical Materials for the Nanjing Massacre*) (Nanjing: Jiangsu Renmin Chubanshe, 2005), 28 volumes.

Zhang Xianwen, *Zhongguo Kang Ri Zhanzheng Shi* (*History of China's War of Resistance*) (Nanjing: Nanjing Daxue Chubanshe, 2001).

Zhang Xianwen, *Zhonghua Minguo Shi* (*History of the Republic of China*) (Nanjing: Nanjing Daxue Chubanshe, 2005).

ZHMGZYSLCB, see under Qin Xiaoyi.

Zhongguo Renmin Jiefangjun Lishi Ziliao Congshu Bianshen Weiyuanhui, eds., *Zhongguo Renmin Jiefangjun Lishi Ziliao: Zong Canmou Bu Huiyi Shiliao* (*Historical Materials for the People's Liberation Army: Recollections from the General Staff Office*) (Beijing: Jiefangjun Chubanshe, 1995).

Zhou Enlai, *Zhou Enlai Shuxin Xuanji* (Selected Correspondence of Zhou Enlai) (Beijing: Zhongyang Wenxian Chubanshe, 1988).

Zhou Gu, ed., *Hu Shi Ye Gongchao Shi Mei Waijiao Wenjian Shougao* (*The Diplomatic Messages of Hu Shi and Yeh Kung-ch'ao as Ambassadors to the USA*) (Taipei: Lianjing Chuban Gongsi, 2001), 6.

ACKNOWLEDGMENTS

In the course of thinking about and researching wartime China, I have incurred many debts. I am deeply grateful to all those who have helped me along the way, including the many whom space restrictions do not allow me to thank individually here. In the early 1990s, Stephen MacKinnon convened a small workshop on wartime China at a lush golf resort in Tucson, Arizona, bringing together the few China scholars who were then undertaking serious work on wartime China, including Diana Lary, Chang-tai Hung, Chang Jui-te, Arthur Waldron, Edward McCord and Joanna Waley-Cohen. That group expanded over time and drew in a younger generation of scholars, with the result that it has now become large and diverse. But the core group never lost its sense of purpose, seriousness and cohesion. We never institutionalised, which ensured that our meetings were easily arranged, our discussions fruitful, and our gatherings informal and friendly. This special group of colleagues has been a great support to me over the years.

The moral support, scholarly enthusiasm and incomparable fundraising abilities of Ezra Vogel ensured that the results of our research gained a far wider hearing than would otherwise have been the case. In the late 1990s, Ezra became troubled by the realisation that the growing attention to wartime events in China and Japan was increasing rather than decreasing the tensions between the two countries. Together with Yang Tianshi of the Chinese Academy of Social Sciences and Yamada Tatsuo of Keio University, Ezra took the initiative in bringing together scholars from China and Japan, as well as Europe and America, in the hope of establishing consensus about the most important events of the Second World War in east Asia. Mobilised by Ezra, our small group helped organise a series of meetings of scholars about such aspects of the war as its main battles, the fate of different regions and foreign relations. Five conferences later – in Boston, Tokyo, Chongqing (twice) and Taipei – and, unsurprisingly, no common narrative has yet emerged. Nonetheless, the results of our meetings have been published in Chinese, Japanese and English and the leading Second World War scholars of all three regions have become colleagues who meet regularly, respect each other's work and understand each other's concerns. A strong basis for continuing dialogue has been put into place. That is no mean achievement in itself.

Historians need archives. In Nanjing, Vice-Director Ma Zhendu of the Second Historical Archives of China facilitated my access to these important archives. Historians also need to talk. My colleagues at the History Department of Nanjing University, especially Zhang Xianwen, Chen Qianping and Chen Hongming, have become lifelong friends. Discussions there and in Beijing with Yang Kuisong, Mao Haijian, Bu Ping, Yang Tianshi, Wang Jianlang, Wang Chaoguang and Wang Qisheng proved profitable, at least to me. In Taiwan, the Academia Historica and the archives as well as the library of the Institute of Modern History proved indispensable to my research, as did conversations with historians there, including Chang Jui-te, Ch'en Yung-fa, Lü Fang-shan and Lin Man-hung. Dr Lin Hsiao-ting, the Curator of the East Asia Collection at the Hoover Institution Library and Archives, facilitated an extremely profitable two-week stay for me there.

Many colleagues have read part or even all of the manuscript. They include John Thompson, Timothy Cheek, Richard Frank, Li Chen, Sheila Miyoshi Jager, Beatrice de Graaf, Stephen MacKinnon, Edward Drea, Diana Lary, Yeh Wen-hsin and Susan van de Ven. They have saved me from making many errors.

Finally, Andrew Franklin of Profile Books proved a perceptive, wise and hugely enthusiastic editor. I thank Rana Mitter for recommending this book to Profile Books and Sally Holloway for smoothing my stylistic awkwardness during the copy-editing stage. Toby Eady, my agent, has always provided wise counsel and found the right people for me to work with. As is the case for all books, it is as much a collective as an individual enterprise. That does not mean, of course, that I am not responsible for any mistakes, of fact or interpretation, that remain.

LIST OF ILLUSTRATIONS

INDEX

Guizhou, Battle for (1944) 188–90
Guo Moruo 101, 268, 276
    'In Commemoration of the 300th
        Anniversary of 1644' 200, 201–2, 217–18, 261
Guo Songling, General 54, 55
Guo Taiqi 119, 175
Guomindang *see* Nationalist Party

H
Hainan 255
Hamilton, Maxwell 174
Han Deqin, General 148
Han Fuju, General 58, 62, 100
Hangzhou 83, 128
Hankow *see* Wuhan
Happy Mountain 216
Harbin 233
Harriman, Averell 157
Hashimoto Guma, Major 59
Hata Shunroku, General 102, 181
He Jian, General 119
He Long, General 144, 255
He-Umezu Agreement (1935) 63, 69, 70
He Yingqin, General 38, 71–2, 203, 204, 206,
    207, 209
He Zizhen 139
Hearnshaw, F. J. C.: *An Outline Sketch of the
    Political History of Europe in the Nineteenth
    Century* 52
Hebei 23, 58, 67, 69–70, 227, 238
    East Hebei Anti-Communist Autonomous
        Council 59, 69
Henan 23, 42, 43, 107, 179, 182–5
Hengyang, Battle of (1944) 186, 195
Herder, Johann Gottfried: *Outlines of a
    Philosophy of the History of Man* 178
Herodotus: *The Histories* 1
Hindenburg, Field Marshal Paul von 102
Hinton, William: *Fanshen: A Documentary of
    Revolution in a Chinese Village* 240, 243
Hirohito, Emperor of Japan 180, 182, 205, 206
Hitler, Adolf 85, 116, 130
Ho Chi Minh 256
Honan 43
Hong Kong 27, 44, 177, 178, 276
    Low Key Club 119
Hongqiao air field 78
Hopei *see* Hebei
Horiba Kazuo, Lieutenant General 114
Hornbeck, Stanley 116–17

Hu Hanmin 28–9
Hu Linyi 23
Hu Shi 90, 109, 119–20, 158
Hu Zongnan, General 100, 184, 198, 254, 256
Huai river 102, 104, 107
Huaihai Campaign (1948-49) 2, 252
Huang Zongxi: *Ming Confucianism* 202
Huangpu river 80
Huangqiao 148
Huayuankou dike 107, 228
Hubei 127, 130, 198, 255
Huiyang 123
Hull, Cordell 40, 157–8, 175, 176
Hunan 136–7, 179
    Battle for Hunan Province (1944) 185–6;
        conference (1938) 112; Winter Offensive
        (1939-40) 127
Hunan Army 113
Hurley, Patrick 180, 193, 212, 213

I
imperialism 27, 152, 153
    British 173, 177, 178; European 178; Japanese
        69; Western 2, 115
India 85, 173–4, 266, 269
inflation 189
infrastructure 35, 49; *see also* railways
Isao Kawada 267–8
Isherwood, Christopher 101
Ishiwara Kanji, Colonel 32, 68
Isogai Rensuke, General 102
Itagaki Seishiro, General 102
Izumo (Japanese flagship) 79, 83

J
Japan
    aggression of 1, 21, 40; air force 76, 77, 80,
        83–4, 116, 124, 125; Anti-Comintern Pact
        (1936) 61–2, 76;
    army 208; China Expeditionary Army 181;
        China Garrison Army 65, 66; Imperial
        Japanese Army 32, 80, 130, 144–5, 163, 186,
        208; Kuantung Army 32, 33, 39, 59, 76, 127;
    autonomous authorities 58; and Battle of
        Henan (1944) 184; and Battle of Shanghai
        (1937) 75–7, 78–87, 88–91; and Battle of
        Taierzhuang (1938) 103, 104–5; and Battle
        of Wuhan (1938) 102, 104–5; bombing
        campaigns 6, 71, 123–6; bombing raids
        on 196; and Chinese Nationalists 41, 114,

115; and Communists 143; Confucianism 264; disarmament of 197; economy 269; First World War 23, 46; food imports 129; imperialism 69; India and 173; isolation 39, 91; in Manchuria 8, 12, 21, 32, 33, 39, 52, 55, 56, 58, 231–2, 248; and Marco Polo Bridge incident 65–9; military operations 116; Nanjing attack 95–6; Nanshin (Southern Expansion Doctrine) 158, 159, 163; Nationalists 6, 267; navy 23, 71, 78, 79, 80; new order 115–16, 121; non-aggression policy (1935) 59; repatriation to 231, 244, 245; resistance to 32, 33, 63; and San Francisco Peace Treaty (1945) 265, 266–7; Second World War 10, 179–82; atomic bombing of 206, 230; Buna-Gona defeat 170; Burma 163, 165; Doolittle Raid 162; Ichigo Campaign (1944) 6, 8, 183–90, 198, 199, 202; Instruction 1380 205–6; invasion of colonies 157;

Pearl Harbor attack (1941) 7, 12, 158, 161; strategies 6–7; surrender 203–9;

Shanghai Expeditionary Army 80; and Soviet Union 76, 116; and Taiwan 267; and Wang Jingwei administration 122; Winter Offensive (1939–40) 126–32

Jiang Baili 36, 103
Jiang Dingwen, General 183, 185
Jiang Qing (Lan Ping) 140
Jiang Tingfu 40–1
Jiang Zemin 180
Jiangsu 23, 147
'Jiangsu–Zhejiang Military Region' 199
Jiangxi 138
Jiangyin 36
Jilin (Kirin) 239
Ji'nan 106
Jinzhou 248, 250
Jiujiang 126
Johnson, Nelson 176

K
Kaifeng 34–5, 126
Kang Sheng 151–2
Katsuki, General 70
Kawamoto Suemori, Lieutenant 32
Kerr, Archibald Clark 236
Kim Il-sung 256, 257, 264
Kirin *see* Jilin
KMT *see* Nationalist Party

Knatchbull-Hugessen, Hughe 85–6
Kong Xiangxi 65, 90, 120
Konoye Fumimaro 68, 69, 101, 118, 120, 122, 123
Korea 177, 212, 230, 256–7
North 256, 257, 261, 264; South 256, 257, 264, 269
Korean War (1950–3) 11, 193, 258–64
Chinese People's Volunteers 260, 261, 263
Kuangtung *see* Guangdong
Kubishev, General N. V. 29
Kunlun Pass 128–9
Kunming 166, 189
Kuomintang *see* Nationalist Party (KMT)
Kurile Islands 212, 266
Kusano Fumio: 'Chinese Communist Guerrilla Warfare' 237, 238–9

L
Lamb, Lionel 238, 252
Lan Ping *see* Jiang Qing
landlords 41, 135, 137, 138, 142, 150, 240, 241
Lattimore, Owen 58, 157, 158
League of Nations 39
Ledo Road 167
Leffler, Melvyn 230, 231
Lei Haizong 109
'National Reconstruction: Anticipating a Third Cycle' 109
Leith-Ross, Frederick 40
LeMay, General Curtis 195
Li Chen, Professor 244
Li Fen 151
Li Pinxian, General 148
Li Yu, Emperor 225
Li Zicheng 32, 200, 201, 217–18
Li Zongren, General 33, 59, 87, 100, 101, 102, 104, 106, 129, 131, 147, 236, 254
Liang Hongzhi 115
Liang Shuming 42, 53, 103, 135
Liao Zhongkai 28–9, 47
Liaoshen Campaign (1948) 2, 244, 248–55
Liaoxi Corridor 237
Liberation Daily 200
Lieberman, Henry 249
Lin Biao, General 144–5, 237, 239, 244–8, 250–1, 255, 259–60, 272
Lin Boqu 199
Lincoln, Abraham 32
Lindsay, Michael 101
Linggu Monastery 47